Speech Freedom on Campus

Speech Freedom on Campus

Past, Present, and Future

Edited by
Joseph Russomanno

With a foreword by
Erwin Chemerinsky

LEXINGTON BOOKS
Lanham • Boulder • New York • London

Published by Lexington Books
An imprint of The Rowman & Littlefield Publishing Group, Inc.
4501 Forbes Boulevard, Suite 200, Lanham, Maryland 20706
www.rowman.com

6 Tinworth Street, London SE11 5AL, United Kingdom

Quotations in chapter 6 from Jonathan Haidt, Interview with author, Tempe, AZ, November 9, 2017. Reprinted with permission.

British Library Cataloguing in Publication Information Available

Library of Congress Cataloging-in-Publication Data

Names: Russomanno, Joseph, editor.
Title: Speech freedom on campus : past, present, and future / edited by Joseph Russomanno ; with a foreword by Erwin Chemerinsky.
Description: Lanham : Lexington Books, [2020] | Includes bibliographical references and index.
Identifiers: LCCN 2020041870 (print) | LCCN 2020041871 (ebook) | ISBN 9781793623607 (Cloth : acid-free paper) | ISBN 9781793623614 (ePub)
Subjects: LCSH: Freedom of speech—United States. | United States. Constitution. 1st Amendment.
Classification: LCC KF4772 .S6494 2020 (print) | LCC KF4772 (ebook) | DDC 342.7308/53—dc23
LC record available at https://lccn.loc.gov/2020041870
LC ebook record available at https://lccn.loc.gov/2020041871

♾™ The paper used in this publication meets the minimum requirements of American National Standard for Information Sciences—Permanence of Paper for Printed Library Materials, ANSI/NISO Z39.48-1992.

This book was largely written, edited, and published during the coronavirus pandemic that began in 2020. It was a time when campus voices were mostly silenced due to their absence. Accordingly, Speech Freedom on Campus: Past, Present, and Future *is dedicated to the return of those voices, and to those—including the scholars whose work appears herein—who strive to protect those voices and to understand those who seek to muzzle them.*

Contents

Foreword

THE ONGOING AND INTRACTABLE DEBATE ABOUT FREE SPEECH ON CAMPUS

Erwin Chemerinsky, Dean and Jesse H. Choper Distinguished Professor of Law, University of California, Berkeley School of Law

Thirty years ago, I participated in many debates over whether colleges should enact free speech codes limiting hate speech on campus. Over 350 colleges and universities adopted such codes, though none survived court challenges. Today, the debate over whether to restrict hateful expression on campus continues. Indeed, I expect the increased attention to anti-blackness and racism will cause more pressure for campuses to punish hate speech.

There are some differences today as compared to three decades ago. Social media and the internet have changed the nature of free speech, including on campuses. Issues of free speech on campus now are primarily about what campuses can do in response to speech over social media and the internet. It used to be possible to draw a distinction between expressions that occurred on campus as opposed to off-campus. But social media and the internet make that distinction meaningless. Of course, this distinction is even more irrelevant in the midst of a pandemic when most or even all campus activities are online.

Also, the debate today is not about campus speech codes. After several courts invalidated them, usually for being unduly vague and overbroad, colleges and universities abandoned them.

The vocabulary has changed somewhat, too, over the last few decades. Now there is much talk about "safe spaces" and "microaggressions." Increasingly, I hear students who object to messages or speakers, describing them as "violence" against people of color. In fall 2019, when Ann Coulter spoke on the Berkeley campus, her presence was described as "violence" against students of color and immigrant students.

Also, difficult issues have arisen as to whether campuses can exclude controversial speakers rather than paying huge amounts of money for safety and security. In fall 2017, my institution, UC Berkeley, spent almost $4 million to allow speakers such as Milo Yiannopoulos and Ben Shapiro to speak on campus. It is unclear how far a campus must go and when it can refuse to allow a speaker rather than pay large security costs.

But ultimately the arguments with regard to hate speech on campus are the same as three decades ago. Those who support restrictions and punishments point to the harms that hate speech inflicts on its targets: students of color, women, gay and lesbian students, Jewish and Muslim students. The arguments are powerful and persuasive. Speech is protected as a fundamental right because it has effects; those can be positive or negative. Free speech is not absolute, and ensuring equality of educational opportunity is certainly a compelling government interest.

On the other side, opponents of restrictions point out that there is no exception to the First Amendment for hate speech. Defining *hate speech* in a manner that is not vague or overbroad is inherently elusive. Giving campus officials the power to punish speech that is offensive is seen as worse than the harms of the speech.

The chapters in this terrific volume are enormously illuminating, but the debate over hate speech seems intractable and unlikely to ever be resolved. Why?

First, there is no way to ever resolve the tension between liberty and equality, which is what underlies the debate over restrictions on hate speech. Those who argue for restrictions on hateful expression point to its effects in undermining equality for its targets. And they are surely right about this impact. But those who argue against these limits point to the importance of free speech, especially on campuses, and the danger of giving officials the power to punish speech they find offensive. And they are right too.

The tension between liberty and equality, of course, is not unique to this debate. It underlies so much of constitutional law and so many areas of social policy. But ultimately is what the debate over hate speech is about.

Second, free speech is not absolute; it never has been and it never will be. The issue always is what harms are sufficient to justify restrictions on speech. Supporters of limits on hate speech point to the many harms it creates and argue that they are comparable, or greater, than what has been found to justify restrictions on speech in the past. Opponents of limits argue that speech never should be restricted because it offends; there would be no limit to the government's power to censor if that were sufficient.

The issue is actually more subtle and more difficult. There are categories of unprotected speech that might apply, but the definitions of these categories are poorly defined. In 1942, the U.S. Supreme Court said that "fighting words"—words that by their very utterance inflict injury—were a category of unprotected speech. The Court never has overruled that holding and on occasion has indicated that it still stands, but nor has the Court upheld a fighting words conviction since 1942.

"True threats" are unprotected speech. But the Court has done little to clarify the standard for when speech rises to this level. As a result, there is a split among the federal courts of appeals as to how to determine whether there is a true threat and whether it is enough that the speech caused a person to reasonably fear for his or her safety, or whether an intent to threaten must be proven.

Harassment can be punished, even when it is entirely through speech. But what is enough to constitute harassment? Must the speech be directed at a person? If it is enough that the speech be pervasive, what is sufficient to meet this requirement?

Third, the problem of vagueness and overbreadth in defining what is hate speech cannot be ignored. Those who oppose hate speech restrictions point to the enormous problems in defining what is prohibited in a constitutionally acceptable way. As mentioned above, this was the basis for the invalidation of several of the hate speech codes. They defined *hate speech* as that which "demeaned or stigmatized" based on race, sex, religion, sexual orientation, age, or disability. But what does "demean" or "stigmatize" mean?

But those who favor restrictions regard this as a problem that can be overcome and not a reason to reject all regulation of hate speech. After all, other categories of unprotected speech—obscenity, incitement, true threats—also defy clear and precise definitions.

Ultimately, the issue of hate speech on campus—like other issues concerning free speech on campus—come down to a basic question: How much latitude do we want campus officials to have in regulating and punishing speech? The chapters in this volume are an excellent exploration of this topic. And it is an issue that will continue as long as there are colleges and universities.

Introduction

Joseph Russomanno

> cam'- pus [kam-puhs]: the grounds and buildings of a university, college, or school.

Though dictionaries are valuable, their definitions are sometimes restricted by the limitation of words. While the above definition is accurate—and to be fair, additional descriptions are typically provided—few would dispute that there is, or should be, much more to a college or university campus. More than a physical entity, it represents the noble pursuit of knowledge. It contains a spirit of learning in the broadest sense possible. It is a social and cultural organism. If the campus is to be a place where knowledge is discovered and shared, then conditions must be conducive to the exchange of information. For learning to occur—not just in the classroom, but in other venues, too—then the campus itself must be a sort of marketplace where various ideas and viewpoints can be offered, exchanged, discussed, and debated—some sampled and considered, then accepted or rejected. And though this dynamic should not be exclusive to the campus, it is what we have come to expect, even demand, at minimum from our colleges and universities.

Complex issues are multi-layered. Speech freedom on campus is no exception. This book examines some of those issues. That is, this book is not exhaustive, nor does it claim to be. Instead, a variety of scholars whose specific areas of expertise allow them to analyze one or more aspects of campus speech share their perspectives here. In so doing, the hope—as it is with any scholarship—is to create knowledge and enhance understanding by sharing it. Not so ironically, and like thousands of others, that is also what we do within our roles on our respective campuses and elsewhere. And also like many others, we believe that those processes are enriched when speech freedom prevails.

Speech freedom on our college and university campuses, like everywhere else, is fragile. There are those who sometimes wish to suppress it, more often than not when the words express ideas, opinions and even facts that conflict with their beliefs. Why does an effort so completely at odds with the foundational values of this country happen? Well, as someone once said, it's complicated.

To be sure, the notion that speech freedom on campus deserves our attention is not universally accepted. For example, in "The Miseducation of Free Speech,"[1] Mary Anne Franks passionately rejects the claim that "America's campuses are in the midst of a free speech crisis." To illustrate these claims, she cites several articles, none of which include "crisis" in either their titles or their narratives. Granted, whether the level of speech suppression on some of America's campuses rises to the level of "crisis" may be in the eye of the beholder (or as Christina Wells addresses this "crisis debate" in chapter 7, we use narrative frames to help us interpret the world). If nothing else, I think we can agree that wherever and whenever in the United States the ability to express thoughts, viewpoints, and opinions is restricted through a concerted and directed effort—or even through a spontaneous response to hearing words that are judged to be unacceptable or dangerous—we have a problem. And that problem is worthy of our attention. We provide some of that attention in the pages that follow.

Before previewing each chapter, a note about them collectively: it is not surprising that they share some concepts. After all, the events and phenomena that these authors examine are similar, as are the authors' academic and scholarly backgrounds. That said, where the similarities appear, they are approached uniquely in each chapter. These concepts include the marketplace of ideas; the campus and classroom as public forums; the role of purpose and mission at colleges and universities; identity and tribe; and perhaps least surprisingly, political perspective and partisanship. This occasional overlap is not only acknowledged here, it is embraced, accompanied by the suggestion that rather than being any kind of liability, it is an asset, contributing to a sort of analytical triangulation while also serving to emphasize the importance of these concepts as instruments of analysis and understanding.

In chapter 1, Geoffrey R. Stone introduces the reader to the issue of free speech on campus and its importance by taking us inside the thinking that ultimately became the well-known "Chicago Principles" that now guide so many colleges and universities. Professor Stone tells us that, yes, we have an issue of law, but it is also much more. The challenge does not originate so much from off campus, or even from administrators, but now often from students themselves.

In chapter 2, Ronald K. L. Collins provides a critical perspective of the marketplace of ideas and the man largely credited with bringing the concept to modern First Amendment jurisprudence, Oliver Wendell Holmes, Jr. This rollicking essay also asks whether the marketplace metaphor is properly applied to defend speech on campus.

Rodney A. Smolla invokes his vast background as an educator—not to mention as a litigator and First Amendment scholar, as well—in chapter 3. He readily acknowledges the complexity and confusing nature of the field he teaches and writes about—a nature that led him to revise his approach. He developed an incredibly insightful, dual-pronged categorization of free speech in America. It is a framework that can be applied to our campus environments, and is especially effective and informative there given its ability to explain the inherent tension between a college's contextual cultures. Included in Dean Smolla's "seminar" is a lesson from a one-time baseball commissioner.

The next three chapters capture the politics of speech freedom on campus in various ways. Much of the work in this book may be seen as steeped in the tradition of liberalism, with an acknowledgment to the ideas of civil liberty, equality, and social justice. In fact, the notion of a right to expression was largely born in the Age of Enlightenment, itself marked by liberal thought. Some have criticized higher education, however, for adopting a liberal orthodoxy, and they instead advocate viewpoint diversity. In chapter 4, Joe Dryden cites an abundance of evidence to support his argument that on-campus speech freedom transgressions—many of which are discussed within these pages—disproportionately affect those who are politically conservative. Like other authors in this volume, he examines the marketplace of ideas, and claims it is broken, and in a way that favors liberals/progressives at the expense of their conservative counterparts.

The political partisanship embedded in speech freedom on campus is front and center in chapter 5. I would be guilty of reaching for low-hanging fruit to write that this chapter is "on FIRE." Its author, Will Creeley, writes about his work at the Foundation for Individual Rights in Education, aka FIRE. This is an organization dedicated to defending student and faculty rights, particularly on freedom of expression. As Will writes, that has given him a front-row seat to witnessing the partisanship that threatens expressive rights for students and ultimately for us all. Chapter 5 also contains a critique of Robert Post's position; Professor Post declined an invitation to respond within these pages.

Some explanations for that partisan divide are offered in chapter 6. There, I explore how a variety of phenomena, largely thought to reside off campus, actually have infiltrated America's colleges and universities, sometimes contributing to efforts to suppress speech. This confluence includes the political polarization—in the form of tribalism and identity politics—that paralyzes much of the nation and is now dividing students. Most of these students are members of iGen, also known as Generation Z. Their unique traits are factors not only in this divide but also in the desire by some to silence perceived sources of danger, including speech.

In the aforementioned chapter 7, Christina E. Wells brings a valuable critical perspective to the issue of speech freedom on campus. After a comprehensive summary of some of the most noteworthy free-speech disputes on American campuses, she examines how we perceive and frame these incidents and the lens through which we view them. Given the primacy of the First Amendment within our belief systems, this chapter may beg the question whether we are victims of that culture and, if so, to what extent.

Our focus remains on the law in chapter 8. There, David L. Hudson, Jr. looks at how the law governing the speech of public employees has evolved, and how that doctrine impacts a particular group of public employees—faculty members at state universities. In particular, Professor Hudson provides a highly critical perspective of a U.S. Supreme Court ruling that he characterizes as "awful."

It will not be surprising to learn that a book with the campus at its core looks at the unique environment of the college classroom from a variety of perspectives. This includes Erica Goldberg's chapter 9 in which she provides a sort of owner's manual for students and especially professors when it comes to classroom discussion. The ever-shifting judgments about acceptable and preferred approaches create a moving target. Hitting the bull's-eye, though never easy, is made more likely with the values-based perspectives that Professor Goldberg provides. Among her many observations, she notes that making judgments in the midst of lively debates can be a function of a particular university's purpose and mission.

University purpose and mission are key elements in chapter 10, written by Brett G. Johnson and Jeremiah P. Fuzy. They posit that the university is an extension of the classroom, with various conclusions flowing from that premise. The "peculiarity" of the college classroom is a notion that catalyzes their analysis. They deftly consider university missions and juxtapose them with legal precedent and doctrine. The authors conclude not only their chapter but also this book with an eye on the future and a recommended path forward.

NOTE

1. Mary Anne Franks, "The Miseducation of Free Speech," *Virginia Law Review Online*, 2019, https://www.virginialawreview.org/volumes/content/miseducation-free-speech#_ftn1.

Chapter 1

Free Speech on Campus

A Challenge of Our Times

Geoffrey R. Stone

I would like to begin by telling you a bit about my world. It is the world of the law. More specifically, it is the world of constitutional law. Law is about stories. It is about real people involved in real disputes with real consequences. So, I shall begin with a story.

This story begins during World War I. As you may or may not know, World War I was not a particularly popular war with the American people, whose sympathies were divided. Many Americans vigorously opposed the Wilson administration's decision to intervene in the brutal conflict that was then raging in Europe, arguing that our intervention was both unwise and immoral.

Not surprisingly, such opposition did not sit well with the government. In 1917 Attorney General Thomas Gregory, attacking the loyalty of war opponents, declared: "May God have mercy on them, for they can expect none from . . . an avenging government."[1] Gregory wasn't kidding about the "avenging" government. In 1918, Congress enacted the Sedition Act, which made it a crime for any person to utter "any disloyal . . . scurrilous, or abusive language intended to cause contempt . . . for the . . . government of the United States, the Constitution, or the flag."[2] True to the Attorney General's threat, during the war federal authorities launched more than 2,000 prosecutions against individuals who wrote or spoke against the war or the draft.

One such prosecution involved five young, Russian-Jewish emigrants. In the summer of 1918, the United States sent a contingent of marines to Vladivostok in Russia. Fearing that this was the first step of an American effort to crush the Russian Revolution, these five self-proclaimed socialists threw several thousand copies of each of two leaflets—one in English, the other in Yiddish—from several rooftops on the lower east side of New York City.

The leaflets, which were boldly signed "The Rebels," were addressed to other Russian emigrants. After stating that the Rebels hated "German militarism," they warned those who worked in ammunition factories that they were "producing bullets, bayonets and cannon to murder not only the Germans, but also your dearest, your best, who are in Russia and who are fighting for their freedom."

The "Rebels" were immediately arrested by the military police. After a controversial trial, they were convicted of violating the Sedition Act of 1918. The trial judge, disgusted by their behavior and their beliefs, sentenced the Rebels to terms ranging up to twenty years in prison. The Rebels appealed their convictions to the Supreme Court of the United States, claiming that their convictions violated the First Amendment, which guarantees that "Congress shall make no law . . . abridging the freedom of speech." In *Abrams v. United States*, the Supreme Court, in a seven-to-two decision, rejected this claim and upheld the convictions. For the majority of the Court, this was an easy case. Because the natural tendency of the defendants' speech was to generate opposition to the war, it was not within "the freedom of speech" protected by the Constitution.

Justice Oliver Wendell Holmes, joined by Justice Louis Brandeis, dissented. Holmes' dissenting opinion in *Abrams* is worth reading, for it remains one of the most eloquent statements ever written by a Justice of the Supreme Court about the freedom of expression. Holmes wrote: "Persecution for the expression of opinion seems to me perfectly logical. If you have no doubt of your premises . . . and want a certain result with all your heart you naturally [want to] sweep away all opposition."[3]

But, he added, "when men have realized that time has upset many fighting faiths, they may come to believe . . . that the ultimate good desired is better reached by free trade in ideas—that the best test of truth is the power of the thought to get itself accepted in the competition of the market, and that truth is the only ground upon which our wishes can safely be carried out."[4] Holmes therefore concluded that "we should be eternally vigilant against attempts to check the expression" even of "opinions that we loathe and believe to be fraught with death, unless they so imminently threaten"[5] compelling government interests that an immediate check is necessary to save the nation.

I first read this passage, written just over a century ago, when I was a law student at the University of Chicago, exactly half-a-century ago. It has engaged my energy and curiosity ever since. Indeed, I think it's fair to say that it was my puzzling over this passage that, for better or worse, put me on the path to my career and, indeed, to writing this chapter.

But now I must change direction, for this is not to be a discourse on the First Amendment. It is, rather, to be a chapter about academic freedom. Happily, these are not unrelated subjects. To the contrary, the longer I have puzzled over the meaning of free expression, and the longer I have thought about education, the more the two seem to me to converge. Indeed, neither really is worth all that much without the other. And, with that in mind, I would like to turn to what I see as the intersection of free expression and education, and to the subject of academic freedom, for it is at this intersection that we will find the most fundamental values of the world of higher education.

I hope to accomplish two things in this part of my chapter. First, I will trace briefly the history of academic freedom, for it is only by understanding where we have been that we can appreciate—in both senses of the word—where we are today. Second, I will offer some thoughts about what all this means for us today and about the responsibilities that we today bear in common.

It is important to understand that, like the freedom of speech, academic freedom is not a law of nature. It does not exist of its own force. It is always vulnerable, and should never be taken for granted. Indeed, until well into the nineteenth century, real freedom of thought was neither practiced nor professed in American colleges. To the contrary, any real freedom of inquiry or expression in American colleges in this era was smothered by the dominance of religion and by the prevailing theory of "doctrinal moralism," which assumed that the worth of an idea must be judged by what the institution's leaders declared its moral value to be.

Thus, through the first half of the nineteenth century American colleges squelched any notion of free and open discussion or intellectual curiosity. Any student or faculty member who dared argue, for example, that women were equal to men, that Blacks were equal to whites, or that homosexuality was not immoral would surely be expelled or fired without hesitation.

Similarly, through the first half of the nineteenth century, as the nation moved toward Civil War, any professor or student in the North who openly defended slavery, or any professor or student in the South who openly challenged slavery, could readily be dismissed, disciplined, or expelled. When a professor at the University of North Carolina expressed sympathy for the 1856 Republican presidential candidate, the students burned him in effigy and he was dismissed by the trustees. When a professor at Franklin College in Pennsylvania admitted he was not an abolitionist, he was promptly fired.

Several decades later, a furious battle arose over Charles Darwin's theory of evolution, with traditionalists charging not only that Darwin was wrong, but also that his beliefs were dangerous, immoral, and ungodly. As a consequence of this conflict in the academy over evolution versus creationism, new academic goals came to be embraced. For the first time, to criticize, as well as to preserve, traditional moral values and understandings became an accepted function of higher education, and by 1892, William Rainey Harper, the first president of the University of Chicago, could boldly assert: "When for any reason the administration of a university attempts to dislodge a professor or punish a student because of his political or religious sentiments, at that moment the institution has ceased to be a university."[6]

But despite such noble sentiments, the battle for academic freedom has been a continuing and fiercely contentious one. In the closing years of the nineteenth century, for example, businessmen who had accumulated vast industrial wealth began to support colleges and universities on an unprecedented scale. But that support was not without strings, and during this era professors who offended wealthy donors by criticizing their business practices were dismissed from leading institutions such as Cornell and Stanford.

Then, during World War I, patriotic zealots persecuted and, as we have seen, even prosecuted those who questioned the wisdom or morality of the war. In the face of such outrage, universities collapsed almost completely in their defense of academic freedom. Students and professors were systematically expelled and fired from colleges and universities across the nation merely for encouraging a spirit of indifference toward the war.

Similar issues arose again, with a vengeance, during the Cold War in the age of Joseph McCarthy. In the late 1940s and 1950s, most colleges and universities excluded those even suspected of Communist sympathies from university life. Yale president Charles Seymour, for example, went so far as to boast that "there will be no witch hunts at Yale, because there will be no witches. We will neither admit nor hire anyone with Communist sympathies."[7]

As this history demonstrates, the freedom to question, the freedom to challenge, and the freedom to inquire are not to be taken for granted. Academic freedom is, in fact, a hard-bought acquisition in an endless struggle to preserve the right of each individual, student and faculty alike, to seek wisdom, knowledge, and truth, free of the censor's sword.

But what does all of this have to do with us? Well, in a radio address to America in 1931, the Irish playwright George Bernard Shaw startled his audience with the following proposition: "Every person who owes his life to civilized society and who has enjoyed . . . its very costly protections and advantages should appear at reasonable intervals before a properly qualified jury to justify his existence, which should be summarily and painlessly terminated if he fails to justify it."[8] I do not advocate such a program. But I do suggest that every one of us who enjoys the protections and advantages of our hard-won system of academic freedom has a responsibility to justify her existence under it.

There are several ways in which we can meet this responsibility. First, we must defend academic freedom when it comes under attack. Like every liberty that is precious to us, the preservation of academic freedom demands vigilance, determination and, sometimes, courage.

Second, we must struggle to define the meaning of academic freedom in our time. As we saw in *Abrams*, the Constitution's guarantee of freedom of speech is not self-defining. Neither is academic freedom. Each generation must give life to this concept in the face of the distinctive conflicts that arise over time.

Today, the principal challenge to academic freedom comes not from outside the academy, but from within it—from students themselves, some of whom demand censorship of ideas that they find distasteful and offensive, and from faculty members and university administrators who, afraid to disappoint their students, too often surrender academic freedom to charges of offense.

To give just a few examples, several colleges and universities, including Johns Hopkins, Brown, and Williams, have withdrawn speaker invitations because of student objections to the views of the invited speakers: Colorado College suspended a student for making a joke that made fun of feminism, the State University of New York denied promotion to a professor who criticized the university's affirmative action program, William & Mary and the University of Colorado disciplined students for criticizing their affirmative action programs, students at Vanderbilt University demanded that a tenured professor be fired for writing an op-ed in which she raised questions about Islam and violence, the University of Kansas disciplined a professor for mocking the National Rife Association, and Louisiana State University fired a professor because some of her women students complained that they had been made to feel uncomfortable by her use of profanity in class.

At Wesleyan University, after the school newspaper published a student op-ed criticizing the Black Lives Matter movement, students demanded that the university defund the school paper; at Amherst College, students demanded that the administration remove posters stating that "All Lives Matter"; at Emory University, students demanded that students who had chalked "Trump in 2016" on the university's sidewalks should be punished because, in their words, a university is "supposed to be a safe place for students and this made us feel unsafe"; and at a number of institutions, including DePaul University, Claremont McKenna, the University of California at Irvine, San Francisco State, the University of Pennsylvania, Middlebury College, and the University of California-Berkeley, students physically obstructed access to venues or shouted down speakers whose views they opposed, causing the events to be cancelled.

To put all this in perspective, a 2015 survey revealed that 72 percent of college students support disciplinary action against any student or faculty member who expresses views deemed by them to be "racist, sexist, homophobic or otherwise offensive."[9]

So, where did all this come from? It was not too long ago when students were demanding the right to free speech. Now, at least some students demand the right to be free from speech that they find to be offensive, upsetting, or emotionally disturbing. What explains this profound shift in attitude?

One often-expressed theory is that at least some members of this generation of students have been raised by the so-called helicopter parents who protected and celebrated them in every way, shielding them at every turn from the risks of failure, frustration, and defeat. On this theory, these students, unlike their predecessors, have never learned to deal effectively with challenge, uncertainty, insult, or fear. They therefore demand the right to be protected from speech that they find to be offensive, hurtful, or demeaning. If this is so, then the proper role of an institution of higher learning is not to shield those students from distressing and offensive ideas, but to prepare them for the challenges of the real world. The goal of a university should not be to insulate students from discomfort and insecurity, but to enable them to be strong and effective citizens of the world—a world that will not shield them from such expression.

Another possible explanation of the current situation is that this generation of students is more attuned than their predecessors to the injustices of society, to the harmful impact of hateful expression, and to the inequalities that poison our nation. To the extent this is so, it might in part be a response to the creation of social media. When I was in college, we were rarely exposed to hateful expression. The media never carried it and although we knew it existed, we rarely confronted it. The world of social media has changed that. Today, it is difficult not to encounter hateful expression. On this view of the matter, students today are not timid, but bold. They seek not shelter, but justice. They understand the ugliness of such expression and they want to protect both themselves and their classmates from the vitriol that now poisons some forms of expression.

Still another possible explanation is that some students, particularly those who come from disadvantaged, marginalized, and discriminated against backgrounds, have *always* felt unwelcome on college campuses, but in the past they simply remained silent. On this view of the matter, this generation of college students, particularly those who themselves feel unwelcome and alienated, deserves credit, because instead of remaining silent in the face of oppression, they have the courage to demand equality and respect.

My own view, for what it's worth, is that there is an element of truth in all of these perspectives. The question is what to do about all this.

Faced with the ongoing challenge to academic freedom at American universities, in 2014 University of Chicago president Robert Zimmer charged a faculty committee with the task of drafting a formal statement for the University on Freedom of Expression. The goal of that committee, which I chaired, was to stake out *our* university's position on these issues. The committee consisted of seven distinguished faculty members from across the university. After broad consultation, we produced a brief, three-page report. At the risk of being self-indulgent, I want to share with you some excerpts from that report:

> Because the University [of Chicago] is committed to free and open inquiry in all matters, it guarantees all members of our community the broadest possible latitude to speak, write, listen, challenge, and learn. Except insofar as limitations on that freedom are necessary to the functioning of the University, the University of Chicago fully respects and supports the freedom of all members of the community "to discuss any problem that presents itself."[10]
>
> Of course, the ideas of different members of the University community will often and quite naturally conflict. But it is not the proper role of the University to attempt to shield individuals from ideas and opinions they find unwelcome, disagreeable, or even deeply offensive. Although the University greatly values civility, and although all members of the University community share in the responsibility for maintaining a climate of mutual respect, concerns about civility and mutual respect can never be used as a justification for closing off discussion of ideas, however offensive or disagreeable those ideas may be to some members of our community.
>
> The freedom to debate and discuss the merits of competing ideas does not, of course, mean that individuals may say whatever they wish, wherever they wish. The University may restrict expression that violates the law, that falsely defames a specific individual, that constitutes a genuine threat or harassment, that unjustifiably invades substantial privacy or confidentiality interests, or that is otherwise directly incompatible with the core functioning of the University. But these are narrow exceptions to the general principle of freedom of expression, and it is vitally important that these exceptions never be used in a manner that is inconsistent with the University's commitment to a completely free and open discussion of ideas.
>
> In a word, the University's fundamental commitment is to the principle that debate or deliberation may not be suppressed because the ideas put forth are thought by some or even by most members of the University community to be offensive, unwise, immoral, or wrong-headed. It is for the individual members of the University community, not for the University as an institution, to make those judgments for themselves, and to act on those judgments not by seeking to suppress speech, but by openly and vigorously contesting the ideas that they oppose. Indeed, fostering the ability of members of the University community to engage in such debate and deliberation in an effective and responsible manner is an essential part of the University's educational mission.

> As a corollary to the University's commitment to protect and promote free expression, members of the University community must also act in conformity with the principle of free expression. Although members of the University community are free to criticize and contest the views expressed on campus, and to criticize and contest speakers who are invited to express their views on campus, they may not obstruct or otherwise interfere with the freedom of others to express views they reject or even loathe. To this end, the University has a solemn responsibility not only to promote a lively and fearless freedom of debate and deliberation, but also to protect that freedom when others attempt to restrict it.

Interestingly, when we wrote this Report, we were thinking only about the University of Chicago. To our surprise, the Report has had a national and even international impact. Indeed, it has now been adopted by some sixty other colleges and universities, including such diverse institutions as Princeton, Columbia, the University of Minnesota, the University of Missouri, Purdue, Johns Hopkins, American University, Amherst College, and the University of Wisconsin, to name just a few.

Now that I've finished congratulating myself, let me elaborate a bit. Why should a university take the position that faculty and students should be free to advance any and all ideas, however offensive, obnoxious, and wrong-headed they might be?

First, one thing we have learned from the bitter experience is that even the ideas we hold to be most certain might in fact turn out to be wrong. As confident as we might be in our own wisdom, experience teaches that certainty is different from truth. If those who believed with absolute certainty that the earth was the center of the universe were wrong, if those who believed with absolute certainty in creationism were wrong, if those who believed that slavery was natural, right, and proper were wrong, if those who believed that a woman's place is in the home were wrong, if those who believed that homosexuals were degraded perverts were wrong, then why should we have the arrogance to think that *we* are unquestionably right about our own beliefs today? The only wise approach, as Justice Holmes made clear, is to acknowledge the risk that *our* certainties might be wrong as well, and that they too must always be open to challenge and question.

Second, experience teaches that the suppression of speech breeds the suppression of speech. If today I am permitted to silence those whose views I find distasteful, I have then opened the door to allow others down the road to silence me. The neutral principle of no suppression of ideas protects us all. This is especially important in the current situation, for in the long run it is likely to be minorities, whether religious minorities, racial minorities, or political minorities, who are most likely to be silenced once censorship is deemed acceptable. Indeed, without a vibrant commitment to freedom of speech, our nation would never have seen a civil rights movement, a women's rights movement, or a gay rights movement, all of which would have been suppressed by intolerant majorities. Censorship is never a one-way street, and this is a door we do not want to open. Indeed, it is important to remember that a robust protection of free speech is especially important to dissenters and to minority groups, because if censorship is permitted it is ultimately they who will suffer the most.

Third, a central precept of free expression is the concern with chilling effect. That problem is especially acute today because of the effects of social media. It used to be the case that students and faculty members were willing to take controversial positions, in part because the risks were relatively modest. One could say something provocative or outrageous, and the statement soon disappeared from view. But in a world of social media, where every comment you make can be circulated to the world and can be called up later by prospective employers or graduate schools or neighbors with the mere click of a button, the potential cost of speaking courageously—of taking controversial positions, of taking risks—is greater than ever before in history. Indeed, according to one study, 65 percent of all college students said that it is "unsafe" for them to express unpopular views,[11] and this clearly has had an effect on faculty as well. In this setting, it is especially important for institutions of higher learning to stand up for free expression.

So, how should this work in practice? Should students, faculty, and other speakers be allowed to express whatever views they want—however offensive they might be to others? Yes. Absolutely.

Should those who disagree and are offended by the views and speech of others be allowed to condemn those views and those speakers in the most vehement terms? Yes. Absolutely.

Should students, faculty, and community members who oppose a speaker be permitted to disrupt an event in order to prevent that individual from speaking? Absolutely not. Although non-disruptive protests are both permitted and encouraged, disruption of the rights of others to speak and to listen is wholly incompatible with the central principle of academic freedom.

Should those who are offended and who disagree with the views of others be allowed to demand that the institution punish those who have offended them? Yes. Absolutely.

Should a university punish those whose speech annoys, offends, and insults others? Absolutely not.

What, though, *should* a university do? First, a university should educate its students and faculty about the importance of civility and mutual respect. As one former student wrote to me, a university "has an obligation to create a community of people as well as 'a community of ideas,' a place where everyone feels certain that they are unambiguously welcomed." This must be a core institutional value, but it is a value that must be reinforced and reaffirmed by education and by example, not by censorship.

Second, a university should encourage free, open, and robust disagreement, argument, and debate. It should educate its students about the history, the importance, and the fragility of free speech, and it should instill in its students and faculty the importance of winning the day by facts, by ideas, and by persuasion, rather than by force, disruption, or censorship. Indeed, for an institution of higher education to fulfill its most fundamental mission, it must be a safe space for even the most loathsome, offensive, and disloyal arguments.

Near the end of his presidency in 2016, Barrack Obama gave some graduating college seniors advice when it comes to handling those whose views they oppose. "Don't try to shut them down, no matter how much you disagree with them," the president said. "Let them talk. . . . Have the confidence to challenge them." Listening and engaging is vital, he added. "If the other side has a point, learn from them. If they're wrong, rebut them. . . . Beat them on the battlefield of ideas. And you might as well start practicing now, because one thing I can guarantee you—you will have to deal with ignorance, hatred, racism . . . at every stage of your life."[12]

Third, a university must recognize that, our society being flawed as it is, the costs of free speech will often fall most heavily on those groups and individuals who feel the most marginalized, unwelcome, and disrespected. All of us feel that way sometimes, but in our often unjust society the individuals who most often bear the brunt of free speech—or at least of certain types of free speech—tend to be racial and ethnic minorities; religious minorities; women; gays, lesbians, and transsexuals; immigrants; ideological dissidents; and the like. Colleges and universities must be sensitive to this reality. Even if they cannot "solve" this problem by censorship, they can and should take other steps to address the special challenges faced by groups and individuals who are most often made to feel unwelcome and unvalued by others.

Institutions of higher learning must take this challenge seriously. They should encourage civility and mutual respect. They should support students who feel vulnerable, marginalized, silenced, and demeaned. They should help those students learn how to speak up, how to respond effectively, and how to challenge those whose attitudes, whose words, and whose beliefs offend, appall, and outrage them. This is a core responsibility of these institutions, for the world is not a safe space, and it is our job to enable our graduates to win the battles they will need to fight in the years and decades to come. This is not a challenge that universities can or should ignore.

Speaking of the responsibility of universities, I should address one other critical facet of these issues. Suppose those who oppose a speaker—whether they be students, faculty, or community members—disregard their responsibility to respect the freedom of speech and threaten violence or otherwise disrupt an event in order to prevent an invited speaker from speaking. What should the university do? After the events of Charlottesville, this is an especially important question. The simple solution is for the institution to "play it safe" and just refuse to permit the speaker to come to campus. Indeed, this is the approach several institutions have now adopted. The University of Florida and Texas A&M, for example, announced that they would not permit alt-right leader Richard Spencer to speak on campus for fear of disruption and even violence.

But if universities adopt this approach, and thus empower those who oppose a speaker to prevent the event from taking place by threatening violence or disruption, what will happen? Such a response will inevitably encourage others who want to exclude speakers to adopt this strategy, knowing that they, too, can shut down speech they oppose merely by threatening violence or disruption. This invites what the Supreme Court has termed the "heckler's veto."

Such a course invites other groups to wield the power of censorship over whatever views they wish to suppress, whether those views be anti-war, pro-Black Lives Matter, anti-immigration, pro-Israel, anti-Trump, pro-abortion, anti-affirmative action, pro-gay rights, or whatever. In effect, the heckler's veto turns the right to free speech over to those who oppose the ideas being espoused.

It is noteworthy, by the way, that the Supreme Court first learned this lesson during the Civil Rights era when white Southerners threatened violence in order to shut down civil rights marches. What the Court concluded is that the responsibility of the city, the police, or the university in such circumstances is to take all reasonable measures to protect the speaker and to enable the event to take place, and that it can terminate the event only if it is impossible for it to prevent a clear and present danger of serious harm. Short of that, though, the heckler's veto cannot prevail.

I should make one other important point about the strategy of disruption. It is counter-productive. It gives the speaker and her ideas greater visibility, turns her into a martyr, and enables her to sell books, get on cable news, and promote her views more effectively than ever. People such as Richard Spencer, Ann Coulter, and Milo Yiannopoulos, for example, were complete unknowns until they were made famous by violent protests against their views. Now, they are household names.

The Southern Poverty Law Center addressed this in a 2017 policy statement:

> When an alt-right personality is scheduled to speak on campus, the most effective course of action is to deny the speaker of the thing he or she wants most—a

> spectacle. Alt-right personalities know that their cause is helped by news footage of large jeering crowds, heated confrontations and outright violence at their events. It allows them to play the victim and gives them a larger platform for their racist message. Denying an alt-right speaker of such a spectacle is the worst insult they can endure.[13]

What the Southern Poverty Law Center wisely recommends instead is that the best strategy is for those who oppose a speaker's views is to "hold an alternative event—away from the alt-right event—to highlight your campus' commitment to inclusion and to our nation's democratic values."[14] This response is the right one across the boards, whether the speaker is a member of the alt-right, an opponent of gay rights, a supporter of abortion rights, or any other speaker whose views you oppose.

It is noteworthy, by the way, that the frequency of incidents involving the suppression of controversial speakers dropped dramatically for a period. Although this is mere speculation, I would guess that three factors have contributed to this development. First, the students who invited these provocateurs to campus have no doubt suffered terribly in their reputations, in no small part because of social media. To the extent this is true, I suspect that their successors have backed away from putting themselves in a similar situation. This is both good and bad. It is good insofar as it has reduced significantly the number of these incidents. It is bad because it is a classic example of chilling effect. To the extent that current students actually want to invite people such as Coulter, Yiannopoulos, and Spencer to campus, it is unfortunate that they do not do so because they are afraid of the consequences to them. Second, it is possible that these speakers understandably grew tired of dealing with these controversies and simply decided that enough was enough. Third, and what I think is the best possible explanation, it may be that the students who oppose these speakers have learned the lesson taught by President Obama, the Southern Poverty Law Center, and others. That is, by not disrupting the event they deny the speakers the attention they crave and thus render the whole enterprise pointless.

Let me now, though, return to my central theme. What is it that makes for a great educational institution? In the words of Robert Hutchins, it is, I submit, "the intense, strenuous and constant intellectual activity of the place . . . . Presented with many points of view, [students must be] compelled to think for [themselves]."[15] At a great educational institution, "the air is electric" with ideas and questions, and it is from that environment that students derive an intellectual stimulation that should last them "the rest of [their] lives."[16] This is the true meaning of education.

The responsibility of universities and colleges to their students is to test what they are taught at every turn, to challenge their teachers, their classmates, and themselves, to choose their own values and their own beliefs. To meet this responsibility, students have to be independent, they have to be daring, and they have to take risks. It is not easy to tell your professor, who has devoted years, perhaps decades, to mastering her subject, that you disagree with her latest observation or theory. But the discourse of a great institution of learning should be an incitement to risk and to boldness. If students find themselves hesitating, if they feel timid, or if they wonder if it's worth it, they should remember the Rebels in *Abrams*. At an age not much older than college students, they dared to take on the government of the United States. Students can certainly take on a mere professor. The faculty of a great institution of higher learning ask nothing of their students that they do not also ask of themselves. Even the most distinguished teacher and scholar routinely suffers frustration and failure. It is only by taking risks, by daring to ask questions no one else has ever asked, that real contributions are achieved. Thus, if professors ask students to take risks, know that they take risks as well. At a serious academic institution, it should never be forgotten that "the only appropriate response to even the most withering question is not resentment, but gratitude."[17]

Fulfilling the responsibility of academic freedom means more than challenging one's classmates and teachers; it also means challenging yourself. It means being willing to reconsider what you yourself have come to accept as true. In 1921, after two years in prison, Mollie Steimer, one of the *Abrams* Rebels, was deported to the Soviet Union. It was not what she expected. Disappointed in the political and economic system she found there, Steimer again agitated against the government. Again, she was arrested, prosecuted, and convicted of sedition. In 1923, she was deported from the Soviet Union. I don't know for sure, but I rather suspect that this was an unparalleled achievement—to be convicted of sedition and deported within five years from both the United States and the Soviet Union. Whatever else one might think of her, Mollie Steimer was not afraid to reconsider her positions.

In 1919, a majority of the Supreme Court in *Abrams* rejected the bold approach of Justice Holmes and opted for a "safe" view of the First Amendment. Fifty years later, the Supreme Court unanimously overruled the majority opinion in *Abrams* and, embracing Justice Holmes' dissenting opinion, held that the government may not punish even speech that we "loathe and believe to be fraught with death"[18] unless that speech is both intended and likely to incite imminent lawless action. To reach this result, the Court had to challenge the first principles of its predecessors and to overturn half-a-century of precedent.

A great university, like a successful Court, must dedicate itself to the rigorous, open-minded, unyielding search for truth. Students will learn in such institutions to ask the hard questions. But it is not enough to examine the premises, beliefs, and assumptions of an earlier time and find them wanting. It is too easy to dismiss those who thought that the earth was the center of the universe, that its resources were boundless, that only men should vote, that marriage is only for people of the opposite sex, or that separate could ever be equal. We must remember that we, too, hold beliefs that our children or our children's children will rightly regard as naïve, foolish, perhaps even obscene. We must be prepared to challenge our beliefs, to reform our world, just as the Rebels in *Abrams* struggled to reform theirs. We, too, must challenge the nature of things.

NOTES

1. Thomas Gregory, "All Disloyal Men Warned," *The New York Times*, November 21, 1917, 3.
2. Espionage Act of May 16, 1918, 40 Stat. 553 (1918).
3. *Abrams v. United States*, 250 U.S. 616, 630 (1919)(Holmes, J., dissenting).
4. Ibid.
5. Ibid.
6. Geoffrey R. Stone, "Free Expression in Peril," *The Chronicle of Higher Education*, August 26, 2016, https://www.chronicle.com/article/Free-Expression-in-Peril/237568.
7. Maurice Isserman, "Who Defines 'Acceptable' Speech?," *The Chronicle of Higher Education*, February 18, 2005, B20.
8. Bernard Shaw, *Selections of His Wit and Wisdom*, ed, Caroline Thomas Harnsberger (Westchester, IL: Follett Publishing Company, 1965), 328.
9. Haley Hudley, "New Survey Exposes New Threats to Free Speech On Campus," Foundation for Individual Rights In Education, October 28, 2015, https://www.thefire.org/new-survey-exposes-threats-to-free-speech-on-campus/.
10. Geoffrey R. Stone, Marianne Bertrand, Angela Olinto, Mark Siegler, David A. Strauss, Kenneth W. Warren and Amanda Woodward, "University of Chicago, Free Speech on Campus: A Report from the University Faculty Committee," January 6, 2015, http://www.law.uchicago.edu/news/free-speech-campus-report-university-faculty-committee.
11. Eric L. Dey, Molly C. Ott, Mary Antonaros, Cassie L. Barnhardt and Matthew A. Holsapple, "Engagging Diverse Viewpoints: What Is the Campus Climate for Perspective-Taking?," American Accociation of Colleges and Universities, 2010, 7, https://www.aacu.org/sites/default/files/files/core_commitments/engaging_diverse_viewpoints.pdf.
12. "Obama's Full Remarks at Howard University Commencement Ceremony," Politico, May 7, 2016, https://www.politico.com/story/2016/05/obamas-howard-commencement-transcript-222931.
13. "The Alt-Right On Campus: What Students Need to Know," Southern Poverty Law Center, August 10, 2017, https://www.splcenter.org/20170810/alt-right-campus-what-students-need-know.

14. Ibid.

15. Geoffrey R. Stome, "Aims of Education Address," University of Chicago, 1996, https://college.uchicago.edu/student-life/aims-education-address-2016-geoffrey-r-stone.

16. Ibid.

17. Ibid.

18. *Abrams v. United States*, 630.

Chapter 2

The Holmesian Experiment and the Democratization of Truth in the Academy

Ronald K. L. Collins

An edgy speaker, who is all the rage in edgy circles, is sought out by a student group seeking to provoke an agitated response on a college campus. This speaker, who revels in being reviled, speaks in enough code to keep himself within inches of the legal line. In the frenzied process he spews out enough of his bigoted creed to send sensitive caring new-age kids racing off to safe spaces surrounded by soothing sounds. It's all part of a spectacle, a kind of theater performed along ideological lines. When pushback comes, which is predictable, it is portrayed as if it were akin to Galileo being persecuted by ecclesiastical inquisitors for defending the heliocentric theory of Copernicus; or so it is billed, this modern-day Miltonian sham of a defense of speech in pursuit of truth. That defense carries the day no matter how vile or farcical the words. After all, by their geocentric measure, their earth is the center of the universe—"deal with it!" is their righteous refrain.

In this marketplace of spectacles, nothing is beyond the pale, no truth beyond doubt, and no falsehood beyond belief—a case of the exploits of social media playing out on college campuses. And as with cable TV, facts are siloed in ideological quarters. In the raucous tumble of this free speech shit fest, everyone is entitled to their fifteen minutes of infamy, this in the name of the First Amendment—that grand symbol of perpetual toleration. Everyone has an opinion with a FUNDAMENTAL RIGHT to espouse in that forum where ideas are said to be exchanged. Of course, it matters not whether such opinions, however absurd or offensive, rise to the level of genuine ideas of the kind associated with more than a modicum of thought. Even to level such a charge smacks of awful authoritarianism, a kind of top-down mindset—the kind that contests the *democratization of truth*. However oxymoronic, that democratization represents the principle that governs all other principles on college campuses at this point in post-modernity.

How did things come to this? How is it that the defense of free speech by those on the Right is every bit as absurd as the objection to it by those on the Left? One side plays the pursuit of truth card; that is the one that requires college administrators to police and protect the ideological compadres of the "Unite the Right" crowd that marched in Charlottesville. On the other side, Bush's Secretary of State is disinvited to speak on campus because her views do not comport with P.C. truths. Oh, what this so-called pursuit of truth has done to vulnerable minds?

To answer such questions, one must proceed down the winding historical paths that lead to a man named Oliver Wendell Holmes, a man who would have sneered at the spectacle of the pursuit of truth being used to deconstruct the pillars of liberal education. Then again as he once told Harold Laski: "If my fellow citizens want to go to Hell I will help them. It's my job."[1] Such a democratic soul!

> *[T]he best test of truth is the power of the thought to get itself accepted in the competition of the market, and that truth is the only ground upon which their wishes safely can be carried out. That at any rate is the theory of our Constitution. It is an experiment, as all life is an experiment.*[2]
>
> —Holmes, J., dissenting
> *Abrams v. United States* (1919)

Holmes' footprint on the American law of free speech is gigantic. Like Atlas, he is a titan in that world. No one else quite casts a shadow so long. While James Madison is the grand *pater* of the historical First Amendment, its modern father figure is surely Justice Oliver Wendell Holmes, Jr. His thought can be found in bold relief in many Supreme Court opinions on freedom of expression, in every contemporary history of the subject, in every casebook used in law schools and every textbook used in colleges, and in every serious scholarly treatment of the matter. This is so, Judge Richard Posner once observed, because "Holmes laid the foundations …for the expansive modern view of free speech."[3] Having done so, he then "left a profound imprint on the law of free speech."[4] Without exaggeration, then, it would be impossible to have any meaningful discussion of modern free speech theory or law, in almost any context, without some consideration of Holmes' views.

But from what well does Holmes' fame spring? Does it derive mainly from three opinions—*Schenck v. United States* (1919),[5] *Abrams v. United States* (1919),[6] and *Gitlow v. New York* (1925)[7]—issued late in the long-life span of this great jurist and scholar? If so, did the ideas for those landmark opinions jet out of his psyche with a singular thrust of insight, or were there some seeds that had been stirring in the soil of his mind for years or even decades before? As with so many other great figures in law, the answer is a combination of both, and other things, too.

Marketplace of Ideas. Every law student, and some college students, and even more college administrators hold (or say they do) to that Holmesian metaphor of free speech. It is noteworthy that a commercial metaphor was employed to conceptualize speech touching everything from politics to education, albeit with a dollop of Enlightenment panache. Trading, exchanging, and bartering for products with an eye to getting the "best deal" was how he invited us to think about First Amendment freedom. By that measure, for First Amendment purposes citizens became consumers. If we hold faithful to the metaphor, the operative principle is to please the customer, which means that *satisfaction* is the end goal. As we will see later, the metaphor became meaningful; its figurative meaning took on literal meaning.

Just to set the record straight at the outset, the Holmesian metaphor (as the epigraph above reveals) was not cast in what has become its familiar wording. As for the actual phrase *marketplace of ideas*, the credit for that precise turn of words in a Supreme Court opinion goes to Justice William O. Douglas as expressed in his concurrence in *United States v. Rumely* (1953): "Like the publishers of newspapers, magazines, or books," Douglas declared, "this publisher bids for the minds of men in the market place of ideas."[8]

With that in the record, let us now turn to the Holmesian phrase *the best of truth*. Why truth and what did it mean to Holmes as he cast it?

WHY ALL OF THIS TRUTH TALK?

The word sounded alien in his mouth, as if spoken by someone else.[9]

—Michael Connelly

Before venturing off to the battlefields of Ball's Bluff and the Civil War / and how that set the psychological stage for Holmes' *Abrams* dissent / and how all that played out afterward / and how that in turn led to the democratization of truth, it may be useful to ask: why? That is, why all this talk about truth and the marketplace in which ideas are supposedly traded? Why the big windup? Why not cut to the doctrinal chase? When litigated, most campus speech codes are handedly struck down under the First and Fourteenth Amendments. There you have it, case closed!

Then again, maybe not. Since the beginning of time people have turned (however disingenuously) to "higher principles" to justify either their defense of liberty or their denial of it. Then again, what is at play here may be nothing more than hubris, an attempt to find meaning in what might be a meaningless universe. To deny truth, or to dismiss the value of the pursuit of it, might be seen in some circles as a crime against men's pride and a wrong against women's faith in their male counterparts. Maybe, if one takes his cues from Nietzsche—"Truths are illusions which we have forgotten are illusions"[10]—that dark side of things might hold.

But if one takes meaning, knowledge, and the pursuit of truth entirely out of the social equation, then as a practical matter anarchy is free to claim its ruinous wants. One does not have to buy into Aristotle's *Politics* to appreciate that any social order must, as a practical matter, lay some claim to knowledge, purpose, and meaning and some faith in facts. How legitimate that claim proves to be is another matter. The problem with "higher principles" is not necessarily that there are none, but that what are labeled as such are too often more fictional than factual in the context of how the world works.

Wherever there is a claim of right, there is typically some reference to a "higher principle" to justify it. One does not, after all, defend pornography in the name of perversion, or commercial speech in the name of exploitation, or defamation in the name of character assassination. To the extent that such forms of expression acquire constitutional legitimacy, they do so because they are linked to some higher value. Consider, for example, John Milton's 1644 defense of free speech as he presented it to the Parliament in his opposition to licensing and (certain forms) of censorship. In his poetic pamphlet John Milton (who had suffered censorship) was eloquent and inspirational: "Let her and Falsehood grapple; who ever knew Truth put to the worse, in a free and open encounter?"[11] Of that pursuit, Milton declared: "Give me the liberty to know, to utter, and to argue freely according to conscience, above all liberties."[12] Holmes flirted with that Miltonian creed though he added more than a spoonful of skepticism to it. In Chapter Two of his *On Liberty* (1859), John Stuart Mill offered a similar rationale grounded in libertarian values checked by a harm principle. Enter thereafter Alexander Meiklejohn, the grand free speech philosopher: "The First Amendment is not, primarily, a device for the winning of new truth," he wrote, "though that is very important. It is a device for the sharing of whatever truth has been won."[13] Put it all together and there is this: the Holmesian metaphor, we were told in *Walker v. Sons of Confederate Veterans* (2015), reminds us that "First Amendment rules [were] designed to protect the marketplace of ideas."[14]

Though more paragraphs and pages could be added, my point is a simple one: The pursuit of truth, and/or its acquisition, is a core First Amendment value in and of itself, and/or because "freedom of speech is essential to freedom of thought"[15] as Erwin Chemerinsky and Howard Gillman put it, and/or because it is vital to the pursuit of self-government. And that is where I want to focus on how and why free speech is so often defended when the First Amendment is invoked to protect various kinds of expression that some find offensive. Just as the righteous like to have God on their side (nod to Bob Dylan[16]), so too is "truth" and/or "self-government" called to the scene of this or that alleged free speech is wrong. And when it does, one soon enough finds herself in the proverbial marketplace of ideas—that Holmesian haunt where administrators and students hang their free speech hats, no matter how ridiculous their claims may be when judged by a truth norm.

Some 800 college professors offer courses on free speech. No doubt, the Holmes name comes up and maybe even his marvelous metaphor, too. But how many impressionable Millennials and Generation Z kids have any idea what influenced the idea of Holmes' metaphor and what he meant by it? And if they did know, might it embolden some to be yet more permissive and others yet more censorial? Probably, but we're not there yet. Hold on.

It is revealing that most commentators have confined their commentary to that corpus of Holmes' free speech jurisprudence that centered around a handful of his later opinions in cases decided between 1919 and 1929. This is so notwithstanding the fact that by the time the Justice sat down to author his two legendary wartime opinions—*Schenck* and *Abrams*—he had already been writing on free speech for several decades in a dozen or so federal and state cases, not to mention his various scholarly publications. And there was something else, something perhaps far more influential that shaped his free speech jurisprudence, something not found in precedents recorded in the *United States Reports*. That something gives us a special insight into the Holmesian metaphor and the soil in which it was rooted.

FROM THE BATTLEFIELDS TO COMPETITION IN THE MARKET

In his near century of living, no single life experience influenced Holmes' thinking about free speech and other matters more than his military service during the Civil War. At age twenty he enlisted in the Union Army. What followed shaped his destiny.

Holmes and the Civil War: it is an epic story. It is also a story of bravery, agony, glory, and the startling impact it had on Holmes—a man who donned a blue uniform on July 10, 1861 to serve in the Twentieth Massachusetts Volunteer Regiment and who did so honorably and at great risk until he was discharged on July 17, 1864. Over those 1,103 days, Holmes witnessed the worst forms of suffering and death on the fields of Antietam, Chancellorsville, Fredericksburg, and Ball's Bluff, where, recalled his Harvard friend and fellow soldier Henry Abbott, "it seemed as if every square inch of air within six feet of the ground was traversed by bullets as they whistled by us."[17] Though

Holmes' wounds were severe and almost fatal, he persevered—he held true to his duty and fought on. Still, the carnage of it all changed him forever. It left a mark on his mind, an indelible mark.

That three-year experience—grounded in the earth of the calamity of the Battle of Ball's Bluff where he almost died—remained with Holmes and shaped his views of life and law. Recall, for example, those lasting lines from his *Abrams* dissent:

> [W]hen men have realized that time has upset many fighting faiths, they may come to believe even more than they believe the very foundations of their own conduct that the ultimate good desired is better reached by free trade in ideas—that the best test of truth is the power of the thought to get itself accepted in the competition of the market.[18]

Earlier, on the occasion of an 1884 Memorial Day Address, he noted that his life and those of his fellow Civil War soldiers had been "set apart by its experience," one that touched the hearts of all who fought "with fire."[19] Or as he put it a decade or so later in his "Soldier's Faith" remarks: "I believe that struggle for life is the order of the world, at which it is vain to repine."[20] That contact with war was the driving force in Holmes' life. Indeed, both literally and metaphorically, it left him a marked man. In a still larger sense, the Civil War also left its mark on the mind of America. While that war alone did not make America modern, it nonetheless helped usher in "the birth of modern America," as Louis Menand put it.[21] There was a transformation in ideas, a different lens by which to view life and law, and also a different way of conceptualizing freedom. Holmes, ever the soldier, played a vital role in that transformation. Hence, to understand Holmes' free speech jurisprudence—especially his *Abrams* dissent—one must have some appreciation of how the Civil War shaped his thinking.

In a world bloated with comfort but bereft of certainty, Holmes hoped to revive the great Phoenix of a soldier's faith—a faith tied to duty and to the value of struggle as a core principle of life. In that Holmesian contest, there are no transcendent truths, no supreme absolutes, no celestial rescues, only victors in the battles of ideas. Or as Holmes so poignantly put it in 1915: "To have doubted one's own first principles is the mark of a civilized man."[22]

That jurisprudence of doubt captured American law in utopian and dystopian ways. On the one hand, it offered the hope of toleration and openness enabling pragmatic survival and the possibility of a more muscular measure of truth. On the other hand, that same jurisprudence in time would pave a path to today's polarized polity where truth collapses into opinion and facts fade into "fake news." In the tumble, the reality of enduring truths seems more fanciful than possible. In effect, the same marketplace of ideas that might save the country is also the one that could portend its downfall. The Holmesian touchstone, after all, was less the enlightenment of humankind than the survival of *any* opinion vetted only by conflict in the marketplace. In that arena, truth might sometimes triumph, but at other times it might as easily surrender to falsehood. Holmes, the soldier turned jurist, was fine with the gamble—such was the lesson he learned from the fields of battle where causes were won and lost.

He went to war in the service of high principles but left believing in no principles. As then-Massachusetts Judge Holmes put it in an 1895 Memorial Day Address:

> In the midst of doubt, in the collapse of creed, there is one thing I do not doubt and that is that the faith is true and adorable which leads a soldier to throw away his life in obedience to a blindly accepted duty, in a cause which he little understands, in a plan or campaign of which he has no notion, under tactics of which he does not see the use, and he has to take the chances of war.[23]

There, so much for this abbreviated account of Holmesian history.

Three points to consider, at least for now: First, what kind and how much stock did Holmes put in the marketplace of ideas and the pursuit of truth? Second, how has his conception of the First Amendment played out in real time, in our post-modern times? Finally, how does this all link up with the curricular trends and free speech activities of today's colleges?

Now onto modernity, or post-modernity if you prefer.

MUSING ON METAPHORS

> *Philosophers have been called poets. And both philosophers and poets live by metaphors. But their motives for making metaphors are not the same.*[24]
>
> —Stephen C. Pepper

It was undeniable: Holmes' ambition made him; his rivalrous mindset invigorated him; his passion delighted him; his wit charmed others; his mind impressed many; and his heroic spirit when expressed in speeches left still others awestruck. Then again, Holmes could be cold, detached, elitist, and even Puritanical at times. He was also someone who knew how to wield a pen in ways that captured men's minds.

Following in his poet father's literary footsteps, the younger Holmes appreciated the value of metaphors as an alternative to the constricting forms of legal writing. Extrapolating from the Pepper quote above, Holmes was not only poet in his use of metaphors, but also philosopher. His importance in law, and especially in the law of the First Amendment, derived in real measure from that talent, from that ability to present his legal reasoning with literary flair.

The market metaphor. A metaphor is not a logical proposition or a legal argument. It is a figure of speech, a symbolic representation, something that is meta-logical or meta-legal. It is an abstraction, a "look-over-there" sort of way of viewing the world. Where others relied on precedent, legal and historical, or to some form of legal reasoning, Holmes (following his poet father) cast his thinking in metaphor. This move gave his words wide conceptual and imaginative latitude. It invited others to fill in the meanings of his metaphor. For some, that meaning circled around the promises of the Enlightenment; for others, that meaning was tied to battle; for yet others, his meaning had a commercial ring to it—and so on and on. What are the contours of the market metaphor? What are its limits? What are its real-world possibilities? On that score Holmes was stoically silent. And perhaps that is exactly where he wanted things to be—at some "subliminal" level as Christy Wampole put it in her book on the ramifications of a metaphor.[25]

In that sense, Holmes' metaphor could mean almost anything one wanted it to be. That possibility made his marketplace metaphor greatly popular with many, regardless of what side of the ideological divide that they sat on or what their views of education are.

CAMPUS CONFLICTS AND THE RACE WARS

The problems of bigotry and discrimination sought to be addressed here are real and truly corrosive of the educational environment. But freedom of speech is almost absolute in our land.

—*UWM Post v. Board of Regents of U. of Wis.* (1991)[26]

It started some thirty-five years ago: "An academic study has found that ten of the twenty largest American universities developed speech codes during 1986 to 1991, and the vast majority of these followed racial incidents that occurred on campus."[27] So wrote Jon Gould in 1999. By the time the Freedom Forum's First Amendment Center issued its 1997 report on campus speech codes, hundreds of colleges had such codes in place. The categories of codes that the Center identified were:

- threats of violence
- breach of peace
- disruption of teaching, research, and so on

- hazing
- obscenity
- intentional infliction of emotional distress
- libel and slander
- fighting words
- lewd, indecent and/or profane expression
- verbal abuse or verbal harassment
- verbal abuse or verbal harassment directed at a member of a specific group

To be sure, and as evidenced by subsequent litigation, many of these regulations were violative of that body of First Amendment law as it had been applied in other contexts such as in parks and on the streets. That said, can it be summarily denied that such types of speech are "corrosive of the educational environment?"[28] Is the civility that is so vital to the educational process compatible with the kind of speech that is expressed in the following ways?

- Yelling for ten minutes, calling a woman a "fucking bitch" and "fucking cunt."
- Calling another student a "piece of shit nigger" in the context of a near-physical altercation.
- Sending messages on a university computer system that read, "Death to all Arabs!! Die Islamic scumbags!"
- Referring to a Black female student as a "fat ass nigger" during an argument.

Those were the kinds of expression that federal district Judge Robert W. Warren was called to rule upon in a 1991 University of Wisconsin campus speech code case.[29] They call to mind something Holmes wrote in his 1929 dissent in *United States v. Schwimmer*: Some speech "might excite popular prejudice, but if there is any principle of the Constitution that more imperatively calls for attachment than any other it is the principle of free thought—not free thought for those who agree with us but freedom for the thought that we hate."[30] "Popular prejudice" and the hate speech that flows from them, is that Holmesian "principle."

As the free speech battle was waged on college campuses, concerns about civility and the educational process were frequently dismissed as the product of the hyper-sensitivities of the "politically correct." Even though Judge Warren granted the plaintiff's motion for summary judgment based on First Amendment law, it is important to note that he also found such speech "truly corrosive of the educational environment." Whatever reason there is for protecting such speech, it is difficult to understand how the environment created by such expression advances truth and knowledge in any market of ideas worthy of the name.

The point: Once the Holmesian rules and rationales, among other doctrines, made their way onto college campuses, they brought with them the battles of the streets, replete with the muscular vernacular and sometimes rowdy ways of "street-fighting men." By that logic, if one could call a police officer a "fuckin' pig" to his face, why not grant the same right when students speak with other students, or with faculty, or with administration officials?

All of this point to the problem of taking the already daring Holmesian view of life and law and then imposing it onto the template of liberal education. When the marketplace left the streets of the city and ventured onto the domain of American campuses, the volume level went up. As it did, more and more voices of reason sought safe harbor in silence.

And there was something more about that street marketplace that was problematic, particularly in the days following the presidential election of 2016. That something had its spillover effects on college campuses.

THE POLITICIZATION OF TRUTH

There's no such thing . . . anymore as facts.[31]

—Scottie Nell Hughes
CNN, November 30, 2016

Ask any college student: Does it matter whether the Shroud of Turin is real? One answer is "no," since facts do not necessarily supersede opinions or beliefs. Thus, as an article of faith, it is of little moment whether there is doubt about the Cloth of Christ. After all, we are in the realm of *religious belief*. What is important for the faithful is that they *believe* it to be so. And if enough of them believed it to be so, would the facts of the matter make any real difference? Just as there is "creation science," perhaps there could be a "miracle science" that could legitimate the Shroud's authenticity. Assuming, of course, that anything named science was even needed for such purposes. Or as the Hughes quote above implies, facts may be a thing of the past.

At this juncture we move from the realm of religious belief to the demands of political truth. In a democratic society, at least of the Madisonian kind, what may pass as truth in the religious realm may fail in the political realm. And why? The answer, the *aspirational* one, is that Madisonian democracy is premised on truth-telling—many of the key Founders were, after all, children of the Age of the Enlightenment. They placed aspirational stock in deliberative democracy, which is a far cry from democracy of the kind that insists on the authenticity of the sacred burial shroud of Christ. As so often claimed by a cadre of free speech scholars (who dabble more in theory than reality), deliberative democracy (another oxymoron?) is the operative premise of the speech and press clauses of the First Amendment. By that guiding norm, it is better that people lose faith in the authenticity of the Shroud than lose trust and confidence in their government. But such theories are all so fanciful, if only because the line between deliberative democracy and the politicization of truth is an imaginary one, a line that James Madison would surely have held to be balderdash.

What happens when the promises of Madisonian norms are ripped away from their ideals and tend toward uninformed belief systems masquerading as truth? In other words, what if the coin of truth becomes devalued to the point that its currency as truth is worthless, or nearly so? What then? And how does this play out in the academy where knowledge is the pursuit but politics is the preference?

In thinking about the devaluation of truth, especially in the college social settings, it is helpful to clear out a little conceptual brush at the outset lest some surmise that there is a groundswell movement of anti-gravity deniers among us or other such groups of truth deniers. Admittedly, Galileo, Brahe, and Newton all had their critics when it came to the orbit of the planets and gravity, but that is another truth-denying story, though not one without its parallels. So let us begin with a dichotomy.

Truth vs. Political Truth. To preface the word *truth* with the word *political* is, as a matter of realpolitik, to devalue the word "truth." (As history reveals, much the same could be said of *religious* truths.) When situated in that environment, truth takes on many meanings and likewise loses many of its otherwise obvious meanings. Cast otherwise, there is something about politics that invites lying in rulers and reliance on lying in those ruled. Though its meaning is different, the expression "lying in wait" takes on novel meaning in the political setting. There, it might be understood as rulers waiting to lie (that opportune moment) as well as those ruled waiting to be lied to (wish-fulfillment anticipation). Lies, after all, sugar coat the unpleasantries of truth; they can even make them appear to disappear. In this game of political sorcery, lying helps rulers maximize power and also pleases those ruled to the extent that they buy into the lie and see it as valuable to them. By this measure, there is opt-in on almost all sides, dissidents notwithstanding.

The problem—the loss of value, the demise of objectivity, and the abandonment of reason in the name of preferred "truths," which are unyieldingly faithful to someone's side in the ideological wars of the moment, whether it be in the political or college marketplace of ideas. As astutely noted by Michiko Kakutani in *The Death of Truth*: "For decades now, objectivity—or even the idea that people can aspire toward ascertaining the best available truth—has been falling out of favor."[32] In matters of domestic policy, foreign policy, economic policy, military policy, and environmental policy, to list but a few areas, the relativism of the Swiss linguist Ferdinand de Saussure's semiology and the deconstructive moves of the French philosopher Jacques Derrida feed the irrational beast of the so-called democratic rule. Of course, they are not the cause of society's fall from reason, but they do serve to legitimate that descent. They give it philosophic staying power. Once such thinking drifted out of the towers of the deconstructive academy and into the crevices of the American mind, something of the same mindset (but of a vulgar sort) was summoned in the service of those who know only the self-serving values of relativism. Then again, the converse might hold to be so—the democratization of truth took hold in the academy.

We live in a time when relativism has captured politics. This maddening mix—something out of the petrifying pages of a Greek or Shakespearean tragedy—wars first with reason and then with everything else in its path, be it the rule of law, the laws of science, the basic tenets of sensible foreign policy strategies, or the way students think and behave on college campuses. It does so by devaluing reason while championing the worst kinds of relativism free of even the most rudimentary kinds of pragmatic norms. Along the way, loyalty to ideology (no matter how deranged) is demanded as if there could be some method in this madness. The purpose: "to normalize the abnormal," as Kakutani casts it.[33]

A lie, as St. Augustine of Hippo wrote in the fifth century, can take on many dizzying forms (he identified eight such types).[34] In modernity, the taxonomy is ever more complex as the messages we convey move from misrepresentations to falsehoods, from bluffing to deception, from half-truths to careless mistakes, from fraud to fabrication, from commercial deception to political propaganda, from guesses to beliefs, and from impression to nonsense.

For a lie to exist, for a falsehood to become manifest, there must be some standard, some truth touchstone. Otherwise, what we communicate and how we act would forever be sucked down into the vortex of a sophistry that values only the knack of persuasion—the kind that Socrates counseled against in Plato's *Dialogues*. In that swirl of the mind, truth is not superior to falsehood; reality is not superior to fantasy; and facts are not superior to fiction. Hence, St. Augustine's taxonomy becomes senseless and gradations of truth become hopelessly blurred.

Fifty-two years ago Leo Strauss echoed a point that traveled from the halls of antiquity through the corridors of modernity: "Man has to choose between peace of mind deriving from a pleasing delusion and peace of mind deriving from the unpleasing truth."[35] Mindful of that, if a ruler senses that his or her subjects crave pleasing delusions, then his or her calculated move is to feed the "Great Beast,"[36] to give it the partisan meat it hungers for. True, in the long run, delusion may starve them to death, but who, asks the manipulative ruler, pays attention to the dangers of tomorrow when they can savor the delights of today? Delusion speaks to now, whereas danger dwells in some distant and unknown future corner. When enough people live in a state of collective denial, when they prefer delusion over deliberation, when they stand ready to ignore the laws of scientific truths, at that point truth is crucified in the marketplace.

All of this points to another question: Even when it knows it, can the human psyche endure the truth? And when that psyche is multiplied in mass form, can a society endure truth? This has long been a question of both social psychology and political philosophy. But whatever the answer is, this much must be near to the mark: the further a society is from those truths that control life, the more endangered that society is. What is at issue here, therefore, is not some grandiose notion of truth or some inflated idea of the role of reason in human affairs. Hardly. More modest, yet nonetheless momentous, concerns drive the point to be brought home. Hence, real peace of mind must hew closer to those unpleasing truths if it is to endure and thrive. Reality (truth's handmaiden) demands its dues; it does not excuse folly born of delusion, no matter how innocent.

Now, consider such matters in light of what happened in the span of political time between the presidential election of 2016 and that of 2020. No sane person (whatever his or her political stripes) should be able to deny that something has gone terribly awry when truth travels down different paths depending on which cable channel it appears, or when Twitter truths trump contradictory facts documented by the institutional press, or when what is touted on Facebook is offered up as an indisputable truth in the quarrels that mold college students' minds?

WHEN THE SUN RISES IN THE WEST

There has been a lot of freedom of thought
over the past few years, but no thought.[37]

—Simone Weil

Justice Abe Fortas (a former Yale Law professor) spoke with considerable confidence[38] when in *Tinker v. Des Moines Independent Community School District* (1969), he declared with "Holmesian flourish"[39] that "[i]t can hardly be argued that either students or teachers shed their constitutional rights to freedom of speech or expression at the schoolhouse gate."[40] But why is that so? The answer Fortas tendered was that "educating the young for citizenship is reason for scrupulous protection of Constitutional freedoms of the individual, if we are not to strangle the free mind at its source and teach youth to discount important principles of our government as mere platitudes." Mind you, if this truism held steadfast for Mary Beth Tinker (a thirteen-year-old junior high school student), it was all the more so for college students.

How then do college educators best realize that Enlightenment ideal is linked to being an informed citizen? Do they, for example, take their educational cues from the kind of education offered at, say, St. John's College in Annapolis where all classes are conducted seminar-style, with faculty facilitating the discussion? Mindful of that version of liberal education, these apprentices of citizenship are enthusiastically exposed to the likes of Homer and Plato, the Old and New Testaments, Maimonides and Machiavelli, Dante and Shakespeare, Hobbes and Locke, Marx and Smith, Lincoln and Douglass, Tolstoy and W. E. B. Du Bois, and of course the Constitution and the *Federalist Papers*. But who chooses to attend St. John's? Its notion of education is so antiquated, so anti-democratic, and so unlike the offerings championed in those institutions of modern mass education. Take, for example, the University of South Carolina that allows its apprentices to major in "Hospitality Management," or the University of Southern California that offers courses in "Food Industry Management." Thirty or more four-year colleges offer these kinds of programs and/or majors in which students can study disciplines such as amusement park and casino managing, cruise directing and room service supervising, and event coordinating and wedding sales managing. To be sure, the U. of South Carolina is far more democratic in its offerings than St. John's College—and it has a remarkable football team (the South Carolina Gamecocks) to boot. Moreover, if one views the marketplace of ideas from a consumer perspective, as previously mentioned, then consumer preferences in college curriculum may well transform civic education into consumer education.

If such comments seem elitist, that is because they are. Yet, if truth be spoken, they are hardly more elitist than the *Tinker* ideal or the pure form of the pursuit of truth in the marketplace of ideas ideal. At best, when tested in the world of realpolitik or in that of modern college education, such ideals are either fanciful or hypocritical—tag them "noble lies" if you will. They make for good Constitution Day speeches but little more. Admittedly (and critics take note here), the St. John's and U. of South Carolina examples are polar ones. Still, modern mass education tends more to the preferred preferences of the latter than to the shunned principles of the former.

Again: The democratization of truth is rooted in such soil. In it facts and truths move ever closer to opinions and beliefs while civic education of the kind vouchsafed in *Tinker* is lost in the mass mix of consumer-oriented education. Such education offers *product* for its consumers, consumer-friendly product, that is. Everything else is fluff, the stuff of which fills *The Federalist Papers* (the Wiki version of it, at least). When the focus of college education moves away from the traditional tenets of liberal education to those of consumer education, when critical thinking bows to democratic preferences, and when the everyday life of college students is preoccupied with the cultural wars of the moment, knowledge itself seems relative— "you have your facts, I have mine." When that occurs, the marketplace of spectacles plays out in spectacular ways that invite provocation, on the one hand, and censorship on the other.

Enter then the sham appeal to the marketplace of ideas, followed by the con-call for toleration, followed by counterfeit claims of victimization. In the deconstructive process everyone is a victim—those who are called out for intolerance and those who must tolerate exposure to views that upset them. What is needed to either stay or reduce the possibility of victimization is thus some happy medium, some safe place where both sides speak their own preferred truths. Here, the competition in the marketplace of ideas is democratized by leveling knowledge and truth. Every person is "their" own measure. In this way the balance of truth is democratically pursued. Of course, there are always those anti-democratic types such as the late Christopher Hitchens who in his *Letters to a Young Contrarian* had the audacity to claim that "[o]n some grave questions there is no difference to be split; one does not look for a synthesis between verity and falsehood; the sun does not rise in the east one day and in the west the next."[41]

When happy-medium approaches fail, colleges predictably turn to speech codes, "trigger warnings," "safe places," and "bias response teams" either to address real bigotry and harassment or to placate those who maintain that anything that offends them, in the least, must be banned and those responsible for such offenses must be punished. When that occurs the politicized university becomes the judicialized university; in either case, liberal education is likely to be the true victim. Predictably, in the last decade or so the number of campus speech cases has exceeded the number of cases in any other category of First Amendment law. What is noteworthy is that when such practices are challenged in court, colleges typically lose, and the Supreme Court has left it at that. This should not be surprising since censorial efforts in this realm (as distinguished from that of middle and high schools) frequently fail, as they should under existing First Amendment precedents.

Let me be clear: When First Amendment claims prevail in the campus speech wars, it is owing more to a libertarian take on the First Amendment than to any pursuit of truth, or any advancement of knowledge principle, or any citizen education ideal operative in some idealized marketplace of ideas world. Nonetheless, whatever the rationale for protecting speech in these instances, that rationale can find some justification in our contemporary free expression jurisprudence, though not for the elevated reasons often accorded it.

THE DISCOURSE OF DONKEYS

> *[W]ithin the legal community today, the* Abrams *dissent of Holmes stands as one of the central organizing pronouncements for our contemporary vision of free speech.*[42]
>
> —Lee C. Bollinger

In the summer of 1925 (July 11th to be precise), Justice Holmes penned a letter to his friend Lewis Einstein, an American diplomat. It was about his much-noticed dissent in the *Abrams* case. Writing from his Massachusetts summer home at Beverly Farms, the great jurist freed himself of the extravagant judicial rhetoric about the grand "principle of the right to free speech" or the "ultimate good desired." Rather, Holmes described his constitutional handiwork in a crude way, one that equated speech freedom with the habits of a dim-witted pack animal:

> I had my whack on free speech some years ago in the case of one Abrams, and therefore did no more than lean to that and add that an idea is always an incitement. To show the ardor of the writer is not a sufficient reason for judging him, I regarded my view as simply upholding the right of a donkey to drool. But the usual notion is that you are free to say what you like if you don't shock me. Of course the value of the constitutional right is only when you do shock people.[43]

The conceptual divide between Justice Holmes' "donkey drool" comment and Professor Bollinger's "central organizing principles" statement, quoted above, is not as distant as may seem at first blush. In fact, the former might be said to inform the latter. Though the ever-capitalist Holmes thought the speech of Jacob Abrams and Mollie Steimer to be of trivial worth, if that, he nonetheless felt that their proletariat voices should have their say in the marketplace. That had less to do with whether their messages had any real value than with the idea that in the battle of words, the government should be a neutral broker. After that, the democratic prize went to the victor, whatever the message, whatever the consequence. He said as much in his dissent in *Gitlow v. New York* (1925): "If, in the long run, the beliefs expressed in proletarian dictatorship are destined to be accepted by the dominant forces of the community, the only meaning of free speech is that they should be given their chance and have their way."[44]

Note the words "proletarian dictatorship." Yes, he linked the word *dictatorship* to the words "free speech." And yes, it was the "*dominant forces* of the community" that must have "their way." As early as 1925 (*Gitlow*), or

1919 (*Abrams*), or 1884 (Memorial Day speech), Holmes had come to realize that truth could be politicized, that uninhibited free speech did not necessarily produce the knowledge of how to get to Larissa.[45] In fact, it might do just the opposite and produce trivia or tyranny. That possibility, that roll-the-dice chance is what it means to democratize truth, to leave truth to the decision of the *demos*. Holmes knew that; he was fine with that, even though he was a devil's cry from being a man of the people.

True, what was said in *Abrams* was cast in the context of politics and political speech. In a democracy, however, concepts are seldom quartered—they find their way into the gaps of every cultural context. Hence, it should surprise no one that the *Abrams* paradigm found its way into a door left open in the academy, the place where Aristotle's *Politics* and the *Federalist Papers* once held cerebral value. Thanks to Holmes (and the forces of post-modernity), the very possibility of their truths is increasingly denied; they are, after all, dead white guys. But the problem does not end at that doorstep. For a while Dr. King's *Stride Toward Freedom: The Montgomery Story* (1958) may find itself into the P.C. curriculum, one wonders how much of his non-violent philosophy (which he traced back to the likes of Aristotle, Thoreau, Marx, Rauschenbusch, and Gandhi) receives serious attention beyond pleasing platitudes that calm consciences.

The point here is not to defend, *carte blanche*, the canons of Western Civilization, which are necessarily incomplete. Rather, it is to say that in this Holmesian realm truth resides with the *prevailing preference*. And with furious fever, that democratic paradigm has assumed an ever more dominant place in the academy. It manifests itself in college classrooms and in college auditoriums where this or that cultural fad demands dominance as its battles against this or that counter-cultural fad that demands denial. In such battles, truth dies a certain death much like the glow of neon light leaves its once brilliant glass tube as its end nears.

But there is even less light at the end of another tunnel. Sometimes truth is not even the measure; at best, it is often sidelined. Take the 2015 case of the Northwestern University students whose vulnerability was on red line alert when an article appeared in a right-wing extremist publication—*The Chronicle of Higher Education*.[46] Yes, you read me right, *The Chronicle*! That article made some students very vulnerable, so exposed to a "terrifying" evil, as one student characterized it in the college paper. And what was this *Mein Kampf*-like form of reactionary literature? Answer: "Sexual Paranoia Strikes Academe" by N.W.U. Professor Laura Kipnis. As described in *The Nation*, the article "argues against her school's ban on sex between professors and students, and more broadly against the growing obsession with trauma and vulnerability among feminists on campus."[47]

In a call to solidarity, "thirty Northwestern anti-rape activists marched to their school's administrative center carrying mattresses and pillows."[48] This theater of the absurd fiasco was not some Camusian play staged as a reaction to a world without meaning (WWM). No, it was much more of a mindfuck. It was the WWM seeking to legitimate itself in a world striving to find meaning, the world of the academy. This form of the prevailing preference knows no allegiance to truth in any form. It is the product of a psychological disposition obsessed with vulnerability and victimization, the kind that if it cannot fall victim to bigotry in demonstrable ways, then substitutes a form of pseudo-bigotry amenable to being hastily tagged as "terrifying."

Jonathan Haidt and Greg Lukianoff rightfully branded this phenomenon "the coddling of the American mind."[49] Allan Bloom was less kind; touc he labeled it "the closing of the American mind."[50] Closing or coddling, the central point remains a constant: the mind and its pursuits must bow to the prevailing preference, which in the Northwestern University case and thousands of others like it is the domain of *feelings*, not so much those that prompt heroic action, but rather those that are self-centered in a world where the psychology (or pathology) of the *self* seeks dominance. Its purported victimization is its claim to power. The flip side of this (though the two work in psychological tandem) is the brash provocateur who seeks out the V.C. (victimization crowd) in the hope of spurting just enough malice to slay their P.C. goat. True to Freudian form, he thereafter plays his own victimization card when calls for censorship float in the theatrical air.

Well, there things sit. In a democracy everyone must have her day, his say, their way. Holmes smiles, or is he sneering? Either way, he lets the shit show go on.

THE HOLMESIAN PARADOX

For all the countless criticisms of the marketplace of ideas paradigm, it still rules the avowed roost in free speech jurisprudence and in those places, such as college campuses, where that metaphor finds a senseless echo. The irony is that the very Holmesian ideal that protects speech often undermines its aspirational value. The paradox: to protect the value of speech in the pursuit of speech, one must abridge speech. This is especially true in our post-modern American culture.[51] Thus, however great the excesses of falsehoods in the political marketplace, or farcicalities in the collegiate arena, the Holmesian paradigm holds, whatever its relationship to knowledge or the pursuit of truth or just simply theatrics.

The modern commonplace practice is an *en masse* approach to education where diversity in the broadest sense is the governing democratic principle.

The idea of *higher education* has taken a back seat to democratic education. The sovereignty of the people in the political marketplace thus becomes the norm in the educational marketplace. In both realms, Mill told us in his *Considerations on Representative Government*, the push "is toward collective mediocrity."[52] When that is the touchstone, the operative principle is that all ideas are created equal in the marketplace. It should thus come as no surprise that even in the dominion of the academy, bigotry is given greater rein, falsehoods are permitted wider freedom, knowledge is more frequently pitched as political, feelings are given more credence even in the face of evidence to the contrary, and all of this as opinions more and more supplant facts in the battle of wills that plays out in the ever-diverse marketplace of spectacles. To cast it another way, the workings of the academy follow the customs of the culture.

If the ideal of democracy is to allow every person to live as he or she likes, and if that ideal is the animating principle in modern colleges, then students should be free to say whatever they like, hear whomever they wish, and censor whomever they please. By that measure, the First Amendment might be seen as anti-democratic; it does not respect the will of the majority. Then again, the opposite might also be said to be true since it demands diversity, base and elevated alike.

When the First Amendment is invoked to defend such diversity, it must sometimes place its thumb on error in the hope that by exposing it, truth will prevail because knowledge demands it to be so. But that the premise is built on a *hope*, which is to say that risk is a central part of the constitutional and educational calculus. But who thinks about hope until it is too late? Preference, after all, precedes hope.

Education in the service of preference, this is the motto of consumer education in the marketplace of ideas when it erects its marquee on the college square. In that realm, bartering and battling are constants with each side claiming to be the victims of oppression. Is this, then, not a paradoxical portrait of education and any claim it might have to being designated "higher"?

When will it end? How will it end? And why? Such questions have been on the minds of many modern Americans. Though unique in their offerings to us, such concerns are not new in the larger philosophical scheme of things. More than a half-century ago, and duly attentive to such types of questions, the sociologist Jules Henry observed that the record of history proves "that man has sometimes been *forced* by misery into enlightenment although he has never accepted it without a bitter fight."[53] As Henry saw it, such a fate might be "[n]ature's plan for *Homo sapiens*, until sometime hence, if he has not destroyed himself, . . . will realize, through misery"[54] that a worthy destiny comes only to a worthy people.

One need not be schooled in Aristotelian logic to prefer informed judgment to ill-informed action. So, too, one need not till the mind fields of Kantian thought to appreciate the value of reason, that ability to apply thought to action. And one need not be versed in the nuances of Simone Weil's philosophy—briefly quoted at the top of a previous section in this chapter—to understand that words empty of meaning can lead to tyranny and barbarity. The aim is not categorical certainty, but rather some sober measure of allegiance to clear-headed thinking, sound expertise, and reasoned discourse combined with some real commitment to civility, especially on college campuses. Such words seem so foreign in our times, so remote from the contemporary experience of political strife in America and political life in the academy.

At a deeper philosophical level, what we are witnessing today is a world polluted with meaninglessness, perhaps more than we have experienced at any time in recent history. In the face of this absurd state of affairs we have two choices: to yield to it as a form of societal suicide or to rebel against it in ways that might give some purpose and value to our lives. Think of that revolt as an all-too-human demand for meaning, a rebellion against a chaotic mix of evil coupled with lunacy in which people live a stupefied kind of existence. What is important is not the realization of perfect meaning so much as the *struggle* for that measure of meaning that lends worth to our lives. It is just that measure of meaning that is being depleted on a perilous scale.

If our lives are cabined in a world of moral equivalence, if value and meaning evade us in the political and educational realms, if reason is questioned as to its worth, if the axis of our world tilts toward a kind of nihilism by any other word, it is in large part owing to our self-indulgence, our unwillingness to rebel against the abnormal becoming normal, and because of our refusal to take stock of what it is in us and in our culture that breeds the malady that afflicts us.

Even some implied or tentative notion of the value of reason in human affairs would be sufficient to improve our collective plight. If meaningful change is possible, it can only occur when enough people rebel, first and foremost, in the way we think about thinking—about being truly attentive to the workings of our physical and political worlds. Such rebellion is a call to cerebral action. It is not a quick fix; it is rather an orientation of the mind. It is not a how-to-save the world formula; it is rather a way to hold onto some measure of our sanity. It is less about ideological politics than liberal education; less about reason seen in absolute terms than reason understood in life-affirming terms; and it is less about categorical certainty than the loss of simple certainty as a way of navigating the conflicts that confront us. True: uncorrupted reason might be beyond our reach, but once politics is beyond the reach of all reason, at that point chaos steps in to claim the spoils.

AND SO HE RETURNS

Are we in danger of accepting him too uncritically?[55]

—Max Lerner

Lerner's question is about Holmes, but it is directed at us, including warnings about a "Holmes cult."[56] Holmes spent much of his time in his I Street home, a three-story house located not far from the White House and west of Farragut Square, working in his second-floor study. There, in that space surrounded by walls of books and adjacent to his secretary's room, he prepared and penned many of the opinions that made him great. Perhaps in that very room Holmes the Justice first penned his commanding metaphor; and indeed it proved to be a most momentous one. Did he have any sense of its afterlife in law and culture? Perhaps. But time was moving on. And so in his late afternoons the elderly jurist would take a break, put aside his legal papers, and read for pleasure. And then there were those times when he dozed off in his easy chair, letting his book fall to the floor. On March 6, 1935, at 2:15 a.m. he took his final rest.

"Canonization." It is the word commonly used, as in the canonization of Justice Holmes. It is an ironic use of the word to describe a man who had little or no interest or belief in "the upward and onward" as he labeled it. "In life, there was little heavenly about the irreverent agnostic, the twinkling skeptic, the down-to-the-ground judicial realist." Fred Rodell added that it took years "to elevate Mr. Justice Holmes from deity to mortality."[57] Since Holmes' life and legacy abound in irony, it is entirely understandable that such words have been used to describe the making of Holmesian memories and myths, including that of the marketplace of ideas. Like Holmes, that metaphor (as reworked by Justice Douglas) took on new life in modernity—it rose from the dead.

Behind the curtain of Holmes' realism was a certain fatalism, a peculiar detachment that bowed to the ubiquity of force. As on the battlefield, he was prepared to yield to the commands of the "dominant power." Still, he valued the fight, the valor, and the contest of wills engaged in Darwinian struggle. At times, it is easy to believe that the contest—that glorious fight for life itself—was the be-all and end-all of human existence. The marketplace metaphor is a remarkable one that says much about the man, his life, and his legacy. In all of them, his world of ideas was never far from his world of war.

This brings us back to the beginning, to the metaphoric quote from the *Abrams* dissent offered as the set piece for this chapter. Recall, that quotation concerned Holmes' fascination with *risk*, with *experimentation*. Yes, diving at night from a mountain cliff into deep dark waters is risky, but it's also gloriously exhilarating. Ah, the rush that comes with taking the existential leap! As for Holmes, there was some diver DNA in him. As Louis Menand urges us to notice, the great jurist "defended free speech in the language of *risk*."[58] Holmes' belief was that since life is an experiment, we can never be entirely certain of anything—thus we must tolerate dissent. Holmes' constitutionalism—from his *Lochner* dissent to and beyond his *Abrams* dissent—was tooled to allow for, and even encourage, social experimentation, including certain experiments that Holmes found personally objectionable, and even potentially ruinous.

The incessant disputes and debates on college campuses in defense of camouflaged bigotry, pointless arguments, feeling fiascos, unjustifiable censorship, or feigned victimization provide a sketch of how the Holmesian market experiment operates in ways that make the democratization of truth ever more real. Admittedly, a few drops of truth do, from time to time, drip into a few minds. But at what cost?

While the Holmesian fight continues, it too often seems to be a senseless one, albeit without any value save for having one's twaddle aired in the flea market of ideas. That, at any rate, appears to be the "fighting faith" of our times. Even though that faith has become ours, either formally or functionally so, few seem to realize its implications, which does not bode well for a constitutional republic ordained as ours was. And yet there is, to echo Dr. Meiklejohn, "dancing in the streets."[59]

As we dance to celebrate that faith, one wonders, to paraphrase Strauss,[60] if we also fiddle while our Rome burns. If so, might we be excused because we do not realize that we fiddle and do not know that Rome burns?[61]

NOTES

1. Oliver Wendell Holmes, letter to Harold Laski, March 4, 1920, in *Holmes-Laski Letters; The Correspondence of Mr. Justice Holmes and Harold J. Laski*, ed. Mark DeWolfe Howe (Cambridge, MA: Harvard University Press, 1953), vol. I, 248–49.

2. 250 U.S. 616, 630 (1919) (Holmes, J., dissenting).

3. Richard A. Posner, ed. *The Essential Holmes* (Chicago: University of Chicago Press, 1997), 192, xii.

4. Richard A. Posner, "Foreword, Symposium: The Path of the Law 100 Years Later: Holmes' Influence on Modern Jurisprudence," *Brooklyn Law Review* 63 (1997): 7–8.

5. 249 U.S. 47 (1919).

6. 250 U.S. 616, 630 (1919) (Holmes, J., dissenting).

7. 268 U.S. 652 (1925) (Holmes, J., dissenting).

8. 345 U.S. 41, 56 (1953) (Douglas, J., concurring).

9. Michael Connelly, *Angels Flight* (New York: Grand Central Publishing, 1999), 1.

10. Friedrich Nietzsche, "On Truth and Lies in a Nonmoral Sense," *Truth: Engagements Across Philosophical Traditions*, ed. David Wood and Jose Medina (Malden, MA: Blackwell Publishing, 2005), 17.

11. John Milton, *Areopagitica* (Cambridge: Cambridge University Press), 1918, 58. For this idea finding expression in the college free speech context, see Robert M. O'Neil, *Free Speech in the College Community* (Bloomington, IN: Indiana University Press, 1997), 87.

12. John Milton, *The Prose Works of John Milton* (London: Westley & Davis, 1835), 117.

13. Alexander Meiklejohn, *Political Freedom: The Constitutional Powers of the People* (New York: Harper, 1960), 75.

14. 135 S. Ct. 2239, 2246 (2015).

15. Erwin Chemerinsky and Howard Gillman, *Free Speech on Campus* (New Haven, CT: Yale University Press, 2017), 24.

16. Bob Dylan, "With God on Our Side," *The Times They Are A Changin'* (Columbia Records, 1964).

17. Henry Livermore Abbott, *Fallen Leaves the Civil War Letters of Major Henry Livermore Abbott*, ed. Robert Garth Scott (Kent, OH: Kent State University Press, 1991), 62.

18. 250 U.S. at 630 (Holmes, J., dissenting).

19. Oliver Wendell Holmes, "Memorial Day Address," May 30, 1884, in *The Fundamental Holmes: A Free Speech Chronicle and Reader – Selections from the Opinions, Books, Articles, Speeches, Letters and Other Writings by and about Oliver Wendell Holmes, Jr.*, ed. Ronald K.L. Collins (New York: Cambridge University Press, 2010), xx.

20. Ibid.

21. Louis Menand, *The Metaphysical Club: A Story of Ideas in America* (New York: Farrar, Straus & Giroux, 2001), 9.

22. Oliver Wendell Holmes, "Ideas and Doubts," *Illinois Law Review* 10 (1915): 1, 2.

23. Oliver Wendell Holmes, quoted in *The Fundamental Holmes*, 394.

24. Stephen Pepper, "Philosophy and Metaphor," *Journal of Philosophy* 25, no. 5 (March 1928): 130.

25. Christy Wampole, *Rootedness: The Ramifications of a Metaphor* (Chicago: University of Chicago Press, 2016).

26. 774 F. Supp. 1163, 1181 (E.D. Wis. 1991).

27. Jon Gould, "The Triumph of Hate Speech Regulation: Why Gender Wins But Race Loses in America," *Michigan Journal of Gender and Law* 6 (1999): 158.

28. 774 F. Supp. 1163, 1181 (E.D. Wis. 1991).

29. Ibid.

30. 279 U.S. 644, 654–55 (1929) (Holmes, J., dissenting).

31. Erik Wemple, "CNN commentator Scottie Nell Hughes: Facts No Longer Exist," *The Washington Post*, December 1, 2016, https://www.washingtonpost.com/blogs/erik-wemple/wp/2016/12/01/cnn-commentator-scottie-nell-hughes-facts-no-longer-exist/.

32. Michiko Kakutani, *The Death of Truth: Notes on Falsehood in the Age of Trump* (New York: Tim Duggan Books, 2018), 17.

33. Ibid., 19.

34. Paul J. Griffiths, *Lying: An Augustinian Theology of Duplicity* (Ada, MI: Brazos Press, 2004), 23–110.

35. Leo Strauss, *Liberalism Ancient and Modern* (Chicago: University of Chicago Press, 1968), 85.

36. Plato, *The Republic* (493-a-493e).

37. Simone Weil, *The Need for Roots: Prelude to a Declaration of Duties Towards Mankind*, trans. Arthur Wills (New York: Routledge 2001), 33.

38. Ironically, and as noted by his biographer (Laura Kalman), when the case first came to the Court, Fortas did not want to have the Justices hear it. See Laura Kalman, *Abe Fortas: A Biography* (New Haven: Yale University Press, 1990), 287.

39. Thomas C. Fisher, "'Whatever Happened to Mary Beth Tinker' and Other Sagas in the Academic 'Marketplace of Ideas,'" *Golden Gate Law Review* 23 (1993): 352.

40. *Tinker*, 393 U.S. 503, 506 (1969).

41. Christopher Hitchens, *Letters to a Young Contrarian* (New York: Basic Books, 2001), 21.

42. Lee C. Bollinger, *The Tolerant Society: Freedom of Speech and Extremist Speech in America* (New York: Oxford University Press, 1986), 18.

43. Oliver Wendell Holmes, letter to Lewis Einstein, in *The Fundamental Holmes*, 280 (July 11, 1925).

44. 268 U.S. 652, 673 (1925).

45. In Plato's *Meno*, the road to Larissa is linked with the knowledge of how to get there.

46. Laura Kipnis, "Sexual Paranoia Strikes Academe," *The Chronicle of Higher Education,* February 27, 2015.

47. Michelle Goldberg, "The Laura Kipnis Melodrama," *The Nation*, March 16, 2015, https://www.thenation.com/article/archive/laura-kipnis-melodrama/.

48. Scott H. Greenfield, "The Consequences of Free Speech Strike Northwestern," *Simple Justice*, March 21, 2015, https://blog.simplejustice.us/2015/03/21/the-consequences-of-free-speech-strike-northwestern/.

49. Jonathan Haidt and Greg Lukianoff, *The Coddling of the American Mind: How Good Intentions and Bad Ideas Are Setting Up a Generation for Failure* (New York: Penguin, 2018).

50. Allan Bloom, *The Closing of the American Mind* (New York: Simon & Schuster, 1987).

51. This point is the focus of *The Death of Discourse* (1996), a book I did with David Skover. See Ronald K.L. Collins and David Skover, *The Death of Discourse* (Durham, NC: Carolina Academic Press, 2005).

52. John Stuart Mill, *Considerations on Representative Government* (West Strand, England: Parker, Son, & Bourn, 1761), 146.

53. Jules Henry, *Culture Against Man* (New York: Vintage, 1965), 477.

54. Ibid.

55. Max Lerner, *Nine Scorpions in a Bottle: Great Judges and Cases of the Supreme Court* (New York: Arcade Publishing, 1994), 124.

56. Ibid.

57. Fred Rodell, *Nine Men: A Political History of the Supreme Court from 1790 to 1955* (New York: Random House, 1955), 179–80 (quoting Walton Hamilton).

58. Menand, *The Metaphysical Club*, 432 (emphasis added).

59. Alexander Meiklejohn, quoted in Harry Kalven, Jr., "The New York Times Case: A Note on 'The Central Meaning of the First Amendment'," *1964 Supreme Court Review* 191, 221 n.125.

60. Leo Strauss, "An Epilogue," in *Essays on the Scientific Study of Politics*, ed. Herbert J. Storing (New York: Rinehart & Winston, Inc., 1962), 327.

61. To think freely and openly, as I have attempted to do in this chapter, ought not to be mistaken as some warrant for censorship in our system of free expression as it is currently constituted (see *The Death of Discourse*). Rather, it is to flag the hypocrisy in much of the campus speech debates (and elsewhere) and likewise to point to the real-world costs of such a system of free speech, costs that may well be unavoidable given our social order. In all of this there is more than a whiff of the absurd, the existential absurd if you will.

Chapter 3

Teaching and Preaching Free Speech

Rodney A. Smolla

REFLECTIONS FROM A BOOK TOUR

While on a "book tour" of sorts before and after the publication of a book entitled *Confessions of a Free Speech Lawyer: Charlottesville and the Politics of Hate*,[1] I've had occasion to be interviewed by or have collegial conversations with many people for whom I have great respect, on the topic of the state of free speech on the modern American university campus. The interviewers have been diverse, from Joseph Russomanno, the editor of this book, to Nadine Strossen, former president of the ACLU, First Amendment scholars Ronald Collins and Mary-Rose Papandrea, to Nico Perrino, of FIRE.

Typically, the conversation moves, often at my own invitation, to the question of what the current generation of college students believe about free speech and the First Amendment.

Anecdotally, a lot of those who live and work on college campuses have been saying for some time that many in this generation "do not understand" freedom of speech.

I tend to frame the issue more neutrally. It is not that this generation does not understand the meaning of "freedom of speech" in the same sense that I understand it as a First Amendment litigator and scholar. It is that many in this generation—perhaps about half—understand it differently. Or to phrase the same proposition in another way: roughly half of this generation understands the meaning of freedom of speech as I embraced it as a college student in the early 1970s, and later as a free speech lawyer and litigator, and the other half disagrees with my understanding.

The impression I have gathered from the anecdotes of colleagues has been reinforced for me firsthand. My own college-age children have challenged my views of free speech, often in the aftermath of hate speech incidents on their own campuses.

Data also supports this anecdotal impression.

John Villasenor, summarizing data collected in a Brookings Institute Report, tells the story succinctly.[2]

Students were asked, "Does the First Amendment protect hate speech?"

The result: 39% "Yes."
44% "No."
16% "Don't know."

Students were posed this scenario and question: "A student group opposed to the speaker disrupts the speech by loudly and repeatedly shouting so that the audience cannot hear the speaker. Do you agree or disagree that the student group's actions are acceptable?"

The result: 51% "Agree."
49% "Disagree."
16% "Don't know."

Students were asked to choose between two options as to the policies that colleges should adopt about their learning environments.

"Option 1: create a positive learning environment for all students by prohibiting certain speech or expression of viewpoints that are offensive or biased against certain groups of people."

"Option 2: create an open learning environment where students are exposed to all types of speech and viewpoints, even if it means allowing speech that is offensive or biased against certain groups of people?"

The result: 53% "Option 1."
47% "Option 2."

The upshot strikes me as pretty clear. Roughly half of those in college, professional schools, or early in their careers as millennials, do not believe that our law or culture should protect hateful speech. About half do not think the Constitution protects it; about half believe it acceptable to heckle and shout down the messages of hate so that they cannot be heard, and about half support policies in which colleges create learning environments that do not permit speech or expression of viewpoints that are offensive or biased against certain groups of people.

So, accepting that this is the state of play, what then, to make of it?

I begin with a division between two opposing conceptions of freedom of speech that in my view have always dominated the American landscape. I call the first conception the "order and morality" theory; the second conception, the "marketplace theory."

I have been preaching about these two opposing conceptions for a long time. I did not originally come up with this simple (or perhaps simplistic) binary approach to thinking about free speech as a scholarly endeavor, but rather simply as a teacher. My purpose was not normative or theoretical, but merely descriptive. I had no grand unifying theory of the First Amendment in mind, but rather began invoking this vocabulary as nothing much more than a teaching tool.

TEACHING FREE SPEECH

Teaching the First Amendment Compared to the Rest of the Constitution

My evolving sensibilities about how to teach free speech law arose from frustration. To put it bluntly, I did not feel I was doing a very good job.

The teaching tool I developed evolved out of my observation of how frustrating it was for students to try to organize and make any coherent sense of the dizzying array of doctrines and tests that populate free speech law. I was struck by how far more disorienting the judicial decisions and legal doctrines governing free speech law were when compared to the cases and doctrines in virtually every other arena of constitutional law.

I have been teaching constitutional law for decades. Many American law schools have for years divided the constitutional law curriculum into more than one course. Criminal procedure, which is largely constitutional law, is always spun off as a world unto itself, typically taken after the course in "substantive" criminal law.

One popular model for the remainder of the constitutional law curriculum is to have one course, typically three to five credit hours, that covers structural elements of constitutional law, such as separation of powers and federalism, the commerce clause, and most civil rights and civil liberties topics other than speech and religion. This "basic" course thus includes judicial review, the presidency, the powers of Congress, the relationship between the federal government and the states, the relationship of the states to each other, equal protection, substantive and procedural due process, the right to bear arms, takings of property, and more. What is then spun off is a separate free-standing course, sometimes required and sometimes optional, typically offered for two or three credit hours, on the First Amendment. The First Amendment course typically covers religion, speech, association, journalism, and related rights.

In undergraduate and other academic programs, most universities, and surely most journalism and communications schools, offer a similar course in First Amendment law.

I love all of American constitutional law and have been a scholar and litigator across much of its expanse, but I have made my strongest mark in litigating and writing about free speech issues. Even so, I found I was a much better teacher in, and intrinsically enjoyed more, the "basic" constitutional law course over the First Amendment course.

For a long time, I chalked this counter-intuitive contradiction up to my own bad habits as a teacher. Perhaps I knew too much about First Amendment law and practice, and my expertise got in the way, as I lost perspective on how much density and detail novice students could plausibly digest. Perhaps too I often gave in way too easily to telling war stories of cases I had litigated.

I still think those bad habits sometimes hurt my teaching, and like any old but not-yet-retired athlete who knows how easy it is to lose one's stride or rhythm or swing, I continue to train against them.

In the self-analysis of my teaching, however, I came to see a deeper problem. In the basic constitutional law course, I have always found it relatively easy to avoid pontification and proselytizing.

I know that many of my university professor colleagues see no problem with using the teaching podium as a bully pulpit. But I have never felt comfortable indulging in partisan advocacy as a professor—at least on most issues. The major exception for me has been my unabashed willingness to take strong stands on professionalism and "what it means to be a lawyer," which includes, in my judgment, cultural sensitivity, and awareness of racism, sexism, homophobia, and other forms of religious, sexual, ethnic, or identity prejudice.

But I am generally scrupulous in *not* taking positions in class on the countless constitutional law issues over which the country remains deeply divided. I do not tip my hand, for example, on whether I privately believe the abortion decisions in *Roe v. Wade*[3] and *Planned Parenthood of Southeastern Pennsylvania v. Casey*[4] were right or wrong, or whether the Supreme Court in *District of Columbia v. Heller*[5] blew it in holding that the Second Amendment embodies a personal right to bear arms.

Particularly during the presidency of Donald Trump, on any given day the material we might be covering in the constitutional law course could devolve into a partisan debate over whether the president did or did not understand or respect the Constitution. I happily moderate these debates, but try to moderate them from a chair of neutrality.

And so in classes in which the topic of the day is abortion, I see my obligation as a teacher as cajoling the students to think deeply and to discuss authentically the deep moral, philosophical, and legal issues posed by abortion, including the core debates over the meaning of "human life" and "potential human life." My goal is to keep this part of the discussion as unstructured and open and authentic, and perhaps as confusing as possible, encouraging the give and take of ideas and positions to swirl through the classroom. I then attempt to bring some order to the chaos, seeking to ensure that whatever a student's subjective views on *Roe* and *Casey* might be, he or she would understand the Court's application of strict scrutiny in the case, understand the notion that women had a constitutional right to an abortion prior to fetal viability, and understand the power of states to regulate abortion on the margins prior to viability under the "under burden" standard. The formal legal doctrines governing abortion turn out to be relatively easy to comprehend—indeed, the doctrines are quite internally logical, in stark contrast to the deep intensity of the philosophical, moral, and policy debates that inform them.

I came to realize, however, that in the First Amendment course, a different dynamic was at work. I was not teaching controversies over hate speech with anywhere near the same teaching acumen that I possessed when teaching controversies over abortion. There were two striking differences, to which I now turn.

My Teaching Blind Spots

To begin, I realized that in teaching free speech I tended to engage in a certain passive-aggressive proselyting and manipulation. It was subtle enough, and perhaps invisible to many students, but on genuine self-introspection, I could not hide it from myself. I was, for the most part, a "true believer" in the marketplace theory (described in more detail below), the wide-open pro-free-speech-let-er-rip-and-let-no-person-come-back-ashamed radical libertarian view of the later Oliver Wendell Holmes and the modern ACLU. My proselytizing, I decided, was getting in the way of authentic and effective teaching.

The second difference, I came to believe, was not so much my fault, but rather a feature of the peculiar way free speech law has evolved. Free speech doctrines constantly present intense "culture war" conflicts—but no more intense than dozens of other constitutional law doctrines. What is peculiar about free speech law, however, is that it appears to lack the elegant architectural balance and symmetry that most other major arenas of constitutional law possess.

Understanding that by nature I exaggerate a bit, what do I mean by the bold (and some may say heretical) assertion that large swaths of constitutional law partake of elegant architectural balance and symmetry? I mean that in the same sense that physicists may see elegance in Einstein's equation that $E = mc^2$, or that both an architect and a historian might see elegance in the Lincoln Memorial—in its columns, in its placement on the Washington Mall, in its seated statue of Lincoln, in its framing by Lincoln's Gettysburg and Second Inaugural Address. Many constitutional law doctrines outside of free speech law at least make a certain satisfying algebraic good sense.

Please do not think me a fool or an apologist. I entirely understand that the basic constitutional law course is not wanting for intensity and controversy. The powers of the judiciary, including the core power to override decisions of the democracy, constraints on judicial power through justiciability doctrines such as standing, ripeness, mootness, and the political question doctrine, the roles of the president and Congress over war and peace, impeachment, the executive order power, race discrimination, sex discrimination, LGBTQ rights, same-sex marriage, abortion, affirmative action, the rights of the terminally ill, the right to travel, the right to keep and bear arms, the balance between property rights and the environment, to name a number of the biggies, are enough to keep any conscientious teacher plenty busy and challenged.

Moreover, I entirely understand that the appropriate resolution of these intense conflicts is a perpetual and dynamic process. My modest claim is that as these conflicts are resolved, for better or for worse, the doctrines that emerge to articulate the resolution tend to be reasonably compressible and well-crafted. The doctrines themselves make internal sense, and those doctrines can usually also be rationally situated against the larger backdrop of constitutional law.

Let me provide some examples.

I have already written about abortion. On an intensity scale, no conflict may match it. Doctrinally, the strict scrutiny standard, the principle of fetal viability, and the undue burden test make reasonable internal and external sense. Candidly, so would a decision to overturn *Roe* and *Casey* and remand the issue to the individual states.

Speaking of individual states, consider the mundane world of the "Dormant Commerce Clause." The Dormant Commerce Clause refers to the powers of states to pass laws that impact interstate commerce. Here are the basic rules: If a state passes a law that discriminates against out-of-state commerce, it is considered a per se violation of the Dormant Commerce Clause. The famous case *Philadelphia v. New Jersey*[6] struck down a law as per se invalid because New Jersey would not allow garbage to be brought in from other states. (Philadelphia's garbage was no better or worse than anybody else's.) States sometimes try to ban people from traveling into a state from other states. This used to be treated as a Dormant Commerce Clause problem—at least when the ban was, for example, banning people without jobs.[7]

Today it would more likely be analyzed under the right to travel.[8] Either way, a ban on people coming into a state from other states would also normally be a per se violation of the Constitution (but see the quarantine exception discussed below).

More commonly, a state will have a neutral rule that does not on its face discriminate against out-of-state commerce, but has the effect of burdening commerce. In such cases, courts apply a balancing test, weighing the negative impact on interstate commerce against the strength of the local interest being advanced by the law. Here is a famous example: Arizona limited the length of freight trains to seventy cars and passenger trains to fourteen cars. This had a major impact on interstate commerce, because most trains traveling across the United States through Arizona were much longer. Arizona claimed the local interest was safety, because longer trains are harder to control and stop. However, it also turned out that Arizona limits meant that twice as many trains would now have to move through Arizona. The Supreme Court struck down the law, because the improved safety appeared to be a wash, but the burden was extreme.[9]

We can add a few additional rules and points. There is a "quarantine exception" that allows states to ban imports from other states that carry disease or other health risks. A typical example is a ban on fruit imports from another state if there is a fungus or insect infestation from that product. This is an exception to the normal per se rule against discrimination from out-of-state imports.[10]

There is also an exception known as the "market participant" exception. This is when the state is in a business itself, and it prefers in-state customers or suppliers over out-of-state customers or suppliers. If the state itself is operating the business, the Dormant Commerce Clause does not apply. A famous example involved a cement factory owned and operated by the state—the state owned the factory and the employees were state employees.[11] In such cases that factory could prefer local suppliers and customers, because it was treated as essentially a private business.

Lastly, the U.S. Congress has an "override" power to regulate interstate commerce. Congress can use its power to regulate interstate commerce to put additional restrictions on states or to ease restrictions on states, if it wanted to. So, for example, under the Dormant Commerce Clause, no state can refuse to take another state's garbage. But Congress could pass a law overriding this rule, enacting legislation that allows a state to refuse to take another state's garbage.[12]

Why have I described, in a book chapter about teaching and preaching on free speech, this mini-dissertation on the "Dormant Commerce Clause?" Because it illustrates the architectural elegance to which I have averred. In a few short paragraphs the core of all Dormant Commerce Clause jurisprudence may be logically articulated and demonstrated.

As a final exemplar, consider equal protection. There is no more deeply troubling and divisive aspect of the American constitutional experience than the meaning of our national commitment to equality, from the ringing natural law assertion in the Declaration of Independence that all men are created equal, to the Emancipation Proclamation, to the Fourteenth Amendment's guarantee of the equal protection of the laws.

The 2020 murder of George Floyd, and the ensuing tsunami of national protest, laid bare our national failure to come to grips with the deepest and most stubbornly persistent elements of our country's entrenched systemic racism. As a teacher, I hope that as students read and absorb in all their ramifications decisions such as *Cherokee Nations v. Georgia*,[13] chronicling the genocidal impulses of whites against native Americans; or *Dred Scott v. Sandford*,[14] reifying slavery; or *Plessy v. Ferguson*,[15] justifying the pernicious racist "separate but equal" doctrine; or *Korematsu v. United States*,[16] upholding the disgraceful internment of Japanese American citizens during World War II; or *Trump v. Hawaii*,[17] sustaining President Trump's immigration ban (though also explicitly overruling *Korematsu*). These cases chronicle the most dreadful dark impulses in the American experience.

Even so, the "make order from chaos" side of me as a teacher welcomes the relative simplicity of equal protection analysis as a *doctrinal* matter. There are three tiers of equal protection scrutiny: "strict scrutiny," which applies to suspect classifications such as race or classifications based on the exercise of fundamental rights, such as the right to marry; "intermediate scrutiny," based on classifications that are deemed quasi-suspect, such as gender; and "rational basis scrutiny," applicable to any classification that does not trigger strict or intermediate review—essentially the vast mine-run of all social and economic legislation.[18]

Strict scrutiny, students learn, requires that the government bear the burden of proving that the law is narrowly tailored to the effectuation of compelling governmental interests. The "gatekeeper" that triggers strict scrutiny review is the "purposeful discrimination" requirement, which requires proof that the government intended to impose a classification based on the suspect category, such as race. If the law merely has, by happenstance, a differential impact—such as affecting blacks more than whites, or women more than men, no heightened scrutiny ("strict" or "intermediate") is triggered.[19]

In class I routinely discuss and debate the propriety of these rules with students. But the *matrix* they impose is logically pleasing. Purposeful discrimination is the key gatekeeper, and if it is demonstrated, then heightened scrutiny—strict or intermediate, as the case may be—is applied.

How Are Students to Make Sense of Free Speech Doctrines?

Contrast the examples from abortion law, the Dormant Commerce Clause, and equal protection jurisprudence, with how free speech doctrine is organized. At first, some semblance of similar logical organization appears promising. Students are taught that there is a fundamental divide between content-based and content-neutral regulation of speech. Content-based discrimination triggers strict scrutiny. "Content-based laws—those that target speech based on its communicative content—are presumptively unconstitutional and may be justified only if the government proves that they are narrowly tailored to serve compelling state interests."[20] Content-neutral regulation triggers some variant of intermediate scrutiny.[21] Students are also taught that "[v]iewpoint discrimination is . . . an egregious form of content discrimination."[22] Laws that discriminate against viewpoints are almost always invalidated through a sort of strict scrutiny on steroids. Even when the viewpoint discrimination is choosing what is manifestly the righteous side of a debate—such as favoring equality and respect for human dignity over racism—the law will be struck down, as the Court did in *R.A.V. v. City of St. Paul*,[23] stating that "St. Paul has no such authority to license one side of a debate to fight freestyle, while requiring the other to follow Marquis of Queensberry rules."[24]

If this were all there were to free speech law, it would remain fascinating in its intensity, but not daunting in its doctrine.

But alas, this is *not* all there is. Unlike equal protection jurisprudence, with its three simple tiers of review and a reasonably coherent "on-off" switch—the "purposeful discrimination" requirement—free speech law presents no comparable easily accessible organizing logic.

First Amendment law in the United States is the accreted experience of 100 years of debate and hundreds of Supreme Court decisions. Free speech law is complicated. I am the author of multiple legal treatises dealing with matters relating to free speech, media, and civil rights laws. They contain scores of chapters and sub-chapters, expounding on a bewildering array of multi-prong tests, and a maze of specialized rules, exceptions to rules, and exceptions to exceptions to rules. Behold the polymath complexity: on top of the big-picture doctrines such as content discrimination, viewpoint discrimination, and content-neutral regulation, free speech law has produced dozens of "mini-tests," governing specific doctrinal arenas. There are definitions and tests for traditional public forums, designated public forums, limited public forums, non-forums, time, place, or manner restrictions, incitement to violence, true threats, obscenity, child pornography, prior restraints, commercial speech, corporate speech, professional speech, government speech, advertising by professionals, speech of government employees, political patronage, campaign finance, regulation of political parties, speech of public school students, speech of public school teachers, academic freedom, student newspapers, student organizations, regulation of print, cable, broadcast, satellite, and internet media, defamation, privacy, infliction of emotional distress, appropriation of name or likeness, copyright, trademark, speech of prisoners, speech of lawyers, and other participants in the legal system, and more. My favorite example of the Court embracing this minute compartmentalizing of First Amendment doctrine is a statement in *Metromedia, Inc. v. City of San Diego*,[25] that each method of communicating ideas is "a law unto itself" and "[w]e deal here with the law of billboards."[26]

Under this approach, on "libel day" I would teach libel law, and on "billboard day" teach billboard law.

Making matters worse, students studying free speech opinions often have a difficult time placing decisions in their temporal context. For classes that cover the history of Supreme Court decisions beginning with the World War I epoch prosecutions, students typically read the Holmes opinions in *Schenck v. United States*,[27] and perhaps also are exposed to Holmes' ruling in *Frohwerk v. United States*,[28] and *Debs v. United States*.[29] In all three cases Holmes sent the protestors to jail. *Schenck* is particularly confusing, because that is where Holmes used his famous phrasing "clear and present danger," which students have often heard bandied about in popular culture as pro-free-speech concept. *Schenck* is also where Holmes used his "shout fire in a crowded theatre" metaphor, another stock cultural cliché. Yet *Schenck* was an anti-free-speech decision, as were *Frohwerk* and *Debs*, neither of which mentioned the clear and present danger test. Then comes *Abrams v. United States*,[30] just months after *Schenck*, *Frohwerk*, and *Debs*, in which Holmes suddenly and famously dissents. Yet Holmes insists in *Abrams* that he thought the results in the prior three cases were correct, and proclaimed no dissonance between his own prior opinions in *Schenck*, *Frohwerk*, and *Debs*, and his dissent in *Abrams*: "I never have seen any reason to doubt that the questions of law that alone were before this Court in the Cases of *Schenck*, . . . *Frohwerk*, . . . and *Debs* . . . were rightly decided."[31]

Place yourself in the position of a student reading all four of these Holmes opinions for the first time. The student might naturally be inclined to expect that somehow they may be harmonized. After all, Holmes himself said so.

It is no wonder many students will be disoriented trying to reconcile the lot of them—because they cannot, with any intellectual honesty and rigor, be harmonized.

Students will typically then soon be exposed to the decision in *Chaplinsky v. New Hampshire*,[32] and this extraordinarily sublime and succinct passage:

> There are certain well-defined and narrowly limited classes of speech, the prevention and punishment of which has never been thought to raise any

> Constitutional problem. These include the lewd and obscene, the profane, the libelous, and the insulting or "fighting" words—those which by their very utterance inflict injury or tend to incite an immediate breach of the peace. It has been well observed that such utterances are no essential part of any exposition of ideas, and are of such slight social value as a step to truth that any benefit that may be derived from them is clearly outweighed by the social interest in order and morality.[33]

But how are students to place this language against the context of the decisions by Justice Holmes in *Schenck* or *Abrams*? And moving forward, how are students to understand this passage in light of the parade of more modern free speech decisions that seem to cut against it, from *New York Times v. Sullivan*,[34] largely immunizing from liability the "libelous," to *Cohen v. California*,[35] holding that the phrase "fuck the draft" was constitutionally protected in a public forum, to cases holding that the First Amendment protected some cross-burnings, such as *R.A.V. v. City of St. Paul*[36] and *Virginia v. Black*[37] (a case I argued in the Supreme Court, defending the Ku Klux Klan—to the dismay of many of my students, then and now)? How are they to harmonize *Chaplinsky* with *Texas v. Johnson*,[38] establishing a First Amendment right to desecrate the American flag, or more recently, *Snyder v. Phelps*,[39] protecting vicious verbal attacks on fallen military heroes at their funerals, *United States v. Stevens*,[40] protecting trafficking in gross images of animal cruelty, indulging the fetish of women crushing small animals in stiletto heels, or *United States v. Alvarez*,[41] protecting cold-blooded lies of persons falsely claiming to have been awarded high military honors?

Is *Chaplinsky* dead, or still good law? If it is dead, why is it still constantly cited? Do the categories of unprotected speech articulated in *Chaplinsky* remain unprotected? Is the list exhaustive, or may more categories be added? And as to methodology, is it still the case that in assessing whether or not speech is protected, courts should weigh the extent to which the speech partakes of anything other than "slight social value as a step to truth," and whether even if there is some slight social value, any benefit that may be derived from the expression "is clearly outweighed by the social interest in order and morality?"

Or has the Court now repudiated this approach to defining levels of First Amendment protection by "categories" identified through such balancing. Such a repudiation might be garnered from the statement in *Stevens* that prior cases "do not set forth a test that may be applied as a general matter to permit the Government to imprison any speaker so long as his speech is deemed valueless or unnecessary, or so long as an ad hoc calculus of costs and benefits tilts in a statute's favor."[42]

These questions do not exhaust the full range of the mystery, but they capture the gist.

How was I, as a teacher, to make some sense of this, or to help my students make some sense of it? My first impulse, and I later came to feel, my worst impulse, was to take sides and proselytize. And in a sense, this worked out pretty well. Holmes was wrong in *Schenck* but then got it right in *Abrams*. As in *Amazing Grace*, "I once was blind but now I see." So too, *Chaplinsky* was wrong, but later *Cohen v. California* (fuck the draft), *Brandenburg v. Ohio*[43] (a racist Klan cross-burning rally), *Virginia v. Black* (cross-burning redux), *Texas v. Johnson*, (burning the American flag), *New York Times Co. v. Sullivan* (public official libel), *United States v. Stevens* (animal crush videos), *Snyder v. Phelps* (vicious attacks at military funerals), *United States v. Alverez* (false military honors) were right.

The Perils of Picking Sides

So, you may be thinking, what would be so wrong with this picture?

I came to see two things wrong with it.

First, I was belittling the opposing side. I was not giving enough attention or credit to the powerful arguments emanating from *Chaplinsky* that in the eyes of many could and should be invoked to reach results opposite those that prevailed in the modern First Amendment "Walk of Fame." Remember the anecdotal tales and survey data presented at the start of this chapter. If I immediately take sides, I immediately marginalize half the student body, who may now think of me as a propagandist for a set of values they do not share.

Second, my approach failed to cogently take account of the myriad decisions in which the "order and morality" values of *Chaplinsky* appeared to *prevail* in modern free speech decisions, as they often continue to do.

The hydraulic pressure of these failures led me to the thesis I advance here, in three parts.

First, I believe all American free speech law may be reduced to a grand debate between two opposing and powerfully attractive conceptions of the meaning of "freedom of speech." I assign the two competing ideas the nicknames "order and morality theory" and "marketplace theory."

Second, both theories are alive and well in modern First Amendment law, and appropriately so. The "marketplace theory" governs in the general open marketplace of discourse. The order and morality theory governs in special settings, such as employment, public schools, prisons, speech within the legal system, and other settings that function as "carve outs" from the general marketplace. This has not always been so. Until the 1960s, the order and morality theory essentially ran the show across-the-board. That is why, when Holmes switched positions in *Abrams*, migrating from his earlier holdings in

Schenck, *Debs*, and *Frohwerk*, all early versions of the "order and morality theory," to his later opinion in *Abrams*, his later opinion was a *dissent*. (And though Holmes would not admit it, it was essentially a dissent from his own prior decisions.)

Third, once the first two propositions above are credited as apt descriptions of free speech law, much of modern free speech law can be cogently explained as a "boundary dispute," in which the salient issue is whether we are in the open public arena, in which the marketplace theory prevails, or a special setting, in which the order and morality theory prevails. This has special poignancy on the modern university campus, in which both theories lay a plausible claim to primacy.

My own view is that the modern campus ought not be regarded as governed by either theory in its entirety, but rather treated as a divided space, in which the marketplace theory governs in certain circumstances, and the order and morality theory in others.

ORGANIZING FREE SPEECH THEORY

Order and Morality

The two American cases that most powerfully illustrate the order and morality theory are *Chaplinsky*, which I have already discussed, and the Supreme Court's 1952 decision in *Beauharnais v. Illinois*.[44]

Joseph Beauharnais was an Illinois racist, the leader of a Chicago racial supremacist group that called itself the White Circle League of America. Beauharnais distributed racist leaflets in Chicago, my hometown and a city plagued, like so many others, with decades of systemic racism. Beauharnais was convicted of violating an Illinois criminal law prohibiting racist attacks.

There was no question that the Beauharnais leaflets violated the Illinois law. The question was whether the Illinois law violated the First Amendment. The Supreme Court held that it did not. Justice Felix Frankfurter, who was Jewish, plainly had in mind Hitler's Holocaust and the use of group libel against Jews when he wrote the opinion affirming Beauharnais's conviction. Echoing the reasoning of Justice Frank Murphy in *Chaplinsky*, Justice Frankfurter's opinion for the Court concluded that considering history and the pernicious tendencies of extreme racial and religious propaganda to promote racial discord, the Illinois law did not violate the First Amendment.

Curiously, not many textbooks and casebooks say much about *Beauharnais*. In the most recent iteration of the constitutional law casebook that I co-edit with my colleague William Banks, however, we have placed *Beauharnais* front and center stage at the beginning of the free speech chapter, right after *Chaplinsky*, to introduce the high-water mark of the order and morality theory.[45] The goal is to make this battle of ideas a somewhat more even fight.

The Marketplace Theory

In a series of landmark decisions beginning in the 1960s and stretching through today, the Supreme Court has largely supplanted the order and morality theory with the marketplace theory *in the general arenas of public discourse*. I have already mentioned the salient cases that represent the ascendency of this view. In presenting it historically, I have students carefully dissect, line by line, the Holmes dissent in *Abrams*, in which he argued for the protection of speech that we loathe and believe is fraught with death, and the subsequent concurring opinion written in 1927 by Justice Louis Brandeis in *Whitney v. California*.[46] Brandeis railed against the suppression of speech that we fear and loathe, arguing that such suppression only makes the evil speech stronger, and that any legislation based on fear may lead to hysterical persecution. In one of the most powerful statements ever written by a Supreme Court Justice, Brandeis admonished: "Men feared witches and burnt women."[47]

The Setting Controls

I am of the view that both the order and morality theory and the marketplace theory are alive and well in modern free speech law. The narrative that I supply to students to help them make sense of it all is that until the 1960s, the order and morality theory dominated. The dissenting opinion of Holmes in *Abrams* and the concurring opinion of Brandeis in *Whitney* were losers, not winners. It was not until the 1960s, in decisions such as *New York Times Co. v. Sullivan* or *Brandenburg v. Ohio* that the tide really began to turn. The tide turned, however, only in the "general marketplace" of American discourse. In many special settings, such as schools, employment, speech within the legal system, or speech *not* in public forums, the order and morality theory remained ascendant. Paul Cohen, I explain to students, could wear a jacket with the word "fuck" in a public forum, but not necessarily to a public school or a public job.

I have spent a good part of my career as a scholar and litigator arguing that it is not the *content* that matters, but the *context*. The issue is not whether the utterance of the word "fuck" is protected by the First Amendment. The issue is when and where it is protected, and when and where it is not. I have written too much and too often on this thesis to repeat myself again here—suffice it to say that for purposes of this chapter, I am arguing that this is, in the descriptive sense, and ought to be, in the normative sense, the governing constitutional divide.[48]

My views on this point will not satisfy those who believe that the marketplace theory should always dominate, in all places and in all times. Nor will my views satisfy those who believe that the order and morality theory should always dominate, in all places and in all times.

My views *do*, however, realistically capture the actual state of modern First Amendment law. And in my judgment, for good reason. There is a fundamental difference, in law, in logic, in experience, in moral intuition, between "taking it to the streets" and "taking to the job" or "taking to the classroom." Again, I have written about this extensively, and do not belabor the point here. The reader may either accept or reject the intuition.

The organizing system I have set out does not work perfectly, I readily admit. Perhaps the biggest sore thumb is obscenity law. The two reigning companion obscenity cases, *Miller v. California*[49]and *Paris Adult Theatre I v. Slaton*,[50] decided on the same day in 1973, are entirely grounded in the order and morality theory. *Miller*, building on the Supreme Court's prior obscenity decision in *Roth v. United States*,[51] observed that "implicit in the history of the First Amendment is the rejection of obscenity as utterly without redeeming social importance. . . . This is the same judgment expressed by this Court in *Chaplinsky*."[52] *Paris Adult Theatre* doubled down on this theme, treating obscenity as a form of moral pollution, holding that prohibiting obscenity, even when accessible only to consenting adults, was justified by "the interest of the public in the quality of life and the total community environment."[53] The Court spoke of the right of government to "maintain a decent society," for which it cited, among other cases, *Beauharnais*.[54] The Court found persuasive the views of Professor Alexander Bickel, who was also channeling the law and morality theory. The Court quoted with approval Bickel's assertion:

> A man may be entitled to read an obscene book in his room, or expose himself indecently there . . . . We should protect his privacy. But if he demands a right to obtain the books and pictures he wants in the market, and to foregather in public places – discreet, if you will, but accessible to all—with others who share his tastes, then to grant him his right is to affect the world about the rest of us, and to impinge on other privacies.[55]

Miller and *Paris Adult Theatre I* remain good law. This actually reinforces one part of my thesis, which is that both the "order and morality theory" and the "marketplace theory" retain some hold on American free speech thinking. That *Miller* and *Paris Adult Theatre* remain good law, however, does certainly upset the neatness of my timeline, in that it cannot be said that suddenly in the 1960s the "order and morality theory" completely lost out in the general marketplace. In this one arena, dealing with hardcore sex, it stubbornly held on.

But unlike physics and math, where a theory is supposed to account for everything, the law is not so linear a science. As Holmes put it, "So judicial dissent often is blamed, as if it meant simply that one side or the other were not doing their sums right, and, if they would take more trouble, agreement inevitably would come."[56]

Accepting that obscenity does not fit my schema, and accepting that my schema might still be generally sound, note that the exception for obscenity opens up a potentially promising line of attack that might be profitably exploited by those on the modern campus who believe that hate speech should be banned, at least from university campuses. For if graphic depictions of hardcore sex are not protected by the First Amendment because a decent society may justly treat such depictions as a form of moral pollution, why should the scourge of racism and other forms hate speech, which undermine a decent society and promote moral rot far more palpable and dangerous than erotica, not also be stripped of constitutional protection?

At the very least, if we accept that society ought to be divided between the reign of the marketplace theory in our open spaces, and the reign of the order and morality theory in special settings, why shouldn't we treat the modern university as outside the general marketplace? Why not treat it as a place of reserve and retreat, dedicated to a shared sense of community and rational discourse?

THE IDEA OF THE UNIVERSITY

A Free and Ordered Space

Once again, I have often in the past opined on how these issues should play out in the context of the modern university, including a book devoted almost entirely to this problem.[57] Yet my pondering remains an open work-in-progress.

I went to Yale to play football. My daughter Corey later went to Yale, making her dad proud, to learn. Yet even as a football player (and not a very good one) I somehow did mature enough to start to show some nascent interest in ideas. While there, one of the professors I most admired was a Dante scholar—go figure—Professor A. Bartlett Giamatti. Bart Giamatti was also a lyrical and romantic American baseball fan. He would go on to become the president of Yale University, and then the Commissioner of Baseball. As the "Comish" he made the courageous and still-controversial decision to ban the

Cincinnati Reds icon, Pete Rose, "Charlie Hustle," from baseball, because Rose had gambled on baseball games.

Whether you count as his highest achievements his scholarship on Dante, his dominion over Major League Baseball, or his leadership of Yale, consider this: through it all Bart Giamatti conceptualized the idea of a university—of Yale University—as "a free and ordered space."[58]

I believe Giamatti was right (about universities—I don't know about Pete Rose). The modern university must have aspects that are robustly free. It must also have aspects that are ordered.

I believe this dual conception is sound as educational policy. It also, in my view, is where the law on the topic, though scant, properly lands. This is as it ought to be, in my view, and, to a large degree, what judicial decisions tell us it actually is.

This is essentially a boundary dispute, and as with any body of law dealing with boundaries, there will be close calls on either side of the line. The examples I recite below are not intended to be exhaustive or definitive, but illustrative.

Publics vs. Privates

As a preliminary note, when we speak of "freedom of speech" or "academic freedom" on American campuses, the "state action doctrine" is implicated. The First Amendment applies only to the actions of governmental actors, and thus only binds public colleges and universities, not privates. Most private universities, however, by custom or contract, effectively "borrow" from formal First Amendment law, voluntarily submitting themselves to free speech principles, typically under the nomenclature of respect for "academic freedom." Even so, private universities and colleges have more latitude in playing with the meaning of academic freedom and might choose to adjust the balance between marketplace values and order and morality values in a manner that differs from what courts would require of their public counterparts.

There is one notable exception to this pattern, in New Jersey. Unlike the federal First Amendment, the free-speech guarantee in the New Jersey Constitution has been extended to bind private actors in certain circumstances. In *State v. Schmid*,[59] the New Jersey Supreme Court held that Chris Schmid, though lacking permission from Princeton, had the right under the New Jersey Constitution to enter the campus, distribute leaflets, and sell political materials.

Universities vs. Lower Grades

An ongoing debate concerning the nature of free-speech protections on college and university campuses is the extent to which the major Supreme Court decisions articulating the standards applicable to the regulation of student speech in the middle and secondary schools apply on university campuses, where the students are adults, not children.

Four famous cases establish the principles that apply to middle and secondary schools. In *Tinker v. Des Moines Independent Community School District*,[60] the Supreme Court upheld the right of a student to wear a black armband as a passive symbol of protest, uttering the celebrated line that students do not "shed their constitutional rights to freedom of speech or expression at the schoolhouse gate."[61] *Tinker* requires schools to demonstrate a risk of substantial or material disruption before they may censor the speech of students that happens to occur on the school campus. In contrast, in *Bethel School District No. 403 v. Fraser*,[62] the Court permitted a school to discipline a student for lewd innuendo during a speech conducted during elections for student government on a school microphone during a school assembly. Then, in *Hazelwood School District v. Kuhlmeier*,[63] the Court upheld the authority of school officials to censor the content of a school-sponsored student newspaper. The Court in *Hazelwood* announced a new test for school-sponsored activities, holding that "educators do not offend the First Amendment by exercising editorial control over the style and content of student speech in school-sponsored expressive activities so long as their actions are reasonably related to legitimate pedagogical concerns."[64]

Lastly, in *Morse v. Frederick*,[65] the Supreme Court held that school officials did not violate the First Amendment in disciplining a high school student, Joseph Frederick, after he and his prankish friends unfurled a 14-foot banner bearing the phrase "BONG HiTS 4 JESUS" as the Olympic Torch Relay parade passed by the Juneau, Alaska High School in 2002, on its way to the winter games in Salt Lake City, Utah. In a 5–4 decision written by Chief Justice Roberts, the Court held it reasonable for school officials to interpret Frederick's cryptic message as advocating illegal drug use. In an opinion heavily emphasizing the menace of drug use by adolescents, the Court decided in favor of school officials.

Morse, however, carries an interesting caveat. Frederick himself disclaimed any profound meaning to his message, essentially dismissing it as gibberish calculated to gain attention. Justice Samuel Alito, joined by Justice Anthony Kennedy, wrote a concurring opinion built on Frederick's lack of any serious intent to convey genuine political content. That concurring opinion is significant because the votes of Justices Alito and Kennedy were needed to comprise the five-Justice majority opinion. Justices Alito and Kennedy claimed to be joining the majority only on the understanding that:

> (1) it goes no further than to hold that a public school may restrict speech that a reasonable observer would interpret as advocating illegal drug use and

> (2) it provides no support for any restriction of speech that can plausibly be interpreted as commenting on any political or social issue, including speech on issues such as the wisdom of the war on drugs or of legalizing marijuana for medicinal use.[66]

Interpreting *Morse*, the U.S. Court of Appeals for the Third Circuit seized on the concurrence of Justice Alito to limit the reach of the *Morse* holding. In *B.H. ex rel. Hawk v. Easton Area School District*,[67] the Third Circuit held that officials could not ban the phrase, "I Love Boobies," distributed by students to promote breast cancer awareness. In support of its holding, the Third Circuit adopted a more constrained interpretation of *Morse*, observing, "Because the votes of Justices Alito and Kennedy were necessary to the majority opinion and were expressly conditioned on their narrower understanding that speech plausibly interpreted as political or social commentary was protected from categorical regulation, that limitation is a binding part of *Morse*."[68]

Whether these decisions, all rendered in the context of public middle and secondary schools, apply to universities, is contested. I am in the camp believing the matrix they create should apply to universities as well. The weight of various interests may shift a bit as one moves from the middle school to high school to post-secondary school contexts, but the basic architecture, with modest adjustments, remains sound.

Several of the decisions I describe with approval in the discussion that follows adopt the view that the principles of *Tinker*, *Fraser*, *Hazelwood*, and *Morse*, with calibrations adjusted for the university setting, do apply to colleges and universities.

Curricular Expression

Students and faculty have their free-speech rights diminished substantially when the expression occurs in curricular settings. The content of assignments, statements made inside classrooms, or the academic work-product of students or faculty may be regulated based on content. Indeed, the idea of a university would be incoherent if professors could not grade papers or exams based on content—how else would they be judged, by "neatness?" So too, decisions on tenure and promotion inevitably require content-based assessments of a faculty member's scholarship or teaching.

The critical divide, well-recognized by custom and sporadically appearing in judicial cases (there are not many, thankfully), is the divide between penalizing a viewpoint and penalizing content based on "neutral" criteria. Universities could not function if they could not critique a student's analysis, creativity, observance of professional or disciplinary norms, academic honesty, or intellectual rigor. To state this divide is not to say that its boundary will always be self-evident. For a professor to say "I am flunking you because I don't like your politics" is plainly out-of-bounds. To say "I am flunking you because your analysis is flaccid and floppy" is not. The danger, of course, is that a professor will treat analysis as flawed only because it partakes of viewpoints with which the professor disagrees. Yet this does not mean that the line itself is invalid. All legal lines may be subverted through cheating. I believe most professors do not cheat. In my world as a law professor, I have faith that my colleagues are unlikely to grade a student more highly or lowly based on whether the student's views are more simpatico with Justice Ruth Bader Ginsburg than Antonin Scalia. But, of course, I know that sometimes abuses do occur, and one hopes that appeals panels and grievance committees can ferret them out.

Forced and Unprofessional Curricular Speech

When curricular speech is implicated, students may at times be forced to engage in expression they find distasteful—such as an assignment to write on a topic from a viewpoint with which they personally disagree—and students may be retained by professional and academic norms regarding the content and tone of their work product.

One of the most vivid exemplars of courts deferring to university officials in their exercise of their pedagogical authority to enforce academic and professional norms is *Brown v. Li.*[69] Christopher Brown was a master's degree student at the University of California at Santa Barbara. He had some issues with educational authorities, which led him to attach a section he entitled "Disacknowledgements" to the end of his master's degree thesis. The section began, "I would like to offer special Fuck You's to the following degenerates for being an ever-present hindrance during my graduate career."[70]

This did not play well. Brown's dropping of the f-bomb resulted in a series of delays in the granting of his degree, including a period in which he was placed on academic probation. Brown sued, claiming his speech was protected by the First Amendment and that the University's disciplinary actions violated it. The Ninth Circuit ruled against Brown and in favor of the university. The court held that Brown's speech was school-sponsored or curricular within the meaning of *Hazelwood*, and that the principles of *Hazelwood* applied to the university and college setting. The court opined "that core curricular speech—that which is an integral part of the classroom-teaching function of an educational institution—differs from students' extracurricular speech and that a public educational institution retains discretion to prescribe its curriculum."[71]

One of the most thoughtful judicial decisions exploring this territory is *Axson-Flynn v. Johnson*,[72] written by Circuit Judge David Ebel on the

U.S. Court of Appeals for the Tenth Circuit, arising from a conflict at the University of Utah. The student, Christina Axson-Flynn, was in Utah's Actor Training Program. She refused to say the word "fuck" or take God's name in vain during classroom acting exercises, because such language offended her Mormon faith.

Judge Ebel's opinion for the court observed that the First Amendment rights of students are not automatically coextensive with the rights of citizens in other settings but must be adjusted in light of the special characteristics of a learning environment. The court held that there were three main types of speech that occur within an educational setting. First is student speech that happens to occur on the school premises. The court characterized this as pure student expression, which the school must tolerate unless it can reasonably forecast that the expression will lead to substantial disruption of or material interference with school activities. A second type of speech in the school setting is "government speech," in which the university is speaking in its own voice—such as a statement by a university president expressing university policy. Under modern First Amendment principles, such speech is not subject to any First Amendment challenge.[73] Finally, there is speech sponsored by the educational institution, the so-called "school-sponsored" speech. As the court observed, here the control of the university is at its apex, noting, "Nowhere is this more true than in the context of a school's right to determine what to teach and how to teach it in its classrooms."[74]

The court concluded, correctly in my view, that Utah's use of plays with such offending language was a valid instructional technique. The court thus held that the decisions of educators to compel such speech were valid as long as the decisions were reasonably related to legitimate pedagogical concerns. As the court observed, "a college history teacher may demand a paper defending Prohibition, and a law-school professor may assign students to write 'opinions' showing how Justices Ginsburg and Scalia would analyze a particular Fourth Amendment question."[75] In imposing these sorts of assignments, universities are simply encouraging critical thinking and acclimatizing students to professional norms.

The Public Forum Spaces of the University

I am confident, as the courts held in *Li* and *Axson-Flynn*, that it is entirely appropriate to characterize certain spaces and places within university life as governed by the "order and morality" theory—the "ordered" part of what Bart Giamatti described as a "free and ordered space."

I am equally confident that other parts of university life should be governed by the principles of the other side of the spectrum, the "free" side of the "free and ordered space." In my view there ought to be programs and places within the university in which the protections of the marketplace theory apply with full force.

We may consider this proposition spatially or geographically. Certain spaces on the campus are governed by one set of principles, other spaces by another set. This merely applies the categories of established First Amendment public forum law to the physical spaces of the campus. We may also consider the proposition more figuratively, conceptualizing the "university" not so much as a physical place but as an ideal. Either way, physical or metaphysical, I am convinced that there must be public forums within a university's operations, akin to the streets, sidewalks, plazas, malls, and parks of First Amendment law outside the boundaries of university campuses.

In staking this claim, I speak as much as an educator as a First Amendment lawyer. If our society, writ large, recognizes that there are wide-open spaces in which the marketplace theory should prevail, and other special settings where the order and morality theory reigns supreme, the university itself should parallel that reality, preparing students for it.

If I were the czar of free speech conflicts on the modern campus, I would not condemn students and faculty who argue that the marketplace theory is itself wrong and should be replaced across-the-board in all segments of society with the order and morality theory. We live in a free country, and if the marketplace theory has any credence then even the marketplace theory itself must always be open to attack. Holmes in *Abrams* said that it is "an experiment, as all life is an experiment."[76] Yet experiments, of course, sometimes fail. I do not dismiss the argument of many students, faculty, and administrators on university campuses who claim that this experiment has failed.

Nor do I indulge the naïve view that in an open marketplace, truth will always prevail over falsity, or good ideas over bad ones. It is no truer that "truth will out" than that "murder will out." We know that people sometimes get away with murder, and often get away with lies.

In my book *Confessions of a Free Speech Lawyer*, I acknowledge a heavy debt to the thinking of Leslie Kendrick, who is Jewish, and a distinguished First Amendment scholar. She is the Vice Dean and Professor of Law at the University of Virginia Law School and lives in Charlottesville, the epicenter of the events I describe in my book. Reflecting on the events in her city and on her campus, particularly the August 2017 events that ended in death, she comes out in much the same place I do, which is to generally support the marketplace theory, but with skepticism and humility. "As a Jewish free speech lawyer living in Charlottesville," she wrote, "I think about August 11 and 12 every day."[77] Kendrick is skeptical of several of the central arguments associated with the marketplace theory. The notion that suppression of extremist speech strengthens it is a proposition that cannot really be empirically proven or disproven, for example. It is just as probable that allowing extremist speech to proliferate only helps it gather strength, as new members are recruited to join evil causes.[78] Yet Kendrick ultimately comes down in favor of the modern protection of hate speech, as better than any plausible alternative. Preventing government from deciding what speech is worthy of protection and what speech is not poses major problems of legitimacy, and the nation has a less than stellar track record on this score. Modern marketplace of ideas principles exist to shelter unpopular views from the power of majorities. As Kendrick points out, this "is true whether the unpopular belief in question is white supremacy in 2017 Charlottesville or equality in 1964 Birmingham."[79]

Professor Kendrick said it more elegantly than I, so I will leave it with her. If I have learned anything as a life-long litigator and scholar navigating the treacherous shoals of free speech law, it is that I have not learned much, beyond the virtue of humility. It is one thing to love the movie *Rocky*, it is another to be self-righteously cocky. "Certitude is not the test of certainty," Oliver Wendell Holmes wrote. "We have been cock-sure of many things that were not so."[80]

NOTES

1. Rodney Smolla, *Confessions of a Free Speech Lawyer: Charlottesville and the Politics of Hate* (Ithaca: Cornell University Press, 2020).
2. John Villasenor, "Views among college students regarding the "First Amendment: results from a new survey," The Brookings Institute, September 18, 2017, available at: https://www.brookings.edu/blog/fixgov/2017/09/18/views-among-college-students-regarding-the-first-amendment-results-from-a-new-survey/.
3. 410 U.S. 113 (1973).
4. 505 U.S. 833 (1992).
5. 554 U.S. 570 (2008).
6. 437 U.S. 617 (1978).
7. See *Edwards v. California*, 314 U.S. 160 (1941) (striking down California's "anti-Okie" law attempting to limit movement into California of persons migrating from the Dust Bowl into California.)
8. *Saenz v. Roe*, 526 U.S. 489 (1999).
9. *Southern Pacific Company v. Arizona*, 325 U.S. 761 (1945).
10. *See Maine v. Taylor*, 477 U.S. 131 (1986) (upholding Maine's ban on importation of out-of-state baitfish).
11. *Reeves, Inc. v. Stake*, 447 U.S. 429 (1980).
12. See *Western & Southern Life Ins. v. State Board of California*, 451 U.S. 648 (1981).
13. 30 U.S. 1 (1831).
14. 60 U.S. (19 How.) 393 (1857).
15. 163 U.S. 537 (1896).

16. 323 U.S. 214 (1944).

17. 138 S.Ct. 2392 (2018).

18. See *Clark v. Jeter*, 486 U.S. 456, 461(1988) ("Between these extremes of rational basis review and strict scrutiny lies a level of intermediate scrutiny, which generally has been applied to discriminatory classifications based on sex or illegitimacy.").

19. See *Washington v. Davis*, 426 U.S. 229 (1976).

20. *Reed v. Town of Gilbert, Arizona*, 576 U.S. 155, 163, 135 S. Ct. 2218, 2226 (2015).

21. See *Ward v. Rock Against Racism*, 491 U.S. 781, 799 (1989).

22. *Rosenberger v. Rector & Visitors of University of Virginia*, 515 U.S. 819, 829 (1995).

23. 505 U.S. 377 (1992).

24. Ibid., 392.

25. 453 U.S. 490 (1981).

26. Ibid., 501.

27. 249 U.S. 47 (1919).

28. 249 U.S. 204 (1919).

29. 249 U.S. 211 (1919).

30. 250 U.S. 616, 624 (1919) (Holmes, J., dissenting).

31. *Abrams v. United States*, 250 U.S. at 627–28 (Holmes, J., dissenting) (internal citations omitted).

32. 315 U.S. 568 (1942).

33. Ibid., 572–73.

34. 376 U.S. 254 (1964).

35. 403 U.S. 15 (1971).

36. 505 U.S. at 377.

37. 538 U.S. 343 (2003).

38. 491 U.S. 397 (1989).

39. 562 U.S. 443 (2011).

40. 559 U.S. 460 (2010).

41. 567 U.S. 709 (2012).

42. *Stevens*, 559 U.S. at 471.

43. 395 U.S. 444 (1969).

44. 343 U.S. 250 (1952).

45. Rodney Smolla and William Banks, *Constitutional Law: Structural Rights in Our Federal System*, 7th Edition (Durham, NC: Carolina Academic Press, 2019).

46. 274 U.S. 357 (1927).

47. Ibid., 376.

48. See Rodney Smolla, *Free Speech in an Open Society* (New York: Alfred A. Knopf, 1992).

49. 413 U.S. 15 (1973).

50. 413 U.S. 49 (1973).

51. 354 U.S. 476 (1957).

52. *Miller v. California,* 413 U.S. 15, 20 (1973).

53. *Paris Adult Theatre*, 413 U.S. at 58.

54. Ibid., 59.
55. Ibid., *quoting* Alexander Bickel, *The Public Interest* 22 (Winter 1917): 25–26.
56. Oliver Wendell Holmes, "The Path of the Law," *Harvard Law Review*, 1897, 457, 465.
57. Rodney Smolla, *The Constitution Goes to College: Five Constitutional Ideas that Have Shaped the American University* (New York: New York University Press, 2011).
58. Ibid.
59. 84 N.J. 535 (1980), *appeal dismissed sub nom. Princeton University v. Schmid*, 455 U.S. 100 (1982).
60. 393 U.S. 503 (1969).
61. Ibid., 506.
62. 478 U.S. 675 (1986).
63. 484 U.S. 260 (1988).
64. Ibid., 273.
65. 551 U.S. 393 (2007).
66. Ibid., 422 (Alito, J., concurring).
67. 725 F.3d 293 (3d Cir. 2013).
68. Ibid., 303.
69. 308 F.3d 939 (9th Cir. 2002).
70. Ibid., 943.
71. Ibid., 950.
72. 356 F.3d 1277 (10th Cir. 2004).
73. *See Pleasant Grove City, Utah v. Summum*, 555 U.S. 460 (2009).
74. *Axson-Flynn*, 356 F.2d at 1285.
75. Ibid., 1291.
76. *Abrams*, 250 U.S. at 630.
77. Leslie Kendrick, "The Answers and the Questions in First Amendment Law," in *Charlottesville 2017, The Legacy of Race and Inequity*, ed. Louis P. Nelson and Claudrena N. Harold (Charlottesville: University of Virginia Press, 2018), 72.
78. Ibid., 73.
79. Kendrick, "The Answers and the Questions in First Amendment Law," 74.
80. Oliver Wendell Holmes, "Natural Law," *Harvard Law Review* 32, no. 1 (November 1918): 40.

Chapter 4

Conservatism and Free Speech in Higher Education

Joe Dryden

"There is rampant discrimination in higher education, and it's not against minorities. . . . It's against Conservatives."[1]

—David French
Senior Fellow, National Review Institute

Institutions of higher education should represent the pinnacle of free speech in an environment where students and professors share, question, and debate ideas without the coercive chill of retaliation, condemnation, or worse. It is through the free exchange of ideas in open debate that students develop a deeper and wider level of interconnected knowledge and an increased capacity for critical reasoning and problem-solving. In *Sweezy v. New Hampshire*,[2] Chief Justice Earl Warren wrote: "Teachers and students must always remain free to inquire, to study and to evaluate, to gain new maturity and understanding; otherwise our civilization will stagnate and die."[3] Unfortunately, the environment on many college campuses has grown increasingly hostile toward some students and professors, but the most common victims do not represent traditionally oppressed groups: increasingly, the victims are conservatives. In 2016, for example, the University of Michigan released the results of a campus climate survey showing that political orientation is the most common form of discrimination on campus—more than race, gender, or sexual orientation.[4] This has produced a chilling effect not only on college campuses but in society at large, where conservatives risk being harassed, threatened, and assaulted for sharing ideas contrary to progressive ideologies.

Freedom of expression is perhaps our most important right. It is through the sharing of ideas and experiences that injustices are highlighted, and the pall of orthodoxy is kept at bay. In times of crisis, our very existence depends on the ability to send and receive messages and to communicate without fear of reprisal. Without the free flow of ideas, progress, creativity, and insight are limited, and tyranny can take root in the darkness.

Over the last several decades, there has been a rising tide of political orthodoxy where the free marketplace of ideas at colleges and universities is starting to resemble more of an echo chamber. According to the Foundation for Individual Rights in Education (FIRE), a non-profit organization dedicated to protecting expression rights in higher education, freedom of expression is at "greater risk now than any time in recent history."[5] Conservative speakers are being excluded under threats of violence and rioting.[6] Conservative students are being harassed and intimidated for expressing ideas that contradict progressive orthodoxy.[7] Conservative professors are increasingly excluded from consideration for job opportunities, grants, and publications.[8]

Sadly, the divide in our country seems greater than at any point in the last several decades.[9] With that divide comes an inability to share ideas that lie outside the political mainstream.[10] Students at New York University reported being afraid because they are ridiculed in class, harassed, and assaulted.[11] Some students at the University of California, Berkeley called for their Republican classmates to be killed,[12] and flyers were posted around the University of North Carolina campus threatening supporters of Donald Trump.[13] Conservative students at UCLA report being harassed, stalked, and threatened.[14] These students feel compelled to change their views on papers submitted in class to match the political views of their professors. They are afraid to share their views on matters of public concern out of fear that they will be stigmatized, ostracized, or worse.[15] According to a survey conducted at the University of North Carolina at Chapel Hill, almost 68 percent of conservative students report self-censoring to avoid potential consequences as opposed to only 24.9 percent of liberal students reporting the same.[16] At Iowa State University, a student organization known as the Young Democratic Socialists of America posted threatening tweets calling for the assassination of the president and the hanging and extermination of capitalists.[17] Trump supporters at the University of Richmond describe "an environment in which . . . one side is vilified to such an extent that open expression of support for Trump could provoke visceral responses and compromise relationships not only with friends but also with the professors who determine their grades."[18] Studies show that the grade point averages of conservative students are substantially lower than those of their liberal classmates when analyzed correctly.[19] Two students who celebrated the election of Donald Trump by driving around campus while waving a Trump flag narrowly avoided expulsion from Babson College by writing apology letters for offending progressive sensibilities.[20]

An article by Seth Ian Yu outlined more than a dozen incidents in which Trump supporters were ostracized, threatened, bullied, and attacked on college campuses across the nation.[21] Strikingly, the article was written before the 2016 presidential election. Since then, the attacks continue, and, if anything, have intensified.[22] A conservative student at North Carolina State was spray-painted in the face. Conservative students at the University of Texas were doxed when they joined conservative student organizations.[23] Three students at Tulane were arrested after they set fire to the dorm room door of the Turning Point USA chapter president.[24] A conservative activist was punched in the face at the University of California, Berkeley.[25] Conservative students at New York's Binghamton College were surrounded and threatened by a mob of students who also shut down an organized speaking event by economist Arthur Laffer.[26] At the University of Washington, a man attempted to chain the doors of an auditorium locking conservative students inside.[27] Students at Chico State destroyed the property and assaulted members of a conservative student group,[28] and pro-life students attending the University of North Carolina at Chapel Hill and the University of Wisconsin-Madison were assaulted.[29]

When students face a hostile environment, they are not free to engage in open debate; their ideas are silenced, and they lose their God-given, constitutionally protected right to freedom of expression. One of the primary trademarks of totalitarian regimes is the suppression of dissent to enable the ruling class to control the message and thereby influence the minds of the governed. Limiting the scope of the marketplace of ideas at some institutions of higher education through the use of hate-speech codes, bias-response teams, the heckler's veto, free-speech zones, and politically partisan hiring practices enables school officials to control the messages which rob students of the opportunity to question, analyze, and evaluate proposed solutions to personal and social challenges.

When students are harassed, threatened, and assaulted for exercising their First Amendment right of expression, the result is the suppression of speech and the marginalization of a substantial portion of the student body and their views. Students are afraid to voice disagreement on important matters of public concern, and the marketplace of ideas is reduced to only that which is acceptable to campus bullies, who at times resort to criminal activity to silence opposing viewpoints.

Conservative professors also face hostile environments and are more likely to suffer adverse employment actions if they express unpopular ideas. Marietta College allegedly fired an assistant professor for his papers examining human genetic variation and its role in physical and psychological adaptation.[30] Providence College shunned and denounced a highly respected professor who questioned the school's diversity agenda.[31] The contract of a popular professor, who ironically taught free-speech courses at UCLA, was not renewed after he used real-life examples to critique how school administrators handled free-speech issues on campus.[32] A professor raised by gay parents was subjected to a lengthy investigation by Cal State Northridge because he shared his concerns about gay parenting; he eventually left the college due to the hostile environment.[33] A professor, and his wife, resigned from Yale under pressure after they questioned the need for the University to proscribe acceptable Halloween costumes.[34] The University of Louisville fired the chair of the Division of Child and Adolescent Psychiatry and Psychology after he, as a panel speaker, suggested that professionals should seek to understand the psychological issues underlying gender dysphoria before providing hormone treatment.[35] A law professor at Cornell faced termination after he was critical of the Black Lives Matter movement in his journal, *Legal Insurrection*.[36] A professor from Riverside Community College won a wrongful termination suit after he was fired for suggesting that environmental factors may be responsible for same-sex attraction.[37] The University of North Texas fired a math professor for his comments about microaggressions, which he claims promote a victimhood mentality and suppress growth through dialogue.[38]

Eliminating professors from campus discussions with conservative perspectives on important social and political issues creates a marketplace with fewer intellectual options, incapable of meeting the demand for the full exploration of our collective intellect. The message to professors with unorthodox views is clear: speak your mind at your own peril—hardly the inclusive atmosphere open to academic freedom, debate, and dialogue. The harassment, or fear thereof, becomes so pervasive that many choose silence to avoid becoming a target of the cancel culture. To speak the truth as one sees it requires courage and the full protection of the First Amendment.

It is undeniable that conservative voices have been and continue to be systematically excluded through institutional policy and practice and through the development of a hostile environment where students and professors are afraid to engage in thoughtful and reasoned debate. When accused of violating unconstitutional hate-speech codes, even if no formal punishment is administered, the process of having to defend one's self becomes the punishment and serves as a warning to others.[39] Tyler Langhofer, Director and Senior Counsel at the Center for Academic Freedom, wrote: "No student or faculty at a college or university should be subjected to threats of punishment simply for expressing a belief on important social issues—even if no punishment is ultimately imposed. This distorts the marketplace of ideas and robs students of the intellectual debate that teaches them how to reason."[40]

It is important to remember that freedom of expression is not designed to protect popular viewpoints; it is designed to protect unpopular viewpoints. Justice Oliver Wendell Holmes, Jr. (Associate Justice of the Supreme Court of the United States, 1902–1932) captured the essence of this principle in

United States v. Schwimmer where he wrote: "[S]peech that demeans on the basis of race, ethnicity, gender, religion, age, disability, or any other similar ground is hateful; but the proudest boast of our free speech jurisprudence is that we protect the freedom to express the thoughts that we hate."[41] Justice William Brennan, in *Texas v. Johnson,* wrote: "If there is a bedrock principle underlying the First Amendment, it is that the government may not prohibit the expression of an idea simply because society finds the idea itself offensive or disagreeable."[42] Sadly, discriminatory hiring practices, hate-speech codes, bias-response teams, free-speech zones, and the use of the heckler's veto erect antithetical barriers to the underlying principles of the First Amendment right of expression. However, it is posited here that these practices are all too often used in higher education to suppress unpopular viewpoints.

Part One of this chapter attempts to provide a reasonable definition of *conservatism* to overcome the pejorative labels that have been applied by the mainstream media with great zeal. The rest of the chapter describes why the use of politically partisan hiring practices, hate-speech codes, bias-response teams, free-speech zones, and the use of the heckler's veto produces a hostile environment and the unconstitutional suppression of protected speech.

WHAT IS CONSERVATISM?

Before discussing the components that enable the systematic silencing of conservative voices in higher education, it is essential to establish an honest definition of *conservatism* as a counterbalance to the defamatory epitaphs repeated ad nauseam by often disingenuous sources.[43] According to Lee Edwards, Distinguished Fellow at the Heritage Foundation, conservatives believe in individual free-will unencumbered from the shackles of arbitrary power.[44] They believe the purpose of government is to preserve individual liberty in an ordered society through the administration of equal justice and due process.[45] They believe that government is a necessary constraint to preserve ordered liberty, but that "government is best which governs least."[46]

According to the *Stanford Encyclopedia of Philosophy*, conservatives tend to be pragmatic. They are skeptical of quick fixes. They are willing to change, but they honor tradition.[47] They are more interested in what works than pie-in-the-sky ideology. As people age, they often develop wisdom and become more conservative because they understand life on a deeper level, recognizing that solutions are far more complicated than those proposed by emotionally charged ideologues.[48] They understand that there is a difference between how things should work when examined superficially and how things do work when examined in depth. Are conservatives always right? Of course not. Do they need to acquiesce to carefully tailored social change?

Absolutely! But conservatives are not the collection of "racist, sexist, homophobic, xenophobic, Islamophobic—you name it" as described by the 2016 Democrat nominee for president.[49] If this is your view, consider the following proposition: within every race, religion, gender, or political perspective, there are both good and bad people, smart and not so smart, kind and mean, altruistic and selfish. Most conservatives believe that people should be judged by their values and character, not by some manufactured intersectionality such as the color of their skin, their religion, or their political orientation. I yearn for a world envisioned by one of the greatest conservatives of all time, Martin Luther King, Jr.,[50] who dreamed of a day when people would "not be judged by the color of their skin, but by the content of their character."[51]

This chapter was submitted at great personal and professional risk, as it seems every day another conservative student or professor is under attack for exercising their right of expression. While the power of free expression sheds light on historical injustice, the current cancel culture resembles a hostile environment where contradictory views, even when based in truth, are met with threats, intimidation, and punishment. These attacks send a warning to other conservatives that if they do not censor their speech, they may be next. As I wrote, I wondered, would I become a target? I asked, "Should I take this risk and accept the invitation of the editor and publisher, or should I succumb and allow my voice to be silenced?" Obviously, I choose the former and stood by the courage of my convictions, but this was not an easy decision. Rather ironic, though, that my desire to contribute to a book focusing on the First Amendment right of expression was almost chilled into silence by the current cultural milieu and its approach to my conservative views.

In the days leading up to my submission of this chapter, a college Division I football coach agreed to forfeit more than $1 million from his contract because he wore a One America News T-shirt.[52] We saw the dean of the nursing school at the University of Massachusetts Lowell lose her job because she condemned acts of violence against people of color but then stated: "BLACK LIVES MATTER, but also, EVERYONE'S LIFE MATTERS. No one should have to live in fear that they will be targeted for how they look or what they believe."[53] A student at Marquette University faced an inquisition and threats that her acceptance would be revoked because she posted a TikTok video expressing her support for President Trump.[54] The current higher education environment has grown into the antithesis of the marketplace of ideas where some students and scholars, who should be free to debate and question, are met with hostility and violence. This disconnect is a disservice to our students, to the search for truth, and ultimately to our collective existence. It casts a pall of orthodoxy which chills freedom of expression and deprives students of the opportunity to critically examine important matters of public concern.

CONSERVATIVE PROFESSORS NEED NOT APPLY

The political disparity between professors at most universities is not a new phenomenon. In 2004, *The New York Times* cited two studies that reported a seven-to-one and nine-to-one disparity in liberal to conservative professors at campuses across the nation. The author of that article, John Tierney, stated that the disparity was likely to increase in the coming decades, and he was right.[55] In 2016, Langbert, Quain, and Klien examined the voter registration records of 7,243 professors at 40 leading U.S. universities and found an overall Democrat to Republican ratio of approximately 11.5:1.[56] Another study of professors in New England reported a ratio of 28:1.[57] John Ellis, Professor Emeritus from the University of California Santa Cruz, stated that when considering junior faculty at the assistant and associate rank, the ratio is 48:1.[58] Within specific disciplines, especially the social sciences, the ratios are even higher, which means some students may go through four years of college without ever having instructors with conservative viewpoints, thus severely decreasing the likelihood of encountering conservative viewpoints on important matters of public concern in the classroom.[59] Granted, not all professors will share their political perspectives in class, but given the scarcity of divergent political ideology, in-class conversations may become echo chambers where students encounter the same perspectives or ideas reinforced without challenge. Two-time Pulitzer Prize–winning journalist Nicholas Kristof describes this as a disservice to students and asserts that liberalism is "collapsing on some campuses into self-parody."[60] He adds that liberals "embrace diversity of all kinds except ideological."[61]

In their definitive work on the plight of conservative professors, Jon Shields and Joshua Dunn describe the disparate representation as a symptom of an underlying culture that is hostile toward conservative professors.[62] Shields and Dunn describe environments where some conservative professors are afraid to share ideas or even to be identified to avoid discriminatory treatment.[63] Furthermore, conservative professors perceive that they have little chance for advancement, a perception supported by research claiming that ideological conformity is the primary factor determining tenure and promotion.[64] As noted at the top of this chapter, David French, a Senior Fellow at the National Review Institute and an Iraq War veteran, goes so far as to say, "There is rampant discrimination in higher education, and it's not against minorities . . . . It's against Conservatives."[65]

Search committees serve as another mechanism of discrimination where conservative professors are sometimes eliminated from the applicant pool through job descriptions or outright exclusion. If the only professors hired are those who proffer liberal perspectives, then students are deprived of conservative perspectives, and the marketplace of ideas becomes monolithic.

Georgetown professor John Hasnas described his experience with search committees. He stated that in every search, school officials remind the committee that they are expected to search for candidates who will increase racial and gender diversity, but nothing is ever said about increasing ideological diversity. "On the contrary," Hasnas says, "I have been involved in searches in which the chairman of the selection committee stated that no libertarian candidates would be considered . . . . Or in which candidates were dismissed because of their association with conservative or libertarian institutions."[66] Ideal candidate descriptions for faculty positions also serve as filters where the ideal candidate is described as one who has a research agenda focusing on issues of social justice or intersectionality.[67] This description, by its very nature, creates a mechanism for anti-conservative discrimination.

HATE-SPEECH CODES ARE UNCONSTITUTIONAL

Labeling certain content as "hate speech" is one of the primary tools used to suppress expressions that some find insensitive or offensive despite the fact that hateful speech is protected by the First Amendment. No legally acceptable definition of *hate speech* exists, and those who attempt to define it often employ vague and ambiguous terms that can be applied in a subjective and discriminatory manner.[68] Nevertheless, or perhaps consequently, it is one of the primary vehicles used for the suppression of conservative voices in higher education. If we cannot uniformly define *hate speech*, it can be used as an amorphous tool to silence anyone with whom we disagree.[69] The vague terminology included in the hate-speech codes does not provide adequate notice to those subject to the policy so that they know what is and is not acceptable.[70] This condition produces a chilling effect on expression rights, limits the marketplace of ideas, and runs afoul of constitutional protections.

The American Bar Association attempts to define *hate speech* as "speech that offends, threatens, or insults groups, based on race, color, religion, national origin, sexual orientation, disability, or other traits."[71] According to this definition, using the term "white privilege" would be considered hate speech because it insults or offends a group of people based on their race. William B. Fisch attempts to define *hate speech* as that which leads to an "'incitement to hatred' . . . primarily against [a person or] group of persons" based on group affiliation, such as race, gender, religion, or ethnic origin.[72] How do we measure hatred when it is a self-reported state of being? How can we distinguish genuine anguish and despair from an overreaction to cognitive dissonance or ideological contradictions? *Hate speech* can only be defined by trying to look into the minds of the victim and the perpetrator to punish thoughts,[73] but thoughts without accompanying acts are insufficient for culpability.[74] John Bennett argues that hate speech allegations now represent a "slanderous epithet for any idea or statement that does not conform to the reigning politically correct dogmas."[75]

Courts have been unequivocal regarding the unconstitutionality of hate-speech codes, often due to the inclusion of terms that are vague, overbroad, or both. As of 2009, every single challenge to campus hate-speech codes—both on and off campus—has been successful,[76] and no contradictory examples have appeared in the interim. In *R.A.V. v. City of St. Paul*, for example, the U.S. Supreme Court struck down the city's hate-speech code because the ordinance prohibited otherwise-protected speech solely as a function of the subjects addressed.[77] Linguistic limitations between words and behaviors invite inconsistent and even discriminatory enforcement practices, which enable officials, in any capacity, to impose speech restrictions on speakers who profess disfavored messages.[78] This leads to viewpoint discrimination.[79] The *R.A.V.* Court acknowledged this consequence when it described the city's ordinance as facially unconstitutional because it imposed special prohibitions on speakers who express views on the disfavored subjects of "race, color, creed, religion or gender."[80] At the same time, it permitted "displays containing abusive invective, no matter how vicious or severe . . . unless they [were] addressed to one of the specified disfavored topics."[81] The holding in *R.A.V.* undermines most justifications for university hate-speech codes due to the same linguistic limitations found in the penumbra of terms. Words such as stigmatize, dehumanize, ostracize, appropriate, civil, legitimate, and acceptable do not have precise meanings or the same meaning to all people. As a result, they can be applied in a biased, discriminatory manner.

Nadine Strossen, former president of the American Civil Liberties Union, questioned the need for hate-speech codes by acknowledging "that we may [already] punish the substantial subsets of hate speech that inflict certain harms that the Court has specifically defined."[82] First, when speech conveys a threat to commit violence, and the targets of that threat reasonably fear that they will be subject to violence, it falls outside of the First Amendment's protection and may be punished.[83] Second, speech that directly targets a specific individual or a small group of individuals, and is sufficiently severe and pervasive, may constitute punishable harassment.[84] Third, we may punish speech that intentionally incites imminent violence.[85] Finally, speech may be punished if it constitutes an element of a crime, such as assault or vandalism.[86] Substantial protections for victims of defamation, harassment, or assault already exist, which, to some extent, render hate-speech codes unnecessary.

Cases Adjudicating University Hate-Speech Codes

Despite numerous cases which consistently hold hate-speech codes as unconstitutional, these codes, and other mechanisms of speech suppression, are still included in many university policy manuals.[87] One of the first cases examining the constitutionality of hate-speech codes in higher education involved a policy at the University of Michigan which prohibited:

> Any behavior, verbal or physical, that stigmatizes or victimizes an individual on the basis of race, ethnicity, religion, sex, sexual orientation, creed, national origin, ancestry, age, marital status, handicap or Vietnam-era veteran status, and that involves an express or implied threat to an individual's academic efforts, employment, participation in University sponsored extra-curricular activities or personal safety, has the purpose or reasonably foreseeable effect of interfering with an individual's academic efforts, employment, participation in University sponsored extra-curricular activities or personal safety; or creates an intimidating, hostile, or demeaning environment for educational pursuits.[88]

The U.S. District Court for the Eastern District of Michigan permanently enjoined the University from enforcing the hate-speech code based on its belief that terms such as "stigmatize" and "demean" were overbroad and vague and had been applied to sanction protected speech without any regard for the intent of the speaker.[89] The court acknowledged that the University could regulate certain forms of speech, such as fighting words[90] and speech which incites imminent lawless action,[91] and it could even provide reasonable time, place, and manner limitations.[92] What the University could not do, "however, was establish an anti-discrimination policy which had the effect of prohibiting certain speech because it disagreed with ideas or messages sought to be conveyed . . . . Nor could the University proscribe speech simply because it was found to be offensive, even gravely so, by large numbers of people."[93]

The University of Wisconsin-Madison faced a constitutional challenge to its version of a hate-speech code in *UWM Post v. Board of Regents*.[94] The U.S. District Court for the Eastern District of Wisconsin described several incidents where students were sanctioned under the policy—usually as the result of profane, sexually, or racially insensitive comments—and ruled that the UMW hate-speech code violated the overbreadth doctrine and was unduly vague.[95] The Fourth Circuit Court of Appeals ruled that George Mason University violated the free-speech rights of students when it sanctioned members of a fraternity for conducting an ugly woman contest.[96] The court classified the actions of school officials as viewpoint discrimination by one administrator who decided to regulate speech not based on any specific policy, but merely on the desire to avoid the discomfort created by unpopular and insulting viewpoints.[97]

In 2007, the U.S. District Court for the Northern District of California prevented the use of a hate-speech code at Reed College in Oregon, which required students to act in accordance with the college's goals and principles and to be "civil to one another."[98] In 2017, Iowa State University settled a First Amendment lawsuit brought by a student who was told that his diploma would be withheld "if he failed to complete the annual sexual harassment and misconduct training required of every student."[99] The student questioned the constitutionality of the policy, which subjected students to expulsion for expressive acts deemed "unacceptable . . . depending on the circumstances" and based on the subjective determination by others as to whether the speech was "legitimate . . . or necessary."[100] The University agreed to award the diploma, pay attorneys' fees, and change its anti-harassment policy.[101]

In *Doe v. Rector & Visitors of George Mason University,* the federal district court for the Eastern District of Virginia stated:

> controversial, and sometimes offensive ideas and viewpoints are central to the educational mission of universities. It follows that university students cannot thrive without a certain thickness of skin that allows them to engage with expressions that might cause "distress" or "discomfort . . ." The coddling of the nation's young adults by *proscribing* any expression on a university campus that is likely to be distressing or discomforting does not protect "the work . . . of the school"; such rules frustrate the mission of the university.[102]

Such proscriptions also frustrate the development of reason and critical analysis because students never have to defend their beliefs in spirited debate. When exposed to divergent viewpoints, we learn that some of our beliefs do not stand up to critical analysis, which opens the door for authentic learning and growth. We all would agree that there is value in diversity, yet political orthodoxy undermines this value by limiting the marketplace of ideas to only what is deemed acceptable by the ruling class. Regardless of one's political perspective, our society is a plurality with many voices that have the right to be heard, even voices that are disagreeable and offensive.

Emotional Distress as a Justification for the Use of Hate-Speech Codes

One justification proffered by those who support the development and use of hate-speech codes, whether on or off campus, is the argument that certain forms of speech, especially speech critical of traditionally oppressed groups, produce emotional distress and perpetuate negative stereotypes leading to further inequities.[103] The Supreme Court torpedoed this justification in *Snyder v. Phelps*[104] when it "explicitly rejected emotional pain as a justification for speech regulation on matters of public concern, even when . . . the speech is 'particularly hurtful,' and even when the speech-based harm goes far beyond 'emotional distress.'"[105] In *Snyder*, members of the Westboro Baptist Church—described as a congregation that pickets military funerals to communicate its belief that God hates the United States for its tolerance of homosexuality, particularly in America's military—held up signs with the words "Thank God for Dead Soldiers" and "You're Going to Hell" 1,000 feet away from the funeral of Marine Lance Corporal Matthew Snyder, who was killed in Iraq in the line of duty.[106] Despite inflicting severe emotional distress on the fallen soldier's father, the Court held that the expressions of the picketers were protected by the First Amendment.[107] The Court characterized the expressions as matters of public interest, displayed peacefully in accordance with local regulations, and stated: "As a Nation, we have chosen a different course—to protect even hurtful speech on public issues to ensure that we do not stifle public debate."[108] Burying a child is the most prolific and egregious loss a person can experience.[109] If the members of the Westboro Baptist Church can display hateful messages at the funerals of fallen heroes and dead children, which is morally reprehensible, then we cannot use the emotional pain experienced by college students to silence the voice of conservatives regarding compelling issues such as, but not limited to, immigration, abortion, political corruption, taxation and spending, the free exercise of religion, or racism.

BIAS-RESPONSE TEAMS

According to FIRE, bias-response teams (BRTs) have the authority to monitor and investigate anonymous reports of biased or offensive speech by students and faculty.[110] While teams do not issue formal punishments, they will direct credible reports of biased speech to campus administrators, or the police for possible action. BRTs are often a collection of students and school administrators with little training in First Amendment jurisprudence.[111] BRTs are in place at hundreds of universities across the country and suffer from the same unconstitutional aliments as hate-speech codes, namely the use of overbroad and vague language.[112] BRTs often act upon the subjective interpretations of sensitive students who believe contradictory statements or differences of opinion constitute acts of violence. The result is chilled expression. At least one university has disbanded its BRT out of a concern over its chilling effect on free expression.[113] Others are sure to follow!

In 2018, Speech First Inc., a non-profit organization dedicated to protecting free speech, sued the University of Michigan claiming the use of a BRT violated students' First Amendment expression rights under a policy so vague and overbroad as to prompt students to limit their speech out of fear that they might be subject to disciplinary sanction, including "individual education" or "restorative justice."[114] The bias-response team at the University of Michigan investigates alleged conduct that "discriminates, stereotypes, excludes, harasses or harms anyone in our community based on their identity."[115] On appeal, the Sixth Circuit ruled that students suffered an injury-in-fact as the result of the policy and were thereby entitled to an injunction.[116] The court recognized that the BRT "acted by way of implicit threat of punishment and intimidation to quell speech,"[117] and referrals led to formal investigations and possible criminal charges. BRTs represent another unconstitutional mechanism to suppress unorthodox views.

FREE-SPEECH ZONES

Free-Speech Zones (FSZs) are anything but free. Often, these small areas are located in remote portions of campus and must be reserved days in advance.[118] Some describe the purpose of FSZs as an effort to prevent students from encountering contrary views except in small designated areas.[119] FSZs further erode the marketplace of ideas through unreasonable restraints as to time, place, and manner of expression.[120] Colleges and universities do not need FSZs; arguably, the entire campus should be an FSZ. The Los Angeles Community College District (LACCD), the largest community college in the United States, settled a lawsuit in 2018 challenging the use of FSZs at its nine campuses, which serve over 150,000 students. The Federal District Court for the Central District of California denied LACCD's motion to dismiss holding that a student, who faced disciplinary action, should he distribute copies of the U.S. Constitution in any place other than FSZs at a designated time, had standing and adequately pleaded violations of his First Amendment rights.[121] The use of FSZs is an unconstitutional attempt by some colleges and universities to prevent the dissemination of ideas that some may find to be unorthodox or offensive.

THE HECKLER'S VETO

According to the Freedom Forum Institute, the heckler's veto is a situation where government officials allow a hostile audience reaction to silence unpopular speakers.[122] In *Roe v. Crawford*,[123] the Eighth Circuit described the heckler's veto as "situations in which the government attempts to ban protected speech because it might provoke a violent response."[124] In *Rosenbaum v. City and County of San Francisco*,[125] the Ninth Circuit described the heckler's veto as an "impermissible content-based speech restriction where the speaker is silenced due to an anticipated disorderly and violent reaction of the audience."[126] Advocating for specific positions related to matters of public concern such as immigration reform, reduced taxation, school choice, or other constitutional limits on government power is not the proximate cause of disorder and violence. The proximate cause is the reaction of the often hypersensitive and often ill-informed heckler. Instead of engaging in violence to silence someone with whom the heckler disagrees, hecklers should develop their own platforms to allow for the expression of contrary views and opinions.

For those who agree with the sentiments of Justice Louis Brandeis in *Whitney v. California*[127]—that the way to counter unpopular and even hateful speech is with more speech, not less[128]—they must understand and acknowledge the need to protect the marketplace of ideas from the suppression of the heckler who uses threats, intimidation, and violence to silence views that contradict the heckler's beliefs. While it may be expedient to silence the voices of agitation, expedience leads to a limited and distorted marketplace of ideas producing a chilling effect on those similarly situated. The Sixth Circuit, in a case not involving schools, saw the heckler's veto for the lawless behavior that it is. That court ruled that the Wayne County Sherriff's Office violated the First Amendment rights of a group called the Bible Believers when its members were escorted from an Arab International Festival to avoid a potential riot.[129] The court stated: "The hostile reaction of a crowd does not transform protected speech into incitement."[130] The Sixth Circuit stated:

> In a balance between two important interests—free speech on one hand, and the state's power to maintain the peace on the other—the scale is heavily weighted in favor of the First Amendment . . . The freedom to espouse sincerely held . . . beliefs, especially in the face of hostile opposition, is too important to our democratic institution for it to be abridged simply due to the hostility of reactionary listeners . . . . If the mere possibility of violence were allowed to dictate whether our views, when spoken aloud, are safeguarded by the Constitution, . . . discourse would be reduced to the "standardization of ideas [held by the] dominant political or community groups." "When a peaceful speaker . . . is confronted by a hostile crowd, the state may not silence the speaker as an expedient alternative to containing or snuffing out the lawless behavior of the rioting individuals."[131]

In *Dariano v. Morgan Hill*, the heckler's veto was successfully used to silence protected speech in K-12 public schools when several high school students wore t-shirts with images of the U.S. flag to school on Cinco de Mayo.[132] Upon seeing the patriotic shirts, several Hispanic students began issuing threats of serious bodily injury in retaliation for the display of the U.S.

flag. The school's assistant principal was warned of impending violence, and he had a choice: he could meet with the angry students threatening violence and use this as a teachable moment for the entire school regarding the First Amendment right of expression, or he could silence the disfavored viewpoint. He chose the latter and required the flag-wearing students to turn their shirts inside-out or be sent home.[133] Their parents sued, alleging that the actions of school officials violated their children's First Amendment expression rights. The Ninth Circuit noted the history of racial tension and gang-related violence at the school,[134] and relied upon cases involving the display of the Confederate flag to argue that when racial tensions are high, and there are warning signs of impending violence, school officials are well within their authority to limit speech which would escalate the situation.[135] This holding gives free rein to hecklers who wish to silence opinions that contradict their subjective sensitivities. The message sent is that it is permissible to orchestrate mobs of people whose intent is to create chaos and mayhem to silence dissenting opinions that are viewed as hateful and insensitive.

Events at the University of California, Berkeley and other universities across the country represent the heckler's veto on a large-scale, coordinated, and well-funded basis. When Charles Murray, co-author of the controversial book *The Bell Curve*, was invited to speak at Middlebury College, he was shouted down by a mob of hecklers in the audience.[136] When his speech was moved to another room with digital-streaming technology, the hecklers congregated outside the room, chanting loudly, and then proceeded to pull the fire alarm.[137] As Murray and a coordinating professor were leaving, they were surrounded and assaulted by a group of masked people.[138] Murray's viewpoint was suppressed by the violent actions of hecklers.

More recently, Christina Hoff Sommers, who critically examined the inflation of campus rape statistics used by the Obama administration to impose unconstitutional disciplinary policies via executive action,[139] was labeled a fascist by some students who seem to equate debate, inquiry, and a search for truth with acts of aggression and violence.[140] Students at Lewis and Clark Law School prevented Ms. Hoff Summers from delivering an invited speech, thereby denying the campus of a relevant and valid perspective on an important sociological issue.[141]

Since the 2016 election, the concept of the heckler's veto has been applied by mostly left-leaning activist groups resulting in violence on and around several college campuses.[142] Colleges and universities face the extraordinary challenge of creating an atmosphere where all voices can be heard, and all parties can be safe, "particularly at institutions where the campus and the community share porous boundaries."[143] Would the analysis and outcome in *Dariano* be different if the events transpired at a post-secondary educational enterprise? Most college students are adults and, having reached the age of majority, possess the right to vote. Arguably, they should no longer need protection from speech that they consider to be highly offensive or hateful. College students should be able to tolerate viewpoints that contradict their deeply held beliefs. Do the First Amendment and the free marketplace of ideas deserve more protection from the heckler's veto on college campuses? Yes, but there are limits. Colleges and universities cannot be expected to be the sole protector of the marketplace. They need the help of the faculty, the student body, and the community at large. If organized violent groups are determined to silence controversial speakers, or any speaker for that matter, then the resources of the state and federal authorities may need to be mobilized to neutralize those who threaten or commit acts of violence or property destruction in response to controversial speakers.

In 2019, the Wisconsin General Assembly passed a measure to protect the marketplace of ideas from the violent heckler.[144] Under the Wisconsin bill, two complaints about a UW System student's conduct during a speech or presentation would trigger a hearing. Students found to have twice engaged in violence or disorderly conduct that disrupts another's freedom of expression would be suspended for a semester. A third offense would mean expulsion.[145] Tennessee implemented the Campus Free Speech Protection Act, which bans public universities in that state from implementing vague-speech codes, establishing FSZs, imposing prior restraints on speech, and disinviting speakers because of the content of their speech.[146] President Trump signed an executive order in March 2019, which threatens to withhold federal funding for colleges and universities that fail to protect freedom of expression.[147]

Whether or not one agrees with the intended messages from conservative speakers who have had speaking engagements canceled via the heckler's veto is not the point. We do not have to agree with their message; the proper response to thoughts and ideas with which we disagree is not property destruction, threat, and violence. The proper response is to provide valid, reasoned counterarguments that explain why our positions make more sense or is a better approach. Unfortunately, the type of response seen on too many college campuses across the nation runs contrary to this suggested approach, and in so doing, interferes with the First Amendment rights of other students, professors, and the entire community. Erwin Chemerinsky, one of the most widely respected First Amendment scholars, who currently serves as the Dean of the University of California, Berkeley Law School, said:

> The law is clear that even in places that are open to speech, there can be time, place, and manner restrictions, so long as there are adequate places for free speech. There is a right to speak on the campus, but there is no right to come into my classroom and shout me down. The central principle of the First

> Amendment—and of academic freedom—is that all ideas and views can be expressed. Sometimes they are ideas and views that we might consider noble, that advance equality. Sometimes they might be ideas that we abhor. But there is no way to empower a government or campus administration [or any other organization] to restrict speech without allowing for the possibility that tomorrow, it will be our speech that is restricted.[148]

Students have every right to express disagreement with ideas that contradict their developing paradigms, but they do not have the right to threaten, intimidate, or assault those with alternative views into silence.

COUNTERING THE HOSTILE ENVIRONMENT

There is a growing recognition of pervasive and insidious discrimination against conservatives, and signs of pushback are emerging. According to Arthur C. Brooks, several top-tier universities are at least giving lip service to the need to promote intellectual diversity, and organizations whose purpose is to foster diversity of thought on college campuses are materializing.[149] There are several examples: Jonathan Haidt, a psychology professor at New York University, founded the Heterodox Academy, a collection of scientists and scholars who want to improve universities by increasing viewpoint diversity;[150] Abby Jackson described the efforts of the University of Colorado-Boulder and Wesleyan University in Connecticut to specifically recruit conservative professors to interject some diversity of thought into the "self-generated bubble" of progressive orthodoxy;[151] and students at Georgetown are asking the University to hire more conservative professors.[152]

States across the country are passing legislation to protect the free-speech rights of students on college campuses through bills that "require public universities to remain neutral on political issues, prevent them from disinviting speakers, and impose penalties for students and others who interfere with these speakers."[153] Iowa and North Carolina considered bills that would require more of an ideological balance in hiring practices among professors, limiting ideological homogeneity to a 10 and 2 percent variation, respectively.[154] Florida approved legislation that bans FSZs and provides a person whose rights have been violated the ability to bring an action for declaratory and injunctive relief and to recover court costs and attorneys' fees.[155] Arizona banned FSZs in 2016 and, in 2018, strengthened its protection of free speech by enabling schools to "suspend or expel students who have repeatedly interfered with others' ability to express themselves."[156] As of early 2018, almost twenty states had either passed or were considering bills that would strengthen free-speech protections on college campuses, and the list continues to grow.[157] Ohio passed a statute in 2020 designed to end FSZs and the use of the heckler's veto to shut down events. Schools in Ohio are required to have a free-speech policy and to report violations to the state legislature.[158]

Students and professors are beginning to stand up against what they perceive as institutional discrimination. The College Republicans at the University of Washington, for example, sued the University after it assessed draconian fees to cover the cost of security at an event that featured a Christian-conservative speaker.[159] The district court granted the students' motion for a temporary restraining order and preliminary injunction, finding that the University's safety and security protocol for events was unreasonable and not viewpoint neutral, and that assessing the fee risks suppression of "speech on only one side of a contentious debate."[160] Without admitting liability, school officials subsequently settled and agreed to pay roughly $123,000 and to rescind the University's unconstitutional and discriminatory policy.[161]

After the mayhem at the University of California, Berkeley in early 2017, school officials instituted two restrictive policies—the High-Profile Speaker Policy (HPSP) and a Major Event Policy (MEP)—in what the Young American's Foundation and Berkeley College Republicans describe as an effort to suppress their First Amendment expression rights and their Fourteenth Amendment rights to equal protection and due process.[162] As a result of the new policies, speaking events featuring conservatives such as Laura Ingraham and Ben Shapiro were canceled or rescheduled.[163] The U.S. District Court for the Northern District of California denied the University's motion to dismiss and found that the HPSP policy gave school officials the unbridled discretion to impose unreasonable time, place, and manner restrictions based on vague and undefined policy language "wholly lacking in standards to guide enforcement."[164] The court held that the conservative student organizations sufficiently argued a First Amendment violation via the implementation of an unreasonable security fee and that the vague language in the HPSP policy violated the student organizations' Due Process rights.[165] Then, the court refused to dismiss the Equal Protection claim, noting a substantial difference in the fees imposed on events featuring conservative versus liberal speakers.[166] Finally, UC Berkeley, in response to its judicial setback, revised its policies for student organizations.[167]

FIRE has also been instrumental in the effort to protect freedom of expression in higher education with its national campaign to eliminate unconstitutional speech codes through targeted First Amendment lawsuits. By imposing a real cost for violating First Amendment rights, FIRE's Stand Up for Speech initiative is resetting the incentives that currently push colleges toward censoring student and faculty speech. Lawsuits are filed against public colleges maintaining unconstitutional speech codes nationwide. After each victory by ruling or settlement, FIRE targets more schools, sending the message that unless public colleges obey the law, they will be sued.[168]

As a result of FIRE's efforts, universities across the country have revised or are in the process of revising their free-speech policies. The results of FIRE's 2019 Spotlight on Speech Codes survey show that fewer institutions "maintain speech codes that clearly and substantially restrict or prohibit constitutionally protected speech," a decrease of 11 percent from 2017, and a 45 percent decrease since 2009.[169] Forty-two institutions received the highest ranking for protecting the marketplace of ideas—up from only eight in 2009.[170] While encouraging, far more needs to be done to return some degree of balance to the free marketplace of ideas, and it starts by protecting conservative voices.

CONCLUSION

According to Ted Gup, "free speech is the single greatest ally of social justice and, even at its most noxious and repulsive, is often a catalyst for reflection and remediation. It is easy to mistake it as a tool for repression, when in fact it is the antidote."[171] This assertion is more than merely a platitude. It is demonstrable fact. It is doubtful that the civil rights or the women's suffrage movements would have succeeded to the degree they have if it were not for the ability to communicate and bring to light inequalities and injustice. Justice Tom Clark, in the seminal case of *W. Va. St. Bd. of Educ. v. Barnette*,[172] wrote: "[E]ducating the young for citizenship is reason for scrupulous protection of Constitutional freedoms of the individual, if we are not to strangle the free mind at its source and teach youth to discount important principles of our government as mere platitudes."[173] That means that "no official, high or petty, shall prescribe what shall be orthodox in politics, nationalism, religion, or other matters of opinion or forcing citizens to confess by word or act their faith therein,"[174] but rather, universities should facilitate the constitutional process by introducing students to the freedoms necessary for its existence.

The primary purpose of institutions of higher education is to provide an environment and professors can explore, inquire, and contribute to the marketplace of ideas. However, this ideal is meaningless to students who are denied the privilege and equal opportunity to express contradictory viewpoints even when those viewpoints are supported by facts and valid research. Universities must protect the First Amendment, but in doing so, they risk seeming insensitive to real and imagined inequalities that can damage a university's reputation, especially in the age of activism via social media. In "A Balancing Act for American Universities: Anti-Harassment Policy v. Freedom of Speech," Bridget Hart wrote: "The challenge then, is to draft policies and legislation that effectively protect students exposed to harassment, while also protecting the free flow of ideas and expression that is highly desired on college campuses."[175] Unfortunately, many universities across the country have yet to find a good way to balance those interests. Universities should review their anti-harassment and hate-speech policies to remove vague and overly broad language. Universities also should follow the lead of Penn State University and include conservative students as a protected class or marginalized group.[176]

It is essential for institutions of higher education to place as much emphasis on protecting the First Amendment as they do on promoting inclusive and safe environments for traditionally oppressed groups. They need to demand that all students and faculty practice the same degree of tolerance that they demand for themselves. Universities and colleges must highlight that a defense of free speech is not an endorsement of the content of what may be perceived as hate speech. We can protect someone's right to express unpopular viewpoints without agreeing with their views.

We cannot allow our most cherished natural right to be marginalized by unconstitutional hate-speech codes, BRTs, discriminatory hiring practices, FSZs, and the use of the heckler's veto. We must protect institutions of higher education from those who wish to limit the choices available in the marketplace of ideas. Colleges and universities sing the praises of diversity. They invest substantial resources into extensive efforts to increase diversity on campuses, but then, too often, they quash protected unorthodox views. Diversity is a compelling government interest, but if we continue to enforce unconstitutional hate-speech policies and practices, then we threaten perhaps the most important diversity of all—ideological diversity—and the marketplace of ideas will become a monopoly with only one idea for sale.

According to Joseph Goebbels, the former minister of public enlightenment and propaganda in Germany:

> If you tell a lie big enough and keep repeating it, people will eventually come to believe it. The lie can be maintained only for such time as the State can shield the people from the political, economic, and/or military consequences of the lie. It thus becomes vitally important for the State to use all of its powers to repress dissent, for the truth is the mortal enemy of the lie, and thus by extension, the truth is the greatest enemy of the State.[177]

Clearly, university administrators who allow the suppression of conservative views are not Nazis, but institutions of higher learning that attempt to repress dissent through the application of hate-speech codes, BRTs, discriminatory hiring practices, FSZs and the acquiescence to the heckler's veto are, in some cases, shielding students from the consequences of potential lies. Social progress can only occur through the interplay of the thesis and antithesis through which new paradigms synthesize.[178] When colleges and universities bury the antithesis, then the song remains the same, and lies perpetuate. Students must be taught not to simply repeat what they learn from their professors, but to question what they learn from their professors. Otherwise, they become automatons lacking the capacity for critical thinking, and they readily accept that which they are fed without question.

In a Supreme Court case involving the removal of books from a public school library, Justice Brennan wrote, "the right to receive ideas is a necessary predicate to the recipient's meaningful exercise of his own right of speech, press, and political freedom."[179] Those who wish to limit the marketplace of ideas to only that which aligns with their subjective concept of social justice undermine students' capacity to exercise their political freedom, and in so doing, enable the growth of tyranny. When ideas cannot withstand critical analysis, they are not worthy of their continued existence in the marketplace of ideas, but this cannot be determined in a marketplace where dissent is repressed and punished.

NOTES

1. David French, "Yes, Universities Discriminate Against Conservatives," *National Review*, April 1, 2016, https://www.nationalreview.com/corner/yes-universities-discriminate-against-conservative-scholars/.
2. 354 U.S. 234 (1957).
3. Ibid., 250.
4. "Results of the 2016 University of Michigan Student Campus Climate Survey on Diversity, Equity and Inclusion," *University of Michigan*, 2016, https://diversity.umich.edu/wp-content/uploads/2017/11/DEI-STUDENT-REPORT-FINAL.pdf.
5. Thomas Healy, "Who's Afraid of Free Speech? What Critics of the Campus Protest Get Wrong About the State of Public Discourse?," *Atlantic,* June 18, 2017, https://www.theatlantic.com/politics/archive/2017/06/whos-afraid-of-free-speech/530094.
6. John Rice-Cameron, "Not Backing Down at Berkeley: Free Speech Under Siege," *Stanford Review*, May 29, 2017, https://stanfordreview.org/not-backing-down-at-berkeley-free-speech-under-siege-b596f2d7939e.
7. James Varney, "Conservative Students Say Free-Speech Rights Assailed by Anti-Kavanaugh Mob," *Washington Times*, October 7, 2018, https://www.washingtontimes.com/news/2018/oct/7/texas-conservative-students-say-free-speech-rights/.
8. David French, "Here's How Anti-Conservative Academic Discrimination Works," *National Review*, July 5, 2017, http://www.nationalreview.com/article/449232/conservatives-face-discrimination-colleges-keith-finks-ucla-case.

9. "Partisanship and Political Animosity in 2016," Pew Research Center, June 22, 2016, http://www.people-press.org/2016/06/22/partisanship-and-political-animosity-in-2016/ ("Partisans' views of the opposing party are now more negative than at any point in nearly a quarter of a century.").

10. Catherine Rampell, Opinion, "Liberal Intolerance is on the Rise on America's College Campuses," *The Washington Post*, February 11, 2016, https://www.washingtonpost.com/opinions/liberal-but-not-tolerant-on-the-nations-college-campuses/2016/02/11/0f79e8e8-d101-11e5-88cd-753e80cd29ad_story.html?utm_term=.786c5263a007 (summarizing survey data that shows college students are more willing to curtail free speech and voicing concern that "student activism may be disparately used to muzzle conservative viewpoints").

11. Melkorka Licea, "NYU Students Who Back Trump Afraid to Show Their Faces," *New York Post,* April 2, 2016, http://nypost.com/2016/04/02/nyu-students-who-back-trump-fear-for-their-safety-on-campus.

12. Kate Tinney, "Campus Graffiti Issues Threaten Berkeley College Republicans," *Daily Californian*, April 13, 2017, http://www.dailycal.org/2017/04/13/campus-graffiti-issues-threaten-berkeley-college-republicans/.

13. Kim Vassiliadis, "Message from University Leadership: Addressing Threatening Flyers," *UNC News Archives*, February 16, 2017, https://uncnewsarchive.unc.edu/campus-updates/message-from-university-leadership-addressing-threatening-flyers.

14. Jillian Frankel, "Conservative Students Face Discrimination, Marginalization at UCLA," *Daily Bruin*, January 18, 2017, http://dailybruin.com/2017/01/18/conservative-students-face-discrimination-marginalization-at-ucla/. (Haley Nieves, the outreach coordinator for the Bruin Republicans, was harassed and threatened when she was hanging up posters announcing a student event. Students followed her back to her apartment shouting at her and calling her a racist.)

15. Ibid.

16. Jennifer Larson, Mark McNeilly and Timothy J. Ryan, "Free Expression and Constructive Dialogue at the University of North Carolina at Chapel Hill," March 2, 2020, https://fecdsurveyreport.web.unc.edu/files/2020/02/UNC-Free-Expression-Report.pdf.

17. Anthony Gockowski, "Socialist Group Calls for the Extermination of Capitalists," *Campus Reform*, October 19, 2017, https://www.campusreform.org/?ID=9991.

18. Damian Hondares, "The Silent Minority: Trump Supporters at Richmond," *Collegian*, November 7, 2016, http://www.thecollegianur.com/article/2016/11/silent-minority-trump-supporters.

19. Jill Barshay, "Calculating Faculty Bias Against Conservative Students," *The Hechinger Report,* June 24, 2019, https://hechingerreport.org/calculating-faculty-bias-against-conservative-students/. (The author claims the difference is quite small but fails to recognize that the distribution of student grade point averages which are highly inflated shows a negatively skewed leptokurtic distribution.)

20. Olivia Quintana and Travis Anderson, "Pro-Trump Babson Students Cleared in Wellesley Incident," *Boston Globe,* December 19, 2016, https://www.bostongl

obe.com/metro/2016/12/19/pro-trump-babson-students-cleared-wellesley-victory-incident/RsIfPd27sNxqiXvnwOrhTJ/story.html.

21. Seth Ian Yu, "College Students Who Openly Support Trump Censored, Threatened, Bullied by Professors, Peers," *College Fix*, September 26, 2016, https://www.thecollegefix.com/college-students-openly-support-trump-censored-threatened-bullied-professors-peers.

22. Alana Mastrangelo, "Top 10 Craziest Attacks on Campus Conservatives of 2019," *Breitbart*, January 1, 2020, https://www.breitbart.com/tech/2020/01/01/top-10-craziest-attacks-on-campus-conservatives-of-2019/.

23. Ibid. (Doxing occurs when a person's personal information such as their address and phone number are published with malicious intent in public forum.)

24. Ibid. (Turning Point USA is a non-profit organization dedicated to identifying, educating and organizing students to promote freedom.)

25. Ibid.

26. Ibid.

27. Ibid.

28. Ibid.

29. Ibid.

30. Bo Winegard, "I've Been Fired. If You Value Academic Freedom, That Should Worry You," *Quillette*, March 6, 2020, https://quillette.com/2020/03/06/ive-been-fired-if-you-value-academic-freedom-that-should-worry-you/.

31. Alexandra Desanctis, "Anthony Esolen Faces the P.C. Onslaught," *National Review*, November 22, 2016, https://www.nationalreview.com/2016/11/anthony-esolen-providence-college-diversity-dispute/.

32. Sarah McLaughlin, "Fire Raises Questions about UCLA Lecturer Keith Fink's Firing," *Foundation for Individual Rights in Education*, August 4, 2017, https://www.thefire.org/fire-raises-questions-about-ucla-lecturer-keith-finks-firing/.

33. Anthony Gockowski, "Conservative Profs 'Blown off' by Academic Freedom Advocates," *Campus Reform*, August 2, 2017, https://www.campusreform.org/?ID=9530.

34. Conor Friedersdorf, "The Perils of Writing a Provocative Email at Yale," *The Atlantic*, May 26, 2016, https://www.theatlantic.com/politics/archive/2016/05/the-peril-of-writing-a-provocative-email-at-yale/484418/.

35. Ryan Everson, "A University Effectively Fired This Professor after He Spoke at a Conservative Think Tank," *Alliance Defending Freedom*, November 18, 2019, http://centerforacademicfreedom.org/a-university-effectively-fired-this-professor-after-he-spoke-at-a-conservative-think-tank/.

36. Jonathan Turley, "Cornell Professors Declare 'Informed Commentary' Criticizing the Protests as Racism," *Jonathan Turley*, https://jonathanturley.org/2020/06/12/cornell-professors-declare-informed-commentary-criticizing-the-protests-as-racism/.

37. "Court Sides with Professor Fired for Expressing Conservative Views in the Classroom," *Pacific Justice Institute*, July 25, 2019. https://www.pacificjustice.org/press/court-sides-with-professor-fired-for-expressing-conservative-views-in-the-classroom/.

38. Samantha Harris, “Fired for his Views: UNT Math Professor Brings Free Speech Lawsuit,” *Foundation for Individual Rights in Education*, April 27, 2020, https://www.thefire.org/fired-for-his-views-unt-math-professor-brings-free-speech-lawsuit/.

39. Tyson Langhofer, “Investigating Speech: When the Process Becomes the Punishment,” *ADF Center for Academic Freedom*, November 7, 2017, http://centerforacademicfreedom.org/team/tlanghofer/.

40. Ibid., para. 18.

41. *United States v. Schwimmer*, 279 U.S. 644, 655 (1929) (Holmes, J., dissenting).

42. *Texas v. Johnson*, 491 U.S. 397, 414 (1989).

43. D.C. McAllister, “The Sordid History of Liberals Calling Republicans Racist,” *PJ Media*, September 13, 2016, https://pjmedia.com/blog/d-c-mcallister/2016/09/13/the-sordid-history-of-liberals-calling-republicans-racists-n5677.

44. Lee Edwards, “What Is Conservatism?” *The Heritage Foundation*, October 25, 2018. https://www.heritage.org/conservatism/commentary/what-conservatism (citing M. Stanton Evans, The Sharon Statement).

45. M. Stanton Evans, *The Sharon Statement*, 1960. https://faculty.atu.edu/cbrucker/Amst2003/Texts/Sharon.pdf.

46. Henry David Thoreau, *Civil Disobedience* (Somerset: Cricket House Books, 2019), 1.

47. Andy Hamilton, “Conservatism,” in *Stanford Encyclopedia of Philosophy*, ed. Edward N. Zalta (Spring 2020 Edition) https://plato.stanford.edu/archives/spr2020/entries/conservatism/.

48. Steve Taylor, “The Politics of Aging,” *Psychology Today*, June 24, 2018, https://www.psychologytoday.com/us/blog/out-the-darkness/201806/the-politics-ageing

49. Kim Hart, “Most Democrats See Republicans as Racist, Sexist,” *Axios*, November 12, 2018, https://www.axios.com/poll-democrats-and-republicans-hate-each-other-racist-ignorant-evil-99ae7afc-5a51-42be-8ee2-3959e43ce320.html.

50. Carolyn Garris, “Martin Luther King’s Conservative Legacy,” *The Heritage Foundation*, January 12, 2006, https://www.heritage.org/conservatism/report/martin-luther-kings-conservative-legacy.

51. Martin Luther King, “I Have a Dream,” in *American Rhetoric: Top 100 Speeches*, https://www.americanrhetoric.com/speeches/mlkihaveadream.htm.

52. “Oklahoma State Football Coach takes Million-Dollar Pay Cut after Player Calls Him Out for Wearing T-Shirt Promoting far-Right News Channel,” Market Watch, July 3, 2020, https://www.marketwatch.com/story/oklahoma-state-football-coach-takes-million-dollar-pay-cut-after-player-calls-him-out-for-t-shirt-promoting-far-right-news-channel-2020-07-03.

53. Madison Dibble, “Dean of Massachusetts Nursing School Fired after Saying Everyone’s life Matters,” *Washington Examiner*, July 2, 2020, https://www.washingtonexaminer.com/news/dean-of-massachusetts-nursing-school-fired-after-saying-everyones-life-matters.

54. Brittany M. Hughes, “Incoming Freshman Says Marquette University Threatened Her Admission over Pro-Trump Video,” *MRCTV*, July 9, 2020, https:/

/www.mrctv.org/blog/incoming-freshman-says-marquette-university-threatened-her-admission-over-pro-trump-video.

55. John Tierney, "Republican Outnumbered in Academia, Studies Find," *The New York Times*, November 18, 2004, https://www.nytimes.com/2004/11/18/education/republicans-outnumbered-in-academia-studies-find.html.

56. Mitchell Langbert, Anthony Quain and Daniel Klien, "Faculty Voter Registration in Economics, History, Journalism, Law and Psychology," *Econ Journal Watch,* September 2016, 422–51, https://econjwatch.org/File+download/944/LangbertQuainKleinSept2016.pdf?mimetype=pdf.

57. Morgan Walker, "Liberal Profs Outnumber Conservatives 28-to-1," *Campus Reform,* July 6, 2016, https://www.thecollegefix.com/liberal-professors-outnumber-conservatives-28-1-region-known-ivy-league/.

58. Mark Levin, "Professor John Ellis Discusses How American Universities Become 'One Party Campuses,'" *Fox News*, June 22, 2020, https://www.foxnews.com/transcript/professor-john-ellis-discusses-how-american-universities-became-one-party-campuses-professor-tim-groseclose-discusses-media-bias.

59. Colleen Flaherty, "Evidence of Liberal Academe," *Inside Higher Ed*, October 3, 2016, https://www.insidehighered.com/news/2016/10/03/voter-registration-data-show-democrats-outnumber-republicans-among-social-scientists.

60. Nicholas Kristof, "The Dangers of Echo Chambers on Campus," *New York Times,* December 10, 2016, https://www.nytimes.com/2016/12/10/opinion/sunday/the-dangers-of-echo-chambers-on-campus.html.

61. Ibid.

62. Jon Shields and Joshua Dunn, *Passing on the Right: Conservative Professors in the Progressive University* (New York: Oxford University Press, 2016).

63. Ibid., 84–92.

64. Ibid., 105.

65. French, "Yes, Universities Discriminate Against Conservatives."

66. John Hasnas, "The One Kind of Diversity Colleges Avoid," *Wall Street Journal*, March 31, 2016, https://www.wsj.com/articles/the-one-kind-of-diversity-colleges-avoid-1459464676.

67. Ibid., n.7.

68. John T. Bennett, "The Harm in Hate Speech: A Critique of the Empirical and Legal Bases of Hate Speech Regulations," *Hastings Constitutional Law Quarterly* 43 (Spring 2016): 445–536.

69. Ibid., 517.

70. Andrew P. Napolitano, "Protecting Hatred Preserves Freedom: Why Offensive Expression Deserves Constitutional Protection," *Journal of Law and Policy* 25 (December 2016): 161–83.

71. Tom Head, "6 Major U.S. Supreme Court Hate Speech Cases," *ThoughtCo.*, July 18, 2019, https://www.thoughtco.com/hate-speech-cases-721215.

72. William B. Frisch, "Hate Speech in the Constitution Law of the United States," *American Journal of Comparative Law* 50 (2002): 463.

73. Richard Cohn, "Laws Won't Rein in Hate," *The Washington Post*, August 4, 2009, https://www.washingtonpost.com/wp-dyn/content/article/2009/08/03/AR2009080302222.html?hpid=opinionsbox1.

74. *Brandenberg v. Ohio*, 395 U.S. 444, 456 (1969).

75. Bennett, 451.

76. Azhar Majeed, "Defying the Constitution: The Rise, Persistence and Prevalence of Campus Speech Codes," *Georgetown Journal of Law and Policy* 7 (November 2009): 484.

77. *R.A.V. v. City of St. Paul*, 505 U.S. 377, 381 (1992).

78. Ibid., 409.

79. Ibid., 391.

80. Ibid., 393.

81. Ibid.

82. Nadine Strossen, "Freedom of Speech and Equality: Do We Have to Choose?" *Journal of Law and Policy* 25 (December 2016): 191.

83. Ibid., n.76.

84. *Davis v. Monroe Cty. Bd. of Educ.*, 526 U.S. 629, 651–52 (1999).

85. Ibid., 447–49, n.74.

86. *Wisconsin v. Mitchell,* 508 U.S. 476, 484 (1993).

87. "Spotlight on Speech Codes 2020," *Foundation for Individual Rights in Education*, https://www.thefire.org/resources/spotlight/reports/spotlight-on-speech-codes-2020/, accessed July 21, 2020.

88. *Doe v. Univ. of Michigan*, 721 F. Supp. 852, 856 (E.D. Mich. 1989).

89. Ibid., 866–67.

90. Ibid., 862 (citing *Chaplinsky v. New Hampshire*, 315 U.S. 568 (1942)).

91. Ibid., 862–63 (citing *Brandenburg v. Ohio*, 395 U.S. 444 (1969)).

92. Ibid., 863 (citing *Heffron v. International Society for Krishna Consciousness*, 452 U.S. 640, (1981)).

93. Ibid.

94. *UMW Post v. Board of Regents*, 774 F. Supp. 1163 (E.D. Wis. 1991).

95. Ibid., 1181.

96. *Iota XI Chapter v. George Mason Univ.*, 993 F.2d. 386, 392 (4th Cir. 1993).

97. Ibid., 393.

98. *College Republicans v. Reed*, 523 F. Supp. 2d 1005, 1009 (N.D. Cal. 2007).

99. Jeff Charis-Carlson, "Iowa State Settles First Amendment Lawsuit: Changes Policy," *Des Moines Register*, April 4, 2017, http://www.desmoinesregister.com/story/news/education/2017/04/04/iowa-state-settles-lawsuit-religious-free-speech-group-changes-harassment-policies/100034314.

100. Tyler Coward, "Iowa State Settles First Amendment Lawsuit, Changes Policy," *Foundation for Individual Rights in Education* April 12, 2017, https://www.thefire.org/iowa-state-university-settles-first-amendment-lawsuit-changes-policies.

101. Ibid.

102. *Doe v. Rector & Visitors of George Mason Univ.*, 149 F. Supp. 3d 602, 627 (E.D. Va. 2016).

103. Ibid., 447–48, n.67.

104. *Snyder v. Phelps,* 562 U.S. 443, 456 (2011).

105. Ibid.

106. Ibid., 448.

107. Ibid., 457.

108. Ibid., 461.

109. Romeo Vitelli, "When a Parent Loses a Child: How Do People Deal with the Emotional Blow Associated with Child Loss?" *Psychology Today*, February 4, 2013, https://www.psychologytoday.com/us/blog/media-spotlight/201302/when-parent-loses-child.

110. "2017 Report on Bias Reporting Systems," *Foundation for Individual Rights in Education*, accessed June 23, 2020, https://www.thefire.org/research/publications/bias-response-team-report-2017/report-on-bias-reporting-systems-2017/#12.

111. Ibid.

112. Ibid.

113. Nadia Dreid, "Amid Concerns About Stifling Speech, Colleges Take a New Look at Bias-Response Teams," *The Chronicle of Higher Education*, September 28, 2016, http://www.chronicle.com/article/Amid-Concerns-About-Stifling/237918 (The University of Northern Colorado disbanded its bias-response team).

114. *Speech First Inc. v. Schlissel*, 939 F.3d 756, (6th Cir. 2019).

115. Ibid., 762.

116. Ibid., 765.

117. Ibid.

118. Ed Feulner, "Zoning Out on Free Speech: First Amendment Winning Fight against Campus Free-Speech Zones," *The Washington Times*, February 12, 2018, https://www.washingtontimes.com/news/2018/feb/12/campus-free-speech-zones-are-dying/.

119. Emerson Sykes and Vera Eidelman, "When Colleges Confine Free Speech to a 'Zone,' It Isn't Free," *ACLU*, February 7, 2019, https://www.aclu.org/blog/free-speech/student-speech-and-privacy/when-colleges-confine-free-speech-zone-it-isnt-free.

120. "Free Speech Zones," *Foundation for Individual Rights in Education*, May 24, 2019, https://www.thefire.org/issues/free-speech-zones/.

121. "Order and Opinion for Motion to Dismiss: Shaw v. Burke," *Foundation for Individual Rights in Education,* January 18, 2018, https://www.thefire.org/order-and-opinion-pierce-college-shaw-v-burke/.

122. David L. Hudson, Jr., "Controversial Speakers and the Problem of the Heckler's Veto," *Freedom Forum Institute*, April 26, 2017, https://www.freedomforuminstitute.org/2017/04/26/controversial-speakers-and-the-problem-of-the-hecklers-veto/.

123. 514 F.3d 789 (8th Cir. 2008).

124. Ibid., 796, n.3.

125. 484 F. 3d 1142 (9th Cir. 2007).

126. Ibid., 1158.

127. 274 U.S. 357 (1927).

128. Ibid., 377.

129. *Bible Believers v. Wayne Cty.*, 805 F. 3d 228, 235–36 (6th Cir. 2015).

130. Ibid., 246.

131. *Bible Believers*, 252.

132. *Dariano v. Morgan Hill Unified Sch. Dist.*, 767 F. 3d 764 (9th Cir. 2014).

133. Ibid., 775.
134. Ibid., 777.
135. Ibid., 780–81.
136. Eugene Volokh, "Protestors at Middlebury College Shout Down Speaker, Attack Him and a Professor," *The Washington Post*, March 4, 2017, https://www.washingtonpost.com/news/volokh-conspiracy/wp/2017/03/04/protesters-at-middlebury-college-shout-down-speaker-attack-him-and-a-professor/?utm_term=.609350a7b3fb.
137. Ibid.
138. Ibid.
139. Tessa Berenson, "1 in 5: Debating the Most Controversial Sexual Assault Statistic," *Time*, June 27, 2014, http://time.com/2934500/1-in-5%E2%C80%82campus-sexual-assault-statistic.
140. Mairead McArdle, "Law-School Students Shout Down 'Known Fascist' Christina Hoff Summers," *National Review,* March 6, 2018, https://www.nationalreview.com/2018/03/christina-hoff-sommers-lewis-clark-law-students-shout-down.
141. Ibid.
142. Christopher Mele and Annie Correal, "Not Our President: Protests Spread after Donald Trump's Election," *The New York Times,* November 9, 2016, https://www.nytimes.com/2016/11/10/us/trump-election-protests.html.
143. Kevin Kruger, "Controversial Speech in a Polarized Climate," *Inside Higher Ed*, February 3, 2017, https://www.insidehighered.com/views/2017/02/03/dealing-controversial-speech-campuses-essay.
144. Wis. Assembly Bill 444, September 13, 2019, https://docs.legis.wisconsin.gov/2019/related/proposals/ab444.
145. Ibid.
146. Campus Free Speech Protection Act, TENN. CODE ANN. § 49-7-2405 2018, accessed July 23, 2020, https://law.justia.com/codes/tennessee/2018/title-49/chapter-7/part-24/section-49-7-2405/.
147. Executive Order on Improving Free Inquiry, Transparency and Accountability at Colleges and Universities, March 21, 2019, https://www.whitehouse.gov/presidential-actions/executive-order-improving-free-inquiry-transparency-accountability-colleges-universities/.
148. Erwin Chemerinsky, Opinion, "The Free Speech-Hate Speech Trade-off," *The New York Times*, September 13, 2017, https://www.nytimes.com/2017/09/13/opinion/berkeley-dean-erwin-chemerinsky.html.
149. Arthur C. Brooks, Opinion, "Don't Shun Conservative Professors," *The New York Times*, September 15, 2017, https://www.nytimes.com/2017/09/15/opinion/conservative-professors.html.
150. "Our Story," *Heterodox Academy,* https://heterodoxacademy.org/our-story/.
151. Abby Jackson, "Liberal Colleges Are Recruiting Conservative Professors to 'Stir up Some Trouble,'" *Business Insider,* August 10, 2017, http://www.businessinsider.com/affirmative-action-conservative-professors-liberal-colleges-2017-8.
152. Mark Judge, "Why Georgetown University Students Want More Conservative Professors on Campus," *National Review*, October 6, 2017, https://www.nationalreview.com/2017/10/georgetown-conservative-professors-students-intellectual-diversity.

153. Jeremy Bauer-Wolf, "Free Speech Mushroom in Wake of Campus Protest," *Inside Higher Ed*, September 16, 2019, https://www.insidehighered.com/news/2019/09/16/states-passing-laws-protect-college-students-free-speech.

154. Colleen Flaherty, "Iowa Bill Would Force 'Partisan Balance' in Hiring," *Inside Higher Ed*, February 21, 2017, https://www.insidehighered.com/quicktakes/2017/02/21/iowa-bill-would-force-partisan-balance-hiring.

155. An Act Relating to Higher Education, Fla. Laws Ch. 2018-4, SB4, March 11, 2018 https://www.flsenate.gov/Session/Bill/2018/4/BillText/Filed/HTML.

156. Postsecondary Institutions; Free Expression Policies, Ariz. Sess. Laws Ch. 267, HB 2563, April 25, 2018, https://legiscan.com/AZ/bill/HB2563/2018.

157. Elizabeth Llorente, "Growing Number of State Laws Are Passed or Introduced Focusing on Campus Free Speech," *Fox News*, February 9, 2018, http://www.foxnews.com/us/2018/02/09/growing-number-state-laws-are-passed-or-introduced-focusing-on-campus-free-speech.html.

158. The Forming Open and Robust University Minds Act, Ohio Laws, Sub. S.B. No. 40.

159. *College Republicans of Univ. of Wash. v. Cauce*, 2018 WL 804497 (W.D. Wash. 2018).

160. Ibid., 3 (quoting *Seattle Mideast Awareness Campaign v. King Cty.*, 781 F.3d 489, 502–503 (2015)).

161. Katherine Long, "UW to Pay $122,500 in Legal Fees in Settlement with College Republicans over Free Speech," *The Seattle Times*, June 18, 2018, https://www.seattletimes.com/seattle-news/uw-to-pay-127000-in-legal-fees-in-settlement-with-college-republicans-over-free-speech/.

162. *Young American Foundation v. Napolitano*, 2018 WL 1947766 (N.D. Ca. 2018).

163. "UC Berkeley BLOCKS Shapiro Event at University on September 14. Shapiro Vows to Fight Back," *Daily Wire*, July 19, 2017, https://www.dailywire.com/news/18778/uc-berkeley-blocks-shapiro-event-university-ben-shapiro.

164. Ibid., 10, n.162.

165. Ibid., 9.

166. Ibid., 11.

167. Brynne Madway, "Berkeley Revises Student Organization Rules in Lawsuit Settlement," *Foundation for Individual Rights in Education,* July 9, 2018, https://www.thefire.org/berkeley-revises-student-organization-rules-in-lawsuit-settlement.

168. "Fire's Stand Up for Speech Litigation Project," *Foundation for Individual Rights in Education,* https://www.thefire.org/cases/fires-stand-up-for-speech-litigation-project/.

169. "Spotlight on Speech Codes 2019," *Foundation for Individ*ual Rights in Education, https://www.thefire.org/resources/spotlight/reports/spotlight-on-speech-codes-2019/.

170. Ibid.

171. Ted Gup, "Free Speech, but Not for All?," *The Chronicle of Higher Education*, April 27, 2017, http://www.chronicle.com/article/Free-Speech-but-Not-for-All-/239909.

172. 319 U.S. 624 (1943).

173. Ibid., 637.

174. Ibid., 642.

175. Bridget Hart, "A Balancing Act for American Universities: Anti-Harassment Policy vs. Free Speech," *Journal of Law and Policy* 25 (December 2016): 399–435.

176. Michael Jones, "Fiery Debate at Penn State After Conservatives Listed as Marginalized Alongside Blacks, Homosexuals, Muslims," *College Fix,* July 6, 2018, https://www.thecollegefix.com/fiery-debate-at-penn-state-after-conservatives-listed-as-marginalized-alongside-blacks-homosexuals-muslims/.

177. Holocaust Education and Archive Research Team, "Joseph Goebbels; 'The Poison Dwarf,'" http://www.holocaustresearchproject.org/holoprelude/goebbels.html, accessed June 29, 2020.

178. Julie E. Maybee, "Hegel's Dialectics," *Stanford Encyclopedia of Philosophy*, June 3, 2016, https://plato.stanford.edu/entries/hegel-dialectics/.

179. *Board of Educ., Island Trees Union Free School Dist. No. 26 v. Pico*, 457 U.S. 853, 867 (1982).

Chapter 5

Doing the Work

Defending Campus Speech Rights in the Culture War

Will Creeley

> Free speech is not a left versus right issue; it is a right that we must preserve, including on college campuses. All of us who believe in America and its freedoms need to make sure powerful institutions and individuals don't shut down speech they don't like, and that includes universities.[1]
>
> —Senator Elizabeth Warren
> Feb. 3, 2020

INTRODUCTION

Today, the defense of freedom of expression on campus is a partisan concern. This is unsurprising; nothing in our United States escapes the pull of partisanship. Even challenges that might presumably be equally daunting to us all, like the global pandemic we now face, soon enough become yet another occasion to demonstrate partisan allegiance.[2] But however unsurprising, evaluating campus speech issues in primarily partisan or ideological terms is reductive and dangerous.

American partisanship is not new, nor necessarily negative.[3] Indeed, the First Amendment's purpose is in large part to shield "core political speech," and when political speech is at issue, the First Amendment's protection is "at its zenith."[4] But protecting partisan speech is one thing. Conceding figurative ownership of the First Amendment itself to one side of the partisan divide is another. In the same way that the Second Amendment and gun ownership are popularly understood today as conservative, Republican concerns, the defense of free speech—particularly on campus—may soon be just as branded.

This development should worry those who care about civil liberties, higher education, and our nation's future. The First Amendment must belong to all Americans. Conceiving of the First Amendment and free expression generally as one party's turf ignores the fundamental democratic necessity of the principled defense of expressive rights for all. The myopic, reflexive, and depressingly common practice of viewing campus speech debates solely through a partisan lens has locked us into a political and social feedback loop that now threatens free speech and academic freedom for today's students and faculty. Worse, the damage done will reverberate. If we allow partisanship to poison a generation's conception of "free speech," the backlash may begin on campus, but will ultimately weaken expressive rights for us all.

Because the First Amendment protects all Americans, in promise if not always in practice,[5] and because our liberal democracy is predicated on the existence of both an informed citizenry and the right to petition our government for the redress of our grievances, preserving freedom of expression as a value that transcends partisan division is of utmost importance.

WORKING AT FIRE

Free expression debates staged on campus grounds have animated partisan actors on both the left and the right for more than a half-century.[6] Arguably, this is just as it should be. What better place than the American university to trade theories with one's instructors? How better to take the measure of one's own beliefs than via daily conversation with a company of classmates? If our college classrooms and their surrounding environs are "peculiarly the marketplace of ideas," as per the Supreme Court's almost wistful characterization, then participating in campus debates—including debates about the contours of expressive rights—is part of the point of matriculating. Discussing campus activism and the danger of what he labeled "dogmatism" in a November 2015 interview, former president Barack Obama described the functional value of campus free speech as providing a kind of education in democracy:

> [We] have these values of free speech. And it's not free speech in the abstract. The purpose of that kind of free speech is to make sure that we are forced to use argument and reason and words in making our democracy work. And, you know, you don't have to be fearful of somebody spouting bad ideas. Just out-argue them. Beat 'em. Make the case as to why they're wrong. Win over adherents. That's how things work in a democracy.[7]

But the campus free speech debate has turned toxic. I know, because I have had a front row seat.[8]

Since 2006, I have worked for the Foundation for Individual Rights in Education, or FIRE, a non-partisan non-profit organization dedicated to defending student and faculty rights, particularly on freedom of expression. Founded in 1999 by a conservative history professor and a liberal defense attorney, FIRE today has critics on both the left and the right. Critics on the left point to our conservative donors and our defense of conservative students and faculty as evidence that our real agenda is the advance of conservative policy.[9] Critics on the right point to our proud identification as a non-partisan organization and our defense of liberal students and faculty as evidence that our real agenda is to "undermine the foundation of America."[10] It is tempting to take the symmetry of this criticism as confirmation that we are "doing something right," but that seems like unearned self-congratulation; if we were doing everything wrong, we'd surely hear plenty of criticism from both sides, too.

Instead, I think the criticism is the inevitable result of our concerted effort to evaluate each case we receive on its own merits. FIRE strives to be an honest broker. When reviewing submissions from our case intake, we do not allow our decisions to be dictated by the popularity or political valence of the speaker or speech at issue, nor our own politics, our boss' politics, our board's politics, or the politics of our donors. Instead, we talk about the applicable law and free speech principles and try our best to get it right. We debate and discuss the question, and sometimes we work through intense disagreement. If we conclude that the speech is protected, we defend it. That means we defend ugly speech, hateful speech, and speech that some or all of us loathe. But that's the job. When we defend speech we like, it almost feels too easy.

FIRE is an interesting and challenging place to work. I have my own partisan commitments, as do my colleagues, and we are arrayed across the political spectrum. Many of us would find little agreement with each other on any substantive question save the importance of protecting civil liberties, but all of us have heard the din of the daily culture war growing louder over the years outside our Philadelphia headquarters. It is now deafening.

The Partisan Fight

Since I began at FIRE, conservatives have continued a decades-long effort to organize students, faculty, and outside partisans in support of expressive freedom on campus. Restrictions on the expressive rights of conservative students and faculty members have been documented and challenged not only on campus, but in the courts and the press by conservative commentators, think tanks, advocacy organizations, policymakers, and state and federal legislators. Conservative actors both on and off campus have aggressively sought to claim the mantle of defenders of campus free expression, criticizing institutions of higher education as liberal city-states explicitly hostile to conservative students, faculty, invited speakers, and ideas.

The initiative has arguably been successful as a policy matter. In the past twenty years, conservative students and faculty have won significant legal victories against institutional speech restrictions, conservative state lawmakers have introduced and passed legislation addressing expressive rights on campus, and a Republican president has signed an executive order on campus speech while surrounded by conservative student-activists in the White House. The initiative has been successful as a media strategy, too. There are at least two online media outlets dedicated to tracking institutional (i.e., liberal) censorship of conservative actors on campus, and their reporting, largely conducted by student stringers, is regularly amplified by national partisan websites or networks. Defending free speech on campus is an issue of intense interest for conservatives.

To be clear (and as described in the previous chapter), conservative students and faculty regularly face campus censorship. The campus speech restrictions criticized by conservatives are often worthy targets, like denials of recognition to conservative student groups because of their beliefs or the imposition of viewpoint-based security fees on conservative speakers because of their message. These and other illiberal restrictions are plainly unconstitutional at public campuses and they flatly violate the promises of free expression made by most private institutions. When these policies and practices are abandoned or reformed, all students benefit. FIRE has successfully fought and won many of these cases. Many did not present particularly close calls.

But while perhaps a boon for conservative activists, the right's messaging success has come at some cost for civil libertarians. The concept of freedom of expression is now relatively unpopular with one of its traditional constituencies: college liberals.[11] Setting aside the legal and policy merits and relative durability of the courtroom victories, legislative acts, and executive initiatives the right has secured in the name of protecting campus expression, the conservative push on campus speech has been met by intense criticism from the left, both on and off campus.

Students, faculty, and commentators point out that the conservative cry for free speech on campus represents a reversal: Conservative actors have historically advocated for restrictions on student and faculty expression,[12] and the foundational student speech cases in both the K-12 and higher education contexts have generally pit students and faculty voicing "liberal" viewpoints against institutional speech restrictions serving "conservative" interests.[13] Noting that the rise in the conservative interest in protecting freedom of expression on campus has tracked the rise in the matriculation of non-white, non-male students, and that wealthy conservative (or libertarian) donors have helped bankroll the effort, commentators on the left have criticized the right's campus speech push. They may variously characterize it as an attempt to preserve the political and socioeconomic status quo, as a proxy attack on peaceful protest and grassroots advocacy for social change, and/or as a means of generating public and political support for ultimately weakening, defunding, or fundamentally altering state institutions.[14]

Liberal students are now less likely than their conservative peers to support the First Amendment's protections, particularly for speech they dislike or find offensive.[15] Faculty on the left critique free speech as a tool to preserve the free-market status quo at best, or, more ominously, to provide ideological cover for the advance of the far right.[16] And though many dutifully acknowledge the institutional importance of academic freedom and freedom of expression, campus administrators nevertheless have come to regard free speech warily.[17] They have seen other campuses struggle with visits from professional trolls with budget-busting security requirements that leave angry and frustrated student bodies in their wake, and they believe that paeans to the value of free speech are unlikely to extinguish social media firestorms, no matter how sincere.

THE MEDIA'S "CRISIS" NARRATIVE AND FIRE'S DAILY WORK

The partisan split on campus speech is reflected and sharpened by media coverage. Media coverage of campus free speech disputes tends to amplify partisan conflicts while paying relatively little if any attention to campus censorship that does not fit neatly into a ready-made culture war frame. For example, a partisan outlet's story about a conservative student group denied recognition by a student government because of its beliefs is virtually guaranteed an audience online and perhaps beyond. If liberal commentators weigh in, they will in turn likely focus on what they perceive as the student group's objectionable viewpoints. Outrage on both sides will ensue on social media, with the loudest voices bringing still more attention. The story is compelling to conservative audiences—not necessarily because they are exercised by the threat to expressive freedom posed by viewpoint-based decision-making by those in power, but rather because it serves to confirm conservative beliefs about the inherent liberalism of our campuses. Liberal reaction will be driven in the other direction. The partisan feedback loop is completed.[18]

Tellingly—and frustratingly for us at FIRE—a press release about, for example, an animal rights group being denied recognition on a public campus for blatantly unconstitutional and illiberal reasons will receive comparatively scant coverage.[19] Animal rights scan as "liberal," but apparently not enough for anyone on either side to don their armor for the daily battle on social media and cable news. This is a recurring problem for FIRE: Because many of the most egregious campus rights abuses involve speech or speakers that are not easily assigned a partisan value, they are simply not covered. For example, after a Northern Michigan University student and sexual assault survivor sought counseling from a university counselor, she received an email from a campus administrator telling her that she could face expulsion for telling her friends about thoughts of self-harm. FIRE intervened, pointing out the obvious First Amendment problems and as well as the possible impact on student mental health, and the school finally told students it would end its practice of threatening discipline against students for talking to other students about self-harm.[20] As shocking a civil liberties abuse as this case was, the student's predicament attracted only minor media attention compared to the sweeping coverage of incidents at Yale University or the University of California Berkeley involving partisan trolls. This problem is only exacerbated if the rights violation occurs at, say, a community college campus, an HBCU or tribal college, or a state school outside of the northeast that doesn't have a successful football or basketball program. The media will not care because people will not care—and vice versa.

Because partisan attention inspires partisan reaction, and because campus free speech flare-ups often prefigure or echo heated national debates, the particular legal or pedagogical harms that result from campus censorship matter far less to outside observers than the viewpoints at issue. In other words, the question of interest for most in the audience isn't whether, say, conscripting student speakers into tiny, highly regulated free-speech zones should be permitted on public campuses bound by the First Amendment and dedicated to serving the public interest. No, what's more determinative is how we feel about the viewpoints of the students being confined to those free-speech zones.[21] It's easier to care about the principle when the voices silenced sound like our own.

Partisanship may be ubiquitous, inevitable, and as old as the nation itself, but it is also distorting. Partisan actors have an incentive to promote partisan narratives that serve partisan needs. When those needs shift, so does the narrative; when a particular case or controversy does not align with the predominant narrative, it is minimized or ignored. Understanding the almost algorithmic partisan calculus of popular attention does not make its effects less corrosive, or less frustrating when censorship of a student or faculty member's protected expression is passed by because it doesn't fit the ready-made frame. If the story doesn't broadly confirm to a pre-existing narrative—"left wing political correctness is out of control on campus," "right wing trolls are at it again on campus," "this liberal professor hates America," "this conservative professor is a bigot"—it is very difficult to garner attention to it.

Instead, we are left with a contrived debate between partisan commentators about whether there is a "free-speech crisis" on campus, an empty exercise that is both boring and obscuring. The argument against the existence of a "crisis" has been written many times now over several years in different venues and at different lengths.[22] Its standard tropes are now familiar: Data, including FIRE's, indicates that free speech is alive and well on campus; there are less speech codes restricting student speech, for example, and the number of outside speakers targeted by disinvitation campaigns is relatively low and dropping.[23] Self-proclaimed free speech warriors ignore more egregious examples of censorship on campus and beyond.[24] The "crisis" narrative is designed to serve the interests of the right.[25]

This debate ignores the reality of the daily work my colleagues and I do defending speech from across the political spectrum. The students and faculty that FIRE defends every day do not care if commentators believe there's a free speech crisis on campus or not. Their crisis has already arrived. FIRE's view is much the same. Our mission commits us to combat the irreparable harm of censorship, without regard to its frequency. One student or faculty member punished for protected speech is one too many. And whether one deems the free speech problem on campus a "crisis" or not, FIRE certainly keeps busy.

Consider our work in 2020 alone.

In January, we revealed that Wright State University (Ohio) had repeatedly censored comments on its Facebook page that supported the faculty union during its nearly month-long strike in early 2019, including posts from faculty union leaders that criticized the censorship as it was occurring.[26] (We'd have more to say about public universities censoring social media commentary in a report released a few months later.) We wrote an emergency letter to Babson College after it fired a professor for a Facebook joke about President Trump's threat to bomb Iranian cultural sites, and joined a public coalition letter, as well.[27] On our site, we highlighted concerns voiced by Yale University faculty about the lack of academic freedom protections at the school's Singapore satellite institute,[28] criticized the University of Connecticut's reaction to two students being arrested after a video recording of them using a racial slur in a campus parking lot went viral,[29] and provided comprehensive analysis of an apparent victory for the student press at Central Washington University, where student news organizations faced defunding for critical coverage of the university until a letter from FIRE and the Student Press Law Center prompted a reversal.[30]

In February, we issued a victory press release after Truman State University (Missouri) reversed its earlier decision to deny official recognition to Animal

Alliance, a prospective animal rights student organization.[31] In initially denying the group's application, administrators cited "the emotional risk of this subject matter" for both club members and "potentially hostile students," and discussed the "reputational risk" of the group's proposed association with PETA. A 2019 open records request from FIRE discovered that Truman State administrators regularly denied official recognition and its attendant benefits to would-be student organizations because of their viewpoints and various administrative concerns about risk. For example, both a proposed Philosophy and Religion Club and a "Consent is so Frat" group were rejected because of "risk management" concerns; a "Love Your Melon" group, which sought to distribute hats to children with cancer, was rejected when administrators concluded it would present too "high of an emotional and physical risk" to student members, who would visit hospitals; and a Vegetarian Club, the mission of which was described as "very very very extreme," was denied because Truman State saw "serious risk in giving students information on what to eat to be vegetarian and where to get it in the Kirksville community."[32] After receiving a letter from FIRE detailing the plain violations of the First Amendment resulting from Truman State's viewpoint-based group recognition process, the university worked with FIRE to revise its policies, which now comply with its First Amendment obligations as a public institution.

In March, we wrote to New York University to criticize a faculty gag order imposed by NYU Grossman School of Medicine and NYU Langone Health. As the COVID-19 pandemic descended upon New York City, medical school faculty were warned that speaking with the press without prior authorization would result in discipline and potential termination.[33] We've successfully fought back against disturbingly corporate "media relations" policies like this on other campuses in recent years, such as the Nassau Community College on Long Island and the Alamo Colleges District in Texas.[34] Unfortunately, these policies remain far too common today—and receive far too little attention.[35]

In April, we reached a $25,000 settlement with Kirkwood Community College (Iowa) on behalf of an adjunct professor who was constructively terminated after a local news outlet discovered his personal Facebook comments, which included a 2019 post on an "Iowa Antifa" Facebook group page hyperbolically suggesting that he would "clock" President Trump with a bat.[36] When reached by the local news station for comment about his Facebook posts, the professor said, "I affirm that I am antifa."[37] Following the inevitable conservative media firestorm that ensued, the college prevented him from teaching, arguing that it was unsafe for him to do so. After the professor resigned to avoid being fired, FIRE came to his defense as his legal counsel.

That same month, we also defended the expressive rights of a Haskell Indian Nations University (Kansas) student kicked out of his dormitory during a statewide stay-at-home order. After a campus facilities employee questioned the student about his student status while the student, a member of the school golf team, was outside practicing, the student asked the employee if he was "on some kind of power trip" and told him he was "being an asshole."[38] On the basis of this brief interaction, the student was evicted from his residence hall and placed on emergency suspension for "threats to federal employees." (Haskell Indian Nations University is a tribal university operated by the federal government.) When the student contacted FIRE, he had been sleeping in his car and had yet to be afforded a hearing weeks after being evicted by the school, in violation of the school's policies and the federal regulations that govern its operations.[39]

Finally, closing out a busy month, we issued a report on the various ways that public colleges and universities censor speech on Facebook via the social media site's filters or by creating custom blacklists of banned words and phrases. Informed by the results of open records responses from 198 public institutions, my colleague Adam Steinbaugh, author of the report, found that 77 percent of the institutions surveyed employed Facebook's filtering system, which restricts an unknown list of words. What's more, roughly 30 percent of institutions created their own list of impermissible phrases or topics. For example, in response to protests against "Silent Sam," a Confederate monument on campus, the University of North Carolina at Chapel Hill censored any comment containing "Silent Sam" or "Nazi." Santa Monica College censored the words "cats," "dissecting," "torture," and "killing" after PETA raised concerns about cats being dissected in an anatomy course. Eighty-seven percent of schools blocked specific users; for example, our records requests revealed that the University of Kansas blocks "Boycott Koch Industries"; Mississippi State University blocks "Legalize Marijuana in Mississippi"; and Georgia State University blocks a "Georgia for Bernie" Twitter account.[40] Each of these various bans are at odds with the emerging judicial consensus that the "interactive space" on government-operated social media accounts constitutes some form of public forum, and thus cannot tolerate viewpoint-based restrictions on speech.[41]

In May, we successfully defended the academic freedom of a professor and department chair at Scottsdale Community College (Arizona). Following social media criticism of the wording of three questions about Islamic terrorism the professor had assigned for a quiz in his "World Politics" class, the professor was told by administrators that he would be investigated by the governing board of the Maricopa County Community College District. After the college stated in an Instagram post that an apology by the professor would be forthcoming, the college's marketing department sent the professor a pre-drafted apology letter, with instructions to "review and edit… so the overall message and tone is authentic."[42] The drafted apology promised that "[n]ot only will the three questions be removed from all future courses, I will be reviewing all of my material to ensure there's no additional insensitivities."[43] On May 11, days after an urgent May 7 letter from FIRE, the chancellor of the district issued his own apology "for the uneven manner in which this was handled and for our lack of full consideration for our professor's right of academic freedom."[44]

THE HARM OF REDUCING CAMPUS SPEECH RIGHTS TO A PARTISAN CONTEST

Reducing campus speech rights to a partisan contest threatens those rights for students and faculty and, by extension, for us all.

Allowing partisanship to define free expression fails students. Most fundamentally, given the mission of higher education, it is a pedagogical failure: Teaching students that freedom of expression is *actually* a tool of the right is both ahistorical and disempowering. Whether that message is sent implicitly or explicitly, it robs students of the agency secured for them by the First Amendment and its jurisprudence, to say nothing of their own democratic power.

Students

This failure to educate may be most damaging to students who already have ample reason to believe that the First Amendment will not protect them as it does others.[45] For example, a Gallup poll taken in April 2015—after a year of student protests on campuses nationwide centering on systemic racism following the fatal shooting of Michael Brown in Ferguson, Missouri—found that "[n]on-Hispanic black college students are less confident than non-Hispanic white college students about the security of all five First Amendment freedoms, but they are especially doubtful about freedom of assembly. Just 39% of black students, compared with seven in 10 white students, say this freedom is secure."[46] This finding is unsurprising when one compares the militarized law enforcement response to the black protesters in Ferguson to the diametrically different, almost *laissez-faire* approach taken by police to the white, armed protesters who took over Charlottesville in 2017 and who swarmed state capitols in 2020. Black students and anyone else paying attention can see the unequal treatment for themselves all too clearly. It is vivid.

But teaching students that this obvious disparity is ultimately beyond our collective power to correct, that free speech is indeed an illusion manipulated by the right and those in power, sells both their futures and our national possibility short. Those arguments may be politically provocative or reflect a half-truth; and easy cynicism may garner clicks or likes. But they do not equip students to redeem the expressive and associational rights they do in fact possess, nor do they explain how the brave exercise of those rights now might again change their country as it has in the past.

Abdicating the conceptual ownership of free speech to partisans means that students learn that free speech is something that will be wielded against them as a cudgel, rather than a collective right that, if equally granted and defended, protects us all from those in power. This is particularly true when pure speech is conflated with violence, as it often is on campus in academic theory and colloquial speech alike.[47] Because tactics that prove useful for one side are soon adopted by the other, both conservative and liberal students now argue that opposing viewpoints voiced by their peers, professors, or visiting speakers make them feel unsafe or attacked.[48] In this conception, free expression is not a tool of liberation and the first threat to dictators; it is itself oppressive.

In coming to understand speech as a harm to be suffered or a risk to be avoided, students rationally learn to respond to protected expression they dislike—whether partisan speech, bigoted speech, or even pornography—with requests for top-down administrative censorship. It is quicker and more effective to call in the proverbial or literal authorities, students learn, than to engage, answer, protest, ridicule, or ignore disagreeable or offensive speakers. Again, both liberal and conservative students have adopted this response.

For example, the conservative Young America's Foundation student organization at George Washington University demanded a formal investigation and discipline for anonymous students who posted flyers satirizing the group's beliefs around campus.[49] A parody of the organization's "Islamo-Fascism Awareness Week," the flyers read, in part, "HATE MUSLIMS? SO DO WE!!!" and were credited to "Students for Conservativo-Fascism Awareness."[50] For its part, the university promptly issued a statement informing students that the "hateful fliers" had been removed because "[t]he university does not tolerate actions that make any member of the GW community feel unsafe."[51] Likewise, at the University of South Carolina, a libertarian student group's public display of posters depicting censorship controversies on other campuses earned the group's members a "Notice of Charge" and a month-long investigation after offended students filed complaints with administrators complaining that the speech was "inflammatory" and "triggering."[52] The fact that the posters had been approved by administrators prior to the event did not preempt the investigation that followed.[53]

These are just two of many such examples. Students have learned well; often, administrators or campus law enforcement don't bother waiting for a student complaint before silencing potentially controversial speech from both sides of the partisan divide. For instance, FIRE filed a First Amendment suit on behalf of student Yvette Salazar against Joliet Junior College (Illinois) after she was detained by campus law enforcement for handing out flyers for the Party of Socialism and Liberation to nearby students who were tabling for the conservative student group Turning Point USA.[54] After distributing the flyers, which read "Shut Down Capitalism," Salazar was told by campus law enforcement prior to being detained and questioned that she shouldn't distribute "these types of flyers" given "the political climate of the country," as doing so "might start something on campus."[55] Similarly, FIRE's student plaintiff in our ongoing lawsuit against Jones County Junior College (Mississippi) was prohibited from discussing marijuana legalization with his fellow students by campus law enforcement and was told by the chief of campus law enforcement that he was "smarter than that."[56]

When we allow free speech to be framed as a problem to be solved by the authorities, students again learn a terrible lesson. Why bother talking? Call the cops on those who disagree with you. Don't just walk by that protest; bring the power of the state to bear on political adversaries or dissidents! By asking the authorities to censor opponents, students cede their own agency to those in power; by setting a dangerous precedent that invites top-down restrictions on their own speech in the future, they are lighting their proverbial house on fire to roast the pig. Transporting this deeply illiberal conception of the contours of one's rights in relation to those of others from campus to larger society will lead to more partisan discord, not less. Figuratively or literally dialing 911 to answer "bad speech" abandons the transformative power of counter-speech, however discomfiting, offensive, or challenging it may sometimes be, for rank authoritarianism.

Instead of seeking to restrict the expressive rights possessed by others, we should empower and encourage students to exercise their own. Because whether achieved by calling in the authorities or assembling a mob, censorship is a fundamentally flawed tactic. Rather than silencing its target, censorship often serves to rebroadcast the speaker it seeks to suppress—either cloaking them with a kind of transgressive allure, like Tipper Gore's "Parental Advisory" stickers on cassette tapes, or simply making them a matter of public interest. For example, Google searches for conservative author Charles Murray spiked to their highest recorded level in March 2017.[57] Murray didn't earn his lifetime high score by releasing a controversial new book or article. Rather, he was shouted down by an angry mob at Middlebury College in a violent protest that left his faculty interviewer with a concussion.[58] The mob didn't silence Murray; they did him a favor.

As that ugly incident demonstrates, censorship's failure is particularly acute at universities.[59] It allows one's political or ideological opponents an easy escape. Instead of debating, rebutting, or ignoring Murray's theories, for example, national conversation instead centered on the campus mob's tactics and free speech. For provocateurs or partisans, talking about "free speech" instead of the substance of one's ideas is generally a winning proposition. The National Organization for Marriage launched a "Free Speech Bus" tour of the East Coast in 2017, parking a bright orange bus in large Northeastern cities (and on Yale University's campus) emblazoned with an anti-transgender message, the hashtag #FreeSpeechBus, and a matching website. Had the organization simply driven an anti-transgender bus, any debate that ensued would likely have focused on that issue. The bus might even have been ignored. But a "Free Speech Bus" came with a built-in news hook, and sure enough, it worked.[60]

Framing freedom of expression as a zero-sum partisan fight teaches students that debate is suspect, that dialogue is complicity, and that violence in response to one's partisan opponents may be justified and necessary. For example, in his recent book *The Case Against Free Speech: The First Amendment, Fascism, and the Future of Dissent*, P. E. Moskowitz argues in conclusion that "[r]ealizing a meaningful definition of free speech—one that encompasses everyone, not just those with privilege who want to uphold our current system—will likely require massively overhauling our government through illegal actions, and perhaps violence. Only then will free speech apply to all."[61] This framing presents a dangerous dead end for students—not only because, as Professor Erica Chenoweth has documented, civil movements that become violent splinter their public support and empower fascists,[62] but because it denies the historical success of free expression as a means of generating social change and political power.[63]

Faculty

Even scholars who care deeply for the protection of the First Amendment and expressive rights have reacted to the focus on partisan controversy on campus by advocating for a conception of the university that diminishes or even rejects freedom of expression on campus. For example, Yale law professor and constitutional scholar Robert Post has argued in recent years that First Amendment doctrine is inapposite on campus, telling students that invoking "abstract principles of freedom of speech and reference our First Amendment" in discussions about campus speech controversies is "going to get you nothing but confusion."[64] Writing for *Vox* in response to controversies about speakers on the right being shouted down or protested on campus, Post argued that while our colleges and universities have "a great responsibility to educate students for citizenship in a country violently split along lines of ideology and identity . . . . the language and structure of First Amendment rights, however, is a misguided way to conceptualize the complex and subtle processes that make such education possible."[65]

Post is consistent. Legal academics will recognize Post's piece for *Vox* as a continuation of his long-standing argument about the First Amendment's incongruity with the educational mission of a public university. In 1991, for instance, as challenges to the constitutionality of public university speech codes began to be considered by courts and scholars, Post drew a distinction between the public square and the public university, concluding that "the constitutionality of restraints on racist speech within public universities does not depend upon the constitutionality of such regulation within public discourse."[66] Both then and now, Post contends that because "state institutions of higher learning are public organizations established for the express purpose of education," and because academic activities like grading or granting tenure involve academic judgments that are incompatible with the First Amendment's prohibitions on viewpoint discrimination, that First Amendment analysis of campus speech controversies is categorically confused at best.[67]

Post's argument warrants criticism. His rejection of the fundamental difference between in-class and on-campus speech abandons the decades of court rulings protecting student expressive rights in public areas of campus. Post thus appears content to weaken student rights in exchange for what he considers a more apt theoretical understanding of a university's mission and the First Amendment's doctrinal coherence.[68] This is not an advantageous trade for the students who are stopped by campus police for trying to talk to their peers about marijuana legalization, socialism, or any other political issue. Likewise, FIRE's case work demonstrates the problem with Post's apparent faith in granting "unlimited discretion to campus officials to exclude or punish any speaker that they deemed to be inconsistent with students' education," as Erwin Chemerinsky put it.[69]

Post writes that "[c]ontemporary controversies about the regulation of speech within universities well illustrate the danger" of the "over-extension of First Amendment rights."[70] Post worries that applying First Amendment analysis to campus controversies debases First Amendment principles, leaving them weaker "when we actually need to call upon them to do serious work to protect the integrity of our political system."[71] But Post's central argument presents a larger danger to student and faculty rights in two respects.

First, by arguing that the First Amendment should have no purchase at our colleges and universities, and that student speech should instead be entrusted to a corporate, bureaucratic academy, Post fails to recognize that empowering students to exercise their First Amendment rights on campus is itself educational. Educating students about their speech rights is an investment in protecting the integrity of our political system. That *is* "serious work." These students will be our future leaders; most are already old enough to fight and die for our nation. A theory that gives powerful institutions free rein to deny students expressive rights because their concerns aren't sufficiently important is a condescending mistake.[72]

Second, Post forgets that censorship is unpopular among those being censorcd. Post's recent commentaries are inspired by the intense partisan focus on campus speech issues following widely covered protests of conservative speakers. Under Post's conception, universities should be able to "regulate speech as necessary to achieve their institutional objectives"; if an invited speaker does not further these objectives, in an institution's own estimation, then that speaker may be denied the ability to speak on campus.[73] But denying an invited speaker access to campus because of their views not only teaches students a terrible lesson about their rights and agency. In our partisan moment, such an exclusion guarantees a partisan counter-reaction that serves to weaken broad public confidence in our institutions of higher education and invites legislative or regulatory overreach.

Imagine if a public university were to prevent a conservative commentator from giving a speech on campus because it deemed his or her message to be irrelevant to the university's educational objectives. Partisans would criticize or applaud the decision, partisan media would seize upon the controversy, and conservative audiences would conclude that universities were inhospitable to conservatives. In turn, conservative lawmakers and regulators would decide that intervention is necessary—and their proposed legislative or policy solutions would likely threaten student and faculty rights, not to mention the institutional autonomy and educational purpose Post sought to protect. Wouldn't the institution have been better served by adherence to the First Amendment's core principle of viewpoint neutrality?

Post contends that the First Amendment cannot be productively applied to the university context, and that invoking expressive rights in college controversies threatens the First Amendment's doctrinal coherence and ultimate sustainability. But compared to institutional censorship or legislative interference, the First Amendment's guarantee of equal access provides comparative stability and certainty, to the lasting benefit of students and faculty.

Legislators

Unfortunately, the hypothetical described above describes what has happened over the past few years. Conservatives have been censored on campus, and partisan media have reported it to concerned audiences. Universities have become increasingly unpopular with conservatives,[74] and conservative policymakers have in turn responded in several states by proposing overreaching legislative or administrative action that would inhibit expressive rights, particularly peaceful protest. While a full survey of the scope of recent legislative and regulatory initiatives concerning campus speech is beyond the scope of this chapter, relevant examples of legislative overreach demonstrate how partisan legislative responses target protected campus speech.

In Wisconsin, for example, state lawmakers have repeatedly introduced deeply flawed state legislation. In 2017, a Republican state senator introduced a bill providing in part that "[n]o person may threaten an invited speaker or threaten to organize protests or riots or to incite violence with the purpose to dissuade or intimidate an invited speaker from attending a campus event."[75] As FIRE pointed out, the bill was flatly unconstitutional: organizing peaceful protests is plainly protected speech, as is peacefully attempting to dissuade invited speakers from coming to campus.[76]

A related bill introduced at roughly the same time in the Wisconsin Assembly served as the framework for regulations adopted by the Wisconsin Board of Regents.[77] While comparatively more precise—the Regent policy requires administrative action against any student who "has engaged in violent or other disorderly misconduct that materially and substantially disrupted the free expression of others"—problems for expressive activity remain. As FIRE noted, civil liberties advocates must watch closely to ensure that the "material and substantial disruption" provision is not applied against protected activity, like walking out of a speech or peacefully protesting outside an event.[78] FIRE also expressed serious concerns about the policy's "mandatory minimum" requirement of certain sanctions, including expulsion, for students found to have repeatedly violated the policy.

We have good reason to remain vigilant, particularly given the history in Wisconsin. While the University of Wisconsin System adopted a free speech statement in 2017, promising "that it is not the proper role of the university to attempt to shield individuals from ideas and opinions they, or others, find unwelcome, disagreeable, or even deeply offensive,"[79] its leadership has not always met that promise. In 2018, system president Ray Cross issued a formal reprimand to University of Wisconsin—La Crosse Chancellor Joe Gow for inviting sex educator, nurse, and former adult film star Nina Hartley to campus as part of the school's "Free Speech Week," where she delivered a lecture titled "Fantasy vs. Reality: Viewing Adult Media with a Critical Eye."[80]

And Wisconsin state legislators have repeatedly threatened to withhold funding to state campuses because of their disapproval of the content of courses offered. In December 2016, the chairman of the Assembly Committee on Colleges and Universities and a state senator threatened to defund the University of Wisconsin-Madison if a course titled "The Problem of Whiteness" was taught as scheduled.[81] (The course appears to have proceeded as planned, and is still offered today.[82]) Months earlier, a state senator called for University of Wisconsin- Madison's defunding because a sociology class included as assigned reading an essay about the intersection of racial attitudes and sexual attraction of gay men.[83]

Unfortunately, Wisconsin lawmakers have plenty of company on this front. In recent years, FIRE has criticized lawmakers who have punished or threatened to punish particular campus speech or course content in Michigan (labor unions),[84] Maryland (screening of adult films),[85] South Carolina (LGBT-related assigned readings),[86] Alabama (faculty member's anti-Trump social media posts),[87] Kansas (faculty social media post critical of the NRA),[88] California (faculty member's social media posts about police),[89] and New York (pro-Palestinian student speech).[90] In Tennessee, state lawmakers preceded the 2017 passage of a commendable campus free speech act[91] with a 2016 act banning the use of university funds for an annual student-organized "Sex Week."[92] These instances generally involve legislators from the right, but Democrats get in on the act as well; in 2019, for example, a Georgia state representative questioned whether a conservative faculty member who had posted sharp criticism of illegal immigration and liberals should remain employed by Georgia Gwinnett College.[93]

Sometimes, legislative threats to campus speech earn bipartisan support, as with "anti-Semitism awareness" acts passed in South Carolina and Florida under strong criticism from FIRE and state ACLU chapters,[94] and effectively enacted at the federal level by executive order in 2019. The laws require institutions to use a broad definition of *anti-Semitism* that includes certain criticisms of Israel or Jewish people—speech unquestionably protected by the First Amendment—when determining whether a student has engaged in discriminatory harassment. And sometimes legislative restrictions on student rights appear to be the result of poor drafting, at best. In Arizona, for example, the state legislature passed and the governor signed into law legislation providing that "[a] university or community college may restrict a student's right to speak, including verbal speech, holding a sign or distributing fliers or other materials, in a public forum."[95] As introduced, the bill declared that institutions "*shall not* restrict a student's right to speak."[96]

For our part, FIRE has authored and supported state and federal legislation that seeks to enshrine existing First Amendment standards into law. Our aim is to secure compliance with First Amendment standards so that censored students and faculty aren't forced to litigate against their public colleges and universities to vindicate their rights. We don't want to make law; we are instead attempting to ensure as a practical matter that existing First Amendment law is followed. To that end, for example, we're proud to have helped secure—with strong bipartisan support—the passage of laws that incorporate well-established First Amendment forum analysis standards to bar public campuses from restricting student speech to tiny, remote "free speech zones."[97] We also play defense. We regularly engage with lawmakers and regulators to attempt to fix or remove provisions in campus speech legislation or regulations, like those described here, that harm or burden student or faculty expressive rights.

It's an uphill battle. Legislators are partisan actors with partisan motivations responding to partisan cues.[98] Troublingly, many lawmakers who proclaim their support for expressive rights when they agree with the speech at issue are quick to call for the censorship of campus speech they or their constituents do not like. When free speech on campus becomes a partisan issue, partisan lawmakers will regularly overreach, moving beyond the protection of free speech to more clearly partisan aims and subjugating protecting the rights of all students to simply the protection of those views they themselves hold. That's a serious problem—not only because legislators may not lawfully abuse their power to silence others, but also because situational, viewpoint-dependent support for freedom of expression is corrosive.

If the same legislators who seek to ensure that no speaker may be barred from campus on the basis of viewpoint also advocate for punishing faculty members for scholarship or social media posts they find objectionable, students are again taught a troubling lesson. Students will rationally conclude that free speech is primarily a partisan tool wielded by hypocrites unbound by principle, and that censorship is justified in certain instances, particularly when someone is voicing a view contrary from your own. Moreover, students might simply conclude that those in power make the rules, and that free speech is no exception. This may be a reasonable lesson in some respects, as such is too often the case. But it is also a deeply regrettable result, and marks a turn away from the First Amendment's promise. For the sake of our democracy, we must do better.

CHANGING THE NARRATIVE

Campus free speech controversies will likely continue to garner intense interest. This is for any number of reasons: Student debates about cultural and political questions may presage the arrival of similar tensions in larger society. Student activism has a long, important, and continuing history in national social and political movements. Student and faculty speech enjoys unprecedented visibility following the advent of social media, and they say interesting, provocative, stupid, and outrageous things. College campuses occupy a central place in the American imagination. Today's college students will one day lead the country. Placing social questions in the framework of "generations" is a popular trope in American commentary. Most members of the media are college-educated. And so forth.

Another reason is that campus debates about free speech are a consistent source of partisan outrage, controversy, and reaction. They will likely continue to be so. But allowing campus free speech debates to be framed in predominantly partisan terms harms students by teaching them, directly or indirectly, the wrong lessons about their expressive rights and by inviting partisan reaction that either dismisses free speech or overreaches in its name.

Advocates for free speech on campus face a challenge. All civil libertarians must quickly grow accustomed to having their defense of the rights of a certain group or individual conflated with a defense of the actions or views of that same group or individual. That comes with the territory, frustrating though it may be, and is the price of standing on principle. But what if the principle itself—here, the idea that free speech on campus is useful and good, and should protect the rights of all—starts to give way under our feet? The balkanization of the current moment and the stark politicization of campus free speech debates make this an urgent question, and prompt another one: Have we lost a generation of students, particularly students on the left, for good?

We'll see. There's work to do.

First, and most importantly, those who claim to care about freedom of expression on campus (and elsewhere) must stand for principle, not party. The viewpoint expressed by the speech at issue cannot determine whether we are willing to defend it.[99] This is hard, lonely, alienating work. But consistency counts. Advocates must show up for the pro-Israel student group denied recognition,[100] for example, *and* show up for the pro-Palestinian student group facing the same problem.[101] Do this work long enough, consistently enough, and without excuse or apology, and the example set may convince skeptics. The function of defending speech takes priority over the content of the speech itself; indeed, if the speech is protected, the view it expresses is irrelevant. In that sense, free speech advocates should emulate plumbers: called to fix a problem, don't care who you voted for. The fact that the kitchen sink is broken is enough reason to get to work.

Second, we must demonstrate to students—again, all students—that freedom of expression may protect and amplify the strength they already possess. This starts by taking their concerns seriously and in good faith. When students ask why the First Amendment protects hateful, dehumanizing speech, we need to recognize that it's a good question and not evidence of thin skin, "snowflake" culture, or a desire to censor their opponents. Advocating for the First Amendment can feel not just deeply counterintuitive, but even dangerous when it protects people who hate you. We must show students that it protects them, too; we should acknowledge the pain of hurtful or dehumanizing speech, but not end the conversation there. The First Amendment protects our right to answer that speech: to name racists, to argue against them, to peacefully protest them.

To move beyond simple talk and the theoretical underpinnings of the First Amendment, we then have to prove that the First Amendment can work to students' advantage. The best way to do so is by showing that it has worked before through concrete examples. First Amendment jurisprudence is full of narratives of breathtaking personal courage that hastened the arrival of hard-earned historic change. I have told thousands of students, faculty members, and administrators from across the country and across the political spectrum some of these stories, and it's a joy.

There is a deep satisfaction to be found in seeing skeptical audiences soften when hearing about the bravery of Billy Gobitas, a Jehovah's Witness and self-described "true follower of Christ" who was expelled from the fifth grade when he refused to salute the flag—"not because I do not love my country, but I love my country and I love God more and I must obey His commandments."[102] Billy lost his First Amendment challenge before the Court, of course, at a time of terrible persecution and violence nationwide against people of his faith.[103] But his willingness to stand up for his freedom of conscience was redeemed in full just a few years later by the Barnett sisters, young Jehovah's Witnesses who had likewise been expelled for refusing to salute the flag. This time, with this First Amendment challenge, the Court got it right, and Justice Robert H. Jackson's majority opinion captures the hope of our democratic pluralism: "If there is any fixed star in our constitutional constellation, it is that no official, high or petty, can prescribe what shall be orthodox in politics, nationalism, religion, or other matters of opinion or force citizens to confess by word or act their faith therein."[104]

Then there's Harry Keyishian enthusiastically challenging a public university loyalty oath to secure his "revenge on the '50s," striking a blow on behalf of the faculty he had seen forced out during McCarthyite purges of the academy.[105] Or the Gay and Lesbian Students Association of the University of Arkansas at Fayetteville, finding the courage to fight back against the naked bigotry they were subjected to by their peers, their university administrators, and even state elected officials after they asked for $165 in student activity funds "to show a historical documentary, 'Before Stonewall,' and sponsor two workshops, one on racism and one on homophobia."[106]

This history is our students' inheritance. The tolerant, pluralistic democracy it points toward seems desperately far away, but its achievement is worth pursuing. It is important for students, educators, commentators, and the public at large to recognize that the availability of the First Amendment's protection is too often contingent upon one's identity. But that recognition should motivate us to get to work, not to abandon the field. There is certainly work to be done. Our publicly supported institutions of higher education and those who care about their preservation have a civic responsibility to teach students how to exercise their expressive rights to engage with their nation, and respect the right of others to do the same. That's how we can avoid partisan fatalism and instead demonstrate the transformative power of the First Amendment's core promise of equal treatment in the eyes of the law.

NOTES

1. "Free Speech Q&A: Elizabeth Warren," PEN America, February 3, 2020, https://pen.org/elizabeth-warren-on-free-expression-in-america.

2. "In this constant state of emergency, there is little room to prize non-ideological values such as governing competence or policy expertise, and any form of compromise with the political opposition is tantamount to capitulation." David A. Hopkins, "Why COVID Was Never Going to Produce National Unity," *Honest Graft*, May 26, 2020, http://www.honestgraft.com/2020/05/why-covid-was-never-going-to-produce.html.

3. Aaron Astor, "Partisanship Is an American Tradition—and Good for Democracy," *The Washington Post*, July 12, 2017, https://www.washingtonpost.com/news/made-by-history/wp/2017/07/12/partisanship-is-an-american-tradition-and-good-for-democracy/.

4. *Buckley v. Am. Constitutional Law Found.*, 525 U.S. 182, 186–87 (1999) (quoting *Meyer v. Grant*, 486 U.S. 414, 425 (1988)).

5. Adam Serwer, senior editor for *The Atlantic*, wrote that he "personally saw Ferguson police use crushing force against protesters for much less than what the Nazis in Charlottesville are doing today. They had snipers trained on unarmed and peaceful crowds merely protesting, before the slightest hint of violence emerged. The first amendment is meant to protect even hate speech. But it often fails to protect the supposedly protected speech of black Americans. So when you say, that Nazis have the right to protest because everyone has that right, remember that not everyone does in practice. To many watching today, it looks like Nazis have an unconditional right to protest, while black Americans have something less than that. This is also how even well-intentioned defenses of free speech can read to some as justifications for selective rights not available to all." Adam Serwer (@adamserwer), August 12, 2017, https://twitter.com/AdamSerwer/status/896413424015560704?s=20.

6. Marjorie Heins, *Priests of Our Democracy: The Supreme Court, Academic Freedom, and the Anti-Communist Purge* (New York: New York University Press, 2013); Joy-Ann Williamson-Lott, *Jim Crow Campus: Higher Education and the Struggle for a New Southern Social Order* (New York: Teachers College Press, 2018).

7. "Obama Praises University of Missouri Protestors," ABC News, November 15, 2015, https://www.youtube.com/watch?v=8PlcALRh6Og&feature=emb_title.

8. In this chapter, I will attempt primarily to be descriptive. I will not make an argument as to the merits of either side's conception of the other's motives or aims—not only because FIRE is a nonpartisan organization, but also because I am unlikely to convince partisans on either side that my account has merit. I will also assume that the general details of certain events mentioned here are familiar to the reader, either by accounts elsewhere in this book or contemporary reporting.

9. Jim Sleeper, "What the Campus 'Free Speech' Crusade Won't Say," *AlterNet*, September 4, 2016, https://www.alternet.org/2016/09/what-campus-free-speech-crusade-wont-say-0/.

10. "Campus Marxists are protected to spread their hateful ideologies, and the courts are gamed – thanks to groups like FIRE – to protect them as they undermine the foundation of America." Trejo, Shane, "ANTIFA Professor Who Wished Genocide on Christians Gets 3+ Years of Pay from College in Settlement," *Big League Politics*, April 28, 2020, https://bigleaguepolitics.com/antifa-professor-who-wished-genocide-on-christians-gets-3-years-of-pay-from-college-in-settlement.

11. Vimal Patel, "Students' Attitudes Toward Controversial Speech Are Changing. Here's Why," *Chronicle of Higher Education*, September 22, 2019, https://www.chronicle.com/article/Students-Attitudes-Toward/247167;Jeremy Bauer-Wolf, "Lukewarm Embrace of Free Speech," *InsideHigherEd*, October 11, 2017, https://www.insidehighered.com/news/2017/10/11/students-opinions-free-speech-divided.

12. Jill Lepore, "Flip-Flopping on Free Speech," *New Yorker*, October 1, 2017, https://www.newyorker.com/magazine/2017/10/09/flip-flopping-on-free-speech.

13. See, e.g., *Papish v. Board of Curators*, 410 U.S. 667 (1973) (reversing expulsion of graduate student for distributing underground newspaper containing profanity), and *Bethel School District v. Fraser*, 478 U.S. 675, 683 (1986) ("The process of educating our youth for citizenship in public schools is not confined to books, the curriculum, and the civics class; schools must teach by example the shared values of a civilized social order.").

14. Sophia A. McClennen, "Enough with the Blue-Baiting: The Biggest Threat on Campus Has Nothing to Do with Free Speech," *Salon*, September 2, 2017, https://www.salon.com/2017/09/02/enough-with-the-blue-baiting-the-biggest-threat-on-campus-has-nothing-to-do-with-free-speech/ ("While everyone gets distracted by debates over free speech, Republican-controlled states are slashing support for higher education at precisely the time when our nation's students need more, not less, funding.");Jamie Piltch, "Free Speech Isn't under Attack on Campuses; It's Just Being Extended to More Groups," *The Washington Post*, December 7, 2017, https://www.washingtonpost.com/news/made-by-history/wp/2017/12/07/free-speech-isnt-under-attack-on-campuses/ ("With student bodies that come from increasingly different backgrounds, universities are being forced to reckon with the fact that they haven't historically valued the free expression of all groups equally."); Clio Chang, "Right Wing Donors Are the Ones Threatening Campus Free Speech, You Idiots," *Splinter*, March 9, 2018, https://splinternews.com/right-wing-donors-are-the-ones-threatening-campus-free-1823651572 ("So when it comes to what is taught on college campuses today, it's clear that wealthy donors exert much more influence than the student activists supposedly suppressing free speech.").

15. "Student Attitudes Free Speech Survey," Foundation for Individual Rights in Education, 2017, https://www.thefire.org/research/publications/student-surveys/student-attitudes-free-speech-survey/.

16. Jason Stanley, "When Fascists Weaponize Free Speech Absolutism," *Literary Hub*, September 12, 2018, https://lithub.com/when-fascists-weaponize-free-speech-absolutism/.

17. Bauer-Wolf, "No End in Sight for Campus Free Speech Battles," *Inside Higher Ed*, March 8, 2018, https://www.insidehighered.com/news/2018/03/08/administrators-still-waging-campus-free-speech-wars.

18. Cass R. Sunstein, "The Law of Group Polarization," John M. Olin Program in Law and Economics Working Paper No. 91, 1999, https://ssrn.com/abstract=199668.

19. "Public University Rejects Animal Rights Club, Citing 'Emotional Risk' to Students," Foundation for Individual Rights in Education, December 10, 2019, https://www.thefire.org/public-university-rejects-animal-rights-club-citing-emotional-risk-to-students/. What little coverage the story did garner came from the right. See, for example: Katherine Timpf, "University Rejects Animal-Rights Club over 'Emotional Risk' Concerns," *National Review*, December 17, 2019, https://www.nationalreview.com/2019/12/truman-state-university-rejects-animal-rights-club-over-emotional-risk-concerns/.

20. "FIRE to Northern Michigan U.: End Ban on Students Discussing Self-Harm," Foundation for Individual Rights in Education, September 22, 2016, https://www.thefire.org/fire-to-northern-michigan-u-end-ban-on-students-discussing-self-harm/.

21. "Most of the debates about free speech, however, are not actually concerned with the First Amendment's protections. As French acknowledges—and he is among the few on the right to do so—what is actually occurring on most college campuses is a conflict between groups over the value of particular ideas, not the censorship of free expression through state power. In any society, ideological and social consensus will lead to some ideas being unacceptable to the majority and consigned to the fringe. The question is which ideas will suffer this fate." Adam Serwer, "A Nation of Snowflakes," *The Atlantic*, September 26, 2017, https://www.theatlantic.com/politics/archive/2017/09/it-takes-a-nation-of-snowflakes/541050/.

22. For an incomplete but representative sample and overview, seeJonathan Chait, "The Right Is Worse Than the Left on Free Speech. So What?," *New York*, March 20, 2018, https://nymag.com/intelligencer/2018/03/the-right-is-worse-than-the-left-on-free-speech-so-what.html.

23. Jeffrey Adam Sachs, "The 'Campus Free Speech Crisis' Is a Myth. Here Are the Facts," *The Washington Post*, March 16, 2018, https://www.washingtonpost.com/news/monkey-cage/wp/2018/03/16/the-campus-free-speech-crisis-is-a-myth-here-are-the-facts/.

24. Jamelle Bouie, "Minor Threat," *Slate*, March 8, 2018, https://slate.com/news-and-politics/2018/03/the-real-threats-to-free-speech-arent-campus-protests.html ("On the list of threats to freedom of expression, left-wing students shouting at prominent writers and speakers—all of whom retain their platforms in major media—seems minor.").

25. Aaron Hanlon, "The Real Threat to Free Speech on Campus Isn't Coming from the Left," *The Washington Post*, October 15, 2019, https://www.washingtonpost.com/outlook/2019/10/15/real-threat-free-speech-campus-isnt-coming-left/.

26. Greg Harold Greubel, "Public Records Reveal Wright State Used Unconstitutional Facebook Page Policy to Censor Pro-union Speech During Historic Faculty Strike," Foundation for Individual Rights in Education, January 24, 2020, https://www.thefire.org/public-records-reveal-wright-state-used-unconstitutional-facebook-page-policy-to-censor-pro-union-speech-during-historic-faculty-strike/.

27. Adam Steinbaugh, "Civil Liberties Advocates, Celebrities Sign Letter Defending Professor Fired by Babson College, Whose Claimed 'Cooperation' with

Police Is in Doubt," Foundation for Individual Rights in Education, January 23, 2020, https://www.thefire.org/civil-liberties-advocates-celebrities-sign-letter-defending-professor-fired-by-babson-college-whose-claimed-cooperation-with-police-is-in-doubt/.

28. Sarah McLaughlin, "After Controversy over Dissent Program's Cancellation at Singapore Campus, Yale Faculty Call for Academic Freedom Protections," Foundation for Individual Rights in Education, January 27, 2020, https://www.thefire.org/after-controversy-over-dissent-programs-cancellation-at-singapore-campus-yale-faculty-call-for-academic-freedom-protections/.

29. Alex Morey and Adam Steinbaugh, "Wrongly Arrested for Racial Slur, UConn Students Sue University over Violation of First Amendment, Court Order [UPDATED]," Foundation for Individual Rights in Education, January 14, 2020, https://www.thefire.org/wrongly-arrested-for-racial-slur-uconn-students-sue-university-over-violation-of-first-amendment-court-order/.

30. Lindsie Rank, "After Scandal, Questions Remain about Central Washington University's New Promise to Support Student Media," Foundation for Individual Rights in Education, January 16, 2020, https://www.thefire.org/after-scandal-questions-remain-about-central-washington-universitys-new-promise-to-support-student-media/.

31. "WHALE DONE: Animal Rights Club Approved by Public University after FIRE's First Amendment Uproar," Foundation for Individual Rights in Education, February 10, 2020, https://www.thefire.org/whale-done-animal-rights-club-approved-by-public-university-after-fires-first-amendment-uproar.

32. "FIRE Letter to Truman State University, December 10, 2019," Foundation for Individual Rights in Education, https://www.thefire.org/fire-letter-to-truman-state-university-december-10-2019/.

33. Shalini Ramachandran, and Joe Palazzolo, "NYU Langone Tells ER Doctors to 'Think More Critically' about Who Gets Ventilators," *Wall Street Journal*, March 30, 2020, https://www.wsj.com/articles/nyu-langone-tells-er-doctors-to-think-more-critically-about-who-gets-ventilators-11585618990.

34. Will Creeley, "Fighting a Faculty Gag Order at NY's Nassau Community College," Foundation for Individual Rights in Education, September 28, 2018, https://www.thefire.org/fighting-a-faculty-gag-order-at-nys-nassau-community-college/.

35. It is necessary to note the tireless efforts of Frank LoMonte, current Director of the Brechner Center for Freedom of Information at the University of Florida and longtime executive director of the Student Press Law Center, to address the danger of gag orders on government employees on campus and beyond. See, for example, Frank LoMonte, "Putting the 'Public' Back into Public Employment: A Roadmap for Challenging Prior Restraints That Prohibit Government Employees from Speaking to the News Media," *Kansas Law Review*, 2019, 1–68.

36. "VICTORY: College Settles with 'Antifa' Professor Fired for Criticizing President Trump on Facebook, Avoids First Amendment Lawsuit from FIRE," Foundation for Individual Rights in Education, April 27, 2020, https://www.thefire.org/victory-college-settles-with-antifa-professor-fired-for-criticizing-president-trump-on-facebook-avoids-first-amendment-lawsuit-from-fire/.

37. Josh Scheinblum, "Kirkwood Professor: 'I affirm that I am antifa,'" KCRG, August 22, 2019, https://www.kcrg.com/content/news/Kirkwood-professor-I-affirm-that-I-am-antifa-557897151.html.

38. "FIRE Letter to Haskell Indian Nations University, April 24, 2020," Foundation for Individual Rights in Education, https://www.thefire.org/fire-letter-to-haskell-indian-nations-university-april-24-2020/.

39. Ibid.

40. "No Comment: Public Universities' Social Media Use and the First Amendment," Foundation for Individual Rights in Education, 2020, https://www.thefire.org/research/publications/miscellaneous-publications/social-media-use-and-the-first-amendment/no-comment-public-universities-social-media-use-and-the-first-amendment/.

41. *See, e.g., Knight First Amendment Inst. at Columbia Univ. v. Trump*, 928 F.3d 226, 237 (2d Cir. 2019); *Robinson v. Hunt Cty.*, 921 F. 3d 440, 447–49 (5th Cir. 2019); *Davison v. Randall*, 912 F.3d 666, 681–87 (4th Cir. 2019).

42. "FIRE Letter to Scottsdale Community College, May 7, 2020," Foundation for Individual Rights in Education, https://www.thefire.org/fire-letter-to-scottsdale-community-college-may-7-2020/.

43. Ibid.

44. "MCCCD Statement on Academic Freedom," Maricopa County Community College District Interim Chancellor Dr. Steven R. Gonzales, May 11, 2020, https://news.maricopa.edu/news-articles/mcccd-statement-academic-freedom.

45. For example, in August 2016, the Department of Justice issued a report following its investigation into the Baltimore Police Department following the 2015 death of Freddie Gray while in custody. The DOJ found that Baltimore's police officers routinely violated the First Amendment rights of African-American citizens, noting that "some BPD officers appear to believe that use of vulgar or profane language provides probable cause to arrest or grounds for ordering a person to leave a location." "Investigation of the Baltimore City Police Department," U.S. Department of Justice, Civil Rights Division, August 10, 2016, https://www.justice.gov/opa/file/883366/download. The fact that American citizens were being arrested solely for cursing or mocking the police—nearly three decades after the Supreme Court made clear in 1987's *Houston v. Hill* that the First Amendment protects such speech—should have been a national scandal. It wasn't. *Houston v. Hill*, 482 U.S. 451 (1987).

46. Lydia Saad and Jeffrey M. Jones, "More College Students Than U.S. Adults Say Free Speech Is Secure," Gallup, April 4, 2016, https://news.gallup.com/poll/190442/college-students-adults-say-free-speech-secure.aspx.

47. For an overview and representative examples, see Suzanne Nossel, "No, Hateful Speech Is Not the Same Thing as 'Violence,'" *The Washington Post*, June 22, 2017, https://www.washingtonpost.com/outlook/no-hateful-speech-is-not-the-same-thing-as-violence/2017/06/22/63c2c07a-5137-11e7-be25-3a519335381c_story.html?utm_term=.3a396ce3995; and Jonathan Zimmerman, "College Campuses Should Not Be Safe Spaces," *Chronicle of Higher Education*, January 17, 2019, https://www.chronicle.com/article/College-Campuses-Should-Not-Be/245505. See also

Lisa Feldman Barrett, "When Is Speech Violence?" *The New York Times*, July 14, 2017, https://www.nytimes.com/2017/07/14/opinion/sunday/when-is-speech-violence.html.

48. See, for example, Adam Steinbaugh, "FIRE Warns University of Georgia and State Attorney General to End Speech-Chilling Investigation into TA's Protected Expression," Foundation for Individual Rights in Education, January 25, 2019, https://www.thefire.org/fire-warns-university-of-georgia-and-state-attorney-general-to-end-speech-chilling-investigation-into-tas-protected-expression/; Elizabeth Nolan Brown, "My Alma Mater American University Cancelled My Title IX 'Hate Speech' Panel," *Reason*, September 29, 2017, https://reason.com/2017/09/29/au-campus-safe-from-title-ix-hate-speech/; Clare Foran, "Trump-Supporting Republicans Face a Backlash on College Campuses," *The Atlantic*, October 31, 2016, https://www.theatlantic.com/politics/archive/2016/10/republicans-trump-racism-sexism/505697/; Ken White, "Some College Thick-Skin Advocates Need a Thicker Skin," *Popehat*, April 18, 2016, https://www.popehat.com/2016/04/18/some-college-thick-skin-advocates-need-a-thicker-skin/; Scott Jaschik, "Justice Scalia, a Law School and Diversity of Thought," *Inside Higher Ed*, February 19, 2016, https://www.insidehighered.com/news/2016/02/19/georgetown-law-debates-intellectual-diversity-and-institutional-neutrality-wake.

49. Justine Coleman, "University Condemns Islamophobic Fliers Wrongly Posted in YAF's Name," *GW Hatchet*, September 9, 2017, https://www.gwhatchet.com/2017/09/09/university-condemns-islamophobic-fliers-wrongly-posted-in-yafs-name.

50. Adam Steinbaugh, "George Washington University Police Investigating Posters Lampooning Conservative Group—Again," Foundation for Individual Rights in Education, September 13, 2017, https://www.thefire.org/george-washington-university-police-investigating-posters-lampooning-conservative-group-again/.

51. "University Statement Regarding Offensive Fliers on Campus," The George Washington University, September 9, 2017, https://mediarelations.gwu.edu/university-statement-regarding-offensive-fliers-campus.

52. "Abbott Notice of Charge Letter," Foundation for Individual Rights in Education, https://www.thefire.org/abbott-notice-of-charge-letter/.

53. FIRE sponsored an ultimately unsuccessful First Amendment lawsuit on behalf of the students against the University of South Carolina. *Abbott v. Pastides*, 900 F.3d 160 (4th Cir. 2018).

54. "Joliet Junior College—Stand Up For Speech Lawsuit," Foundation for Individual Rights in Education, https://www.thefire.org/cases/joliet-junior-college-stand-up-for-speech-lawsuit/.

55. "Amended Complaint, *Salazar v. JJC*," Foundation for Individual Rights in Education, March 27, 2018, https://www.thefire.org/amended-complaint-salazar-v-jjc-pdf/.

56. "Complaint – *Brown v. Jones County Junior College*," Foundation for Individual Rights in Education, September 4, 2019, https://www.thefire.org/complaint-brown-v-jones-county-junior-college/.

57. "Google Trends: Charles Murray," Google, https://trends.google.com/trends/explore?date=all&geo=US&q=%22charles%20murray%22.

58. Allison Stanger, "Understanding the Angry Mob at Middlebury That Gave Me a Concussion," *The New York Times*, March 13, 2017, https://www.nytimes.com/2017/03/13/opinion/understanding-the-angry-mob-that-gave-me-a-concussion.html.

59. As one critic of the right's campus free speech push wrote: "The activist practice of no-platforming—denying public figures platforms, like speaking engagements or articles, through protest or other means—has become an irresistible motif for the media. It is a terrible tactic for a number of reasons, for both academic freedom and the advancement of progressive causes. In the current moment, liberal ideas are dominant at universities, but it's not hard to imagine a world in which they are considered dangerous. More urgently, in the age of social media and conservative trolls, no-platforming turns into amplification on steroids; it does the very opposite of what it aims to do." Mari Uyehara, "The Free Speech Grifters," *GQ*, March 19, 2018, https://www.gq.com/story/free-speech-grifting.

60. Elyse Wanshel, "Transphobic 'Free Speech Bus' to Tour U.S. With Message of Hate," *Huffington Post*, March 23, 2017, http://www.huffingtonpost.com/entry/transphobic-free-speech-bus-anti-lgbtq_us_58d3ce1be4b0b22b0d1a5022.

61. P.E. Moskowitz, *The Case Against Free Speech: The First Amendment, Fascism, and the Future of Dissent* (New York: Bold Type Books, 2019).

62. "If any part of the resistance sacrifices its strength in numbers to play to the opponent's expertise in violence, it won't stand a fighting chance." Erica Chenoweth, "Violence Will Only Hurt the Trump Resistance," *The New Republic*, February 7, 2017, https://newrepublic.com/article/140474/violence-will-hurt-trump-resistance.

63. In reviewing Moskowitz's book, Stephen Rohde noted that Moskowitz had chosen to "[i]gnore Gandhi, Lawson, and King, ignore the great movements for social change in America that succeeded through nonviolent resistance; ignore voting rights; ignore the students at Stoneman Douglas High School; ignore Indivisible, People Power, and the thousands of churches, mosques, temples, and civil rights and social justice organizations struggling every day to achieve economic, gender, and racial equality." As Rohde wrote, "Moskowitz is lucky we have a First Amendment, which protects a book advocating the violent overthrow of the government." Stephen Rohde, "A Failed Case against Free Speech," *Los Angeles Review of Books*, March 17, 2020, https://lareviewofbooks.org/article/a-failed-case-against-free-speech/.

64. Ben Shumate, "Robert Post Talks Freedom of Expression," *Brown Daily Herald*, November 15, 2016, https://www.browndailyherald.com/2016/11/15/robert-post-talks-freedom-expression/.

65. Robert C. Post, "There Is No 1st Amendment Right to Speak on a College Campus," *Vox*, December 31, 2017, https://www.vox.com/the-big-idea/2017/10/25/16526442/first-amendment-college-campuses-milo-spencer-protests.

66. "Although the Supreme Court has often held that 'the First Amendment rights of speech and association extend to the campuses of state universities,' and

even that 'the campus of a public university, at least for its students, possesses many of the characteristics of a public forum,' in fact state institutions of higher learning are public organizations established for the express purpose of education. The Court has always held that 'a university's mission is education' and has never construed the first amendment to deny a university's 'authority to impose reasonable regulations compatible with that mission upon the use of its campus and facilities.' The Court has explicitly recognized 'a university's right to exclude . . . First Amendment activities that . . . substantially interfere with the opportunity of other students to obtain an education.' Thus student speech incompatible with classroom processes may be censored; faculty publications inconsistent with academic standards may be evaluated and judged; and so forth." Robert C. Post, "Free Speech and Religious, Racial, and Sexual Harassment: Racist Speech, Democracy, and the First Amendment," *William & Mary Law Review* 32 (1991): 318.

67. Ibid.

68. Ronald K. L. Collins, "Recent Developments Regarding Free Speech on College Campuses," The Free Speech Center, October 27, 2017, https://mtsu.edu/first-amendment/post/65/recent-developments-regarding-free-speech-on-college-campuses.

69. Erwin Chemerinsky, "Hate Speech Is Protected Free Speech, Even on College Campuses," *Vox*, December 26, 2017, https://www.vox.com/the-big-idea/2017/10/25/16524832/campus-free-speech-first-amendment-protest.

70. Robert Post, "The Classic First Amendment Tradition under Stress: Freedom of Speech and the University," Yale Law School, Public Law Research Paper No. 619, September 28, 2017, https://papers.ssrn.com/sol3/papers.cfm?abstract_id=3044434.

71. Ibid. (quoting description in abstract).

72. Kelly Sarabyn, "The Twenty-Sixth Amendment: Resolving the Federal Circuit Split Over College Students' First Amendment Rights," *Texas Journal on Civil Liberties and Civil Rights*, 2008.

73. Ibid.

74. Kim Parker, "The Growing Partisan Divide in Views of Higher Education," Pew Research Center, August 19, 2019, https://www.pewsocialtrends.org/essay/the-growing-partisan-divide-in-views-of-higher-education.

75. "AN ACT to create 36.02 and 38.05 of the statutes; relating to: free speech at the University of Wisconsin and technical college systems and granting rule-making authority," https://www.wispolitics.com/wp-content/uploads/2017/05/170503VukmirJarchowBill.pdf.

76. "Just as the First Amendment protects the rights of any speaker—no matter how controversial their ideas may be—to speak on a public campus where they have been invited, it also protects the rights of others to peacefully protest that speaker. Nonviolent protest that does not materially interfere with the rights of others is one of the quintessential forms of protected speech, so certainly organizing lawful protests is also protected. . . . Encouraging institutions, organizations, or persons to reconsider invitations to a speaker, or encouraging a speaker to avoid speaking or to change their views, are examples of protected speech. FIRE agrees that calls for disinviting

speakers are at odds with the purpose of higher education and criticizes those demands accordingly, but those campaigns, so long as they are not accompanied by true threats or violence, are protected under the First Amendment."Joe Cohn, "Second Wisconsin Bill Addressing Free Speech Presents Significant First Amendment Problems," Foundation for Individual Rights in Education, May 5, 2017, https://www.thefire.org/second-wisconsin-bill-addressing-free-speech-presents-significant-first-amendment-problems/.

77. "Regent Policy Document 4-21: Commitment to Academic Freedom and Freedom of Expression," University of Wisconsin System Board of Regents, https://www.wisconsin.edu/regents/policies/commitment-to-academic-freedom-and-freedom-of-expression.

78. Joe Cohn, "New Wisconsin Regents Policy Has Problems and Promise," Foundation for Individual Rights in Education, October 10, 2017, https://www.thefire.org/new-wisconsin-regents-policy-has-problems-and-promise/.

79. "Board of Regents Agenda and Materials, October 6, 2017," University of Wisconsin System Board of Regents, https://www.wisconsin.edu/regents/download/meeting_materials/2017/october/Board-of-Regents-Friday-Agenda-and-Materials---October-2017.pdf.

80. Colleen Flaherty, "Free Speech for Some, Not All?" *Inside Higher Ed*, November 29, 2018, https://www.insidehighered.com/news/2018/11/29/adult-film-stars-invite-campus-gets-wisconsin-chancellor-trouble-some-see-hypocrisy.

81. Joe Cohn, "Wisconsin Lawmakers Once Again Threaten Academic Freedom," Foundation for Individual Rights in Education, December 21, 2016, https://www.thefire.org/wisconsin-lawmakers-once-again-threaten-academic-freedom/.

82. "African 405: The Problem of Whiteness," African Cultural Studies, University of Wisconsin–Madison, https://african.wisc.edu/courses/african-405-the-problem-of-whiteness/.

83. Alex Morey and Adam Steinbaugh, "Wisconsin Legislator's Threat to Slash UW Budget over Reading Assignment 'Cuts to the Core of Academic Freedom,'" Foundation for Individual Rights in Education, July 8, 2016, https://www.thefire.org/wisconsin-legislators-threat-to-slash-uw-budget-over-reading-assignment-cuts-to-the-core-of-academic-freedom/.

84. Susan Kruth, "Michigan Senate Subcommittee Proposes Penalty for Speech about Labor Unions," Foundation for Individual Rights in Education, April 1, 2014, https://www.thefire.org/michigan-senate-subcommittee-proposes-penalty-for-speech-about-labor-unions/.

85. "University of Maryland: State Senators Pressure University to Cancel Controversial Film Screening," Foundation for Individual Rights in Education, https://www.thefire.org/cases/university-of-maryland-state-senators-pressure-university-to-cancel-controversial-film-screening/.

86. Will Creeley, "Ignoring Academic Freedom, South Carolina Legislators Aim to Punish Public Colleges for Choice of Books," Foundation for Individual Rights in Education, February 21, 2014, https://www.thefire.org/ignoring-academic-freedom-south-carolina-legislators-aim-to-punish-public-colleges-for-choice-of-books/.

87. Brooks, Mo, (@RepMoBrooks), August 25, 2019, https://twitter.com/RepMoBrooks/status/1165706990926086144.

88. Robert Shibley, "The University of Kansas Controversy: Defending the Freedom to Tweet," Foundation for Individual Rights in Education, September 23, 2013, https://www.thefire.org/the-university-of-kansas-controversy-defending-the-freedom-to-tweet/.

89. Sawsan Morrar, "'He should Be fired': Lawmaker's Resolution Urges Dismissal of UC Davis Prof over Cop Comments," *Modesto Bee*, March 21, 2019, https://www.modbee.com/news/california/article228181294.html.

90. Adam Steinbaugh, "New York Legislators Threaten CUNY Funding, Call for Banishment of Pro-Palestinian Student Group," Foundation for Individual Rights in Education, March 30, 2016, https://www.thefire.org/new-york-legislators-threaten-cuny-funding-call-for-banishment-of-pro-palestinian-student-group/.

91. "2017 Tennessee Code, Title 49 – Education, Chapter 7 - Postsecondary and Higher Education Generally, Part 24 - Campus Free Speech Protection Act," available at https://law.justia.com/codes/tennessee/2017/title-49/chapter-7/part-24/.

Writing for *Academe*, the blog of the American Association of University Professors, John K. Wilson described the enacted legislation as "to my complete shock, a really good law that strongly protects free speech on campus." John K. Wilson, "The Tennessee Legislature's Defense of Campus Free Speech," *Academe*, May 11, 2017, https://academeblog.org/2017/05/11/the-tennessee-legislatures-defense-of-campus-free-speech/.

92. Joe Cohn, "Tennessee Bill to Punish UT for Sex Week Becomes Law," Foundation for Individual Rights in Education, May 23, 2016, https://www.thefire.org/tennessee-bill-to-punish-ut-for-sex-week-becomes-law/.

93. Alex Morey, "Georgia Legislator Suggests Professor Be Punished for Comments on Illegal Immigration," Foundation for Individual Rights in Education, June 10, 2019, https://www.thefire.org/georgia-legislator-suggests-professor-be-punished-for-comments-on-illegal-immigration/.

94. Joe Cohn, "Problematic Anti-Semitism Bill Passes in South Carolina," Foundation for Individual Rights in Education, April 17, 2018, https://www.thefire.org/problematic-anti-semitism-bill-passes-in-south-carolina/; Joe Cohn, "First Test of Florida's Commitment to Campus Free Speech Looms," Foundation for Individual Rights in Education, April 30, 2019, https://www.thefire.org/first-test-of-floridas-commitment-to-campus-free-speech-looms/; "UPDATED: FIRE Statement Regarding Executive Order on Campus Anti-Semitism," Foundation for Individual Rights in Education, December 10, 2019, https://www.thefire.org/fire-statement-regarding-executive-order-on-campus-anti-semitism/.

95. House Bill 2563, State of Arizona House of Representatives, 2018, https://www.azleg.gov/legtext/53leg/2R/laws/0267.htm.

96. House Bill 2563, State of Arizona House of Representatives, 2018, https://www.azleg.gov/legtext/53leg/2R/bills/HB2563P.pdf (emphasis added).

97. For example, see "Florida Becomes Ninth State to Ban Restrictive Campus Free Speech Zones," Foundation for Individual Rights in Education, March 12, 2018, https://www.thefire.org/florida-becomes-ninth-state-to-ban-restrictive-campus-free-speech-zones/.

98. Conor Friedersdorf, "A Wisconsin Legislator Models Political Correctness for Students," *The Atlantic*, December 21, 2016, https://www.theatlantic.com/politics/archive/2016/12/a-wisconsin-legislator-models-political-correctness-for-university-students/511337/.

99. "And conservatives, liberals, and libertarians should all be able to agree that consistent, principled defenses of free speech norms are indispensable at institutions of higher education, and that their absence is most damaging to marginalized students. Uniting against illiberalism on the right and left is the best course. Otherwise, political groups will waste their efforts on an interminable fight to censor one another, instead of defending the values that serve them all. By definition, marginalized groups will never win." *Ibid.*

100. Sarah McLaughlin, "After Viewpoint-based Denial, Williams Initiative for Israel Finally Receives Recognition," Foundation for Individual Rights in Education, May 16, 2019, https://www.thefire.org/after-viewpoint-based-denial-williams-initiative-for-israel-finally-receives-recognition/.

101. Marieke Tuthill Beck-Coon, "After Two-plus Years in Court, Students for Justice in Palestine Wins Recognition at Fordham," Foundation for Individual Rights in Education, August 7, 2019, https://www.thefire.org/after-two-plus-years-in-court-students-for-justice-in-palestine-wins-recognition-at-fordham/.

102. Billy Gobitas, "Letter to Minersville, Pennsylvania, School Directors, Explaining Why the Young Jehovah's Witness Refused to Salute the American Flag, 5 November 1935," Library of Congress, https://www.loc.gov/item/mcc.016/.

103. *Minersville School District v. Gobitis*, 310 U.S. 586 (1940). Due to an error, Gobitas was misspelled "Gobitis."

104. *West Virginia State Board of Education v. Barnette*, 319 U.S. 624 (1943) 319 U.S. 624, 642 (1943). Again, due to error, the plaintiffs' last name—Barnett—was misspelled as "Barnette."

105. Heins, 4.

106. *Gay & Lesbian Students Ass'n v. Gohn*, 850 F.2d 361, 364 (8th Cir. 1988).

Chapter 6

A Confluence on Campus

Joseph Russomanno

Why? Why have speech-related incidents on America's college and university campuses increased in both number and visibility? There are many reasons, undoubtedly far more than this chapter examines. As with so many issues, a confluence of developments coalesce, creating a sort of "perfect storm" that produces conditions conducive to certain outcomes. Some of those conditions are considered here.

Colleges and universities do not exist in vacuums, removed from the dynamics that permeate all corners of society. Instead, political, economic, and social phenomena—both global and national—not only affect campuses and their inhabitants, they are observed and studied there perhaps more intently than anywhere else. As Yale law professor Justin Driver observes, the same issues "that pervade the larger society often flash where the law and education converge."[1] Many of these happenings that contribute to speech-related clashes on America's campuses parallel those that are occurring nationwide. Campus conflicts, including those over speech, writes Ezra Klein, "reflect the reality that something deeper and more fearful in us is being activated. These are proxy wars for bigger, more fundamental concerns over the direction of the culture."[2]

Nationwide, there has been a decades-long decline in trust and confidence not just in government generally, but also in public institutions. Pew Research, for example, shows that confidence in U.S. government institutions has dropped steadily for seventy years.[3] When coupled with what George Packer called Donald Trump's successful "war on American institutions,"[4] the results are profound. Trump's "antidemocratic propensities" led to "attacks on cornerstones of American democracy, including the free press, the judiciary, and other political institutions," write political scientists Marc

Hetherington and Jonathan Weiler.[5] "We live in an anti-institutional age," according to Gen. James Mattis. "When you tear down institutions you tear down the scaffolding on which society is built."[6] As the political framework seems to break down, individual well-being follows. In investigating what she calls democracy grief, Michelle Goldberg spoke to mental health therapists, one of whom said, "It's about this general feeling that the institutions that we rely on to protect us from a dangerous individual might fail."[7] In early 2020, *The New York Times* editorial board wrote that it was "rattled by the weakness of the institutions that we trusted to undergird [important] values."[8] Yuval Levin believes that Americans are living through a social crisis due to a "failure of" and "a collapse of confidence in institutions."[9] At the root of an American shift from an institution-based society to being transaction-based, according to Nicholas Lemann, was the loss of faith in institutions and their ability to protect, defend, and promote the dreams of so many.[10] The distrust and dismantling of institutions is so serious, wrote Harvard's Danielle Allen, that "we have arrived at a point where no issue is as important as restoring the institutions of democratic participation."[11]

No institution is more critical to democratic participation than the ability to speak out, particularly against government and its officials. Among the first to articulate this notion was U.S. Supreme Court Justice Louis Brandeis. In a 1927 opinion, he wrote, "The greatest menace to freedom is an inert people; that public discussion is a political duty; and that this should be a fundamental principle of the American government."[12] The right—and even obligation—of citizens to criticize government officials has been recognized as the central meaning of the First Amendment,[13] which according to law professor Harry Kalven, Jr., is "a core protection without which democracy cannot function."[14]

Trust in the institution of speech freedom is eroding, however. The foundational faith in the idea that over time, freedom—particularly freedom of speech—ultimately produces results superior to those in societies that constrain certain speech is losing devotees. As a 1974 Yale University report on freedom of expression asserted, "We take a chance, as the First Amendment takes a chance, when we commit ourselves to the idea that results of free expression are to the general benefit in the long run, however unpleasant they may appear at the time."[15] Fewer people, including college students, are willing to take that chance. According to a 2017 Brookings Institution study, half of college students believe their schools should prohibit "certain speech or expression of viewpoints that are offensive or biased against certain groups of people."[16] Whereas their predecessors protested *for* free speech, demonstrations *against* those who would use speech to share their ideas are now more common on campus. The same speech freedom that once seemed to be a solution to problems is being perceived more often as the problem itself, inflaming already volatile issues. That said, Harvard historian Jill Lepore believes that the lessons of the past provide hope: "If the commitment to these difficult freedoms has sometimes flagged—and it has—it has just as often been renewed."[17]

Some of the episodes of the recent history of the U.S. Supreme Court, the most prominent shaper of the First Amendment doctrine and itself a highly polarized—some might say broken—institution, has done little to enhance its credibility. Ostensibly independent jurists there rarely rule against the ideology of the president who nominated them. In April 2020, for example, in a "party line vote," the Court ruled 5–4 that in-person voting in Wisconsin must proceed despite the health risks stemming from the COVID pandemic.[18] Previously, the Court stopped an electoral recount, allowing a candidate who had fewer votes than his opponent to assume the presidency.[19] Its membership consists of two men who dodged accusations of sexual harassment and/or assault.[20] Another member is there because the Senate majority leader hijacked the confirmation process of another nominee.[21] In the name of the First Amendment, the Court: allowed for the personification of corporations for the purpose of campaign contributions;[22] struck down laws that would have limited the distribution of animal "crush" videos[23] and violent video games;[24] gave members of a radical church the right to taunt family members of fallen soldiers;[25] denied equal protection under the law for bakery patrons;[26] and consistently protected offensive and hateful speech.[27] (Some of these rulings compelled First Amendment scholar Steven Shiffrin to write *What's Wrong with the First Amendment?*[28]) Granted, there are strong constitutional arguments that support these decisions. But those rationales often fail to resonate with many Americans. When perceived justice is elusive due to the arguably inappropriate application of speech freedom, then the confidence in—and respect for—the institution diminishes. When people believe that institutions break down, failing to work as they should, some may compensate by taking matters into their own hands. That includes preventing those whose words and ideas they believe are dangerous, but constitutionally protected, from speaking at all.

This thought progression has become part of a mindset that provides license to casting aside traditionally accepted norms, often done with the hope of achieving results radically different from the status quo. Though various pieces of this puzzle were in place prior to the 2016 presidential campaign, many observers agree that Donald Trump is responsible for legitimizing hate, bias, and anger. In analyzing a speech-based protest that turned violent on her campus, Middlebury College Professor Allison Stanger wrote that college students took note of what they witnessed on the national political stage. "Much of the free speech [that Trump] has inspired—or has refused to disavow—is ugly, and has already had ugly real-world consequences," she wrote. "College students have seen this, and have taken note: Speech can become action."[29] Moreover, action *against* speech was endorsed. According to Jeremy Peters, "President Trump's victory was, to many of his supporters, a defiant uprising against what they saw as a cultural and political elite that told them their values were wrong and their beliefs bigoted."[30] It may not be coincidental that speech-on-campus conflicts accelerated post-2016. A common technique: Protesters bullying their opponents.

Granted, there are claims that some invited campus speakers improperly legitimize racism, classism, or other undesirable traits. A University of California, Berkeley protester, for example, took satisfaction in shutting down a scheduled speech by provocateur Milo Yiannopoulos in 2017, saying it was about sending a message: "We aren't about to allow white supremacist views to be normalized."[31] It is acknowledged here that scholars such as law professor Charles Lawrence have justifiably advocated that it is impossible to fully understand the nature of racist/hate speech absent the firsthand experience of the harm it inflicts.[32] Regulating that (or any other) kind of speech, however, may mask the underlying problems rather than confronting them. Preventing expression addresses neither the thoughts at its root nor any behavior that reveals those feelings. Professor James Weinstein, for example, argues that hate speech legislation "can be seen as just another quick fix that Americans are so fond of—splashy, superficial remedies that do nothing to address the complex issues underlying large societal problems but may well detract from finding real solutions."[33] The U.S. Supreme Court has repeatedly granted First Amendment protection to hate speech.

As institutions fail, polarization increases. Ironically, one response was the rise of some institutions and groups to combat polarization. Duke University's Polarization Lab, for instance, brings together scholars from many fields "to develop new technology to bridge America's partisan divide." Recognizing a "degree of civil rancor that threatens our democracy," Better Angels took root not long after the 2016 election. In its Red/Blue workshops, people are taught depolarization skills by finding areas of commonality. A virtual cottage industry of books addressing polarization in various ways emerged—for example, *Prius or Pickup?* by Hetherington and Weiler. Within the context of higher education, a political divide that "increasingly began to fracture our country" is the target of on-campus discussions led by BridgeUSA. And the Heterodox Academy strives to combat orthodoxy in scholarship by promoting open inquiry and viewpoint diversity. Among other goals, these efforts seek to confront tribalism.

TRIBALISM

In another example of how the American campus reflects society at large, college students are no different than other citizens in grouping themselves along several fault lines—socioeconomic, political, cultural, racial, and ethnic, to name a few. This kind of grouping has occurred since even before humans emerged from the caves. To seek and form "tribes" is a deep-seated instinct. For most of human history, the tribe was the only form of social organization. Survival meant not only gravitating to those like ourselves, but also excluding those who were different.

Though survival may now be less dependent on this tribal instinct, it remains prevalent, shaping our thinking and decision-making. People act in ways that both reinforce their status within tribes and exclude non-members. This results in an us-versus-them thinking. In *Political Tribes*, Yale law professor Amy Chua called this "the darkest side to the tribal instinct: the ease with which we dehumanize outsiders and the satisfaction we derive from doing so."[34] As Klein wrote, "Nothing brings a group together like a common enemy."[35] Not only is a common enemy important in the forming and maintenance of a tribe, it serves as a motivating factor.

The degree to which tribalism is part of us cannot be overstated. It is universal and the instinct is deep-seated. It is not merely one aspect of human existence, but the default mode, according to Andrew Sullivan.[36] Chua said that humans are "*very* tribal, and it distorts the way we think and feel."[37] That includes what can be described as an irrational approach when confronted with information that is counter to our tribe, its interests and its beliefs. "In tribal mode, we seem to go blind to arguments and information that challenge our team's narrative," according to Greg Lukianoff and Jonathan Haidt.[38] Harvard's Steven Pinker added that political tribalism is "the most insidious form of irrationality today."[39] That irrationality can occur to even harmful degrees. Nicholas Kristof, for example, reported that attitudes toward the flu "diverged based on ideology."[40] People in red states are less likely to get vaccinated—and more likely to die from the flu. Similarly, irrational tribal divisions with potentially harmful outcomes occurred during the coronavirus outbreak in 2020. In the United States, various polls showed "stunning differences"[41]—splits along party (i.e., tribal) lines, where Democrats were much more likely than Republicans to see the coronavirus as a threat to the country's health and to fear for their family's well-being.[42] This dynamic surfaced "despite the fact that medical experts and epidemiologists have warned that the virus could affect many millions of Americans, regardless of political party or state."[43] As Goldberg noted later that year, the president and his followers "polarized the response to the coronavirus, turning defiance of public health directives into a mark of right-wing identity."[44] Referring to the pandemic, Packer says, "even as it spread from blue to red states, attitudes broke down along familiar partisan lines."[45] These divisions rooted in tribalism are sometimes the products of the politics of deception, an effort to convince at least 51 percent of the voting populace of alternate "facts." Those for whom truth still matters are left to confront the challenge of navigating the unstable airspace populated by the gullible whose unconscious calculus obliges them to maintain the psychic comfort of their tribal memberships rather than breaking free from the inertia that binds them. Suffice it to say that contemporary politics is not only replete with tribalism—note how those in high office consistently pit Americans against one another—it serves as an accelerant in sowing the seeds of division. (See the discussion of framing in Chapter 7.)

Tribes build themselves around belief systems. Within a tribe, beliefs are the ultimate currency. As Bruce Rozenblit asserts, all of reality is filtered or altered to enhance the tenets of the beliefs within a tribe: "The belief must prevail, and we can't let a little thing like reality get in the way."[46] Members sometimes fail to investigate facts that the tribe has come to consider as normal and acceptable. It is an uncritical, conformist tendency that spawns "alternative facts" and "fake news." Within tribes there is often pressure to conform—and sometimes to demonstrate beliefs avidly—or risk losing membership. Therefore, as Rozenblit wrote, complete buy-in is essential. Decisions are "made on an all-or-nothing basis. A person can't be half a tribe member."[47]

The tribal instinct coalesces around identification. It is continually necessary to assess who is "in," and at least as importantly, who is "out." Group identification "is both innate and almost immediate," said Chua.[48] Thus, there is a link between tribalism and identity politics. For example, political scientist Francis Fukuyama described identity politics as being driven by the quest for recognition by groups that have been marginalized.[49] That marginalization can take the form of group members feeling that they are forced to abandon their identities, but resisting the process and both clinging to and defending their tribe. Those who are marginalized tribalize anew.

Klein referred to "mega-identities"[50]—the several personal identities that an individual possesses at the same time—for example, geography, a specific political viewpoint, race, religion, and level of income and education. When one identity is activated, all of them may be triggered. Just as important, because multiple identities can be threatened simultaneously, a perceived threat increases exponentially. As the stakes rise, according to Klein, so does "our willingness to do anything to make sure our side wins."[51]

Today's tribes are not unlike what concerned James Madison during America's founding era—factions. In *Federalist No. 10*, he described faction in a way that today could be substituted for tribe: "a number of citizens. . .

who are united and actuated by some common impulse of passion, or of interest."[52] Because factions could trample the rights of others—including those of other factions—Madison determined that the solution resided in allowing them to compete and to provide them the space to do so. Today, that space can be what universities and colleges are uniquely positioned to provide—a marketplace of ideas that is as open and free as possible.

The link between tribalism and the institutions in which confidence has eroded is highly relevant. Many of those institutions were established, in part, to combat tribal instincts. Pinker wrote that institutions stem from the Age of Reason and Enlightenment whose thinkers established what we now call humanism. It privileges the well-being of people over "the glory of the tribe, race, nation, or religion,"[53] Pinker wrote. Because those institutions are products of reason, they struggle with other aspects of human nature, including loyalty to tribe. Consequently, some institutions fail to achieve their purpose and trust in them has steadily declined, with a corresponding rise in populist movements that are tribal and authoritarian. "Authoritarian populism," according to Pinker, "can be seen as a pushback of elements of human nature—tribalism, authoritarianism, demonization, zero-sum thinking—against Enlightenment institutions that were designed to circumvent them."[54] As institutions fail—or as people *perceive* that they have failed—those who once depended on them to resolve problems, including college students, seek alternate solutions.

Tribalism fuels and structures contemporary campus activism. While campus activism is not a new phenomenon, the dynamics that drive it do change over time. Due to the polarization inherent in contemporary campus tribalism, social justice movements were rekindled and—in some cases where perceived injustice due to the unresponsiveness of institutions occurs—with newfound vigor. According to sociologist Bradley Campbell, "Many campus activists . . . have attacked the ideals of free speech and academic freedom."[55] University environments have been especially susceptible to the dynamics that include restricting the speech of those whose views some groups (i.e., tribes) oppose. "Americans generally support free speech on campuses," wrote Christopher Ellis, "but sometimes they're willing to restrict it. How they would restrict it varies by partisan identity."[56] People on campus learn that speech is power, particularly when social settings are perceived as zero-sum situations. Denying speech to others may be seen as a means of securing or reclaiming some degree of power.

iGEN ON CAMPUS

Tribalism and identity politics permeate every aspect of society. As suggested above, the college campus is no exception. As much as the campus reflects society, however, it is unique in a way that is central to this chapter: those who are now overwhelmingly the majority of campus inhabitants belong to iGen, sometimes also referred to as Generation Z. As a 2019 Knight Foundation report observed, "College campuses have recently undergone a pivotal generational shift . . . . Undergraduates on campus now hail from the tip of the next age cohort known as Generation Z. They are the true digital natives born into an always-on world."[57] So why does this matter? In short, the confluence of iGen's emergence and an escalation in tribalism have combined to create an environment in which many campus inhabitants find convenient exceptions to free-speech principles at best, or at worst, reject those principles outright.

First recognized as a distinct generation by psychologist Jean Twenge in 2017, these post-millennials, born after 1995, tend to be uniquely insecure.[58] Physically and psychologically linked to their iPhones and social media, Twenge found that those who "spend more time on smartphone screens are less happy and more depressed"[59] than those who devote less time to screens and social media. "It's not an exaggeration to describe iGen as being on the brink of the worst mental-health crisis in decades," Twenge wrote.[60] Members of iGen were raised in a culture of "safetyism" according to Lukianoff and Haidt, possessing "an obsession with eliminating threats (both real and imagined) to the point at which people become unwilling to make reasonable trade-offs demanded by other practical and moral concerns."[61] The threats they seek to eliminate sometimes include speech they believe to be menacing. Some iGen'ers who find themselves on college campuses, sometimes away from family for the first time—thus, experiencing increased levels of insecurity and anxiety—are driven to seek others for protection, drawn together and bonding according to identity and reinforced by particular aspects of campus culture. Like all tribes, these groups are formed according to shared beliefs, oftentimes with passionate members who—well-meaning and protective—advocate silencing those who would express views deemed disagreeable, offensive, or potentially harmful.

The link between iGen's inherent insecurity, the fear of harmful speech, and the downward trend in the perceived value of free speech is apparent. Twenge's discovery of widespread insecurity among today's college students helps to explain the sudden increase in the number of anti-speech campus incidents. "Many protests focus on eliminating not just discrimination," she wrote, "but offensive speech."[62] Some campus tribes form to combat social injustice, with certain speech viewed as contributing to the injustices they fight. It is very unlikely that the frequency of clashes over speech increased as iGen'ers arrived on campuses is merely coincidence. In part, their fears were directed at ideas and viewpoints that exacerbated their insecurity. They sought safety in numbers, joining groups whose beliefs and fears paralleled their own. Moreover, in some cases, their commitment to fight back by silencing those with whom they disagree is a bonding factor.

This is not to suggest that the safety hyper-sensitivity possessed by many college students in any way absolves universities from their obligation to provide safe learning environments. That said, balancing safety concerns with free speech requires a level of needle-threading that can be extremely challenging. The famous Benjamin Franklin quote comes to mind: "Those who would give up essential Liberty, to purchase a little temporary Safety, deserve neither Liberty nor Safety."[63] If nothing else, the takeaway might be that liberty and safety are not mutually exclusive, on campus or off. Moreover, any suggestion that achieving complete safety in any context is likely unrealistic. Wesleyan University president Michael Roth suggests that achieving complete safety and security is not only impractical, but also unwise to try because it requires a level of handholding that stunts students' emotional and intellectual growth.[64] "The history of intellectual growth and discovery," according to the conclusion of Yale's Woodward Report, "clearly demonstrates the need for unfettered freedom, the right to think the unthinkable, discuss the unmentionable, and challenge the unchallengeable."[65] This was reaffirmed by Lukianoff and Haidt in their original incarnation of "The Coddling of the American Mind" in 2015, a ground-breaking *Atlantic* article. As suggested by the title, the concern focused on students being overly sheltered: "Rather than trying to protect students from words and ideas that they will inevitably encounter, colleges should do all they can to equip students to thrive in a world full of words and ideas that they cannot control."[66]

Creating and enhancing a culture of tolerance in which a variety of ideas and viewpoints can be expressed, and where it will be respected, is the responsibility of any administering institution, including the university or college. Those who believe that their views will be heard are more likely to be tolerant of others expressing their ideas and opinions. Ideally, speech is valued and the expression of ideas, if not rewarded, is certainly is not punished. Because many campus clashes over speech begin with students who feel marginalized and powerless, this kind of recognition can be a potent remedy. Thus, creating and supporting a campus culture in which students believe that they have access to platforms for expression and that their views are heard is vital. This free-speech culture includes the knowledge that there may be particular times, places, or manners in which the expression of ideas may be limited, but that the opportunity to communicate views in some way always will be available. While some students may not like some of the ideas articulated on campus, it is important for them to know that there are opportunities for them to respond. It is an environment of free speech, a culture of tolerance in which all ideas can be expressed.

This is a path rooted in the belief that speech freedom ultimately produces outcomes preferred to those when speech and thoughts are restricted. It is not unlike the route historically taken by many of the nation's colleges and universities. Pursuing this kind of path creates and shapes a particular kind of national consciousness that favors liberty and autonomous decision-making. In this way we are taught, Columbia University president and First Amendment scholar Lee Bollinger wrote, to deal calmly with differences of opinion and scathing dissent. We redefine *tolerance* "as a matter of courage rather than weakness and signify[ ] the importance of developing a democratic temperament."[67] The zone for freedom of expression, Bollinger adds, tests our ability to live in a society defined by conflict and controversy.

Achieving campus safety should not occur by insulating students from words and ideas. A cue can be taken from the University of Chicago and the principles that stem from its declarations on these issues. (Dozens of universities and colleges have adopted the Chicago Principles; see Chapter 1). "It is not the proper role of the University to attempt to shield individuals from ideas and opinions they find unwelcome, disagreeable, or even deeply offensive."[68] This is at the heart of any free-speech defense—tolerance even of ideas contrary to one's beliefs or values, and accepting the possibility that an open mind could lead to new understanding. U.S. Supreme Court Justice Oliver Wendell Holmes believed that the Constitution calls for the principle of free thought—"[N]ot free thought for those who agree with us but freedom for the thought that we hate."[69] This approach has been echoed repeatedly by the Court.

Contentious speech on campus has revolved around two linked categories: invited speakers and what might be characterized as the day-to-day business of college—lectures, conversations, and discussions, for example. The political correctness effort that grew in the 1980s was escalated by a movement that took root in the twenty-first century in which concern over words that wound demand self-censorship by those who might otherwise insult or oppress. Concerned that those who lead the basic functions of university life lack the sensitivity and perspective necessary to achieve fairness, social justice, and proper recognition, advocates of this movement seek to address in particular how individuals and groups are regarded and identified. According to Lukianoff and Haidt, "Students claimed that certain kinds of speech—and even the content of some books and courses—interfered with their ability to function."[70] Terms such as "trigger warnings," "micro-aggressions," and "safe spaces" became more common on campuses as those fearful of offense and oppression sought to limit how—and in some cases, what—ideas could be expressed. The effects are multi-layered, and include chilling speech. The movement's tenets were advocated with many of the hallmarks of tribalism: passion, self-interest, and demands for respect and recognition.

This movement developed concurrently with—and sometimes in response to—the expansion of liberal education. Columbia University professor Mark Lilla observed that, as the curricula of the American university developed, the "study of identity groups. . .seemed the most urgent scholarly/political task, and soon there was an extraordinary proliferation of departments, research centers, and professorial chairs devoted to it."[71] Some aspects have been arguably counter-productive, according to Chua, who adds that shifts in tone, rhetoric, and logic have made identity politics divisive: "For some, especially on college campuses, anyone who doesn't swallow the antioppression orthodoxy hook, line, and sinker—anyone who doesn't acknowledge 'white supremacy' in America—is a racist."[72] An ideology results, according to Lilla, that is "institutionalized in colleges and universities that fetishes our individual and group attachments."[73] According to Lukianoff and Haidt, these approaches "used in universities today may be hyperactivating our ancient tribal tendencies."[74] Thus, the tendency to tribalize, already extant throughout society, is arguably accelerated within the kind of campus culture bred at some colleges and universities. In an interview with me, Jonathan Haidt suggested another way in which the university culture interacts with this dynamic: "Young people are learning to judge peoples' moral worth by their race and gender, [with the] college campus as the locus of this phenomenon."[75] Thus, a cyclical phenomenon unfolds in which environment and inhabitants mutually propel one another, often toward an end that includes the hallmarks of tribalism explored herein.

The movements described above—in particular, those marked by heightened sensitivity to identity and other "liberal interests"—were sometimes met with pushback. Seen as political correctness run amok, some conservative student groups responded by inviting to campuses speakers whose views, in some cases, were extreme and provocative by any objective measure. In turn, the self-identifying liberals protested against what for decades their ideological ancestors had supported: people expressing their viewpoints with words—that is, free speech. Students acknowledged that they, sometimes with the support of faculty and administrators, increasingly attacked the ideals of free speech.

Understandably, these conservative speakers and their hosts expected—even demanded—that their speech freedom merited protection at the same level as that granted to anyone else. Almost as equally expected, some liberals saw it differently. Since the Free Speech Movement of the 1960s, the political left defended robust debate, with the conservative right often opposed. Lepore documents how then-California gubernatorial candidate Ronald Reagan targeted college students, complaining that undergraduates were "malcontents," in denouncing speaking invitations at the University of California, Berkeley.[76] That created a left–right tension when it came to speech freedom, particularly on college campuses. Now, some analysts suggest that vigorous speech protection is embraced by conservatives, with liberals—buoyed by the cause of social justice—largely being those who attempt to preempt the expression of what they perceive to be offensive or harmful ideas. Professor Stanger described the core dynamic of this tension: "One side sees the free exchange of ideas as fundamental and non-negotiable. The other side sees inclusivity and social justice as the supreme value."[77] Sizable student segments now approach these situations with mindsets far different than their predecessors of decades past. As some, such as Nat Hentoff, have noted, the predominant approach often seems to be guided by the principle, "Free speech for me, but not for thee."[78]

Somewhere along the path to the twenty-first century, "the left and the right would appear to have switched sides," wrote Lepore, "the left fighting against free speech and the right fighting for it."[79] Lepore referred to philosopher Herbert Marcuse, who argued that liberals' commitment to open debate was absurd, because free speech had become a form of oppression. In his essay "Repressive Toleration," Marcuse provided "a blueprint . . . for an oppressive campus life dominated by left-wing hegemony," according to Jeffrey Tucker.[80]

It is doubtful whether many people, if any, are seeking to make campus life oppressive. That said, there is no denying that some have tried to suppress the speech of others. "Campus protesters have tried to silence not only alt-right gadflies," wrote Lepore, "but also serious if controversial scholars and policymakers."[81] Because these provocative speakers are often invited by student groups, another shift has occurred: Rather than fighting the state for speech rights as in past eras, students are now fighting other students. As Haidt said, "The problem we have on campus is the fear not of government, but of each other."[82]

Lepore's analysis echoes what others have called the "weaponizing" of the First Amendment. *The New York Times'* Adam Liptak reported on the rise of this sentiment just after the U.S. Supreme Court's 2017–2018 term.[83] In a harsh dissenting opinion, Justice Elena Kagan not only invoked the concept of First Amendment weaponization, but accused her conservative colleagues of engaging in the practice.[84] Others followed suit, including law professor Burt Neuborne: "The [political] right, which had for years been hostile to and very nervous about a strong First Amendment, has rediscovered it."[85] In part, it is the adoption of a libertarian position that is skeptical of speech regulation. Cato Institute lawyer Ilya Shapiro observed, "That used to be an uncontroversial and nonideological point. What's now being called the libertarian position on speech was in the 1960s the liberal position on speech."[86] Professor Louis Seidman explained, what to many, was the disturbing aspect of this turnabout: "Instead of providing a shield for the powerless, the First

Amendment became a sword used by people at the apex of the American hierarchy of power."[87] Liptak notes that an increasingly conservative judiciary has been "more than a little receptive to this argument."[88] Within the context of this chapter, this development, regardless of its label, may also help to explain the on-campus clashes over speech. That is, like their judicial brethren, conservative student groups have also been receptive to the idea that they can utilize First Amendment protection to their advantage. In response, as Liptak notes in an observation that squarely addresses one element of the contemporary campus clashes, "Many on the left have traded an absolutist commitment to free speech for one sensitive to the harms it can inflict."[89] To be both fair and clear, the right's newfound power of the First Amendment can be viewed as nothing more than members of one tribe seeking the rights and constitutional protection that are available to all tribes. College conservatives are following the lead of the U.S. Supreme Court that, according to a study led by Professor Lee Epstein of Washington University, more than any modern court, "has trained its sights on speech promoting conservative values."[90]

Among the ideals that have historically been in place is the availability of free-speech opportunities that are administered equally, regardless of the speaker and message content. However, that, too, is now being rejected more often by iGen students. As Wesleyan's Roth wrote, "Many students do not accept the view that neither the content of speech nor the identity of the speaker should matter; they are skeptical of the commitment to having one set of procedures for all people (or organizations) no matter what the content."[91] Students, he added, "are suspicious of any acontextual appeal on pure principle."[92] Thus, principle and tradition aside, the history and identity of speakers are relevant to more and more students in determining whether they should be allowed to speak. Students believe that some of those invited are underserving of having their voices heard, particularly those with a history of expressing hatred or what may be perceived as offensive, dangerous ideas. For some students, that is enough to trigger a response to prevent further expression. The same Brookings survey cited above also reports that "a surprisingly large fraction of students believe that it is acceptable to act—including to the extent of resorting to violence—in order to shut down expression they consider offensive. And a majority of students appear to want an environment that shields them from being exposed to views they might find offensive."[93] In their 2018 book, Bradley Campbell and Jason Manning address a culture of victimhood on the nation's campuses.[94] That is, some students believe that they are casualties of those who would do them harm, including with words. In this environment, hostility toward free speech is not an uncommon response to unwelcome ideas. Moreover, Campbell and Manning echo the Brookings findings in noting that the distinction between speech and violence is blurred. In other words, some believe that expressing certain ideas is a form of violence. Thus, preventing those ideas from being expressed is viewed as justifiable, sometimes including through violent means.

An incident at Northwestern University in late 2019 is instructive in understanding iGen. The event followed the template provided by many other speech-related campus clashes. Former U.S. Attorney General Jeff Sessions was invited by a conservative student group, "Young Americans for Freedom," to speak on the Evanston campus. The event attracted protesters who opposed Sessions and his political ideology. Some attempted to disrupt the speech. The student newspaper, *The Daily Northwestern*, covered the event, including posting photos of some protesters on social media platforms. *Daily* reporters used a student directory to obtain phone numbers of some protesters, then called them to ask for permission to interview them. In an editorial a few days later, the newspaper apologized for the trauma that these common journalistic techniques may have caused. The student-journalists were upset about covering peers—again, something commonplace in journalism. The apology had iGen's fingerprints all over it: students were traumatized for what they thought traumatized other students—members of their own tribe. "[W]e recognize that we contributed to the harm students experienced. Some protesters found photos posted to reporters' Twitter accounts retraumatizing and invasive."[95] Editorial board members were so concerned, they suppressed their own speech, removing information that had been posted because "nothing is more important than ensuring that our fellow students feel safe."[96] The editorial attracted harsh criticism from the journalism community. Northwestern's journalism school dean, Charles Whitaker, wrote that the coverage "was in no way beyond the bounds of fair, responsible journalism."[97] In an ironic coda, two months later, Northwestern University's student government voted to table a resolution in support of the First Amendment and freedom of speech on campus.

A WAY FORWARD

Solutions to the emergence of iGen and its convergence with an escalation in tribalism begin to materialize in examining the model provided by American law and free-speech doctrine. Absent elements such as harassment or threats, hate speech is protected by the First Amendment. This approach has been echoed repeatedly, including in the 2017 U.S. Supreme Court ruling *Matal v. Tam* that characterized this as a "bedrock First Amendment principle,"[98] and reiterating the long-held principle, "Speech may not be banned on the ground that it expresses ideas that offend."[99] The justification includes the notion that applies to many aspects of speech protection: On the whole, it is preferable to prevent government from regulating speech and its content rather than criminalizing certain content, and thus requiring categorization imbued with subjective judgment of what speech does and does not cross the line of acceptability.

Because of government involvement in deciding content questions, a similarly problematic approach lies in legislation that would require universities to ensure political and ideological balance to all on-campus speaking events. A bill proposed in early 2020 in Arizona is an example—a content-based regulation mandating each of the three universities governed by the state's board of regents to establish an Office of Public Policy Events. This office would oversee the organizing and staging of debates, lectures, and discussions with guests from "multiple, divergent and opposing perspectives."[100] Clearly violating the First Amendment, measures like this open Pandora's Boxes in unique ways. This includes necessary assessments to determine whether specific invited speakers are "representative enough" of a particular perspective. This bill adheres to the template established by the Campus Intellectual Diversity Act[101] which surfaced in 2019, at about the same time that President Donald Trump signed an executive order requiring institutions of higher education that receive federal funds to guarantee free speech to those on American college and university campuses. The order included a stipulation that institutions must "avoid creating environments that stifle competing perspectives."[102]

The dangerous precedent of addressing campus speech challenges through legislation or executive order is addressed by University of Chicago president Robert Zimmer. Such measures, he wrote, would actually threaten the mission of institutions of higher education. "They would do so by creating the specter of less rather than more free expression, and by deeply chilling the environment for discourse and intellectual challenge. . . . It makes the government, with all its power and authority, a party to defining the very nature of discussion on campus."[103] The Supreme Court had, in its 1943 ruling in *West Va. Board of Education v. Barnette,* already established that the Constitution forbids officials from prescribing what is "orthodox in politics, nationalism, religion or other matters of opinion."[104] Justice Felix Frankfurter followed in 1957, writing in *Sweezy v. New Hampshire*, "A university ceases to be true to its own nature if it becomes the tool of Church or State or any sectional interest."[105]

To the extent that any campus discussion should be managed, an open marketplace of ideas should be its guiding principle, with the issues that are debated free to take their own course. At the core of free speech on campus is the purpose of higher education. Among the authoritative resources are the two aforementioned university-generated reports. First, Yale's 1974 Woodward Report embraced free speech as central to university goals, starting with its first words: "The primary function of a university is to discover and disseminate knowledge by means of research and teaching. To fulfill this function a free interchange of ideas is necessary not only within its walls but with the world beyond as well. It follows that the university must do everything possible to ensure within it the fullest degree of intellectual freedom."[106]

Second, to the extent that the University of Chicago's 2015 report addresses higher education's purpose generally, it does so focused on the role that free speech should play. A free and open marketplace of ideas is central to the approach:

> [T]he University's fundamental commitment is to the principle that debate or deliberation may not be suppressed because the ideas put forth are thought by some or even by most members of the University community to be offensive, unwise, immoral, or wrong-headed. It is for the individual members of the University community, not for the University as an institution, to make those judgments for themselves, and to act on those judgments not by seeking to suppress speech, but by openly and vigorously contesting the ideas that they oppose.[107]

A key tenet of this marketplace tradition, wrote Vincent Blasi, "is that all propositions are subject to perpetual testing."[108] That testing, in turn, suggests that accepted premises may be shown to be wrong. "In short," Blasi added, "no matter how elegant and coherent the explanation and supportive the current data, we might be wrong."[109] This approach that resonates of the scientific method was most notably introduced to American law by Oliver Wendell Holmes: "Certitude is not the test of certainty. We have been cocksure of many things that were not so,"[110] he wrote in a *Harvard Law Review* article, followed a year later by his famous dissenting opinion in *Abrams v. United States* in which he invoked the concepts of "free trade in ideas" in the "competition of the market."[111] Holmes championed the notion that absent the ability to both access a variety of ideas and to accept that held beliefs might be wrong—that is, fallibilism—the foundation of this structure crumbles.

Just as Holmes addressed "the best test of truth," Lepore writes that "an unflinching search for the truth and the fearless unmasking of error" is the work of the university.[112] Channeling John Milton, and as noted above, she adds that the university has an obligation to speech freedom, "whose premise, however idealized, is that, in a battle between truth and error, truth, in an open field, will always win. If the commitment to these difficult freedoms has sometimes flagged—and it has—it has just as often been renewed."[113] Lepore suggests that this search for truth and its required element not be confined to celebratory periods or to specific zones on campus: "Free speech is not a week or a place."[114]

The marketplace approach echoes the doctrines established by philosophers, scholars, and jurists whose works remain pillars of free-speech approaches, on campus and elsewhere. First, the U.S. Supreme Court has, through multiple rulings, made clear its standing on the university environment. Again in *Sweezy*, Justice Frankfurter wrote, "The essentiality of freedom in the community of American universities is almost self-evident,"[115] stressing the importance of free inquiry. A decade later, Justice William Brennan added that education depends on exposure to a "robust exchange of ideas," rather than "through any kind of authoritative selection."[116] As is stressed in Chapter 10, in 1972, Justice Lewis Powell described the college classroom, "with its surrounding environs," as "peculiarly the marketplace of ideas."[117]

In his book about higher education, appropriately entitled *The Marketplace of Ideas*, Louis Menand asserted, "Americans are committed to the principle that the production of knowledge should be uninhibited and access to it should be universal."[118] He calls this a democratic ideal—that producing information and making it available improves our chances of making good decisions. "Americans therefore make a large social investment in institutions whose purpose is simply the production and dissemination of knowledge,"[119] he wrote.

There is no more appropriate venue and one no more ideally suited to be the quintessential marketplace of ideas than the university/college campus. The core purposes of institutions of higher education include the free and open exchange of concepts and viewpoints, discussion and debate, and the discovery and sharing of knowledge. While it is acknowledged that no approach is flawless, the perfect should not be the enemy of the good. Roth, for example, while generally supportive of the marketplace approach, writes that calling for the free exchange of ideas no matter the cost to some people not only approaches authoritarianism, but does not resonate with most of today's college students. They recognize that not all ideas make it to the market because it is not always free and open.[120] Thus, while there are flaws in the marketplace metaphor, colleges and universities are among the institutions best positioned to remedy them by ensuring that they are truly open and free. It is here, in fact, where institutions of higher education can take a page from the James Madison playbook. Though competing tribes can produce chaos, Madison believed that the competition of factions—the "tribes" of the founding era—in the marketplace of ideas was not only productive but necessary for the survival of the new republic. Ideological collisions among widely disparate interests would make it difficult for any one group to dominate. (It is believed that Madison embraced an observation by Voltaire: "If there were only one religion in England, one would have to fear despotism; if there were two, they would cut each other's throats; but they have thirty, and they live happy and in peace."[121]) That is, more factions—enough to compete against one another and, in turn, check their effects—would more likely materialize across a large territory. This way, no single faction/tribe would dominate.[122] The key, however, is the space for tribes to co-exist. In Madison's era, that meant geographic space—that is, territory. Today, it can mean virtual space, as well. Thus, on campuses, technology can create accessible marketplaces of ideas across multiple platforms. Moreover, whereas members of iGen are predisposed to not only safety and security, but also to social media, they are more likely to adopt an approach that allows them to remain within the sanctuary of their iPhones.

Madison's contribution to this issue does not end with his perspective on factions/tribes. A major element of his checks-and-balances approach to government was trust and where to place it—in the government or in the people. As Professor Forrest MacDonald wrote, "Madison and other men of his temperament did not trust themselves and therefore did not trust power in anyone's hands."[123] To be sure, Madison had doubts about human nature: "If men were angels, no government would be necessary. If angels were to govern men, neither external nor internal controls on government would be necessary."[124] Thus, there was concern in both arenas. But Madison also distrusted power and those who held it. Presciently, he noted that "Enlightened statesmen will not always be at the helm."[125] Ultimately Madison favored the notion of trusting the people rather than government.

The corollary to Madison's observations regarding trust is mistrust and the fear that accompanies it. In his era, mistrust and fear of other factions was common; today, it revolves around tribes and identity. Same concepts, different labels. On campus, the attachment to security and safety by members of iGen cannot be separated from fear. As Susanna Schrobsdorff wrote of this group, "They are the post-9/11 generation, raised in an era of economic and national insecurity. They've never known a time when terrorism and school shootings weren't the norm. They grew up watching their parents weather a severe recession, and, perhaps most important, they hit puberty at a time when technology and social media were transforming society."[126] With that backdrop, it should be surprising neither that some students may be fearful of what others say, nor that they may be willing to protect themselves and others like them from those words.

Fear is central to this entire issue. Fear of words and ideas is rooted in the belief that they will "negatively" affect the thinking and behavior of others. This is why for ages, those with power and those who seek it strive to control messaging. On the one hand, speech, particularly by prominent figures, can affect an environment by influencing the thinking of individuals, even providing a degree of legitimacy to thoughts and behavior previously viewed as unacceptable. On the other hand, those effects tend to be limited, with the speech often activating sentiments or actions to which an individual is predisposed. In other words, rather than speech effects being direct and powerful, they are more often indirect and limited.

This perspective especially began to surface in the early twentieth century as the scientific method, and later the social sciences, gained a foothold. Professor Jennings Bryant suggested that early twentieth-century assumptions about powerful effects reflected the prominence of stimulus response models in psychology—that is, a cause-and-effect link between a catalyst and a behavioral outcome.[127] The field's jargon of the period was revealing, and included the "firing" of messages that entered the consciousness like "magic bullets," or the implication that messages were injected in a drug-like fashion with a "hypodermic needle" resulting in immediate effects. The concern then was that "bad" speech inevitably led to bad behavior by those who heard or read the words. Though people like philosopher Alexander Meiklejohn focused attention on the inappropriate juxtaposition of fear of words and the role of speech in a democratic society—"To be afraid of ideas, any ideas, is to be unfit for self-government"[128]—that fear remains in place today for some people.

The concern permeated the law and First Amendment jurisprudence. From "clear and present danger" to "bad tendency," from "incitement of imminent lawless action" to "direct causal link," at the core of the debate has been where to draw the line between speech that should be permitted into the marketplace of ideas and speech that results in improper action or influence. As law professor David Rabban wrote, "A general hostility to free expression permeated the judicial system," and more commonly in higher courts.[129] That received wisdom prevailed for years, especially as courts embraced the notion that speech had the potential to directly cause dangerous effects in individuals. As the acceptance of limited effects began to disperse in the first half of the twentieth century, however, so did speech freedom. That is, as evidence grew that speech effects are limited—and thus fear of speech is often unfounded because of its relative harmlessness—judicial leaders such as Holmes and Brandeis began to advocate for its First Amendment protection.

For Justice Brandeis, in fact, unfounded fear of words became a lynchpin of his free-speech doctrine.[130] He lived in an era, the late nineteenth and early twentieth centuries, permeated by fear. A contemporary and fellow U.S. Supreme Court Justice, Felix Frankfurter, wrote that the years bracketing World War I were "dominated by fears—the fear of change, the fear of new ideas."[131] Brandeis confronted this fear with an approach that serves any speech-challenged context, including the campus setting. He determined that, with various issues, speech was often the solution, not the problem. Thus, rather than seeing it as something to be feared, Brandeis believed that speech should be viewed as a liberator from fear. It is an approach readily applied to campus speech. According to Brandeis, the words alone of undesirable speakers should not engender fear. As suggested by the incidents of violent protest, the primary imminent danger often lies not in the speech, but in those who wish to prevent it.

Providing counsel that can be applied to the contemporary campus, Brandeis wrote, "If there be time to expose through discussion the falsehood and fallacies, to avert the evil by the processes of education, the remedy to be applied is more speech, not enforced silence."[132] Not only can students and administrators embrace this value and the wisdom behind the words, it is incumbent on universities to create platforms that provide opportunities for those who wish to respond to speech that they may consider offensive or disagreeable. In linking his free-speech doctrine to constitutional principles, Brandeis extracted his rationale from the nation's founding generation:

> Those who won our independence . . . knew that order cannot be secured merely through fear of punishment for its infraction; that it is hazardous to discourage thought, hope and imagination; . . . the path of safety lies in the opportunity to discuss freely supposed grievances and proposed remedies; and that the fitting remedy for evil counsels is good ones. Believing in the power of reason as applied through public discussion, they eschewed silence coerced by law—the argument of force in its worst form.[133]

These features—encouraging thought, hope, and imagination; discussing freely grievances and remedies; and believing in the power of reason—correspond to the purposes of higher education. Recognizing this parallel and the call to realize each idea's essential worth will benefit everyone on American campuses. Those who are members of the higher education community can help their institutions to achieve their core missions not by silencing voices, or by allowing tribalism's worst instincts to intensify out of sight, but by recognizing, promoting, and adhering to the values initiated by America's founding generation (f-Gen?) and rekindled by Justice Brandeis nearly a century ago.

NOTES

1. Justin Driver, *The Schoolhouse Gate: Public Education, the Supreme Court, and the Battle for the American Mind* (New York: Vintage Books, 2018), 10.
2. Ezra Klein, *Why We're Polarized* (New York: Avid Reader Press, 2020), 124.
3. Gretel Kauffman, "US No Longer a 'Full Democracy' in 2016 Democracy Index," *Christian Science Monitor*, January 26, 2017, http://www.csmonitor.com/USA/2017/0126/US-nolonger-a-full-democracy-in-2016-Democracy-Index-Where-do-we-go-from-here.

4. George Packer, "How to Destroy a Government: The President Is Winning His War on American Institutions," *The Atlantic*, April 2020, 54–74.

5. Marc Hetherington and Jonathan Weiler, *Prius or Pickup? How the Answers to Four Simple Questions Explain America's Great Divide* (New York: Houghton Mifflin Harcourt, 2018), 159.

6. James Mattis, "The Enemy Within," *The Atlantic*, December 2019, 104.

7. Michelle Goldberg "Democracy Grief Is Real," *The New York Times*, December 13, 2019, https://www.nytimes.com/2019/12/13/opinion/sunday/trump-democracy.html.

8. Opinion, "The Democrats' Best Choices for President," *The New York Times*, January 19, 2020, https://www.nytimes.com/interactive/2020/01/19/opinion/amy-klobuchar-elizabeth-warren-nytimes-endorsement.html.

9. Yuval Levin, "How Did Americans Lose Faith in Everything?," *The New York Times*, January 19, 2020, 4.

10. Nicholas Lemann, *Transaction Man: The Rise of the Deal and the Decline of the American Dream* (New York: Farrar, Straus and Giroux, 2019).

11. Danielle Allen, "The Road to Serfdom: How American Can Become Citizens Again." *The Atlantic,* December 2019, 100.

12. *Whitney v. California*, 274 U.S. 357, 375 (1927) (Brandeis, J., concurring).

13. *New York Times Co. v. Sullivan*, 376 U.S. 254, 273 (1964) (Brennan, J.).

14. Harry Kalven, Jr., "The New York Times Case: A Note on 'The Central Meaning of the First Amendment,'" *Supreme Court Law Review* (1964): 208.

15. C. Vann Woodward et al., "Report of the Committee on Freedom of Expression at Yale," December 23, 1974, https://yalecollege.yale.edu/get-know-yale-college/office-dean/reports/report-committee-freedom-expression-yale.

16. John Villasenor, "Views Among College Students Regarding the First Amendment: Results from a New Survey," Brookings Institution, September 18, 2017, https://www.brookings.edu/blog/fixgov/2017/09/18/views-among-college-students-regarding-the-first-amendment-results-from-a-new-survey/.

17. Jill Lepore, "Flip-Flopping on Free Speech: The Fight for the First Amendment on Campuses and Football Fields, From the Sixties to Today," *New Yorker*, October 1, 2017, https://www.newyorker.com/magazine/2017/10/09/flip-flopping-on-free-speech.

18. *Republican National Committee v. Democratic National Committee*, 140 S.Ct. 1205 (2020).

19. *Bush v. Gore*, 531 U.S. 98 (2000).

20. See, e.g., Sabrina Siddiqui, "Kavanaugh Hearing Recalls Clarence Thomas Case," *Guardian*, September 27, 2018, https://www.theguardian.com/us-news/2018/sep/27/brett-kavanaugh-clarence-thomas-anita-hill-hearings.

21. See, e.g., Ariane de Vogue, "How McConnell Won, and Obama Lost, the Merrick Garland Fight," CNN, November 9, 2016, https://www.cnn.com/2016/11/09/politics/merrick-garland-supreme-court/index.html.

22. *Citizens United v. FEC*, 558 U.S. 310 (2010).

23. *United States v. Stevens*, 559 U.S. 460 (2010).

24. *Brown v. Entertainment Merchants Association*, 564 U.S. 786 (2011).

25. *Snyder v. Phelps*, 562 U.S. 443 (2011).

26. *Masterpiece Cakeshop, Ltd. v. Colo. Civil Rights Comm'n*, 138 S.Ct. 1719 (2018).

27. See, e.g., *R.A.V. v. City of St. Paul*, 505 U.S. 377 (1992).

28. Steven H. Shiffrin, *What's Wrong with the First Amendment?* (Cambridge: Cambridge University Press, 2016).

29. Allison Stanger, "Understanding the Angry Mob at Middlebury That Gave Me a Concussion," *The New York Times,* March 13, 2017, https://www.nytimes.com/2017/03/13/opinion/understanding-the-angry-mob-that-gave-me-a-concussion.html.

30. Jeremy W. Peters, "In Coulter's Free Speech Battle, The Right's Latest Rallying Cry," *The New York Times*, April 26, 2017, A1.

31. Matt Saincome, "Berkeley Riots: How Free Speech Debate Launched Violent Campus Showdown," *Rolling Stone*, February 6, 2017, http://www.rollingstone.com/culture/features/berkeley-riots-inside-the-campus-showdown-over-free-speech-w465151.

32. Charles R. Lawrence III, "If He Hollers Let Him Go: Regulating Racist Speech on Campus," 1990 *Duke Law Journal*: 431–83.

33. James Weinstein, *Hate Speech, Pornography, and the Radical Attack on Free Speech Doctrine* (Boulder: Westview Press, 1990), 155.

34. Amy Chua, *Political Tribes: Group Instinct and the Fate of Nations* (New York: Penguin Press, 2018), 105.

35. Klein, *Why We're Polarized*, 63.

36. Andrew Sullivan, "America Wasn't Built For Humans," *New York*, September 18, 2017, https://nymag.com/intelligencer/2017/09/can-democracy-survive-tribalism.html.

37. Chua, *Political Tribes*, 41.

38. Greg Lukianoff and Jonathan Haidt, *The Coddling of the American Mind: How Good Intentions and Bad Ideas Are Setting Up a Generation for Failure* (New York: Penguin Press, 2018), 58.

39. Steven Pinker, *Enlightenment Now: The Case for Reason, Science, Humanism, and Progress* (New York: Viking, 2018), 383.

40. Nicholas Kristof, "Beware the Contagion Spread by Blowhards," *The New York Times*, March 8, 2020, SR9.

41. Ronald Brownstein, "Red and Blue America Aren't Experiencing the Same Pandemic," *The Atlantic*, March 20, 2020, https://www.theatlantic.com/politics/archive/2020/03/how-republicans-and-democrats-think-about-coronavirus/608395.

42. Janet Hook, "Even the Coronavirus Can't Bridge America's Partisan Divide," *The Los Angeles Times*, March 20, 2020, https://www.latimes.com/politics/story/2020-03-20/coronavirus-crisis-cant-bridge-partisan-divide.

43. Susan Milligan, "The Political Divide over the Coronavirus," *U.S. News & World Report*, March 18, 2020, https://www.usnews.com/news/politics/articles/2020-03-18/the-political-divide-over-the-coronavirus.

44. Michelle Goldberg, "The Phony Coronavirus Class War," *The New York Times*, May 19, 2020, A27.

45. George Packer, "Underlying Conditions," *The Atlantic*, June 2020, 11.

46. Bruce Rozenblit, *Us Against Them: How Tribalism Affects the Way We Think* (Kansas City: Transcendent Publications, 2008), 116.

47. Ibid., 49.

48. Chua, *Political Tribes*, 34.

49. Francis Fukuyama, *Identity: The Demand for Dignity and the Politics of Resentment* (New York: Farrar, Straus and Giroux, 2018), 22.

50. Klein, *Why We're Polarized*, 69–70.

51. Ibid., 74.

52. James Madison, "The Federalist No. 10," in *The Federalist Papers*, ed. Clinton Rossiter (New York: Penguin Books, 1961), 78.

53. Pinker, *Enlightenment Now*, 10.

54. Ibid., 333.

55. Bradley Campbell, "The Free Speech Crisis on Campus Is Worse Than People Think," *Quillette*, November 14, 2018, https://quillette.com/2018/11/14/the-free-speech-crisis-on-campus-is-worse-than-people-think.

56. Christopher Ellis, "Do Americans Support Free Speech on College Campuses? Absolutely. Except Sometimes," *The Washington Post,* November 8, 2017, https://www.washingtonpost.com/news/monkey-cage/wp/2017/11/08/do-americans-support-freespeech-on-college-campuses-absolutely-except-sometimes.

57. Evette Alexander, "First Amendment Vitals," Knight Foundation, May 13, 2019, https://knightfoundation.org/articles/first-amendment-vitals-gen-z-expression-inclusion

58. Jean Twenge, *iGen: Why Today's Super-Connected Kids Are Growing Up Less Rebellious, More Tolerant, Less Happy – and Completely Unprepared For Adulthood* (New York: Atria Books, 2017).

59. Jean Twenge, "How the Smartphone Affected an Entire Generation of Kids," *New York Observer*, August 22, 2017, https://observer.com/2017/08/how-thesmartphone-affected-an-entire-generation-of-kids-millennilals-igen.

60. Ibid.

61. Lukianoff and Haidt, *The Coddling of the American Mind*, 32.

62. Twenge, *iGen,* 249–50.

63. J.A. Leo Lemay, *The Life of Benjamin Franklin*, vol. 3 (Philadelphia: University of Pennsylvania Press, 2009), 474.

64. Michael S. Roth, *Safe Enough Spaces: A Pragmatist's Approach to Inclusion, Free Speech, and Political Correctness on College Campuses* (New Haven: Yale University Press, 2019).

65. Woodward, "Report of the Committee on Freedom of Expression at Yale."

66. Greg Lukianoff and Jonathan Haidt, "The Coddling of the American Mind," *The Atlantic*, September 2015, https://www.theatlantic.com/magazine/archive/2015/09/the-coddling-of-the-american-mind/399356.

67. Lee C. Bollinger, *Uninhibited, Robust and Wide-Open: A Free Press View for a New Century* (New York: Oxford University Press, 2010), 50.

68. Geoffrey R. Stone, Marianne Bertrand, Angela Olinto, Mark Siegler, David A. Strauss, Kenneth W. Warren and Amanda Woodward, "University of Chicago, Free Speech on Campus: A Report from the University Faculty Committee," January

6, 2015, http://www.law.uchicago.edu/news/free-speech-campus-report-university-faculty-committee.

69. *United States v. Schwimmer*, 279 U.S. 644, 655 (1929) (Holmes, J., dissenting).

70. Lukianoff and Haidt, *The Coddling of the American Mind*, 6.

71. Mark Lilla, *The Once and Future Liberal: After Identity Politics* (New York: Harper, 2017), 83–84.

72. Chua, *Political Tribes*, 183.

73. Lilla, *The Once and Future Liberal*, 132–33.

74. Lukianoff and Haidt, *The Coddling of the American Mind*, 70.

75. Jonathan Haidt, Interview with author, Tempe, AZ, November 9, 2017. See also, Joseph Russomanno, "Tribalism on Campus: Factions, iGen and the Threat to Free Speech," *Communication Law and Policy* 24, no. 4 (2019): 563, n.157.

76. Jill Lepore, *These Truths: A History of the United States* (New York: W.W. Norton & Company, 2018), 625.

77. Alison Stanger, "Middlebury, My Divided Campus," *The New York Times*, April 3, 2017, ED22.

78. Nat Hentoff, Free Speech For Me – But Not For Thee: How the American Left and Right Relentlessly Censor Each Other (New York: Harper Collins, 1992).

79. Lepore, "Flip-Flopping."

80. Jeffrey A. Tucker, "Why Free Speech on Campus Is Under Attack: Blame Marcuse." Foundation for American Freedom, April 22, 2017, https://fee.org/articles/why-free-speech-on-campus-is-under-attack-blame-marcuse/. https://fee.org/articles/why-free-speech-on-campus-is-under-attack-blame-marcuse/.

81. Lepore, "Flip-Flopping."

82. Haidt interview.

83. Adam Liptak, "How Conservatives Weaponized the First Amendment," *The New York Times*, June 30, 2018, https://www.nytimes.com/2018/06/30/us/politics/first-amendment-conservatives-supreme-court.html.

84. *Janus v. AFSCME, Council 31*, 138 S. Ct. 2448, 2501 (2018) (Kagan, J., dissenting).

85. Liptak, "How Conservatives Weaponized the First Amendment."

86. Ibid.

87. Ibid.

88. Ibid.

89. Ibid.

90. Lee Epstein, Andrew D. Martin and Kevin Quinn, "6+ Decades of Freedom of Expression in the U.S. Supreme Court," June 30, 2018, http://epstein.wustl.edu/research/FreedomOfExpression.pdf.

91. Roth, *Safe Enough Spaces*, 91.

92. Ibid.

93. Villasenor, "Views Among College Students."

94. Bradley Campbell and Jason Manning, *The Rise of Victimhood Culture: Microsaggressions, Safe Spaces, and the New Culture Wars* (New York: Palgrave Macmillan, 2018).

95. Troy Closson, Catherine Henderson, Kristina Karisch, Peter Warren, Christopher Vazquez, Sneha Dey, Evan Robinson-Johnson, Amy Li, "Addressing *The Daily*'s Coverage of Sessions Protests," *The Daily Northwestern*, November 10, 2019, https://dailynorthwestern.com/2019/11/10/lateststories/addressing-the-dailys-coverage-of-sessions-protests/.

96. Ibid.

97. Charles Whitaker, "Northwestern's Jeff Sessions Protest Controversy: 'Give the Young People a Break,'" *USA Today*, November 19, 2019, https://www.usatoday.com/story/opinion/2019/11/19/northwestern-university-students-journalists-apology-editorial-jeff-sessions-column/4230002002.

98. *Matal v. Tam*, 137 S.Ct. 1744, 1751 (2017).

99. Ibid.

100. Helena Wagner, "Lawmaker's Bill Aims to Guard Free Speech at Arizona Universities. Critics Decry Censoring," *AZcentral,* February 17, 2020, https://www.azcentral.com/story/news/politics/legislature/2020/02/17/house-bill-2238-sponsored-anthony-kern-would-add-oversight-speakers-arizona-campuses/4626386002/.

101. Stanley Kurtz, "The Campus Intellectual Diversity Act: A Proposal," *National Review*, February 12, 2019, https://www.nationalreview.com/corner/the-campus-intellectual-diversity-act-a-proposal/

102. "Executive Order on Improving Free Inquiry, Transparency, and Accountability at Colleges and Universities," March 21, 2019, https://www.whitehouse.gov/presidential-actions/executive-order-improving-free-inquiry-transparency-accountabilitycolleges-universities/.

103. Robert J. Zimmer, "President Zimmer's Message on Free Expression and Federal Action," *UChicago News*, March 4, 2019, https://news.uchicago.edu/story/president-zimmers-message-free-expression-and-federal-action.

104. *West Virginia Board of Education v. Barnette*, 319 U.S. 624, 642 (1943).

105. *Sweezy v. New Hampshire*, 354 U.S. 234, 262 (1957).

106. Woodward et Al., "Report of the Committee on Freedom of Expression at Yale."

107. Stone et al., "University of Chicago, Free Speech on Campus."

108. Vincent Blasi, "Holmes and the Marketplace of Ideas," *The Supreme Court Review*, 2004, 19.

109. Ibid.

110. Oliver W. Holmes, "Natural Law," *Harvard Law Review* 32, no. 1 (November 1918): 40.

111. *Abrams v. United States,* 250 U.S. 616, 630 (1919) (Holmes, J., dissenting).

112. Lepore, "Flip-Flopping."

113. Ibid.

114. Ibid.

115. *Sweezy v. New Hampshire*, 250.

116. *Keyishian v. Board of Regents*, 385 U.S. 589, 603 (1967).

117. *Healy v. James*, 408 U.S. 169, 180 (1972).

118. Louis Menand, *The Marketplace of Ideas* (New York: W.W. Norton & Co., 2010), 13.

119. Ibid., 14.

120. Roth, *Safe Enough Spaces*, 99.

121. Richard Hofstadter, *The Idea of a Party System* (Berkeley: University of California Press, 1969), 61, n.20.

122. Madison, "The Federalist No. 10," 83.

123. Forrest McDonald, *Novus Ordo Seclorum: The Intellectual Origins of the Constitution* (Lawrence: University of Kansas Press, 1985), 205.

124. Madison, "The Federalist No. 51," 322.

125. Madison, "The Federalist No. 10," 80.

126. Susanna Schrobsdorff, "Teen Depression and Anxiety: Why the Kids Are Not Alright," *Time*, October 26, 2016, http://time.com/4547322/american-teens-anxious-depressed-overwhelmed.

127. Jennings Bryant, "Media Effects, History of Research On," in *Encyclopedia of Children, Adolescents and the Media*, ed. Jeffrey Jensen Arnett (Thousand Oaks, CA: Sage Publications, 2007), 509–10.

128. Alexander Meiklejohn, *Free Speech and Its Relation to Self-Government* (New York: Harper & Brothers, 1948), 27.

129. David M. Rabban, *Free Speech in Its Forgotten Years* (New York: Cambridge University Press, 1997), 175.

130. *Whitney v. California*, 274 U.S. 357, 375 n.2 (Brandeis, J., concurring).

131. Felix Frankfurter, "The Supreme Court and the Public," *Forum* 83 (1930): 333.

132. *Whitney v. California,* 377.

133. Ibid., 375.

Chapter 7

Beyond Free Speech Rhetoric

Framing Campus Free Speech Conflicts

Christina E. Wells

Over the last several years, college campuses have erupted in protests as speakers have tried to ply their (admittedly controversial, usually conservative, sometimes offensive) ideas on unyielding young minds. In response to this simple attempt at an exchange of ideas, frenzied (overwhelmingly liberal) student protestors responded as censorial mobs, calling for disinvitations of speakers, heckling or shouting them down, and resorting to violence, all leading to a full-blown First Amendment crisis. As one commentator put it, college students are "'unlearning liberty,' carrying the virus of censorship and oppression beyond the university and into the nation."[1] This is the dominant view of recent campus protests. In fact, the "claim that America's campuses are in the midst of a free speech crisis has been made so often and so emphatically that it has widely become accepted as fact."[2] As a result, several states have adopted laws—many of them based on a model law drafted by the conservative Goldwater Institute—that punish students who disrupt or interfere with the free speech rights of others.[3]

But the extent to which a free speech crisis really exists on our college and university campuses is highly debatable.[4] Rather than objective fact, the argument promoting the existence of such a crisis is based in narrative choice, specifically the choice of a particular narrative frame. Narrative frames are the cognitive devices we use to "shap[e], focus[], and organiz[e]" the world around us.[5] We use frames to help us interpret and make sense of the world and strategically to persuade others about our points of view.[6] Indeed, our frames can "incite conflicts."[7] Furthermore, we usually formulate frames in line with our own interests.[8] For example, when we perceive others as threatening the values and principles that underlie who we believe we are, we act to defend our sense of self and our beliefs, including blaming or demonizing others.[9]

Those embracing the existence of a free speech crisis employed a frame that embraces two aspects of free speech jurisprudence—the U.S. Supreme Court's protection of offensive speech and universities as places of tolerance and exchange of ideas.[10] By strategically combining these aspects of the Court's jurisprudence, critics of student protestors created an argument that student protestors are censors who silence speech merely because they find it offensive. This frame is not only built on long-standing free speech traditions, it is built on our belief in the transcendent value of the First Amendment.[11] Accordingly, it resonated with many people on both sides of the political spectrum and became the dominant view of protestors.

Unfortunately, this dominant frame ignores the ambiguities associated with free speech law. The constitutional framework governing offensive speakers faced with disruptive protests lacks clarity and gives officials great leeway to subjectively enforce the law. This is especially problematic given our tendency to overlook information when our beliefs are threatened.[12] In this case, that tendency allows people to overlook the fact that many of the protests fell far short of the kind of disruption that was so heavily criticized. In addition, the dominant frame ignores the context in which the campus protests arose. Many are situated within larger university or community conflicts involving racial or other social injustices. By focusing on free speech issues, the dominant frame deflects discussion from important substantive issues or fails to credit the protestors with raising such issues, by refusing even to recognize their actions as speech. Accordingly, this narrative frame is likely to perpetuate conflict rather than aid in resolving it.

This chapter first discusses several campus free speech conflicts between protestors and speakers, the critical responses to the protests, and the culmination of that criticism in campus free speech protection laws in recent years. It next reviews the scholarly literature on framing and applies it to the criticism of protests to try to understand how this criticism became the dominant frame for understanding campus protestors. Finally, the chapter discusses problems arising with the dominant frame.

RECENT CAMPUS PROTESTS AND THE CRITICS' RESPONSE

Beginning in 2015, colleges and university campuses across the country seemingly experienced an exponential increase in student protests. These protests occurred for a variety of reasons although they generally fell into one of a two general categories: (1) student protests against faculty or administrative responses to student complaints about racial injustice, and (2) student protests against outside speakers.

Student Protests against University Actions

In the first category, students at Evergreen State College in Olympia, Washington protested Professor Bret Weinstein's actions in the spring of 2017. The protests arose, in part, out of Weinstein's objections to the school's decision to change a long-standing practice associated with its "Day of Absence," which was designed to show the importance of the presence of people of color on campus.[13] Rather than have students, faculty, and staff of color leave on that day to gather and discuss issues associated with race, as was the norm, the school proposed in 2017 to have people of color stay on campus while asking white people to stay away voluntarily as a show of solidarity.[14] Weinstein wrote an email objecting to this proposal, arguing that it was a form of discrimination, "a show of force, and an act of oppression in and of itself."[15] These objections echoed Weinstein's earlier concerns about the school's Equity Action Plan, which he argued prioritized a racial viewpoint in faculty hiring and would not benefit students.[16]

In the weeks following the email, and after a highly publicized encounter in which the police detained two Black students (but not two white students) following a cafeteria altercation, students confronted Professor Weinstein about his emails.[17] The confrontations were antagonistic, with students calling Professor Weinstein a racist, challenging him, and demanding his resignation—during his class in at least one instance.[18] Protestors also confronted the college president about Weinstein and other long-simmering racial issues, demanding, among other things, that Weinstein be fired, that various changes be made to police resources, and that the university deal more directly with problems of institutional racism.[19]

Students posted videos of these encounters, which quickly went viral.[20] Soon, critics lamented the students' lack of tolerance and loss of civil debate on campus; others called the students fascists.[21] Still others worried about the trend of intolerant students reflected in the Evergreen State College protestor actions. As one observer noted, "[t]he Weinstein saga is just the latest installment in a series of similar instances of illiberalism on American campuses."[22]

In fact, the Evergreen protests occurred within a year and a half of two similar encounters between students and administrators/faculty at other universities. In the fall of 2015 student protestors at the University of Missouri, who were also frustrated with the university's lack of responsiveness to complaints about the racial environment on campus, engaged in a series of escalating protests, including blocking the Homecoming parade in order to talk to the university president, a hunger strike by one student, camping on the university quad in support of that student, and, ultimately, a boycott of athletic events by the football team.[23] These protests resulted in the resignations of both the chancellor and the president of the university.[24] At the celebration of the president's resignation, which took place on the university quad outdoors, students and some press representatives had contentious encounters as the students did not want to allow press members into their (admittedly large) protective circle for interviews; two members of the press who disregarded this wish were escorted out, berated, and told they had no right to take pictures or interview students who asked them to leave.[25] One member had an especially contentious encounter when a faculty member pushed his hand away and called for "muscle" to escort him out.[26]

Similarly, that same fall at Yale University, students protested what they considered to be a particularly problematic email sent by one of their professors, Erika Christakis, who was also headmaster at one of their residential colleges. The email raised the question of whether requests to avoid offensive Halloween costumes infantilized college students and also questioned the difference between adult and childhood desires to dress-up. It further suggested that students "look away" if they were offended by a Halloween costume.[27] Over 700 outraged students and alumni wrote a letter, pointing out that the professor's email had—quite literally—equated childhood dress-up play with offensive and racist adult costumes.[28] According to the students and alumni, "[g]iving 'room' for students to be 'obnoxious' or 'offensive,' as you suggest, is only inviting ridicule and violence onto ourselves and our communities, and ultimately comes at the expense of room in which marginalized students can feel safe."[29] Eventually, students protested outside the residential college headed by the professor. This protest ended in an extremely contentious encounter with the professor's spouse, who was also a Yale professor; students yelled at and over the professor and demanded the couple's resignation as head of their residential college.[30]

As with Evergreen State College, critics condemned the protestors at Yale and Missouri, arguing that they engaged in censorship or interfered with free speech rights of the press (in the case of Missouri) or the faculty couple (in the case of Yale).[31] One commentator described the protestors' actions as a "left-wing coup" from a "tantrum generation" that has learned to use "political correctness [to] silence[] dissent on campus."[32] Another critic argued that the protests were a lesson in how "[i]nsufficient tolerance for disagreement is undermining campus discourse."[33]

Student Protests against Outside Speakers

Students' objections against outside speakers have been even more pronounced than those against their own faculty or administration. Again, such objections take various forms. Some occur as demands that the university "disinvite" outside speakers or protests in response to university refusal to do so that ultimately result in the speaker's withdrawal. In other instances, counter-protests occur during the speaker's appearance and can include heckling, shouting, and physical disruption.

As examples of the first scenario, consider the separate attempts of Ann Coulter and Milo Yiannopoulos to speak at the University of California, Berkeley in early 2017. Coulter, a right-wing media pundit and author, was scheduled to speak about immigration issues at the invitation of student groups in April 2017.[34] Acting on tips regarding potential violence, university officials said they could not guarantee her safety on the day that Coulter requested to speak and offered her an alternative date a week later.[35] Coulter refused because she and the students believed the alternative date to be unsatisfactory given that it would occur when school was not in session due to final exams.[36] Coulter threatened to show up on the original date; nevertheless, the speech did not occur although she eventually spoke on such issues in 2019 where large protests took place.[37]

Some student leaders of the groups inviting Coulter blamed the university for being unwilling to guarantee her safety on the original invitation date, arguing that the school was suppressing their free speech rights by "cancelling" her event.[38] Coulter herself said she was sickened by how easily a "thuggish institution like Berkeley" could "snuff out the cherished American right of free speech."[39] Other critics were equally unsparing. Senator Bernie Sanders, for example, criticized the students' inability to engage with Coulter, noting that "[i]f you can't ask Ann Coulter in a polite way questions which expose the weakness of her arguments, if all you can do is boo, or shut her down, or prevent her from coming, what does that tell the world?"[40] David Cole, head of the ACLU condemned the "unacceptable threats of violence that have led to the 'hecklers' veto' of Ann Coulter's speech."[41]

The Coulter event occurred just months after violence erupted on Berkeley's campus in response to a planned speaking event featuring Milo Yiannopoulos, who was at the time an editor of the right-wing Breitbart News and a provocateur known for his inflammatory homophobic, racist, and sexist remarks.[42] The event was part of Mr. Yiannopoulos' "Dangerous Faggot" tour on campuses around the country, which was marked by protests.[43] Other campuses had withdrawn invitations to Mr. Yiannopoulos or cancelled his speech over security concerns.[44] Over a hundred faculty members wrote a letter calling for the administration to cancel Yiannopoulos' talk, arguing that he engaged in "harassment, slander, defamation, and hate speech."[45] The administration, however, resisted these calls.[46] Eventually, on the day of the event but before Mr. Yiannopoulos' talk, some protestors not associated with the university turned violent, forcing the university to lock down the campus and cancel the event.[47]

As with the Coulter event, critics accused the university of ignoring freedom of speech. The Heritage Foundation argued that the protests were evidence that "even the most liberal, open-minded campuses in our country harbor intolerance for those that disagree with them."[48] Some original members of Berkeley's Free Speech Movement from the 1960s wrote a letter expressing concern about the effect of the Yiannopoulos protests on "Berkeley's free speech tradition;" the Berkeley College Republicans posted the statement "the Free Speech Movement is dead" on their Facebook page.[49] President Trump threatened to cut off funds to the university, although that threat sparked a backlash of its own with others variously calling it "counterproductive" or "blackmail."[50]

In addition to incidents where student or faculty protests resulted in cancellation of speaking events prior to their occurrence, campus protests have also occurred *during* speaking events. In March 2017, for example, students, faculty, and community members protested at Middlebury College at a talk given by Charles Murray, author of *The Bell Curve*, a book about the academic achievement gap between Black and white students that is widely considered to rely on racist assumptions.[51] When the university refused to accede to earlier calls to cancel the talks, over 400 people protested at the talk itself, standing up, holding signs, and chanting or shouting to the point that Murray was forced to move his talk to a live stream from a different room.[52] Violence eventually erupted as Murray was leaving the event when protestors confronted him and a Middlebury professor as they were walking to their car.[53]

As in other episodes, critics were quick to condemn the protestors' violation of the speaker's free speech rights. *Washington Post* columnist Richard Cohen hinted that the protestors' actions had antecedents in fascism.[54] The *New York Times* editorial board criticized the students for engaging in intimidation and interfering with the "sacred right" of free speech.[55] A Middlebury faculty member lamented that the episode "reflected an institutional failure" on Middlebury's part because students "don't understand the value of free speech at a college and what free speech really means."[56]

In the fall of 2017 students protested at several other universities that hosted speakers, heckling them, interrupting them, and/or effectively preventing them from continuing with their prepared remarks. At the University of Florida students shouted and jeered at Richard Spencer, leader of the alt-right National Policy Institute and purveyor of white separatism.[57] Spencer's speech "devolved into a futile shouting match" with his audience that "left him unable to make a sustained speech" as he exchanged taunts with students after claiming that their persistent shouts of "Go home" and "Nazis are not welcome" here violated his free speech rights.[58]

At the University of Oregon, a few dozen student protestors interrupted the annual "State of the University" address by university president Michael Schill, shouting slogans such as "Nothing About Us, Without Us," and carrying signs stating "Take Back Our University." President Schill, who was going to make a major gift announcement, was forced online to complete his address.[59] The protestors raised issues related to campus climate for minority students, including recent issues of hateful actions, as well as rising tuition costs.[60] Similarly, at William and Mary, students affiliated with Black Lives Matter prevented an ACLU leader from finishing her talk on freedom of speech, shouting slogans such as "ACLU, free speech for who?," "The oppressed are not impressed," and "ACLU, you protect Hitler, too."[61] According to the students, they were protesting the ACLU's decision to "hid[e] behind the 'rhetoric of the First Amendment' to defend white supremacists."[62]

Again, the student protestors were generally criticized. President Schill wrote an editorial, published in *The New York Times*, lamenting the students' "tactic of silencing" and "resistance" to all opposition and arguing that "our future as a nation, depends upon our willingness to hear voices different from our own and engage in meaningful discussion."[63] The president of William and Mary similarly lamented the students' failure to engage in "respectful dialogue, especially in disagreement," with the speaker or to "listen and learn from views that differ[ed] from [their] own."[64] In contrast, most commentators seemed to believe that the University of Florida had sufficiently protected Spencer's free speech rights—after spending $600,000 for security—and that the students' actions there fell under the heading of "counter-protests."[65]

The Fallout: Campus Free Expression Statutes

Although the above protests bore similarities to one another, each had its own unique set of circumstances. Nevertheless, as the above discussion indicates, critics' responses to the protests took characteristically similar approaches, casting the protestors as intolerant snowflakes who turned to censoring speech that offended them rather than using more rational, dialogue-based approaches.[66] Also evident was the desire to link much of this response to universities' institutional failures to instill appropriately tolerant values of open-mindedness.[67] Policy advocates and legislators picked up on this theme.

In 2017, for example, the Goldwater Institute proposed a model law regulating some of these protests. According to the Institute:

> Speakers who challenge campus orthodoxies are rarely sought out, are disinvited when called, and are shouted down or otherwise disrupted while on campus. . . . When protestors disrupt visiting speakers, or break in on meetings to take them over and list demands, administrators look the other way. Students have come to take it for granted they will face no discipline for such disruptions. Administrators also focus enforcement on silencing "offensive" speech and give short shrift to due-process protections for students accused of

> wrongdoing. . . . Substantial sections of the faculty have abandoned the defense of free speech. . . . In short, as both a deeply held commitment and a living tradition, freedom of speech is dying on our college campuses and is increasingly imperiled in society at large.[68]

As a result of this threat to campus tolerance, the model law proposed several provisions. Referencing the Supreme Court's jurisprudence protecting speech on public property,[69] the model law proposed making "all public areas of campus" into "traditional public forums" subject only to reasonable content-neutral time, place, and manner regulations that leave open ample means to communicate. (Sections 1C&E) Similarly, one provision required universities to make a statement that "[i]t is not the proper role of the institution to shield individuals from speech protected by the First Amendment, including, without limitation, ideas and opinions they find unwelcome, disagreeable, or even deeply offensive." (Section 1B) It also proposed provisions requiring campuses be open to any speaker invited by a member of the campus community and that the university take all reasonable efforts to ensure the safety of such speakers. (Sections 1F&G) Finally, the model legislation made clear that while "[a]ny person lawfully present on campus may protest or demonstrate[,] . . . protests and demonstrations that materially and substantially infringe upon the rights of others to engage in or listen to expressive activity shall not be permitted and shall be subject to sanction." (Section 1D) Under the proposal, students who violate this requirement could be disciplined and, ultimately, suspended for multiple violations. (Sections 1I–J)[70]

Within a few years of the Goldwater Institute's proposal, approximately twenty states adopted, and several more proposed, legislation involving free expression on college and university campuses.[71] Many of these laws adopted aspects of the model legislation. Some, such as Missouri and Virginia, enacted provisions designating public spaces as traditional public forums and limited the creation of "free speech zones."[72] These laws were primarily a response to long-standing university actions that corralled protesters in small areas of campus.[73] In addition, some states adopted (or required schools to adopt) a provision preventing discrimination against outside speakers based on their viewpoint.[74] Finally, many states, including Alabama, Arizona, Arkansas, Florida, Georgia, Iowa, Kentucky, Louisiana, North Carolina, Oklahoma, South Dakota, and Texas, adopted provisions similar to the model provisions that prohibited students from disrupting others' expression.[75] Some included sanctions as punishment.[76] Several statutes also required universities to affirmatively embrace the notion that it was not their place to protect students from "ideas and opinions they find offensive, unwise, immoral, indecent, disagreeable, conservative, liberal, traditional, radical, or wrong-headed."[77]

UNDERSTANDING THE CRITICS' FRAMING OF CAMPUS PROTESTS

The views reflected in the above criticism of campus protestors and the resulting state legislation have some basis in the First Amendment. The Supreme Court has consistently affirmed that the "college classroom with its surrounding environs is peculiarly the 'marketplace of ideas'" open to those who seek to express themselves.[78] Similarly, the Court has stated on numerous occasions that officials may not regulate speech "because the speaker's message may be offensive to his audience"[79] or because of the viewpoint expressed.[80] Thus, images of heckling protestors shouting down others or resorting to physical obstruction—even violence—to stop them seems utterly inconsistent with First Amendment values and jurisprudence. Indeed, such protestors arguably engage in the "heckler's veto" that the Court's doctrine is designed to protect against.[81]

Nevertheless, the dominant frame used to describe campus protestors is less objective and allows for less honest discussion than its proponents want to admit. This section discusses the academic literature regarding framing and its application to the critics' characterization of campus protestors. This discussion suggests that a powerful narrative arose based on the primacy of the First Amendment within our belief system and the strength with which criticism of protestors resonated with much of the public.

Understanding Framing Basics

"Frames" are our interpretive lenses. People use frames to understand the world around them. We create frames to "name situations in which we find ourselves, identify and interpret aspects that seem to us key in understanding the situation, and communicate that interpretation to others."[82] We also use frames to help us with conflicts.[83] "When we frame a conflict, we develop interpretations about what the conflict is about, why it is occurring, the motivations of the partners involved, and how the conflict should be settled."[84] People or groups in conflict usually have inconsistent frames that share similarities but emphasize different aspects of their experiences.[85] These inconsistent interpretations of the issues and events contribute to and perpetuate the conflict.

Framing scholars have identified several types of frames that can contribute to conflict. "Identity frames" involve a person or group's core conception of who they are—that is, their sense of self.[86] A common source of identity involves demographic characteristics, such as race or gender.[87] In addition, people can base their identity on institutions with which they associate (such as employment or social/political groups) or interests and beliefs (such as the belief that gun control violates the Constitution).[88] Challenges to a person's identity can seem especially threatening because they "call into question the beliefs and values that undergird who people believe they are."[89] As a result of this identity threat, conflict almost inevitably arises as individuals or groups take defensive action to preserve their identity, including ignoring information and perspectives that threaten their self-concept, reinforcing affiliations with like-minded people or groups, blaming others for the conflict, and demonizing those who oppose them.[90] (See the discussion of tribalism in Chapter 6.)

If identity frames are based on a conception of self, "characterization frames" are effectively the opposite—based on a conception of others. Thus, characterization frames "are reductionist labels, associating positive or negative characteristics with individuals or groups."[91] Characterization frames are often related to identity frames in that one who perceives another person or group as seriously threatening their identity often negatively characterizes that other person or group.[92] Scholars have noted that characterization frames are powerful primarily because they can be communicated to like-minded individuals or groups and used to undermine the legitimacy of one's opponents or cast doubt on their motivations.[93]

Individuals and groups use additional frames not just to make sense of conflict, but also strategically to persuade others or even incite or prolong conflict.[94] When people speak of conflicts, for example, they use phrases that favor their interests, including choosing "which fairness measures will benefit them most."[95] As Professor Barbara Gray, a prominent expert in the field, has explained people often use "grievance frames"[96] to mobilize others for social movements:

> The frames invoked typically portray a particular group as victims who have suffered unjustly at the hands of others. This type of framing is called diagnostic framing because it defines the existing circumstances as unfair and attributes to others the responsibility for the injustice. Prognostic framing follows this and offers the victims a roadmap for how to address or remedy the unjustice [sic] they have experienced. Finally, motivational framing provides an impetus for the victims to take action on the proposed solutions.[97]

Such frames allow us to justify our own actions as we decide what "ought" to be and whether others live up to our expectations.[98]

Understanding the Dominant Campus Protest Frame

The critics' response to the raucous campus protests implicates these frames. In particular, the preceding criticism of the protestors suggests that an identity frame plays a role. The critics' comments reflect a strong concern about the

First Amendment's protection of freedom of speech. Thus, critics expressed outrage at heckling protestors who allegedly resorted to violence and obstruction of speakers, describing them as "snuff[ing] out the cherished American right of free speech," "interfering with the "sacred right" of free speech or claiming that "freedom of speech [was] dying on our college campuses."[99] More indirectly, they lamented the protestors' failure to use civil dialogue and debate.[100] As noted above, it is common to form interest-based identities that reflect "shared concerns about particular issues, causes or values."[101]

The critics' identification with the First Amendment is not surprising given the reverence with which many citizens view freedom of speech. As Chapter 3 author Dean Rodney Smolla has noted, "'freedom of speech' is a value that has become powerfully internalized by the American polity. [It] is a core American belief, almost a kind of secular religious tenet, an article of constitutional faith."[102] That the protestors' actions appeared to undermine the First Amendment on college and university campuses arguably could have contributed to identity threat, especially given the Supreme Court's statement that "[t]he essentiality of freedom in the community of American universities is almost self-evident."[103] Interrupting or blocking speakers seems counter to the open debate and dialogue integral to effective education in universities. Thus, such protests arguably undermine important values associated with institutions of higher education as well as the First Amendment.

Identity threats often lead people to become defensive, which can cause them to demonize others and fuel conflict. Critics of the campus protestors portrayed the protestors negatively—that is, identity threat triggered a negative characterization frame of the protestors. Thus, critics described the protestors as engaging in a "left-wing coup," "thuggish," a "tantrum generation," "fascists," or "intolerant," and implied that their actions were censorial or acts of intimidation.[104] These descriptions involve characterization frames as they described the protestors in order to differentiate them from the critics, who believed themselves to be protectors of the First Amendment.

The critics' frames also seem strategic. As is common with grievance frames, critics of the protestors adopted a diagnostic frame that cast the protestors' actions as unfair and the speakers as victims who unjustly suffered as a result of the protests. Furthermore, these characterizations spread easily as many of the criticisms were published in national newspapers and journals, such as *The New York Times*, *Washington Post*, and the *Atlantic*.[105] As one observer noted, "[a] chorus of critics darkly warns that college students' departures from liberal norms of open public debate threaten free speech values on U.S. campuses."[106] From there, some critics use these characterizations to justify action, essentially moving to a prognostic frame. In this instance, that frame took the form of proposed legislation ostensibly designed to protect free expression on campus. Such legislation includes provisions punishing discrimination against outside speakers or protestors who interfered with free expression on campus. The Goldwater Institute legislation, for example, makes clear that these provisions build on characterizations of speakers as victims who have been treated unjustly at the hands of universities or protestors. Its model legislation references speakers who are "disinvited . . . shouted down, or otherwise disrupted while on campus[,] . . . faculty [who] have abandoned the defense of free speech," and the fact that "freedom of speech is dying on our college campuses."[107]

These frames coalesced to create a dominant frame of campus protestors as intolerant, disruptive, and sometimes violent to the point of being censorial. That frame has been "repeated by politicians, civil libertarians, university administrators, media outlets, and scholars" and has resonated with the public "to the point of becoming accepted as fact."[108] Framing research suggests that frames resonate when they are credible, can point to empirically credible evidence, and involve beliefs central to the groups that one is trying to mobilize.[109] As such, this overarching frame seems credible because those who espouse it span an ideological spectrum (and thus seem to have no ideological axe to grind), can point to evidence to support their claims (i.e., the protests themselves), and involve beliefs central to our way of life (thus making it easy to mobilize citizens to action on this issue).

THE DOMINANT CAMPUS PROTEST FRAME AND THE PERPETUATION OF CONFLICT

Although the dominant campus protest frame resonates with many people, it is nevertheless narrow and distorted, an unsurprising fact given that people in identity conflicts often ignore inconsistent information or selectively attend to information relevant to their frames.[110] In this case, that frame's portrayal of campus protestors as sometimes-violent censors who violate the letter and spirit of the First Amendment when facing ideas they dislike ignores both the ambiguity associated with free speech law and the facts underlying these protests. As a result, the frame further perpetuates these conflicts.

Misunderstanding Free Expression Issues

The Heckler's Veto

The dominant frame's characterization of campus protestors as often violent and censorial assumes that all of the protests discussed earlier fit within this frame. Yet many such protests fall far short of this notion. While some protests, such as those at Berkeley and Middlebury, included incidences of violence, that violence occurred before or after (not during) the speaking event. In both instances, outsiders committed the violence rather than students. Similarly, many Middlebury protestors heckled and shouted during Charles Murray's presentation, requiring that he move to a different room to finish his remarks via live stream. Arguably, the protestors interfered with Murray's remarks because he did not deliver them in the manner he intended; on the other hand, he did deliver them. Accordingly, it is not clear that their actions fit within the dominant frame's notion of violent, censorial protestors shutting down speakers.

Other situations fall even further short of the dominant narrative. Students at Missouri and Yale, for example, engaged in extremely angry and contentious arguments with faculty—to the point of calling for faculty resignations or telling reporters to leave a public space that students occupied and escorting them out. But these actions are not censorship. Students at Evergreen College condemned Professor Weinstein for his emails, protested and called for his dismissal. They did not, however, censor him in any way. Yet critics of the students, including the Goldwater Institute's report, frequently likened them to intolerant censors responsible for the death of the First Amendment on campus.

By compressing all protests together, the dominant frame perpetuates free speech problems rather than solving them. For example, the Goldwater Institute's bill builds on the dominant campus protest frame by punishing students for materially or substantially "infringing" the free expression rights of others.[111] The proposed law, however, does not define the term "infringe." Given the ease with which critics included disparate protests within their notion of "censorial" and "intolerant," using such a broad and undefined term will likely allow officials to regulate many non-disruptive protests. Some states attempted to refine the Goldwater Institute's standard by narrowly defining terms like "infringe" or "disrupt," limiting them to protests that involved primarily violence or physical interference.[112] Even some of these suffered from vagueness problems—by, for example, including a catchall phrase at the end punishing disruption of any protest that "significantly hinders" an audience's participation in a speaker's presentation. Thus, many state statutes suffer from the same arbitrary application problems as the Goldwater Institute's proposal.

Arguably, the Supreme Court's doctrine on the heckler's veto—that is, when an audience prevents someone from speaking—could limit arbitrary application of the model statute and related laws. As early as the 1940s, the Supreme Court recognized that hostile audience reactions were no reason to censor speakers. According to the Court in *Terminiello v. Chicago*,[113] speech may

> best serve its high purpose when it induces a condition of unrest, creates dissatisfaction with conditions as they are, or even stirs people to anger. Speech is

> often provocative and challenging. It may strike at prejudices and preconceptions and have profound unsettling effects as it presses for acceptance of an idea. That is why freedom of speech, though not absolute is nevertheless protected against censorship or punishment, unless shown likely to produce a clear and present danger of a serious substantive evil that rises far above public inconvenience, annoyance, or unrest.[114]

Numerous subsequent cases reaffirm the principle that the government has an obligation to protect speakers in the face of hostile audiences.[115] Thus, one could argue that existing free speech law heavily favors interpreting campus free expression statutes in favor of the speakers.

Although the Supreme Court has reaffirmed its antipathy to the heckler's veto, it has not given us a detailed legal framework with which to work. As Professor Frederick Schauer has noted, "[o]n the surface, it appears that we now have a considerable amount of law on the problem[.] . . . But appearances can be deceiving."[116] While the Court's cases tell us that police and other officials must protect speakers' rights by providing adequate police protection, they rarely provide specific direction regarding how much police protection and at what cost.[117] Counter-protestors also have expressive rights in these situations, including the right to heckle and jeer a speaker.[118] But because there is little case law on when counter-protestors cross the line into unacceptable disruption, state officials have great discretion to determine whether protestors interfere with another speaker's free expression rights. Given the state of the case law, the likelihood remains that the laws will be arbitrarily applied.

This is especially true given our propensity to filter information in a manner that favors our interests, including choosing "which fairness measures will benefit [us] most."[119] For those favoring the speaker, protestors' heckles take on the characteristics of disruption, intolerance, and censorship. For those favoring the protestors, they are legitimate counter-protests. An examination of responses to two of the speakers discussed earlier explores this further. At Middlebury College, critics decried campus protestors who interrupted Charles Murray's remarks, drove him to a different room to complete them, and then possibly—but probably not— engaged in violence after his remarks. Less criticism was directed at similar protests at Richard Spencer's University of Florida speech. Protestors there also interrupted his remarks, causing him to engage in a widely reported back and forth taunting match. Yet, most accounts described the Florida students as "counter-protestors" rather than use the dominant frame's language of "intolerant" or "censorial." In fact, Charles Murray delivered his remarks although via different means than anticipated, while Richard Spencer barely did, if at all. At the very least, both were subject to heckling counter-protestors. Yet the public response condemned Murray's protestors but not Spencer's, suggesting that dominant frame regarding protests broke down with the latter.

Many factors could explain this. People may have found Spencer's white nationalism more repugnant than Murray's more academic if arguably still racist remarks.[120] The timing of Spencer's remarks, coming soon after the August 2017 violence associated with white nationalist groups in Charlottesville could have affected the lenses through which people viewed the Florida protests, making them more sympathetic to the protestors. The widely reported violence occurring after the Middlebury protests, as opposed to the largely peaceful Florida protests, could have affected the response to the Middlebury protestors as well.[121] Although violence did not occur before or during Murray's remarks, nor were Middlebury students apparently involved, the dominant frame has linked contentious and angry protests to violence in a manner that "no doubt contribute[s] to Americans' antipathy toward public protest."[122] Regardless of the actual reason, the differential treatment of the Spencer and Murray protestors reveals how easily frames can affect our views of protestors and our subsequent applications of the law.

Disinviting Campus Speakers

One important difference between the Middlebury and Florida situations could be that Murray was invited by a student organization while Spencer availed himself of Florida's policy allowing outside speakers to rent its facilities.[123] Earlier criticisms of the protests involved a sense that angry and contentious protests or demands that universities disinvite speakers were inconsistent with free speech. Thus, there were negative characterizations of protestors as "thuggish," "intolerant," or engaging in a heckler's veto.[124] Consistent with these characterizations, the Goldwater Institute proposed rules requiring campuses to be open to any speaker invited by a member of the campus community, that the university take all reasonable efforts to ensure the safety of such speakers, and that students be subject to discipline for infringing on a speaker's expression. Several states followed suit, enacting laws making it difficult to disinvite or cancel an invited speaker based on perceived viewpoint bias.[125]

Some free speech scholars agree that rescinding an invitation violates an outside speaker's free speech rights. Referring to Milo Yiannopoulos' invitation to speak at Berkeley, Law School Dean Erwin Chemerinsky stated that "if [the] Chancellor . . . were to exclude speakers based on their viewpoint, she would get sued and lose."[126] According to Chemerinsky, "[t]he law is clear that a public university may not exclude a speaker based on his or her views, nor may students or faculty be punished for the views they express."[127] In contrast, Professor Robert Post argued that First Amendment rights, including the heckler's veto, were developed in the rough-and-tumble political arena but that "universities are not Hyde Parks. Unless they are wasting their resources, . . . [universities] can support student-invited speakers *only* because it serves university purposes to do so. And these purposes must involve the purpose of education."[128] Although Post acknowledged that it is typically not acceptable to punish someone who spews hateful speech in public, he argued that the university's mission to inculcate critical thinking to help students develop as democratic citizens means that "universities must be free to regulate speech in ways that are inconsistent with First Amendment rights, at least as ordinarily interpreted."[129] Accordingly, "if a campus speaker hurls personal insults at students—if he outs them or individually intimidates them—he has no business on campus."[130]

The Chemerinsky/Post debate reflects the complexity surrounding the free speech rights of outside speakers—a fact that the dominant frame and related statutes overlook. The statutes' relatively simple frameworks make it difficult to deal with the nuances of questions that arise from protests associated with invited speakers. Arizona's statute, for example, requires that universities "make reasonable efforts and make available reasonable resources to address the safety of an invited speaker" and their audience, and prohibits them from charging security fees "based on the content of the speech." It does, however, allow universities to "restrict the use of its nonpublic facilities to invited individuals."[131] Universities that fail to protect speakers may be subject to a civil suit for injunctive relief and actual damages.[132] Although the statute tracks the legal doctrine, it does not aid in answering questions such as how much money universities must spend or how many police officers must be present to satisfy the "reasonable efforts and reasonable resources" requirement. Nor does it keep critics from questioning a university's actions in hindsight if a crowd becomes violent despite a university's efforts. This seemingly objective statute, filtered through our individual subjective lenses, will likely result in the arbitrary application of these laws just like the earlier laws prohibiting protestors from disrupting the free expression of others.

Beyond Free Speech Rhetoric: Giving Context to Campus Protests

None of this is to say that freedom of speech lacks importance. The protection of free and open debate, including contentious and angry speech, is a foundational First Amendment principle. But the Supreme Court's First Amendment rules simply do not answer many of the questions that arise in these scenarios. In fact, campus protest scenarios are as much conflict problems as they are free speech problems. As much as context matters when applying free speech rules, it similarly matters when discussing the actions of campus protestors more generally. Understanding the context in which these protests are grounded suggests that the dominant frame is overly narrow and reductionist and makes the conflicts of which these protests are part harder to resolve.

Critics of the protestors often overlook that the immediate protests they criticize are usually situated within larger, ongoing conflicts. At Evergreen College, Middlebury, and Missouri the contentious protests occurred in the midst of larger discussions about the universities' continuing failure to make progress on issues regarding race relations. The campus protestors in those cases engaged in extended discussions about the particular issues prior to the contentious protests or encounters with these particular speakers. At Yale the students and alumni tried to raise the issue of Halloween costumes as part of a broader societal issue and then tried to engage in extended discussions afterward. In these instances, the protestors' relationships to the speaker's actions were not simply instances of knee-jerk intolerance about a speaker's message or right to be heard. Rather, they were an evolving response after a series of interactions.

The protests against speakers such as Richard Spencer at Florida and Ann Coulter and Milo Yiannopoulos at Berkeley also occurred within broader societal conflicts. Coulter was invited to speak by a student group at Berkeley on immigration issues, a subject on which she has particularly controversial—some argue racist—ideas.[133] Her stance is part of a larger conflict in the United States about how we treat immigration, especially after the Trump administration's decisions to separate families at the U.S. border and effectively ban immigration from some countries.[134] Yiannopoulos' often sexist, homophobic, and racist statements are part of his self-proclaimed position as protector of "cultural libertarianism," which an observer has described as the practice of "a lot of people on the internet saying intentionally offensive stuff."[135] His speech sits within the United States' larger conflict over hate speech.[136] Spencer's white nationalism is also located within our nation's attempts to come to grips with long-standing and systemic racial discrimination and violence.[137] Campus protests against him sit within a larger history of similar anti-racist protests.[138] Even the William and Mary protests against the ACLU speaker sit within this broader context as part of the debate over hate speech and its protection.

Understanding that campus protests are largely situated within broader university and community conflicts helps us dismantle and reframe the dominant narrative. For example, by failing to present the campus protests in their larger contexts, the dominant frame characterized them as irresponsible and thoughtless overreactions to offensive speakers and further lamented the protestors' failure to use reasoned dialogue and debate. Yet contentious tactics like protests are a natural evolution of conflict if other attempts at resolving a conflict have not worked. Thus, if "lighter" contentious tactics, such as ingratiation, promises, or persuasive argumentation have not worked, it is common to move to more "coercive" tactics including shaming, protests, boycotts, sit-ins, and the like.[139] In fact, that escalative sequence signals to others that the people using these tactics are "reasonable" and not simply using heavy coercive tactics for no reason.[140] Accordingly, the fact that campus protestors in several situations had engaged with university administration or professors on these issues, and that the universities and the nation were also immersed in racial justice issues, gives context to the protests. At the very least it suggests that the protests were not simply unexplainable overreactions by Gen Z (or iGen) snowflakes.

This broader context also allows us to view the campus protests not as an attempt simply to shout down or prevent another person's expression, but as an expressive contribution in its own right. The tactics chosen by the protestors were undoubtedly contentious. They involved shouting, angry, mocking, and shaming speech. Students sometimes turned their backs or heckled during another's speech. Some called for universities to cancel speakers' invitations. All of these are expression even if the form they took was sometimes uncivil.[141] In *Terminiello v. Chicago*, the Supreme Court made clear that the First Amendment protects speech even when it is "provocative and challenging . . . [or has] profound unsettling effects as it presses for acceptance of an idea."[142] This view of protestors stands in stark contrast to their critics, who seem to view the protestors' emotion or contentiousness as casting their behavior outside the bounds of the First Amendment.[143]

Locating the campus protests within this larger context also shows how the dominant frame deflects from the broader substantive issues associated with the protests. By dismissing the potential legitimacy of the protestors' actions under the First Amendment, the dominant narrative assumes either that we no longer need or that there no longer is an effective way to engage with the protestors.[144] Although such deflection is common with identity conflicts, it nevertheless leads to frames "defining a conflict in ways that cloud the real issue or problem."[145] Accordingly, by focusing on the campus protestors' actions, the dominant frame neglected to discuss the issues they raised, which often focused on continuing racial injustices and whether the universities involved were (1) doing enough to respond to ongoing student concerns, (2) how the universities involved were situated within larger issues of racial injustice, and (3) whether the universities involved should host speakers that arguably perpetuate racial or other social injustices.

Failure to engage on these substantive issues has consequences. Many of the campus protests are part of a larger, enduring conflict over racial injustice in this country.[146] In fact, past responses to civil rights activists trying to fight racial injustice were nearly identical to those involving campus protestors. They included "demonization, fear, and criticism," which left us "with a narrative that silences the voices and diminishes the concerns of those who would call attention to racial injustice today."[147] Our failure to engage on these issues when campus protestors raised them, not only effectively silenced them at the time, it further contributed to the enormous pain and public reckoning currently underway.[148] This result was entirely predictable given the energy that people bring to avoiding conflict and the devastating consequences that can follow, such as long-simmering anger and resentment.[149] Our need to directly engage with and discuss these issues is paramount.

CONCLUSION

The dominant frame is too narrow. Campus protestors unquestionably open themselves up to First Amendment criticism if violence or physical disturbance ensues. But lesser "disruptions" raise far murkier free speech questions. By framing the issue as primarily one involving students violating obvious free speech principles, the dominant frame also deflects from an examination of the broader university and social context in which the protests are situated—and, as a result—further perpetuates conflict.

NOTES

1. David French, "It's Time to Crush Campus Censorship," *National Review*, April 24, 2017, https://www.nationalreview.com/2017/04/free-speech-campus-censorship-congress-must-punish-universities-indulging-student-mob/.

2. Mary Anne Franks, "The Miseducation of Free Speech," *Virginia Law Review Online,* December 2019, 218, https://www.virginialawreview.org/volumes/content/miseducation-free-speech.

3. Jeremy Bauer-Wolf, "Free Speech Laws Mushroom in the Wake of Campus Protests," *Insider Higher Ed*, September 16, 2019, https://www.insidehighered.com/news/2019/09/16/states-passing-laws-protect-college-students-free-speech.

4. Franks, "Miseducation," 218; Rob Kahn, "The Anti-Coddling Narrative and Campus Speech," *University of St. Thomas Law Journal* 15 (2018): 5–12; Gregory P. Magarian, "When Audiences Object: Free Speech and Campus Speaker Protests," *University of Colorado Law Review* 90 (2019): 551; Christina E. Wells, "Free Speech Hypocrisy: Campus Free Speech Conflicts and the Sub-legal First Amendment," *University of Colorado Law Review* 89 (2018): 533.

5. Barbara Gray, "Framing of Environmental Disputes," in *Making Sense of Intractable Environmental Conflicts: Frames and Cases*, ed. Roy J. Lewicki et al. (Washington, DC: Island Press, 2003), 11.

6. Deborah Shmueli, Michael Elliott, and Sanda Kaufman, "Frame Changes and the Management of Intractable Conflicts," *Conflict Resolution Quarterly*, 24, no. 2 (Winter 2006): 208–209, https://doi.org/10.1002/crq.169.

7. Barbara Gray, "Strong Opposition: Frame Based Resistance to Collaboration," *Journal of Community and Applied Social Psychology* 14 (2004): 167, https://doi.org/10.1002/casp.773.

8. Shmueli et al., "Frame Changes," 209.

9. Gray, "Framing Environmental Disputes," 21–22.

10. *Terminiello v. Chicago*, 337 U.S. 1 (1949); *Healy v. James*, 408 U.S. 169 (1972).

11. Wells, "Free Speech Hypocrisy," 535.

12. Shmueli et al., "Frame Changes," 211.

13. Matt Driscoll, "There's More to the Race Protests at Evergreen that Biology Professor and Viral Videos," *News Tribune (Tacoma)*, June 1, 2017, https://www.thenewstribune.com/news/local/news-columns-blogs/matt-driscoll/article153694734.html.

14. Ibid.; Walker Orenstein, "Read the Email Exchange that Sparked Protests Against an Evergreen Professor," *News Tribune (Tacoma)*, June 1, 2017, https://www.thenewstribune.com/news/politics-government/article153826039.html.

15. Driscoll, "More to Race Protests;" Katherine Long, "Long Simmering Discord Led to The Evergreen State College's Viral Moment," *Seattle Times*, June 10, 2017, https://www.seattletimes.com/seattle-news/education/discord-at-evergreen-state-simmered-for-a-year-before-it-boiled-over/; Orenstein, "Email Exchange."

16. Ivette Feliciano and Zachary Green, "Evergreen Copes with Fallout, Months after 'Day of Absence' Sparked National Debate," January 7, 2018, *PBS*, https://www.pbs.org/newshour/show/evergreen-copes-with-fallout-months-after-day-of-absence-sparked-national-debate.

17. Noah Berlatsky, "How Right-Wing Media Has Tried to Stifle Student Speech at Evergreen State College," *Pacific Standard*, July 10, 2018, https://psmag.com/education/the-real-free-speech-story-at-evergreen-college.

18. Ibid. See also Feliciano & Green, "Evergreen Copes with Fallout."

19. Berlatzky, "Right-Wing Media;" Driscoll, "More to Race Protests."

20. Susan Svrluga and Joe Heim, "A Washington State College, Caught Up in Racial Turmoil, Remains Closed Friday after Threat of Violence," *Washington Post*, June 2, 2017, https://www.washingtonpost.com/news/grade-point/wp/2017/06/02/evergreen-state-caught-up-in-racial-turmoil-remains-closed-friday-after-threat-of-violence/.

21. Ibid.

22. Bari Weis, "When the Left Turns on Its Own," *New York Times*, June 1, 2017, https://www.nytimes.com/2017/06/01/opinion/when-the-left-turns-on-its-own.html.

23. Wells, "Free Speech Hypocrisy," 539–42.

24. Ibid., 541.

25. Ibid., 541–42.

26. Ibid., 542.

27. Erika Christakis, "Dressing Yourselves," Email to Silliman College (Yale) Students on Halloween Costumes, *FIRE,* October 30, 2015, https://www.thefire.org/email-from-erika-christakis-dressing-yourselves-email-to-silliman-college-yale-students-on-halloween-costumes/.

28. Wells, "Free Speech Hypocrisy," 544–45.

29. "Open Letter to Associate Master Christakis," *Down Magazine*, October 31, 2015, https://downatyale.com/open-letter-to-associate-master-christakis/; Wells, "Free Speech Hypocrisy," 544–45.

30. Ibid., 545.

31. Conor Friedersdorf, "The Perils of Writing a Provocative Email at Yale," *Atlantic,* May 26, 2016, https://www.theatlantic.com/politics/archive/2016/05/the-peril-of-writing-a-provocative-email-at-yale/484418/; Haley Hudler, "Yale Students Demand Resignations from Faculty Members over Halloween Email," *FIRE*, November 6, 2015, https://www.thefire.org/yale-students-demand-resignations-from-faculty-members-over-halloween-email/.

32. Suzanne Fields, "The Closing of the American Mouth," *Washington Times*, November 11, 2015, https://www.washingtontimes.com/news/2015/nov/11/suzanne-fields-colleges-teaching-students-what-to-/.

33. Friedersdorf, "Perils."

34. Susan Svrluga and William Wan, "UC-Berkeley Readies police, Concerned Ann Coulter Plans to Speak in Public Plaza on Campus," *Washington Post*, April 25, 2017, https://www.washingtonpost.com/news/grade-point/wp/2017/04/25/uc-berkeley-readies-police-as-ann-coulter-plans-to-speak-in-public-plaza-on-campus/; Chris Quintana, "At Berkeley, A Speaker's Cancellation Spurs New Battles Over Free Speech," in *Dealing With Controversial Speakers*, ed. The Chronicle of Higher Education (2017), 10.

35. Franks, "Miseducation," 223; Quintana, "Speaker Cancellation," at 10–11.

36. Thomas Fuller and Stephanie Saul, "Berkeley Is Being Tested on 2 Fronts: Free Speech and Safety," *New York Times*, April 21, 2017, https://www.nytimes.com/2017/04/21/us/berkeley-ann-coulter-speech.html.

37. Quintana, "Speaker Cancellation," at 10; Jaclyn Cosgrove and Shelby Grad, "Arrests Made as Hundreds Protest Ann Coulter Speech at UC Berkeley," *Los Angeles Times*, November 20, 2019, https://www.latimes.com/california/story/2019-11-20/arrests-made-as-hundreds-protest-against-ann-coulter-at-uc-berkeley.

38. Fuller and Saul, "Berkeley Tested;" Quintana, "Speaker Cancellation," at 11.

39. Quintana, "Speaker Cancellation," at 10.

40. Franks, "Miseducation," 223.

41. Ibid.

42. Sarah Brown and Katherine Mangan, "Trump Can't Cut Off Berkeley's Funds by Himself. His Threat Still Raised Alarms," in *Dealing with Controversial Speakers*, ed. The Chronicle of Higher Education (2017), 7.

43. Ibid.

44. Thomas Fuller, "A Free Speech Battle at the Birthplace of a Movement at Berkeley," *New York Times*, February 2, 2017, https://www.nytimes.com/2017/02/02/us/university-california-berkeley-free-speech-milo-yiannopoulos.html.

45. Ibid.

46. Beth McMurtrie, "Mayhem at Berkeley Hardens New Battle Lines on Free Speech," in *Dealing with Controversial Speakers*, ed. The Chronicle of Higher Education (2017), 4.

47. Brown and Mangan, "Berkely Funds," 7.

48. McMurtrie, "Mayhem at Berkeley," 5.

49. Fuller, "Free Speech Battle."

50. Brown and Mangan, "Berkeley Funds," 7; McMurtrie, "Mayhem at Berkeley," 6.

51. Wells, "Free Speech Hypocrisy," 546–47.

52. Ibid., 547.

53. Ibid., 547–48.

54. Richard Cohen, "Protestors at Middlebury College Demonstrate 'Cultural Appropriation' – Of Fascism," *Washington Post*, May 29, 2017, https://www.washingtonpost.com/opinions/protesters-at-middlebury-college-demonstrate-cultural-appropriation--of-fascism/2017/05/29/af2a3548-4241-11e7-9869-bac8b446820a_story.html.

55. "Smothering Speech at Middlebury (Editorial)," *New York Times*, March 7, 2017, https://www.nytimes.com/2017/03/07/opinion/smothering-speech-at-middlebury.html.

56. Stephanie Saul, "Dozens of Middlebury Students Are Disciplined for Charles Murray Protest," *New York Times*, May 24, 2017, https://www.nytimes.com/2017/05/24/us/middlebury-college-charles-murray-bell-curve.html.

57. "Richard Bertrand Spencer," *Southern Poverty Law Center*, https://www.splcenter.org/fighting-hate/extremist-files/individual/richard-bertrand-spencer-0.

58. Clay Calvert, "College Campuses as First Amendment Combat Zones and Theatres of the Absurd: The High Price of Protecting Extremist Speakers For Shouting Matches and Insults," *First Amendment Law Review* 16 (Spring 2018): 456–57; Andrew Pantazi and Nate Monroe, "Shouting Match; Hostile Audience Drowns Out White Nationalist's Speech," *Florida Times-Union (Jacksonville)*, October 20, 2017, at A-1; "Richard Spencer Speech At Florida Campus Sparks Mass Protest," *BBC*, October 20, 2017, https://www.bbc.com/news/world-us-canada-41683713.

59. Nick Roll, "Blocking a President from Talking," *Inside Higher Ed*, October 9, 2017, https://www.insidehighered.com/news/2017/10/09/speaker-interruptions-continue-controversial-policy-adopted-wisconsin.

60. Therese Bottomly, "Student Protestors Disrupt University of Oregon's Announcement of $50 Million Gift," *Oregonian*, October 6, 2017, https://www.oregonlive.com/education/2017/10/protesters_disrupt_announcemen.html.

61. Jeremy Bauer-Wolf, "Free Speech Advocate Silenced," *Inside Higher Ed*, October 6, 2017, https://www.insidehighered.com/news/2017/10/06/william-mary-students-who-shut-down-aclu-event-broke-conduct-code.

62. Ibid.

63. Michael H. Schill, "The Misguided Student Crusade against 'Fascism,'" *New York Times*, October 23, 2017, https://www.nytimes.com/2017/10/23/opinion/fascism-protest-university-oregon.html.

64. Wesley Wright, "William and Mary Students Protest ACLU Speaker, White Supremacy," *Virginia Gazette (Williamsburg)*, October 6, 2017, https://www.dailypress.com/virginiagazette/news/va-vg-aclu-protest-1007-story.html.

65. Joe Heim, Lori Rosza, Abigail Hausloner, Susan Svrluga, "'Go Home Spencer!' Protestors Disrupt White Nationalists Speech at the University of Florida," *Washington Post*, October 19, 2017, https://www.washingtonpost.com/news/grade-point/wp/2017/10/18/uf/; Cindy Swirko, "Behind Scenes Logistics at Protests Let Officers Control Chaos, *Gainesville Sun*, October 20, 2017, https://www.gainesville.com/news/20171020/behind-scenes-logistics-at-protest-let-officers-control-chaos.

66. Greg Lukianoff and Jonathan Haidt, "The Coddling of the American Mind," *Atlantic*, September 2015, https://www.theatlantic.com/magazine/archive/2015/09/the-coddling-of-the-american-mind/399356/.

67. Ibid.

68. Stanley Kurtz, James Manley and Jonathan Butcher, *Campus Free Speech: A Legislative Proposal* (Phoenix: Goldwater Institute, 2017), 3–4, https://goldwaterinstitute.org/wp-content/uploads/2019/03/Campus-Free-Speech-A-Legislative-Proposal_Web.pdf.

69. *Hague v. CIO*, 307 U.S. 496 (1939); *Perry Educ. Ass'n v. Perry Local Educators' Ass'n*, 460 U.S. 37 (1983).

70. The "Campus Free Expression Act" is appended near the end of Kurtz, Manley and Butcher, "Legislative Proposal," 20–21.

71. Between 2014 and 2020, Alabama, Arkansas, Arizona, Colorado, Georgia, Kentucky, Iowa, Louisiana, Maryland, Missouri, Nevada, North Carolina, North Dakota, Oklahoma, South Dakota, Tennessee, Texas, Utah, Vermont, and Virginia enacted laws regulating expression on campus. Although some focused on protecting student journalists, most tracked provisions of the Goldwater Institute's law or an earlier proposal by the Foundation of Individual Rights in Education (FIRE). See Teri R. Day and Danielle Weatherby, "Speech Narcissim," *Florida Law Review* 70 (July 2018): 875–78; Frank D. Lo Monte, "The Legislative Response to a Perceived 'Free Speech Crisis' On Campus," *Communications Lawyer* 34 (Winter 2019): 8–9; "Missouri Governor Signs Law Banning Campus Free Speech Zones," *FIRE*, July 15, 2015, https://www.thefire.org/missouri-governor-signs-law-banning-campus-free-speech-zones/.

72. Mo. Rev. Stat. § 173.1550 (2015); Va. Code Ann. § 23.1-401 (2019).

73. Thomas J. Davis, "Assessing Constitutional Challenges to University Free Speech Zones Under Public Forum Doctrine," *Indiana Law Journal* 79, no. 1 (2004): 267–69.

74. Ariz. Rev. Stat. §§ 15-1864(E) (2019); N. Dak. Cent. Code Ann. § 15-10.4-02(3) (2019); Tenn. Code Ann. § 49-7-2405(17) (2018); Tex. Educ. Code Ann. § 51.9315(h) (2019).

75. Ala. Code § 16-68-3 (2020); Ariz. Rev. Stat. § 15-1864, § 15-1865 (2019); Ark. Code Ann. § 6-60-1003 (2019); Fla. Stat. Ann. § 1004.097 (2019); Ga. Code Ann. § 20-3-48 (2018); Iowa Code Ann. § 261H.4 (2019); Ky. Rev. Stat. § 164.348 (2019); La. Rev. Stat., tit. 17, § 3399.35 (2018); N.C. Gen. Stat. §§116-300 -116-304

(2018); Okla. Stat. tit. 70, § 2120 (2019); S. Dak. Codified Laws § 13-53-51 (2019); Tex. Educ. Code Ann. § 51.9315 (2019).

76. Lo Monte, "Legislative Response," 9–10.

77. Tenn. Code Ann. § 49-7-2405(5) (2018); see also Ark. Code Ann. § 6-60-1002(7) (2019); La. Rev. Stat., tit. 17, § 3399.35(2) (2018).

78. *Healy v. James*, 408 U.S. 169, 180 (1972); *Keyishian v. Board of Regents*, 385 U.S. 589, 603 (1967); *Sweezy v. New Hampshire*, 354 U.S. 234, 249–50 (1957) (plurality opinion).

79. *Hill v. Colorado*, 530 U.S. 703, 716 (2000); see also *Snyder v. Phelps*, 562 U.S. 443, 460–61 (2011); *Texas v. Johnson*, 491 U.S. 397, 414 (1989); *Hustler v. Falwell*, 485 U.S. 46, 55–56 (1988); *Cohen v. California*, 403 U.S. 15, 21 (1971); *Cantwell v. Connecticut*, 310 U.S. 296, 310 (1940).

80. *R.A.V. v. City of St. Paul*, 505 U.S. 377, 382 (1992).

81. Wells, "Free Speech Hypocrisy," 554.

82. Shmueli, et al., "Frame Changes," 208. See also Gray, "Framing Environmental Disputes," 12.

83. Gray, "Frame-Based Resistance," 167.

84. Gray, "Framing Environmental Disputes," 12.

85. Boris H. J. M. Brummans, Linda L. Putnam, Barbara Gray, Ralph Hanke, Roy J. Lewicki, and Carolyn Wiethoff, "Making Sense of Intractable Multiparty Conflict: A Study of Framing in Four Environmental Disputes," *Communication Monographs* 75, no. 1 (March 2008): 28, https://doi.org/10.1080/03637750801952735.

86. Gray, "Frame-Based Resistance," 167–68; Shmueli et al., "Frame Changes," 211.

87. Gray, "Framing Environmental Disputes," 22.

88. Ibid., 22.

89. Ibid., 21.

90. Ibid., 168; Gray, "Framing Environmental Disputes," 21–22; Alison Peck, "Identity-Based Conflicts in Public Policy: Hydraulic Fracturing in Pennsylvania," *University of Pittsburgh Law Review* 79 (Spring 2018): 445; Shmueli et al., "Frame Changes," 211.

91. Shmueli et al., "Frame Changes," 211.

92. Peck, "Identity-Based Conflicts," 449; Shmueli et al., "Frame Changes," 212.

93. Shmueli et al., "Frame Changes," 211.

94. Gray, "Frame-Based Resistance," 167; Shmueli et al., "Frame Changes," 209.

95. Shmueli et al., "Frame Changes," 209.

96. Gray, "Framing Environmental Disputes," 17–18.

97. Gray, "Frame-Based Resistance," 167. See also Robert D. Benford and David A. Snow, "Framing Processes and Social Movements: An Overview and Assessment," *Annual Review of Sociology* 26 (2000): 615–18.

98. Gray, "Framing Environmental Disputes," 17.

99. "Smothering Speech;" Kurtz, Manley and Butcher, "Legislative Proposal," 3–4; Quintana, "Speaker Cancellation," at 10.

100. Franks, "Miseducation," 223; Schill, "Misguided Crusade."

101. Gray, "Framing Environmental Disputes," 23.

102. Rodney A. Smolla, "Speech Overview," *Freedom Forum Institute*, https://www.freedomforuminstitute.org/first-amendment-center/topics/freedom-of-speech-2/speech-overview/.

103. *Sweezy v. New Hampshire*, 354 U.S. 234, 250 (1957).

104. Cohen, "'Cultural Appropriation' Of Fascism;" Fields, "Closing of American Mouth;" Friedersdorf, "Perils;" Quintana, "Speaker Cancellation," at 10.

105. Cohen, "'Cultural Appropriation' of Fascism;" Editorial Board, "Smothering Speech;" Friedersdorf, "The Perils of Writing;" Lukianoff and Haidt, "Coddling;" Schill, "Misguided Student Crusade;" Svrluga and Heim, "Threat of Violence;" Weis, "Left Turns on Own."

106. Magarian, "When Audiences Object," 553.

107. Kurtz, Manley and Butcher, "Legislative Proposal," 3–4.

108. Franks, "Miseducating Free Speech," 218, 220.

109. Bedford and Snow, "Framing Processes," 619–20.

110. Shmueli, et al., "Frame Changes," 211.

111. Kurtz, Manley and Butcher, "Legislative Proposal," 3–4.

112. Ariz. Rev. Stat. § 15-1861(2) (2018); Ark. Code Ann. § 6-60-1003(6) (2019); Okla. Stat. tit. 70, § 2120(3) (2019).

113. *Terminiello v. Chicago*, 337 U.S. 1 (1949).

114. Ibid., 4.

115. *Bachellar v. Maryland*, 397 U.S. 564, 567 (1970); *Street v. New York*, 394 U.S. 576, 592 (1969); *Gregory v. City of Chicago*, 394 U.S. 111 (1969); *Cox v. Louisiana*, 379 U.S. 536 (1965); *Edwards v. South Carolina*, 372 U.S. 229 (1963).

116. Frederick Schauer, "The Hostile Audience Revisited," *Knight First Amendment Institute*, November 2, 2017, https://knightcolumbia.org/content/hostile-audience-revisited.

117. Ibid.

118. Wells, "Free Speech Hypocrisy," 554–55.

119. Shmueli, et al., "Frame Changes," 209.

120. Wells, "Free Speech Hypocrisy," 546–47.

121. Jeremy Bauer-Wolf, "Spencer Gets to Speak," *Insider Higher Ed*, October 20, 2017, https://www.insidehighered.com/news/2017/10/20/spencers-talk-florida-met-protests-and-attempts-shout-him-down.

122. Magarian, "When Audiences Object," 560.

123. Wells, "Free Speech Hypocrisy," 546; Susan Svrluga, "Richard Spencer Gets OK to Speak at the University of Florida, His First Campus Event Since U-Va.," *Washington Post*, October 5, 2017, https://www.washingtonpost.com/news/grade-point/wp/2017/10/05/richard-spencer-gets-ok-to-speak-at-the-university-of-florida-his-first-campus-event-since-u-va/.

124. Quintana, "Speaker Cancellation," 10; McMurtrie, "Mayhem at Berkeley," 5.

125. Ariz. Rev. Stat. §§ 15-1864(E) (2019); N. Dak. Cent. Code Ann. § 15-10.4-02(3) (2019); Tenn. Code Ann. § 49-7-2405(17) (2018); Tex. Educ. Code Ann. § 51.9315(h) (2019).

126. Erwin Chemerinsky, "Hate Speech Is Protected Free Speech, Even on College Campuses," *Vox*, October 25, 2017, https://www.vox.com/the-big-idea/20

17/10/25/16524832/campus-free-speech-first-amendment-protest. See also Kenneth Lasson, "The Decline of Free Speech on the Post-Modern Campus: The Troubling Evolution of the Heckler's Veto," *Quinnipiac Law Review* 37 (2018): 39.

127. Chemerinsky, "Hate Speech is Protected."

128. Robert C. Post, "There Is No 1st Amendment Right to Speak on A College Campus," *Vox*, December 31, 2017, https://www.vox.com/the-big-idea/2017/10/25/16526442-first-amendment-college-campuses-milo-spencer-protests/.

129. Ibid.

130. Ibid.

131. Ariz. Rev. Stat. §§ 15-1864(F) (2019).

132. Ariz. Rev. Stat. §§ 15-1864(I)-(J) (2019).

133. "Ann Coulter: It's Not Just Illegal Immigration That's the Problem; It's All Immigration," Dallas Morning News, June 3, 2015, https://www.dallasnews.com/opinion/commentary/2015/06/03/ann-coulter-it-s-not-just-illegal-immigration-that-s-the-problem-it-s-all-immigration/.

134. Michael D. Shear and Helene Cooper, "Trump Bars Refugees and Citizens of 7 Countries," *New York Times*, January 27, 2017, https://www.nytimes.com/2017/01/27/us/politics/trump-syrian-refugees.html; Joel Rose and Marisa Peñaloza, "Protestors across the U.S. Decry Policy of Separating Immigrant Families," *NPR*, June 1, 2018, https://www.npr.org/2018/06/01/616257822/immigration-rights-activists-protest-trump-administration-child-separation-polic.

135. Zack Beauchamp, "Milo Yiannopoulos: Breitbart's Star Provocateur and Trump Champion, Explained," *Vox* (February 20, 2017), https://www.vox.com/2016/4/4/11355876/milo-yiannopoulos.

136. Richard Stengel, "Why America Needs a Hate Speech Law," *Washington Post*, October 29, 2019, https://www.washingtonpost.com/opinions/2019/10/29/why-america-needs-hate-speech-law/; James Kirchick, "No, America Doesn't Need a Hate Speech Law," *Washington Post*, November 7, 2019, https://www.washingtonpost.com/opinions/2019/11/07/no-america-doesnt-need-hate-speech-law/.

137. *A Social History of Racial Violence*, ed. Allen Grimshaw (New York: Routledge, 2017).

138. Linda Poon and Marie Patino, "CityLab University: A Timeline of U.S. Police Protests," *Bloomberg*, June 9, 2020, https://www.bloomberg.com/news/articles/2020-06-09/a-history-of-protests-against-police-brutality.

139. Dean G. Pruitt and Sung Hee Kim, *Social Conflict: Escalation, Stalemate, and Settlement*, 3rd Edition (New York: McGraw Hill, 2004), 64, 81.

140. Ibid., 64.

141. Wells, "Free Speech Hypocrisy," 558–59.

142. *Terminiello v. City of Chicago*, 337 U.S. 1, 4 (1949).

143. Wells, "Free Speech Hypocrisy," 560–61.

144. Bernard Mayer, *Staying With Conflict: A Strategic Approach to Ongoing Disputes* (San Francisco: Jossey-Bass, 2009), 64

145. Ibid. Shmueli et al., "Frame Changes," 211.

146. David Montgomery, "The Endless Call," *Washington Post Magazine*, June 11, 2020, https://www.washingtonpost.com/graphics/2020/lifestyle/magazine/the

-endless-call-for-racial-equity-and-justice-in-photos-and-quotes/?itid=hp_magazine-left-8-12_maglead-ans%3Ahomepage%2Fstory-ans.

147. Katie R. Eyer, "The New Jim Crow Is the Old Jim Crow," review of *Mothers of Massive Resistance: White Women and the Politics of White Supremacy*, by Elizabeth Gillespie McRae and *A More Beautiful and Terrible History: The Uses and Misuses of Civil Rights History*, by Jeanne Theoharis, *Yale Law Journal* 128 (2019): 1019.

148. Evan Semones, "Enough Is Erough: Thousands Descend on D.C. for Largest George Floyd Protest Yet," *Politico*, June 6, 2020, https://www.politico.com/news/2020/06/06/george-floyd-blm-protest-washington-304635.

149. Mayer, *Enduring Conflict*, 55–68.

Chapter 8

The Awful Ruling of *Garcetti v. Ceballos* and Its Application at the University Level

David L. Hudson, Jr.

> The essentiality of freedom in the community of American universities is almost self-evident. No one should underestimate the vital role in a democracy that is played by those who guide and train our youth. To impose any strait jacket upon the intellectual leaders in our colleges and universities would imperil the future of our Nation. No field of education is so thoroughly comprehended by man that new discoveries cannot yet be made. Particularly is that true in the social sciences, where few, if any, principles are accepted as absolutes. Scholarship cannot flourish in an atmosphere of suspicion and distrust. Teachers and students must always remain free to inquire, to study and to evaluate, to gain new maturity and understanding; otherwise our civilization will stagnate and die.[1]
>
> —Chief Justice Earl Warren,
> *Sweezy v. New Hampshire* (1957)

The U.S. Supreme Court created a new categorical bar for public employees in *Garcetti v. Ceballos*,[2] ruling that such employees have no First Amendment rights when they engage in official, job-duty speech.[3] It doesn't matter how important the speech is to society at large. It doesn't matter if the public employee is the purest of whistleblowers. Instead, if the public employee spoke as an employee instead of a citizen, there is zero free-speech protection. The decision is the "Dred Scott" decision for public employees, sacrificing their free-speech rights on the altar of categorical exclusion.[4]

This ruling upset the traditional calculus in this area of law, a careful balance created by the Supreme Court in *Pickering v. Board of Education*[5] and later in *Connick v. Myers*.[6] But, the Court did not decide in *Garcetti* whether this new categorical bar would apply with the same force when it comes to professorial teaching and scholarship, an area assumed to have extra protection under the concept of academic freedom. The Supreme Court has not answered the question even in the face of a pressing circuit split. If applied to the professorial scholarship, research, and speech of academics, the decision becomes even worse and poses a grave threat to academic freedom.[7]

This chapter begins by recounting the development of the free-speech rights of public employees from the late nineteenth century and specifically on the modern view created in the 1960s. Next, the chapter examines the Supreme Court's creation of a new categorical rule in *Garcetti v. Ceballos*. This is followed by a discussion of the debate over whether *Garcetti* applies with full force, or any force at all, in the college and university setting.

DEVELOPMENT OF FREE-SPEECH RIGHTS OF PUBLIC EMPLOYEES

Historically, public employees possessed no free-speech rights on the job. Justice Oliver Wendell Holmes famously referred to this state of affairs in a case involving a police officer named John J. McAuliffe who was doing some political canvassing. Holmes wrote: "Petitioner may have a constitutional right to talk politics, but he has no constitutional right to be a policeman."[8] The idea was that public employees willingly relinquished their free-speech rights when they accepted public employment.

However, the U.S. Supreme Court changed course in the 1960s, culminating in what is still the landmark public employee free-speech decision, *Pickering v. Board of Education*.[9] The case involved a high school science teacher named Marvin Pickering who believed that the school board was too concerned with finishing a new football facility, rather than in putting needed money into academics. For example, Pickering wrote that "To sod football fields on borrowed money and then not be able to pay teachers' salaries is getting the cart before the horse."[10] He added, "That's the kind of totalitarianism teachers live in at the high school, and your children go to school in."[11] The school board fired Pickering for what it claimed were false statements in the letter.[12]

Pickering could not get another teaching job in the state of Illinois, having been blacklisted. He had to work in a Chicago-based soup factory for several years, as his case progressed through the court system.[13] "Sure I missed teaching," he told me in a 2001 interview. "But I had to support my family and I had always been independent."[14]

Pickering lost in the Illinois state court system, including the state high court in a 3–2 decision. Pickering then pursued his case to the Court of Last

Resort. The Court ruled 8–1 in his favor. Writing for the majority, Justice Thurgood Marshall—whose career was marked by a consistent protection for the free-speech rights of employees and other individuals[15]—explained that "[t]he problem in any case is to arrive at a balance between the interests of the teacher, as a citizen, in commenting upon matters of public concern and the interest of the State, as an employer, in promoting the efficiency of the public services it performs through its employees."[16]

The Court reasoned that Pickering's letter was a matter of public importance to the community and that his comments in the letter did not harm the "close working relationships" he had at the school with fellow teachers and administrators.[17] In other words, Marvin Pickering's speech did not negatively impact his fellow teachers or his students or his principals. He criticized the school board.

Notably, the Court also emphasized that as a public school teacher, Pickering was in the best position to offer information to the public about how the school board operated.[18] In other words, he had keen insight as a public school teacher of how the school board was doing with regard to spending money on academics and athletics. That speech was valuable to people in his community.

The Court later refined the *Pickering* balancing test in *Connick v. Myers*, a case involving an assistant district attorney who was fired after circulating a questionnaire at the office that criticized office practices.[19] Sheila Myers had been upset that she had been transferred to a different division.[20] She then circulated a questionnaire on the job that asked questions, such as whether employees had confidence in the word of superiors in the office and whether employees felt pressured to support political candidates supported by the district attorney, Harry Connick, Sr.[21]

Connick asked Myers if she circulated this questionnaire, which a deputy district attorney had described as creating a "mini-insurrection" in the office. When Myers said yes, Connick fired her.[22] Myers responded by filing a lawsuit in federal court. The case eventually reached the U.S. Supreme Court.

The Court ruled 5–4 in favor of Connick. The Court reasoned that Myers, the assistant district attorney, had negatively impacted the operation of the district attorney's office even though one of the questions in her questionnaire touched on matters of public importance.[23] The Court wrote that "[w]hen close working relationships are essential to fulfilling public responsibilities, a wide degree of deference to the employer's judgment is appropriate."[24]

Thus, the Court had created a balancing test that became known as the *Pickering-Connick* test, a test that dominated public employee free-speech jurisprudence for decades.[25] Under this approach, the Court first asked whether an employee spoke on a matter of public concern or if the employee merely engaged in a personal grievance. If the speech was a private grievance, there was no First Amendment protection. If the speech touched on a matter of public concern, then the Court balanced the employee's right to engage in speech on a matter of public concern versus the employee's interests in an efficient, disruptive-free workplace.[26]

GARCETTI: THE CREATION OF A NEW CATEGORICAL BAR

That all changed with the case of Los Angeles deputy calendar District Attorney Richard Ceballos, who ran afoul of his superiors when he wrote a memorandum to his bosses recommending dismissal of criminal charges in a case based on perjured law enforcement testimony.[27] Ceballos believed that a sheriff's deputy had given false testimony in a search warrant affidavit.[28] Ceballos wrote his memo and later testified for the defense. As a result of this, his superiors stripped him of supervisory duties and transferred him to a less desirable location.[29]

Ceballos sued in federal court, alleging retaliation based on his protected speech. A federal district court ruled in favor of the government, finding that Ceballos had no First Amendment protection in his work memo.[30] The U.S. Court of Appeals for the Ninth Circuit reversed, finding that "Ceballos's allegations of wrongdoing in the memorandum constitute protected speech under the First Amendment."[31] The appeals court first noted that Ceballos' speech in the memo was inherently a matter of public concern.[32] The Ninth Circuit then proceeded to the balancing test and found in favor of Ceballos, noting that his memo did not cause any disruption in the workplace.[33]

The government appealed to the U.S. Supreme Court. The case was argued twice before the U.S. Supreme Court. Initially the Court appeared sharply divided. The Court may have been leaning toward a 5–4 vote in favor of Ceballos.[34] However, the Court composition changed with Justice Samuel A. Alito Jr. replacing the newly-retired Justice Sandra Day O'Connor. Without O'Connor, the Court faced the prospect of a 4–4 split.[35] The Alito-O'Connor change resulted in the Court hearing oral arguments again and ruling in favor of the district attorney's office. Justice John Paul Stevens subsequently confirmed in his memoir that the initial vote of the Justices in *Garcetti* after the first round of arguments was 5–4 in favor of Ceballos, not the government.[36]

However, the Court's composition changed and the Court ruled 5–4 against Ceballos. Justice Anthony Kennedy wrote the Court's majority opinion. He noted that the Court should not "constitutionalize the employee grievance."[37] The Court emphasized that it was Ceballos's job to write the memo in question.[38] Kennedy then created the new threshold categorical rule: "We hold that when public employees make statements pursuant to their official duties, the employees are not speaking as citizens for First Amendment purposes, and the Constitution does not insulate their communications from employer discipline."[39]

Kennedy also explained that "[r]estricting speech that owes its existence to a public employee's professional responsibilities does not infringe any liberties the employee might have enjoyed as a private citizen."[40] He also stressed the importance that public employee supervisors must have the ability to ensure that their employees' official communications are "accurate, demonstrate sound judgment, and promote the employer's mission."[41] Kennedy even invoked the constitutional principles of federalism and separation of powers to justify the new rule, writing that "judicial intervention in the conduct of governmental operations" could threaten these seminal constitutional precepts.[42]

Three justices—John Paul Stevens, David Souter, and Stephen Breyer—authored separate dissenting opinions. Stevens emphasized that the all-or-nothing description of employee speech as citizen speech or employee speech "is quite wrong."[43] He also noted that it "seems perverse to fashion a new rule that provides employees with an incentive to voice their concerns publicly before talking frankly to their superiors."[44]

Justice Souter wrote a lengthier dissent, proposing a modified *Pickering-Connick* test but against the categorical exclusion created by *Garcetti*.[45] He wrote that "private and public interests in addressing official wrongdoing and threats to health and safety can outweigh the government's stake in the efficient implementation of policy, and when they do public employees who speak on these matters in the course of their duties should be eligible to claim First Amendment protection."[46]

Justice Breyer emphasized that Ceballos, as a prosecutor, had independent professional responsibility obligations to voice his concerns over potentially perjured law enforcement testimony.[47] To Justice Breyer, these "professional and special constitutional obligations" counseled in favor of protecting such employee speech.[48]

The *Garcetti* decision upset the careful balance of *Pickering-Connick*, a jurisprudence that had lasted decades.[49] However, the Court's decision in *Garcetti* changed the game in a negative way for countless employees. Many criticized the *Garcetti* decision as unsound. For example, Professor Paul Secunda explained that "[t]hrough its holding, the Court has now made it nearly impossible for conscientious public servants to speak out in the best interests of the public without jeopardizing their career."[50] Professor Sheldon Nahmod wrote that "*Garcetti* is unsound as a matter of First Amendment policy because it under-protects public employee speech that is vital to self-government."[51]

The decision spelled doom for public employees across the country, leading many plaintiffs' attorneys to refer to the phenomenon of being "Garcettized."[52]

GARCETTI IN THE UNIVERSITY SETTING

In *Garcetti*, Justices Kennedy and Souter sparred over whether the majority's holding of no First Amendment protection for official, job-duty speech would apply to the expression of university professors and academics. In his dissent, Souter warned that the holding would imperil the speech of university professors and academic freedom, writing:

> This ostensible domain beyond the pale of the First Amendment is spacious enough to include even the teaching of a public university professor, and I have to hope that today's majority does not mean to imperil First Amendment protection of academic freedom in public colleges and universities, whose teachers necessarily speak and write "pursuant to . . . official duties."[53]

Souter then cited a litany of passages from older U.S. Supreme Court decisions that spoke of the importance of freedom of speech at the university level and the impact of the concept of academic freedom.[54] Souter noted that the Supreme Court had referred to academic freedom as a "transcendent value to all of us"[55] and the fact that "[t]he vigilant protection of constitutional freedoms is nowhere more vital than in the community of American schools."[56]

Kennedy responded to Souter's warnings. He noted that "[t]here is some argument that expression related to academic scholarship or classroom instruction implicates additional constitutional interests that are not fully accounted for by this Court's customary employee-speech jurisprudence."[57] But Kennedy ultimately avoided the question, writing: "We need not, and for that reason do not, decide whether the analysis we conduct today would apply in the same manner to a case involving speech related to scholarship or teaching."[58] Thus, as some scholars have noted, the state of additional First Amendment protection for academic freedom in the college and university setting remains unsettled.[59]

Only two federal circuits have ruled that *Garcetti* does not apply in the university setting—the Fourth Circuit and the Ninth Circuit.[60] The Fourth Circuit first rejected *Garcetti* in the university academic setting in a case involving Michael Adams, an associate professor of criminology at the University of North Carolina Wilmington.[61] He alleged that university officials denied him promotion to the rank of full professor because of his Christian and conservative viewpoints reflected in his columns and books.[62] A federal district court denied his claims in part based on *Garcetti*.

On appeal, the U.S. Court of Appeals for the Fourth Circuit reinstated his First Amendment claims. The Fourth Circuit explained: "We are also persuaded that *Garcetti* would not apply in the academic context of a public university as represented by the facts of this case."[63] The appeals court reasoned that applying Garcetti to the facts of this case "could place beyond the reach of First Amendment protection many forms of public speech or service a professor engaged in during his employment."[64]

The Ninth Circuit also rejected *Garcetti* in an academic setting in the case of David Demers, a tenured associate professor at Washington State University.[65] Demers claimed that university officials retaliated against him by lowering his evaluation scores because of a pamphlet called "the 7 Step Plan" and his book, *The Ivory Tower of Babel*.[66]

A federal district court granted summary judgment to university administrators. On appeal, the Ninth Circuit reversed, noting that "Demers presents the kind of case that worried Justice Souter."[67] The Ninth Circuit determined that "*Garcetti* does not—indeed, consistent with the First Amendment, cannot—apply to teaching and academic writing that are performed 'pursuant to the official duties' of a teacher and professor."[68] Instead, the Ninth Circuit held that cases involving academic freedom and scholarship at the university level are best resolved by application of the traditional Pickering balancing test.[69]

Other circuits have not embraced this approach. For example, the Second U.S. Circuit Court of Appeals recently ruled that *Garcetti* foreclosed the First Amendment claim of a university adjunct professor who alleged he was not rehired after he revealed student cheating.[70] A federal district court in Ohio declined to adopt the reasoning of the Fourth and Sixth Circuits and instead evaluated a college professor's under the Garcetti framework.[71] A federal district court in Kansas also determined that *Garcetti* applied to a professor's free-speech claim.[72]

CONCLUSION

The *Garcetti* decision unnecessarily threatens the free-speech rights of public employees across the country. The Supreme Court hopefully will revisit its decision at some point and provide public employees with the protection they had under the *Pickering-Connick* framework. However, the *Garcetti* decision certainly should not apply when it comes to professorial classroom speech, research, and scholarship. Those activities form the essence of academic freedom, a concept the U.S Supreme Court called "a transcendent value" and "of special concern to the First Amendment."[73] At some point the U.S. Supreme Court will clarify that *Garcetti* does not apply to teaching and scholarship.[74]

NOTES

1. 354 U.S. 234, 250 (1957).
2. *Garcetti v. Ceballos*, 547 U.S. 410 (2006).
3. Ibid., 421.

4. David L. Hudson, Jr., "The Supreme Court's Worst Decision in Recent Years – Garcetti v. Ceballos, the Dred Scott Decision for Public Employees," *Mitchell Hamline Law Review* (forthcoming 2020).

5. 391 U.S. 568 (1968).

6. 461 U.S 138 (1983).

7. Owen R. Griffin, "Academic Freedom and Professorial Speech in the Post-Garcetti World," 37 *U. Seattle L. Rev*. 1, 20 (2013) (A general decision that First Amendment protection does not extend to the speech of public-sector employees offered in performance of their official job duties would strike a tremendous blow to professorial expression at public colleges and universities.").

8. *McAuliffe v. Mayor of New Bedford*, 155 Mass. 216, 220 (1892).

9. 391 U.S. 563 (1968).

10. Ibid., 577.

11. Ibid.

12. Ibid., 566.

13. David L. Hudson, Jr. "Teachers Looks Back on Letter That Led to Firing – and Supreme Court Victory," Freedom Forum Institute, July 20, 2001, https://www.freedomforuminstitute.org/2001/07/20/teacher-looks-back-on-letter-that-led-to-firing-and-supreme-court-victory/

14. Ibid.

15. David L. Hudson, Jr., "Justice Thurgood Marshall, Great Defender of First Amendment Free-Speech Rights for the Powerless," *Howard Human & Civil Rights Law Review* 2 (2018): 167.

16. *Pickering*, 391 U.S. at 568.

17. Ibid., 570.

18. Ibid., 572.

19. *Connick v. Myers*, 461 U.S. 138 (1983).

20. Ibid., 140.

21. Ibid., 141.

22. David L. Hudson, Jr., "Connick v. Myers: Reflections on Landmark Public Employee Free-Speech Case," Freedom Forum Institute, April 10, 2001, https://www.freedomforuminstitute.org/2001/04/10/connick-v-myers-reflections-on-landmark-public-employee-free-speech-case/.

23. Ibid., 151–52.

24. Ibid.

25. David L. Hudson, Jr., "Balancing Act: Public Employees and Free Speech," Freedom Forum, December 2002, 23, https://www.freedomforuminstitute.org/wp-content/uploads/2014/09/fac_firstreport_public-employees-free-speech.pdf.

26. Ibid., 23–24.

27. *Garcetti*, 547 U.S. at 414.

28. Ibid., 414.

29. Ibid.,415.

30. Ibid.

31. Ibid., quoting *Ceballos v. Garcetti*, 361 F.3d 1168, 1173 (9th Cir. 2004).

32. Ibid., 416.

33. *Garcetti*, 547 U.S. at 416, citing *Ceballos*, 361 F.3d 1180.

34. Marty Lederman, "Ceballos v. Garcetti – What Difference Will Alito Make?," Scotusblog, February 19, 2006, https://www.scotusblog.com/2006/02/ceballos-v-garcetti-what-difference-will-alito-make/.

35. Lyle Denniston. "Court to Rehear Public Employee Speech Case," Scotusblog, February 17, 2006, https://www.scotusblog.com/2006/02/court-to-rehear-public-employee-speech-case/.

36. John Paul Stevens, *The Making of a Justice: Reflections on My First 94 Years* (New York: Little, Brown and Company, 2019), 456. (Stevens noted that "astute observers of the Court correctly inferred that Sandra had provided the decisive vote for the opposite result in all three before she retired. Otherwise there would have been no need to reargue any of them.").

37. *Garcetti*, 547 U.S. at 420, quoting *Connick*, 461 U.S. at 154.

38. Ibid., 421.

39. Ibid.

40. Ibid., 421–22.

41. Ibid., 422–23.

42. Ibid., 423.

43. Ibid., 427 (J. Stevens, dissenting).

44. Ibid. (J. Stevens, dissenting).

45. Ibid., 428 (J. Souter, dissenting).

46. Ibid. (J. Souter, dissenting).

47. Ibid., 448 (J. Breyer, dissenting).

48. Ibid. (J. Breyer, dissenting).

49. Sonya Bice, "Tough Talk from the Supreme Court on Free Speech: the Illusory Per Se Rule in Garcetti as Further Evidence of Connick's Unworkable Employee/Citizen Speech Partition," *Journal of Law in Society* 8 (Winter 2008): 54 (noting that the Supreme Court had a balancing test in place for "four decades" until Garcetti).

50. Paul M. Secunda, "Garcetti's Impact on the First Amendment Speech Rights of Federal Employees," *First Amend. Law Review* 7 (Fall 2008): 117.

51. Sheldon Nahmod, "Public Employee Speech, Categorical Balancing, and §1983: A Critique of Garcetti v. Ceballos," *University of Richmond Law Review* 42 (January 2008): 563.

52. David L. Hudson, Jr., "Garcettized! 06 Ruling Still Zapping Speech," Freedom Forum Institute, January 5, 2010, https://www.freedomforuminstitute.org/2010/01/15/garcettized-06-ruling-still-zapping-speech/.

53. *Garcetti*, 547 U.S. at 438 (J. Souter, dissenting).

54. Ibid., 439 (J. Souter, dissenting).

55. Ibid. (J. Souter, dissenting), quoting *Keyishian v. Board of Regents*, 385 U.S. 589, 603 (1967).

56. Ibid. (J. Souter, dissenting), quoting *Shelton v. Tucker*, 364 U.S. 479, 487 (1960).

57. Ibid., 425.

58. Ibid.

59. Lauren K. Ross, "Pursing Academic Freedom after Garcetti v. Ceballos," *Texas Law Review* 91 (2013): 1281.

60. David L. Hudson, Jr. "Are Free Speech and Academic Freedom under Assault at Colleges and Universities?" *ABA Journal*, October 1, 2018, http://www.abajournal.com/magazine/article/free_speech_academic_freedom_buchanan.

61. *Adams v. Trustees of the University of North Carolina-Wilmington*, 640 F.3d 550 (4th Cir. 2011).

62. Ibid., 557.

63. Ibid., 562.

64. Ibid., 564.

65. *Demers v. Austin*, 746 F.3d 402, 406 (9th Cir. 2014).

66. Ibid., 406–407. See David Demers, *The Ivory Tower of Babel: Why the Social Sciences Are Failing to Live Up to Their Promises* (New York: Algora Publishing, 2011).

67. Ibid., 411.

68. Ibid., 412.

69. Ibid.

70. David L. Hudson, Jr. "No First Amendment Protection for Professor Who Spoke Out Against Cheating Students," Freedom Forum Institute, October 24, 2017, https://www.freedomforuminstitute.org/2017/10/24/court-rules-no-first-amendment-protection-for-professor-who-spoke-out-about-cheating-students/.

71. *Meriwether v. Trustees of Shawnee State Univ.*, 2019 U.S. Dist. LEXIS 151494 (S.D. Ohio)(9/5/2019) (noting that "Thus, the Court is bound to analyze plaintiff's First Amendment retaliation claim under *Garcetti*.")

72. *Klaassen v. Atkinson*, 348 F. Supp. 3d 1106 (D. Kan. 2018).

73. *Keyishian*, 385 U.S. at 603.

74. David L. Hudson, Jr. "Academic Freedom for Public University Professors: Unsettled Questions in the Wake of Garcetti v. Ceballos," Freedom Forum Institute, April 26, 2017, https://www.freedomforuminstitute.org/first-amendment-center/topics/freedom-of-speech-2/free-speech-and-government-employees-overview/academic-freedom-for-public-university-professors-unsettled-questions-in-the-wake-of-garcetti-v-ceballos/.

Chapter 9

Free Speech Values in the Classroom

Erica Goldberg

When I was a law student, a professor of mine began our seminar on Wrongful Convictions by telling the class that we may express any idea we would like in the class, so long as we did so respectfully.[1] Although I learned so much about the fallibility of evidence in that class, I cannot remember if the class discussions that followed were robust, with a variety of viewpoints represented, or if they skewed dramatically defendant-friendly, given the nature of the class. But I was so affected by the professor's introduction that, now as a professor myself, I deliver some version of it in every class that I teach.

For all of my classes, and especially when I teach free speech classes, I want students to accommodate new perspectives into their own thinking and to learn to engage civilly, even when they are confronted with ideas (or facts) they find objectionable. We live in an era where people's political engagement often consists of uncritically re-posting memes and simplified slogans in superficial social media interactions, and where people have become weary of hostile, angry debates that solve nothing. The classroom should be the antidote to this cultural pathology. Classroom discussions can exemplify the main justifications for free speech. Open communication assists in the search for truth, allows individuals room to express themselves, and legitimizes our democracy by providing voters necessary information to make informed choices.[2]

I want students to sincerely question their own worldviews. Because we are less critical of arguments with which we agree, and because we interpret facts and data in line with our existing beliefs,[3] discussion with our ideological or political adversaries can expose the flaws in our reasoning and provide facts and interpretation we may not have considered.

Unfortunately, the ideal of facilitating meaningful, open discourse on a variety of topics is more easily articulated in theory than practiced in reality, especially given the current cultural and political climates. Even starting from a position of wishing to foster truly open discussion—although it is not a given that every professor should use that approach—difficult questions abound. Imagine a conversation on the proactive policing practice of "stop and frisk," discussed in *Terry v., Ohio*,[4] a case I cover in my Criminal Procedure class. My job is to teach students the current state of the law and what is permitted by the Fourth Amendment, but also to have them question whether the doctrine is logically sound and leads to good results. There is some evidence that stop and frisk deters crime.[5] However, the police practice is also applied in ways that lead to racial harassment by law enforcement.[6] Engaging students on stop and frisk is highly consequential and relevant, but the issues are sensitive and difficult to confront for a variety of reasons.

For one, we all have different views about what are acceptable and appropriate topics of inquiry in the classroom, and which assertions are no longer reasonably debated. We can surely discuss the trade-offs of crime prevention with the intrusiveness of stop and frisks and abstractly weigh the tension between community security and personal liberty. And we can debate whether stop and frisk necessarily entails racial harassment, or whether the evidence does not support this assertion. Somewhat more controversially, reasonable minds can differ on whether this police practice helps or harms minority communities, perhaps reducing crime but affronting the dignity of innocent citizens in the process. But can a student suggest that racial profiling is acceptable if it is effective? Or, have we as a society determined that this sort of view is morally and legally beyond the pale?

Students—even bright, sincere students—often express ideas that other students will find demeaning, not just illogical or even objectionable. Some topics intersect with questions of identity, which seem to undermine a student's experience more than other types of potentially objectionable classroom content. When teaching Torts, we covered a case involving civil liability damages for a woman dragged some distance by a city bus.[7] I was asked a provocative question about what the intangible damages for loss of quality of life for an unmarried, childless, middle-aged woman should be, given that her future looked unpromising anyway. My female students, over a year later, mentioned that question to me, evidencing that they were affected and surprised by the question.

A somewhat similar incident occurred in another class, one on the Establishment Clause. There, we covered whether prayers at graduation ceremonies were coercive enough to be unconstitutional.[8] A student noted that she would not feel compelled to stand for an Islamic prayer at her graduation, because she would never worship in that way, so she wondered why non-Christians would feel compelled to participate in Christian prayers at a graduation. Both of the students mentioned here were excellent pupils making sincere points and had been encouraged by me to share all of their views, but the potential for offending other students on the basis of identity characteristics was there.

Additionally, what is acceptable for a student to say in the classroom may be different than what a professor can or should say. Professors, to some degree, need to look out for the emotional well-being of their students—all of their students—whose views and interests often conflict, while ensuring that each student feels included in the conversation. Navigating the fault lines of when to intervene or how to set the terms of debate is a difficult task. If I intervened in the Torts and Establishment Clause examples above to chastise students for their comments—which may have offended other students (and sometimes offended me)—that intervention would undermine the spirit of allowing all ideas to be pursued, if logically supported. If I simply added some context or color to these comments, I still compromise my neutrality, which is often necessary in enabling many viewpoints to flourish. I would be taking sides. If I said nothing, some students would feel alienated, or excluded, and I would allow certain biases to become part of the discussion.

Students want different things from their professors, and often have contradictory views about when a professor's intervention into a class discussion is unwarranted or unfair. For example, when I was a Legal Research and Writing Instructor on a fellowship, I met with my students in groups of two to discuss their legal briefs. I vividly remember two students coming in for a meeting close to tears, offended at a viewpoint expressed by another student during a discussion on rape in a Criminal Law class taught by another professor. The students were dismayed that this professor had not intervened more. The very next meeting, a different brief-writing pair told me how classmates had bullied an international student for expressing particular views, perhaps unartfully, and the professor seemed to pile on instead of coming to the aid of the student. From these meetings, I learned that students can emerge from the same class discussion with very different perspectives, both on how they wish a professor to behave and even on their perception of how the professor actually behaved, depending on their prior beliefs about what is appropriate and desirable in classroom discussions on difficult topics. If the professor had intervened more to protect the student with the controversial view, some students would have been severely distressed. However, not protecting the student also has costs, both to the student and to the openness of class discussion.

The role of the professor is partially amorphous because the university has a variety of functions, often existing in tension with each other. One scholar has articulated these functions, extracted from statements by university professors and other prominent figures, as

> [L]earning and research; anti-discrimination; providing educational opportunities and making societal contributions; advancement of knowledge; freedom of expression and communication; promoting economic growth; disinterested scholarship; serving as societal critic; moral cultivation of the students; professional training; preparation for competent democratic citizenship; reflecting or determining status and opportunity hierarchies or promoting social mobility; and fundamental personal transformation.[9]

Different professors may choose to emphasize some of these functions over others, and different students will wish to gain different skills and benefits from their education. Figuring out how actively I wish to guide conversations about policy or doctrine, especially on sensitive topics, is more difficult than the still tricky but less political issue of how much I want to influence students' modes of reasoning or abstract approaches to legal questions. More so than other law professors, I am a "legal formalist."[10] I think the quality of reasoning of opinions and the formal categories created by the law do and should control the outcomes of a case. Other law professors, who are more of the "legal realist"[11] persuasion, may spend more class time putting a case in its historical context or questioning the biases of a judge or Justice to understand the outcome of a given case.

A further complexity animating these issues is that public universities are constitutionally required to uphold the First Amendment rights of students and professors,[12] and both public and private universities often afford professors the academic freedom to set curriculum and make decisions about how to run their classrooms.[13] Further, school administrators have their own agendas and views about what is acceptable in the classroom. Some amount of First Amendment institutional academic freedom is bestowed upon universities as institutions to set pedagogical goals,[14] and this institutional academic freedom may conflict with an individual faculty member's academic freedom. Incidents involving professors being fired for statements made in the classroom, or students being punished or expelled, get national attention. Some of these incidents appear to violate the Constitution in addition to professional and ethical academic freedom values.[15]

Even assuming schools respect the dictates of the Constitution and academic freedom norms, there is still a lot of leeway for professors to decide how to run their classrooms. A variety of classroom approaches are open to public university professors, and private schools have even more leeway. Indeed, free speech doctrine—the mandates of the First Amendment—and free speech values—the rationales supporting the First Amendment—sometimes support each other but sometimes conflict. Sometimes, in order to foster free speech values, professors need to establish classroom rules that seem to undermine our strongest protections under First Amendment rules and doctrine. As an example, if every student were permitted to utter every hateful bit of speech protected by the First Amendment, classroom discussions would surely suffer instead of being productive.

This chapter continues by discussing the legal and ethical protections that govern classroom discussions and the range of approaches teachers can take in facilitating classroom discussions, which are critical to student learning. I will first explore ways in which the highest levels of First Amendment protections, which usually govern private interactions in private spaces as against government censorship, may actually conflict with the free speech values justifying the First Amendment, especially in the university classroom. I will then explain the free speech rights that do apply to teachers and students in the classrooms of public universities, a forum that is owned by the government. I will also describe the academic freedom protections often afforded to professors at both public and private universities. Private universities, which are not the government's, may have greater leeway to censor students' and professors' speech, but ethical and professional academic freedom norms still apply to the university classroom. Given that there is still much discretion in how professors should facilitate classroom dialog, I will finally detail the virtues and vices of several possible styles that professors can adopt regarding their roles in facilitating discussions in the classroom.

COMPETING FREE SPEECH VALUES AND FIRST AMENDMENT DOCTRINE

The First Amendment's protection of the freedom of speech is anything but simple or clear. Defining what constitutes protected speech is a contested question, as is determining how the government may regulate speech on its own property, especially in its schools. In spaces not owned by the government, such as in general society or in my home, First Amendment protections are at their apex. The government cannot, for example, punish me for expressing a controversial view inside my own home, unless the speech fits into an unprotected category, such as defamation or incitement—that is, speech that is designed to and is reasonably likely to provoke someone else to imminent lawless action.[16] The so-called "hate speech" is fully protected in general society.[17] I cannot be arrested or sued for expressing demeaning or derogatory views about a particular minority group or even displaying particularly horrifying symbols or signs.[18]

Speech on government property, by contrast, is subjected to what the courts term "forum analysis."[19] In a traditional or designated public forum, such as streets, parks, or public property intentionally opened up for expressive activity, First Amendment protections apply as if the government did not own the property.[20] Here, protections are at their apex. The government can place reasonable "time, place, and manner" restrictions on speech, such as controlling the volume at public concert halls, but cannot discriminate on speech based on its content (i.e., subject matter) or viewpoint (opinion within that subject matter).[21] In a more limited public forum, where the government has not opened up its property for free-ranging expressive activity, the government may make content-based distinctions on speech, but may not discriminate on the basis of viewpoint.[22] For example, on a city bus, a town could prohibit all political advertising, but could not prohibit advertising just by Democrats, or just by Republicans.[23]

As will be detailed in the next sub-section, the First Amendment protections that apply to a public university classroom have not been entirely specified by the courts. It is unclear whether this setting is treated like a designated public forum or a more limited forum. Complicating the issue is that the strongest dictates of First Amendment doctrine may clash with the values that justify First Amendment doctrine, especially in the classroom.

As noted above, there are generally considered to be three main rationales for protecting the freedom of speech.[24] The marketplace of ideas rationale, first articulated in American law by Justice Oliver Wendell Holmes in a dissenting opinion, provides that unfettered dialog best leads to the ascertainment of truth, both factual and moral.[25] Second, the democratic legitimacy rationale supports the idea that citizens or residents need access to free and open dialog in order to properly participate in their democracy and make informed voting choices.[26] Finally, the expressive autonomy rationale, which perhaps supports the most robust First Amendment protections, suggests that in order for individuals to be their fully-realized selves, they require the ability to express who they are, regardless of who is listening.[27]

These free speech values, which justify First Amendment rights, may sometimes not be served by the strongest First Amendment protections. Sometimes the government's intervention into the marketplace of ideas actually strengthens the search for truth, even though the government's affirmative intervention constitutes some degree of censorship. For example, when the government punishes false speech, say through libel laws, this may end up chilling the speech of others who wish to utter truths, impoverishing the marketplace of ideas. But if libel laws did not exist, we could not trust the facts of what we read or see. In the case of libel, some degree of abridgment of speech, so long as it is sufficiently speech protective, may actually serve free speech values.[28] The key is to set the bar high enough so that the government does not chill truthful, important speech. In America, because of our robust free speech protections, public figures cannot successfully sue for libel unless they prove that the falsehood that injured their reputation was known to be false or if the truth was recklessly disregarded.[29]

The clash of free speech values is heightened in the classroom. For example, imagine a professor who told her students that she will treat and grade all students fairly. However, she believes that women, on average, become more emotional during classroom discussions and she would like to ensure that all classroom discussions proceed only on the basis of logic. In her day-to-day life, the professor surely has some First Amendment right to say this; she cannot be arrested by the government for expressing this view. However, expressing this view in the classroom may undermine the marketplace of ideas rationale if female students feel discouraged from participating in class discussions. Then, the professor's robust exercise of her First Amendment freedoms compromises one of the rationales animating the First Amendment. Or perhaps not. No one is demanding that female students do not participate; nothing in the way of criminal prosecution or academic sanctions actually prohibits them from doing so, whereas punishing the professor would attach sanctions to her speech. Still, it is easy to see how allowing certain comments from students or professors, in the name of robust, academic discourse, may actually stifle open discussion or discourage certain ideas from being shared, impoverishing the debate. Managing the marketplace of ideas involves a difficult balance. Professors should not, and often cannot, punish the expression of certain views, but still must be mindful of students' sensibilities. On the other hand, if professors are too attuned to the sensitivities of certain students, the discussion may become one-sided or banal, with everyone—especially those with controversial or non-mainstream views—feeling chilled in their expression.

When free speech doctrine and free speech values conflict in the classroom, professors must find a way to reconcile them. In order to do this, professors and universities must first appreciate what the actual free speech liberties of their students are, and the extent of professors' and institutions' own First Amendment rights, when engaging in classroom discussion. Then, once faculty and administrators understand what students and professors cannot be prevented from expressing, professors can choose among a variety of styles, including more interventionist versus more neutral styles.

FIRST AMENDMENT PROTECTIONS AND ACADEMIC FREEDOM CONCERNS IN THE CLASSROOM

Because a public university campus is government property, some degree of forum analysis controls the First Amendment rights of students and faculty at these institutions. The Supreme Court "has recognized that the campus of a public university, at least for its students, possesses many of the characteristics of a public forum[,]"[30] where the First Amendment is most protective of speech. As discussed above, in a traditional public forum, like a park, speech cannot be punished for its content (i.e., its subject matter) or its viewpoint (i.e., a particular opinion within a given subject), unless the speech falls into an unprotected category, like true threats or obscenity.[31] In the areas of a university that are deemed a public forum, administrators can reasonably control the time, place, and manner of how speech is uttered, but administrators are generally not permitted to decide which topics are permissible and especially cannot dictate which viewpoints within those topics can be abridged.[32]

However, the question of which parts of a public university are treated like a public forum has not been fully resolved by the U.S. Supreme Court. "A university differs in significant respects from public forums .... A university's mission is education, and decisions of [the Supreme] Court have never denied a university's authority to impose reasonable regulations compatible with that mission upon the use of its campus and facilities."[33]

Some forum analysis issues in this context have been resolved. The Supreme Court has held that a student activities fee by a public university is explicitly considered a "limited public forum," where the university can discriminate on the basis of content but not on the basis of viewpoint.[34] In *Rosenberger v. Rector*, for example, a university violated the First Amendment by refusing to recognize and fund a religious publication.[35] Speech that acknowledges a deity or higher power is speech on a particular viewpoint, and the government may not discriminate on the basis of viewpoint, even in a limited public forum.[36] Thus, a public university can require all student groups to accept all members;[37] for example, it cannot fund a College Democrats student group but not a College Republicans student group.

The classification of other areas of a university has not been fleshed out explicitly by the courts. Critically, the protections afforded to professors and students in the classroom setting of a public college or university have not entirely been specified, perhaps because the classroom setting must be both tightly controlled and open for discussion. The public university classroom merits greater First Amendment protections than a public high school or elementary school classroom,[38] but lines have not been clearly drawn.

There are reasons to think that students and professors in the public university classroom deserve close to the highest levels of First Amendment protection—a classroom may be the quintessential marketplace of ideas. As the Supreme Court articulated in *Healy v. James*,[39] "[t]he college classroom with its surrounding environs is peculiarly the 'marketplace of ideas,' and we break no new constitutional ground in reaffirming this Nation's dedication to safeguarding academic freedom."[40]

There are also reasons to think university administrators may regulate the classroom more than other spaces on campus, like grassy areas between buildings. For students, the content of their class-related speech must be regulated. Their speech, after all, is what forms the basis for professors to assess whether they have learned the material. The speech must relate to the subject being taught and display rigorous thought and understanding of the material. For professors, the classroom is part of their professional duties, and the government is acting as their employer, not as their sovereign. This relationship diminishes the professor's First Amendment rights.[41] However, she has her own First Amendment academic freedom rights that the Supreme Court has not fully fleshed out,[42] but some lower courts have provided as a matter of First Amendment law.[43] The classroom, although perhaps the place best suited to open discussion, may not warrant free speech protections as strong as in other areas of a public university or public spaces generally.

Another consideration in determining what professors and students must be permitted to say without fear of reprisal is federal law, such as Title VI of the Civil Rights Act,[44] and Title IX of the Education Amendments of 1972.[45] These provisions prohibit discrimination on the basis of status characteristics such as race, national origin, and gender, and they apply to all public or private universities that receive federal funding. Title IX provides that "[n]o person in the United States shall, on the basis of sex, be excluded from participation in, be denied the benefits of, or be subjected to discrimination under any education program or activity receiving Federal financial assistance."[46]

The Supreme Court has held that if a student is subjected to severe or pervasive harassment in a way that undermines the benefits she receives from education, the student can sue the university under Title IX.[47] An errant classroom comment will likely not suffice to trigger the anti-discrimination provisions of Title VI or Title IX,[48] especially given First Amendment protections that apply to public universities. According to the Supreme Court,

> funding recipients are properly held liable in damages only where they are deliberately indifferent to sexual harassment, of which they have actual knowledge, that is so severe, pervasive, and objectively offensive that it can be said to deprive the victims of access to the educational opportunities or benefits provided by the school.[49]

However, schools are wary of repeated offenses that create a hostile environment for students.

Because the Constitution supersedes federal law, Title VI and Title IX cannot be interpreted in ways that violate the First Amendment. Lower courts appear to be quite sensitive to First Amendment concerns in the classroom, overturning campus harassment policies if they are vague or overbroad, meaning they reach a substantial amount of protected speech.[50] As a typical example, the Third Circuit Court of Appeals struck down a university's sexual harassment policy after a student alleged that the policy prevented him from discussing the role of women in the military.[51] The court of appeals held that some "harassing" speech is still protected by the First Amendment, and that the university harassment policy must include a severity and pervasiveness requirement, excluding speech only if it "objectively and subjectively creates a hostile environment or substantially interferes with an individual's work" so as not to interfere with "core, protected speech" about "gender politics and sexual morality."[52]

Some believe that the only way to reconcile the Civil Rights Act with the First Amendment is for courts to hold that in order to punish a student for speech, a college would need to show that the "speech created a hostile environment or substantially deprived the victims of access to opportunities, *and* that it was not an expression of a moral or political conviction."[53] This standard would allow all political expression or views about morality in the classroom. The professor could grade a student down for flaws in logic or disrespecting viewpoint-neutral classroom rules, but not for their conclusions, views, or beliefs, no matter how insulting to other students. Currently, however, not all courts adhere to this broad a view of what the First Amendment requires. One district court, for example, believed the classroom to be a place where the university's interests in avoiding intimidation or a hostile environment through insulting speech are most significant.[54]

Although the current state of free speech protections in the public university classroom has not been fully resolved by the Supreme Court, professors and administrators likely may not discipline or discriminate against students on the basis of their viewpoints, because viewpoint discrimination is never permissible in any forum.[55] Because First Amendment protections may be somewhat relaxed in the college classroom, professors have room to reconcile the ways in which honoring the strongest dictates of First Amendment doctrine undermines the values animating the First Amendment.

Although the issue has not fully been resolved by the Supreme Court, administrators also likely cannot punish professors for their viewpoints at public universities, although they can demand that professors conform to professional standards.[56] Difficult cases are thus created where a professor believes he is being impermissibly targeted by the university for his viewpoints, whereas the university maintains he is being disciplined for violating norms of professionalism.

The First Amendment does not protect students or professors at private schools from decisions made by professors or administrators.[57] (The government cannot, of course, censor speech at these private universities, but the government is generally not making decisions there.[58]) Some have argued that private universities are bound by contract law, if their documents promise student rights to the full extent of the First Amendment, and if those documents are treated as binding.[59]

Academic freedom norms also protect professors in both public and private universities and colleges.[60] Some courts have held that public university professors deserve academic freedom as part of their First Amendment rights.[61] Most often, however, academic freedom is a professional norm that protects both private and public college professors in expressing unpopular views in their scholarship and affords them some amount of discretion in designing their curriculum and managing their classroom.[62] "Classic discussions of academic freedom stress the freedom of the professor to investigate, teach, and publish, subject only to scholarly standards and professional ethics."[63] Institutions also have academic freedom rights to make administrative decisions about pedagogy that may conflict with the academic freedom rights of professors.[64]

At private universities, academic freedom does not comprise legally enforceable norms. However, colleges often respect the traditions of academic freedom, designed to ensure that higher education remains a place of true inquiry, even if that inquiry is not socially or culturally popular, or politically popular with the university. Even at a private university, where the First Amendment is inapplicable, academic freedom norms mean that professors should have a great deal of freedom not only in their scholarship, but in how they run their classrooms. Professors, not administrators, are the subject matter experts in their disciplines, and they also have critical ideas about which materials should be given to best educate students on the topic, how best to engage students in discussions on the topic, and what the best pedagogical approach to the subject is. As an example, it would violate academic freedom norms for universities to require professors to provide trigger warnings on certain content, although professors could decide to do so based on their own pedagogical approach.[65]

All this is to say that professors have a lot of leeway in determining how to run their classrooms. At public universities, they must respect their students' First Amendment rights, but they can still decide how much to intervene in discussions, how much to insert their own views, and how to manage (or avoid) classroom controversies. Plus, universities can ensure that professors act with professionalism, but must also respect professors' First Amendment rights. At private universities, professors have more ability to control the speech of their students, but the First Amendment is not relevant to their speech because their employer is not the government. At both public and private universities, academic freedom norms mean that professors should govern how to teach the curriculum and how to best inspire class discussions.

Given all this discretion, the question becomes how professors should best approach facilitating class discussions, especially on controversial topics, to best promote free speech values. The professor has options for her own involvement and also options for her expectations on and rules about student involvement. In some instances, the highest levels of First Amendment protection are not required in the classroom, given that the classroom is not exactly like a public forum. Indeed, giving these types of protections may actually undermine the free speech values that provide the rationale for the First Amendment.

The final section of this chapter details the different types of approaches, on a variety of axes, that professors can take when leading classroom discussion.

CHOICES PROFESSORS MAKE WHEN PROMOTING FREE SPEECH VALUES IN THE CLASSROOM

The Professor's Goal

The most primary choice professors must make involves her goals in educating her students. Professors have to decide whether their commitments are to process or to outcome. If a professor's commitment is to the process of education, she focuses on teaching students to think critically about the material, no matter the students' ultimate opinion on a particular topic. A process-based educator predominantly focuses on instilling thinking, reading, and writing skills. If a professor's commitment is instead to outcome—for example, a social justice aim of dismantling social or economic hierarchies—he or she may emphasize certain readings and be more vocal about his own views in an attempt to educate his students in what he believes to be the logically and morally correct position.

My preference, as is likely apparent, is for a more process-based, neutral teaching goal. Students often come to college or graduate school with serious deficits in their critical thinking, reading comprehension, and writing skills. I view my job as one that teaches students how to best absorb, organize, and transmit information. In my field of law, I also want to assist students in engaging with and learning from one another as they develop their views on legal doctrine, legal interpretation, and policy outcomes. We live in a culture of unfriending, of intolerance to opposing views, and of increased political polarization (and, I believe, extremism) based on self-selecting bubbles of facts and opinions. To the extent that discussion is the best path to moderate incorrect, un-nuanced, or extreme views, the process-based method requires students to engage with each other and come to their own conclusions, through guided class discussions and learning *how* to think, not *what* to think.

In this way, the classroom can and should be a true marketplace of ideas, where students try out new ideas and perhaps alter their own perspectives. I also model critical thinking skills by showing students that I can question both sides of an argument and find logical fallacies in a variety of opposing positions. I find that the more vocal a professor is about her views, the less students with opposing views feel comfortable speaking up, and class discussion atrophies. This was my own experience as a law student, and I developed the notion that professors who use their classroom as a way to push a particular perspective have abused their power, which should be to educate, not indoctrinate. Even in my First Amendment classes, I challenge the students to think about whether the protections I cherish are necessary, good, or consistent with the text and history of the free speech clause. Of course, even if I do not try to impart ultimate views about the legal doctrine onto my students, I am still accepting as fundamental more meta-level, abstract norms, such as fidelity to the rule of law or belief in the legal system as generally fair and just. This is why some believe a process-based approach is an impossible ideal, although I believe that the less a professor promotes specific, base-level political views and the more she perhaps incorporates more abstract ideals, the less chance there is for indoctrination, and the more students will feel comfortable expressing themselves in the classroom.

On the other hand, many believe that professors are being paid to impart their perspectives, not just their teaching skills. Plus, neutrality, many believe, favors the status quo; if professors do not affirmatively advance particular social justice perspectives or provide counter-narratives, some believe that students will not receive them. Education is not simply about facts and figures, but about values. Additionally, every time a professor chooses to emphasize sharing some facts over others, that professor is making a decision about what is important. Thus, there is no truly neutral, process-based professor. So long as a professor does not penalize students for disagreeing with their ultimate views (I am somewhat skeptical that professors never do this, even if they think they are intellectually honest as instructors), a professor should be free to teach with an ideological persuasion, even if class discussion may sometimes suffer. Many believe that students are strong enough to handle an opinionated professor and still feel comfortable disagreeing anyway, and that this dynamic can enrich discussion. I tend to think that because professors know so much more than students on their area of expertise, it is too easy to present a biased factual account that students are not sufficiently equipped to discredit.

The Professor's Role

Both the process-based and the outcome-based professor can choose to assume either a hands-off or a hands-on role to classroom discussion. A truly unfettered classroom discussion, once the professor has finished imparting what the students need to know, might involve a more hands-off approach, lest the professor's interventions into the discussion be taken to mean that the professor is actually inserting her own agenda into the classroom environment. Professors may opt for a strong listener model, notions of which animate First Amendment doctrine outside the classroom. For example, when considering regulations of advertising, a rational listener model assumes that audiences are "rational, skeptical, and capable of sorting through masses of information to find truth" in addition to being non-impulsive and thick-skinned.[66] In this context, a strong student model would presume that students are thick-skinned, do not need to be cajoled to enter discussions, and will speak up even if the discussion environment is not perfectly suited to their comfort.

That said, students often want and need a referee, and some types of comments are so injurious that they short-circuit students' ability to remain fully controlled. Encouraging a range of views, but buffering the views in case they become offensive to students, might help ease the tension created around sensitive topics. Professors may opt for a model that recognizes that all students are not strong students, and that some will feel excluded from conversations that alienate them and will feel uncomfortable participating, impoverishing the debate. In addition, the harm from some student comments may be felt disproportionately on minority student populations. For example, when my student in the Establishment Clause class noted that she would never feel compelled to stand for a Muslim prayer if one occurred at her graduation, I mentioned that those of a minority religion might feel more compelled to participate in prayers than those belonging to a majority religion. I also noted that it would be wonderful if a Muslim cleric were to deliver a graduation speech, but that usually does not happen. In this way, my student could express her views about the Establishment Clause, but I could ensure that Muslim students felt included and not inadvertently disparaged.

There is a spectrum of how much a professor can intervene in class discussion. On one end, a professor intervenes to protect only certain members of the class or share particular perspectives. On the other end, a professor never intervenes. In the middle, which may be optimal for cultivating free speech values in the classroom, a professor jumps in to add context or ensure that all perspectives are being appreciated, so that unpopular opinions can receive airtime. Professors can also massage comments, recasting them to make them more palatable to the class. If the professor does this in an even-handed way, discussions should not suffer. Further, students can be broken into small groups, where they sometimes feel more emboldened to really engage with each other on difficult topics because there is a smaller audience.

Of course, a totally neutral approach to intervening in class discussions may promote unfortunate false equivalencies between competing viewpoints on a topic. Some opinions should rightly fall out of favor. But I believe there is a danger to professing that instructors cannot be neutral, or that silence is complicity. The famous quote by Eli Wiesel that "neutrality helps the oppressor"[67] should not be imported into this context. Neutrality is an animating force behind free speech doctrine—the government is not permitted to choose sides in a way that dramatically skews the debate. No one person has a monopoly on truth, so those in power must remain viewpoint neutral. Of course, the government (or, in the classroom scenario, the professor) may engage in her own speech, but must do so in a way that does not censor others from speaking.

We as a society have become too adept at drawing lines about what is acceptable speech and when there is room for debate in a place that is too close to our own personal opinions, boxing out so many reasonable views that simply are not ours. Students must learn that there are acceptable views and approaches besides their own, even if these views and approaches initially seem beyond the pale. What may, at first blush, appear to be an unholy position may come from the speaker's own experiences, and may be less extreme, or more sophisticated or developed, than first believed. Whole frameworks of analysis can be shared between people who can learn to view the world through an entirely different lens. And thus, professors should work to bring many lenses to bear on their curriculum, and many types of facts, and allow students to scrutinize them all.

The Professor's Persona

The process-based and outcome-based professors, and the hands-off versus hands-on professors, can also assume one or two different personas: the persona of someone who attempts to remain as neutral as possible—*the non-discloser*—or the persona of *the discloser*, someone who discloses her biases and views, but is nonetheless open to discussion. In my early career, I attempted to hide my inclinations about certain cases, certain doctrines, or certain policies from students, worried they would feel pressured to agree with my approaches and that classroom discussion would suffer. I found that students attempted to guess my views anyway—sometimes correctly, sometimes incorrectly. Now, I tend not to share my views with students in class, but will readily give those views outside class.

The virtue of not disclosing one's own views is that the professor's views cannot supersede other views, because the professor is actively trying not to show her ultimate opinion. The virtue of disclosing is that a professor's views may seep out anyway, and perhaps the best approach to an honest discussion involves everyone admitting her biases, especially if there is no true neutral.

There are many other axes upon which professors can determine their own approaches to facilitating classroom discussion. In Torts class, where a lot of the cases involve gruesome injuries, I sometimes insert levity, even dark humor, which appeals to many students and eases tensions but may be off-putting to others. Reasonable minds can differ about the best way to foster dialog in the classroom, especially given that free speech values sometimes exist in tension with each other and with First Amendment doctrine, although some approaches may make students more open to sharing than others.

Perhaps the solution to truly accommodating free speech values in the classroom is for professors to be process-based, intervene less often, and never disclose their biases. But perhaps not. The First Amendment, and academic freedom, promotes permitting professors an ability to navigate these decisions without much intervention from the institution. Perhaps students are best served by experiencing professors who employ a diversity of approaches. This way, students can benefit from the discussion-welcoming atmosphere of a professor whose goal is to encourage critical thinking. But the same students can also learn moral courage and values-based education, or see how a narrative is developed, by encountering a professor who has a strongly held worldview and moral commitments and teaches his class from that thoroughly developed perspective. Academic freedom may best be promoted by allowing professors to run their classrooms as they see fit, within the bounds of constitutional dictates, even though some styles may be more conducive to free and open discourse than others.

NOTES

1. Sharon Driscoll, "The Wrongful Convictions Seminar." *Stanford Lawyer*, November 4, 2010, https://law.stanford.edu/stanford-lawyer/articles/the-wrongful-convictions-seminar-2/.

2. Kent Greenawalt, "Free Speech Justifications," *Columbia Law Review* 89 (January 1989): 130–45.

3. Yagoda Ben, "Your Lying Mind: The Cognitive Biases Tickling Our Brain," *The Atlantic*, September 2018, https://www.theatlantic.com/magazine/archive/2018/09/cognitive-bias/565775/.

4. *Terry v. Ohio*, 392 U.S. 1 (1968).

5. Jeremy Gorner, "Study Blames 'ACLU Effect' For Spike In Chicago's Crime in 2016, But Experts Differ," *The Chicago Tribune*, March 26, 2018, https://www.chicagotribune.com/news/breaking/ct-met-chicago-violence-2016-aclu-effect-20180315-story.html.

6. Dylan Matthews, "Here's What You Need to Know about Stop and Frisk—and Why Courts Shut It Down," *The Washington Post*, August 13, 2003.

7. *Seffert v. Los Angeles Transit Lines*, 56 Cal. 2d. 498 (Cal. 1961).

8. *Lee v. Weisman*, 505 U.S. 577 (1992).

9. R. George Wright, "Campus Speech and the Functions of the University," *Journal of College and University Law* 43 (2017): 10–11.

10. Jason Iuliano, "The Supreme Court's Noble Lie," *University of California, Davis Law Review* 51 (February 2018): 921–38.

11. Ibid., 938–56.

12. Erwin Chemerinky and Howard Gilman, *Free Speech on Campus* (New Haven and London: Yale University Press, 2018), 143–47.

13. David M. Rabban, "Does Academic Freedom Limit Faculty Autonomy," *Texas Law Review* 66 (1988): 1421.

14. *Grutter v. Bollinger*, 539 U.S. 306, 324 (2003).

15. Lauren Lumpkin, "University of Massachusetts Professor Removed from Classroom after Showing Hitler Parody," *The Washington Post*, December 16, 2019, https://www.washingtonpost.com/local/education/university-of-massachusetts-professor-removed-from-classroom-after-showing-hitler-parody/2019/12/16/9534a852-1de6-11ea-87f7-f2e91143c60d_story.html.

16. *United States v. Stevens*, 559 U.S. 460, 468–69 (2010).

17. Adam Liptak, "Hate Speech or Free Speech? What Much of West Bans Is Protected in the U.S." *The New York Times*, June 11, 2008, http://www.nytimes.com/2008/06/11/world/americas/11iht-hate.4.13645369.html

18. *Snyder v. Phelps*, 562 U.S. 443 (2011).

19. *Perry Educational Association v. Perry Local Educators Association*, 460 U.S. 37, 45 (1983).

20. Ibid.

21. Ibid.

22. *Rosenberger v. Rector*, 515 U.S. 819, 829 (1995).

23. *American Freedom Defense Initiative v. Suburban Mobility Authority for Regional Transportation*, 698 F.3d 885, 894 (6th Cir. 2012).

24. Erica Goldberg, "Competing Free Speech Values in an Age of Protest," *Cardozo Law Review* 39 (August 2018).

25. *Abrams v. United States*, 250 U.S. 616, 630 (1919).

26. Goldberg, "Competing Free Speech Values," 2164, n.1.

27. Ibid.

28. *New York Times v. Sullivan*, 376 U.S. 254, 280 (1964).

29. Ibid.

30. *Widmar v. Vincent*, 454 U.S. 263, 267 n.5 (1981).

31. *United States v. Stevens*, 559 U.S. 460, 468–69 (2010).

32. Ibid.

33. *Healy*, 268, n.5.

34. *Rosenberger v. Rector*, 515 U.S. 819, 829 (1995).

35. Ibid., 836–37.

36. Ibid., 831.

37. *Christian Legal Society v. Martinez*, 561 U.S. 661, 694–95 (2010).

38. *DeJohn v. Temple University*, 537 F.3d 301, 315 (3d Cir. 2008).

39. 408 U.S. 169 (1972).

40. Ibid., 180–81.

41. *Garcetti v. Ceballos*, 547 U.S. 410 (2006).

42. Ibid., 425.

43. *Kerr v. Hurd*, 694 F.Supp.2d 817, 843–44 (S.D. Ohio 2010).

44. 42 U.S.C. § 2000d et seq.

45. 20 U.S.C. §§ 1681–88.

46. 20 U.S.C. § 1681(a).

47. *Davis v. Monroe County Board of Education*, 526 U.S. 629, 650 (1999).

48. Ibid., 652.

49. Ibid., 650.

50. Alexander Tsesis, "Campus Speech and Harassment," *Minnesota Law Review* 101 (May 2017): 1903–906.

51. *DeJohn*, 317–18.

52. Ibid.

53. Patrick Miller, "University Regulation of Student Speech: In Search of a Unified Mode of Analysis," *Michigan Law Review* 116 (May 2018): 1319 (emphasis in original).

54. *Roberts v. Harrigan*, 346 F.Supp.2d 853, 872–73 (N.D. Tex. 2004).

55. Joseph Blocher, "Viewpoint Neutrality and Government Speech," *Boston College Law Review* 52 (May 2011): 703–704.

56. Chemerinsky and Gilman, *Free Speech on Campus*, 76–77.

57. *Margee v. Trustees of Hamline University*, 747 F.3d 532, 536 (8th Cir. 2014).

58. *University of Pennsylvania v. E.E.O.C.*, 493 U.S. 182, 198 n.6 (1990).

59. "Private Universities," *TheFire.org*, https://www.thefire.org/resources/spotlight/public-and-private-universities/.

60. Chemerinsky and Gilman, *Free Speech on Campus*, 9.

61. Wright, "Campus Speech and the Functions of the University," 21–22.

62. Rabban, "Academic Freedom," 1421.

63. Ibid.

64. Erica Goldberg and Kelly Sarabyn, "Measuring 'A Degree of Deference': Institutional Academic Freedom in a Post-*Grutter* World," *Santa Clara Law Review* 51 (November 2010): 221–24.

65. Chemerinsky and Gilman, *Free Speech on Campus*, 148.

66. Lyrissa Barnett Lidsky, "Nobody's Fools: The Rational Audience as First Amendment Ideal," *University of Illinois Law Review* (2010): 804–49.

67. Eli Wiesel, Acceptance Speech on the occasion of the award of the Nobel Peace Prize, Dec. 10, 1986, http:// www.nobelprize.org/nobel_prizes/peace/laureates/1986/wiesel-acceptance_ en.html).

Chapter 10

Managing the Peculiar Marketplace in the Face of Extremism

Brett G. Johnson and Jeremiah P. Fuzy

It is no secret why Richard Spencer and other far-right extremists target public universities for speaking engagements. Public universities have a unique blend of attributes that make them ideal loci for First Amendment activities: multiple large public spaces that can facilitate large crowds; large audiences made up of young, impressionable, and active individuals; and a culture of allowing ideas to compete in a free marketplace, both inside and outside of the classroom.[1] Add to this mix a concomitant culture of fostering criticism of the status quo, leading to a popular perception of public universities as taxpayer-funded havens of liberal thought (or, indoctrination, depending on your political persuasion). Thus, Spencer, et al. have an extra incentive to provoke progressive students and administrators into censorial reactions, as doing so allows them to cast themselves as free-speech martyrs at the hands of the "tyrannical left."[2]

It is, therefore, no surprise that public universities—and the extent to which their policies restrict freedom of expression—have long been the focus of so much attention from First Amendment advocates. Restricting speech on college campuses, even that of ultra-conservative provocateurs, evokes several ghastly specters: the greasing up of a slippery slope for more restrictions on speech by other state actors; the tarnishing of a collective memory of robust exercising of free speech rights, which have fueled (mainly progressive) social movements since the 1960s; and a lost opportunity to influence the very course of our nation. Add in the concern that universities' paternalistic restrictions on speech in the name of "protecting" students will end up *harming* students by making them ill-prepared for the harsh realities beyond the quadrangle, and the volume of the debate on free speech on campus reaches a fever pitch.[3]

In the din of this debate, Justice William Brennan's statement that the college "classroom is *peculiarly* 'the marketplace of ideas'"[4] offers an opening for an alternative perspective that we seek to advance here.[5] We believe this perspective can move the debate on controversial outside speakers beyond an otherwise starkly dichotomous framing of a choice between complete freedom or complete restrictions.[6] We argue that public university campuses are an extension of the classroom, and the *peculiar* fact that a marketplace of ideas is created there suggests that, when it comes to outside speakers, this marketplace should be affirmatively managed to meet the mission of the university. We qualify the argument by focusing only on outside speakers for two reasons. First, these speakers are often the source of the most *visible* (if not the most significant) debates on freedom of expression on college campuses. Second, scholars and jurists generally agree that the outcomes of public forum analyses involving public universities (which we discuss in greater detail below) often hinge on the relationship between the class of speaker (from inside or outside the university community) and the university's educational mission.[7]

Our argument begins with a close reading of Brennan's statement. The word "peculiarly," an adverb, modifies the verb "to be" in his sentence. This suggests the marketplace is not only peculiar by nature, but also by way of its creation. Constructed differently, it reads, "It is peculiar that the classroom is a marketplace of ideas." What explains this peculiar creation? In brief, the classroom is a microcosm of the mission of the university to foster free inquiry in a setting managed by a professor. Herein lies the peculiar creation: free inquiry arises from a *managed* setting. A limited number of individuals who meet a certain set of requirements that allows them to occupy a scarce number of seats, and who bring with them a unique set of experiences and worldviews, assemble to train their academic focus on a limited set of topics that a professor has selected to fill the limited timeframe of a course. The range of ideas the class uses to study these topics may freely, yet reasonably, expand and contract: principles of physics may be evoked to facilitate the study of chemistry; quoting Shakespeare could reasonably be employed to do the same; but entertaining a tenet of white supremacy would not be so reasonable. The inquiry in the classroom is no less free in the absence of this last topic. Therein lies its peculiar, organic creation.

The premise on which our call for a managed marketplace is based—that the university is an extension of the classroom—is not as big of a stretch as it may seem at first blush. First, like classrooms, public universities must shepherd scarce resources in the service of educating their students. These include financial resources, physical spaces, personnel, and time, among others. Second, the educational mission of universities, while much broader than the discrete missions of learning certain topics in a classroom, still has its own reasonable boundaries. These two factors (scarcity and the reasonable bounds of their mission) will be discussed in greater detail below. For now, we contend that these factors afford public universities the ability to manage their marketplace of ideas, particularly when they are faced with the prospect of having prominent (and sometimes controversial or even extremist) figures seeking access to that marketplace.

This argument has both an "is" and an "ought" component; it is as much about what the law surrounding the First Amendment on college campuses actually says as it is about policy prescriptions for public universities moving forward. The "is" part of the argument focuses on how courts have applied public forum doctrine to public universities and, for the most part, concluded that public universities consist of mostly limited or non-public forums subject to rational basis review, with a reasonability standard tied to the educational mission of these universities. The "ought" portion of the argument is an extension of the "is." We argue that public universities should not be considered marketplaces of ideas in the traditional libertarian sense, open to any outside speaker without any type of regulation and operating on the misguided assumption that all speakers have equal access to a platform. Rather, these schools, guided by their mission to serve American democracy, judiciously and transparently should manage the peculiar marketplaces that have arisen in them, thereby allowing them to be a bulwark against the most extremist of outside speakers. Such a policy will allow public universities to reveal to the rest of American democracy that extremist ideas (particularly of white supremacy), while perfectly allowable under the First Amendment, should be relegated to the fringes of the great American public discourse.

In outlining both the "is" and the "ought" of this argument, we hope to equip public universities with a powerful tool for managing extreme outside speakers, while also ensuring that this tool is only used in narrow circumstances. The scope of this argument has nothing to do with other hot-button issues involving free speech on college campuses. It is not designed to be applied to the speech of the university's own students or how faculty design their courses. It is not an argument that applies to "trigger warnings" or other issues that attract criticism for coddling the sensibilities of "snowflake" students. Indeed, we argue that the most appropriate way to debate issues related to free speech on campus is to handle each unique issue separately. In taking such an approach, we are able to see in clearer relief that managing extreme speakers allows public universities to assert themselves as powerful institutions guiding the course of public discourse in a democracy. This approach does not preclude the creation of a comprehensive set of governing principles that can be applied to various situations involving First Amendment issues facing public universities. Rather, if that is the end goal, we contend the best way to reach it is to first examine each issue one-by-one and build a set of principles from the ground up.

This chapter will be structured as follows. First, we will discuss the development of the "educational mission" standard in cases involving First Amendment issues at public universities. The goal of this section is to come to a better understanding of how courts have applied this standard generally—that is, in cases involving outside speakers seeking access to universities' forums (the focus of this chapter) and cases involving other First Amendment concerns—so that a solid foundation can be laid for building universities' strategies for managing extreme outside speakers. This section will address cases in which courts have both upheld and struck down universities' policies, as well as cases in which courts have inferred both greater and lesser importance of free speech to universities' educational mission. The purpose of having such a broad focus is to build consensus over the meaning of the marketplace of ideas within the context of public universities, grounded in the context of the *Keyishian* case from which Justice Brennan gave us the notion of peculiarly created marketplaces of ideas and its foundation in affirmative First Amendment theory. Perspectives from secondary scholarship will be reviewed here as well to buttress our argument.

Second, we will offer empirical evidence from public universities' own mission statements. These mission statements are not designed to form the bases of legal tests for future First Amendment litigation involving extreme speakers, and we do not intend to make them so by reviewing them here. Rather, the goal of this evidence is to build a better understanding of how public universities conceive of their educational missions today so that we can appreciate their unique positions as institutions equipped to guide public discourse in American democracy. Perspectives from secondary scholarship on public universities' missions will be reviewed here as well to allow for a more comprehensive discussion of the mission of these institutions and its application to managing their marketplace of ideas. We close the chapter with some thoughts on how public universities might best craft policies geared toward managing extreme speakers seeking access to their forums.

UNIVERSITIES' EDUCATIONAL MISSION AND CONSTITUTIONAL REVIEW

To understand the role of public universities' educational mission in First Amendment cases involving outside (often extremist) speakers on college campuses, we must begin with the U.S. Supreme Court's reasoning in *Widmar v. Vincent*.[8] The case came as the wave of cases applying public forum analysis to government property was rising, and the Court was asked to determine what type of forum existed in the classrooms of a public university (the University of Missouri-Kansas City). In holding that such classrooms are limited public forums, the Court articulated a lower standard of review for constitutional challenges to the use of university classrooms for expressive purposes. Namely, courts in such cases only need to apply a rational-basis level of scrutiny, which merely requires that the universities prove that their restrictions on speech are reasonable in light of the university's educational mission and not based on viewpoint discrimination.[9] Regarding the basis for this reasonableness standard, the Court said:

> [A public] university's mission is education, and decisions of this Court have never denied a university's authority to impose reasonable regulations compatible with that mission upon the use of its campus and facilities. We have not held, for example, that a campus must make all of its facilities equally available to students and nonstudents alike, or that a university must grant free access to all of its grounds or buildings.[10]

In short, the Court held that universities have the right "to make academic judgments as to how best to allocate scarce resources."[11]

Since *Widmar*, lower courts have relied on the reasonableness standard when adjudicating challenges to public universities' management of their limited or non-public forums. In doing so, courts have relied on various definitions of a university's mission to determine reasonableness. Most definitions cite educational goals or functions. For some, the mission is rather basely described as being "primarily pedagogical,"[12] but most courts frame the mission in loftier terms, such as a university's mission being about "intellectual enrichment and research."[13] At least one court used a very broad definition of educational mission: "the fundamental mission of the University [is] protecting its relationship with its students."[14] But the most common theme was for courts to consider not just what universities' missions were, but how they could best be fulfilled. One concurring judge on the U.S. Court of Appeals for the Fourth Circuit wrote, "Certainly, the most fundamental concern of a university is to provide the optimum conditions for learning."[15] In the context of allowing outside speakers access to the university's marketplace of ideas, the notion of "optimum conditions" begets refusal. As the U.S. Court of Appeals for the Eighth Circuit put it, "A university's purpose, its traditional use, and the government's intent with respect to the property is quite different because a university's function is not to provide a forum for all persons to talk about all topics at all times. Rather, a university's mission is education and the search for knowledge."[16] The U.S. Court of Appeals for the Fourth Circuit relied on some more poetic language in defining the scope of the educational mission and attempts to preserve it:

> The state college is dedicated to the pursuit of vigorous debate in a halcyon educational setting. To that end, the Board of Regents, and the college itself, have taken rather commendable steps to open the campus, allowing both on- and off-campus groups the use of school facilities for educational and cultural activities. However, the college fastidiously has avoided transforming the campus area into an unlimited arena for charitable, political, or commercial solicitation. It had a right to take steps to safeguard the traditional academic atmosphere.[17]

The U.S. Court of Appeals for the Ninth Circuit echoed the Fourth Circuit in holding that a university "may preserve such tranquility as the facilities' central purpose requires. . . . [A] university [must] have the power to foster an atmosphere and conditions in which its educational mission can be carried out."[18] This case did not involve an extreme speaker, but rather a person who was not part of the university community who challenged on First Amendment grounds a restraining order the school placed on him after he was cited for stalking two female students. In upholding the constitutionality of the order restricting the person's access to the public campus, the court held, "Not only must a university have the power to foster an atmosphere and conditions in which its educational mission can be carried out, it also has a duty to protect its students by imposing reasonable regulations on the conduct of those who come onto campus."[19]

We do not seek to extend the court's language of "protecting students" to the context of managing extreme speakers. For one, the court here connects protection with conduct (such as stalking), not speech. More importantly, as we noted above, our purpose in articulating universities' ability to manage extreme speakers is not based on an abstract goal of "protecting" students, whether physically or emotionally. Rather, we cite the language of the Ninth Circuit here to note that reasonable concerns for safety in the context of restrictions on outside speakers can be consistent with a university's mission, particularly given the scarce resources universities have to work with to ensure safety. As the U.S. Court of Appeals for the Eleventh Circuit put it, "Maintaining safety, efficiency, and order on campus are crucial to the furtherance of the University's mission of providing a proper educational environment."[20] As long as a public university does not kowtow to an angry mob of students seeking to enact a heckler's veto on a controversial outside speaker, then a policy on how that university marshals scarce security resources to advance its mission to promote a marketplace of ideas free from *physical* harm would almost certainly be considered reasonable.

Judge James Dennis of the U.S. Court of Appeals for the Fifth Circuit, in a 2010 opinion dissenting to that court's upholding the constitutionality of several policies of a public university designed to restrict outside speakers, articulated several aspects of a public university's mission that might rise to significant state interests: "(1) maintaining public safety, (2) preventing the disruption of education, (3) conserving the university's resources, and (4) fostering diversity."[21] The first three of these interests we have seen so far. The fourth is new, and has served as the catalyst for many recent First Amendment controversies. Several other courts have also identified fostering diversity and preventing discrimination as making up part of a university's reasonable mission.[22] As will be discussed below, fostering diversity and preventing discrimination are not trivial—they are part of an existential crisis that public universities face as the nation's demographics and social values change. We do not seek to brush them aside, just as we do not seek to make them sufficient criteria on their own for meeting the reasonableness standard governing public universities' ability to manage speech. We point them out here for two reasons. First, simply put, they exist, and courts have recognized them as significant as they pertain to public universities' educational mission. Second, we believe that they should form a part of the calculus in the narrow context we highlight here of public universities' ability to manage their marketplace of ideas when confronted with extreme outside speakers.

It is important to point out that courts have not been unanimous either in their definition of a public university's mission or in their application of that mission to First Amendment issues. The Fifth Circuit's Judge Dennis, for one, argued in his dissenting opinion that freedom of expression must be afforded more weight in the calculus of determining the reasonableness of a university's mission:

> By concluding that a university must be allowed to regulate expressive conduct which runs directly counter to its mission, I do not mean to imply that a university has the unrestricted power to silence entirely certain perspectives. I wholeheartedly believe that the free exchange of ideas and debate are fundamental to a place of learning. Yet, they comprise only part of a university's mission and must be balanced against a university's other interests, especially those interests which rise to the level of constitutional significance.[23]

Other courts have gone further, holding that an unfettered marketplace of ideas is central to a university's mission. Indeed, the U.S. Supreme Court held that "student life in its many dimensions includes the necessity of wide-ranging speech and inquiry and that student expression is an integral part of the University's educational mission."[24] Lower courts have zeroed in further on the instrumental purpose of free speech for fulfilling universities' mission. According to one court, "the very mission of higher education is to challenge basic values instilled during childhood at a time when an individual student has the intellectual maturity to choose between competing beliefs."[25] That same court concluded, "the very mission of the University is to expose developing young adults to a universe of new ideas and beliefs, most of which the University claims no special allegiance to."[26] The U.S. Court of Appeals for the Third Circuit focused on the contrapositive of protecting speech on campuses, holding that "the chilling of protected speech in a university setting . . . is harmful to the core mission of the university."[27] Another court went even further, tying the protection of extreme speech to the development of students' character and fortitude:

> In short, controversial and sometimes offensive ideas and viewpoints are central to the educational mission of universities. It follows that university students cannot thrive without a certain thickness of skin that allows them to engage with expressions that might cause "distress" or "discomfort" . . . . The coddling of the nation's young adults by proscribing any expression on a university campus that is likely to be distressing or discomforting does not protect "the work...of the school;" such rules frustrate the mission of the university.[28]

Some courts have shown a willingness to defer to universities' interests in fulfilling their educational mission, yet have held that policies in place to uphold them were too vague, overly broad, or placing too much unbridled discretion over policing speech in the hands of one administrator. In holding that a public university failed to meet its burden in defending its speech policies, the U.S. Court of Appeals for the Sixth Circuit noted that the university had "not specified the 'significant interests'" behind its policy or "elaborated on an 'educational mission.' They have not explained how the policy at issue maintains order or prevents interruption of an educational mission."[29]

We do not disagree with the argument that free speech is a major part of (if not central to) the educational mission of public universities. What's more, the courts that upheld universities' management of outside speakers would also not disagree with that argument. It is even possible that courts upholding universities' policies have been somewhat "myopic."[30] The central question is what the marketplace of ideas at these institutions should look like, or rather, how public universities can (peculiarly) create them.

The best place to start answering that question is the case from whence Justice Brennan gave us the line about classrooms peculiarly being marketplaces of ideas: *Keyishian v. Regents of the University of the State of New York*.[31] Here, the Court struck down a New York law allowing public universities to require their faculty members to sign a statement averring they were not members of the Communist Party. Writing for the majority and citing Judge Learned Hand, Justice Brennan held that "[t]he Nation's future depends upon leaders trained through wide exposure to that robust exchange of ideas which discovers truth out of a multitude of tongues, [rather] than through any kind of authoritative selection."[32]

Keyishian thus made an integral connection between diversity of viewpoints and the robust exchange of ideas. In doing so, the Court applied the seldom-used affirmative First Amendment theory. Rather than conceiving of the First Amendment as exclusively granting individuals "freedom from" government interference with their expression (as is the main thrust of negative First Amendment theory), affirmative theory sees government as playing an important (if not essential) role in facilitating the robust participation of a multitude of speakers in the name of democratic self-governance (i.e., granting them a "freedom to" speak on matters of public concern).[33] These two schools of thought are best distinguished in terms of how they conceive of the marketplace of ideas metaphor. Negative theory sees the marketplace of ideas as the domain of rational individuals, and no idea should be prevented from entering that marketplace to compete for acceptance in an arena where human reason is the only referee. Affirmative theory does not negate the central role of human reason in judging the validity of ideas, but it sees the marketplace as a venue that should be regulated to varying degrees (depending on the context) by some government entity in a way that enhances the robustness of the discourse that takes place within that venue. These two attributes—placing faith in government actors' ability to manage the marketplace of ideas, and the vague nature of both the goals and standards cited as reasons to manage it—often become fatal flaws for affirmative theory in a legal and political culture based on viewpoint neutrality.[34]

However, in certain contexts, affirmative theory ends up being both constitutionally sound and politically desirable. One of these contexts is broadcast regulation. In *Metromedia v. FCC*,[35] the Supreme Court upheld the constitutionality of an FCC policy designed to increase the number of minority owners of broadcast licenses.[36] Extolling the social benefits of the policy, Justice Brennan wrote:

> [T]he diversity of views and information on the airwaves serves important First Amendment values. . . . The benefits of such diversity are not limited to the members of minority groups who gain access to the broadcasting industry by virtue of the ownership policies; rather, the benefits redound to all members of the viewing and listening audience.

Justice Brennan's opinion underscores one of the key characteristics of affirmative theory: speakers who may not have been able to access the marketplace in the absence of state action are given privileged treatment through state action—possibly, though not necessarily, at the expense of speakers who could access the marketplace without state action—yet the marketplace of ideas becomes richer as a result, allowing the benefits of such policies to be felt broadly.

Another area in which affirmative First Amendment theory informs doctrine (one closer to the focus of this chapter) is in the area of affirmative action in the context of university admissions. In *Regents of the University of California v. Bakke*,[37] a fractured Court held that the University of California-Davis Medical School's use of race as one criterion for admissions, in general, was constitutional, even if its specific program of using a quota system for admitting minority students was not.[38] Citing *Keyishian*'s "truth out of a multitude of tongues" maxim, Justice Lewis Powell wrote that the UC-Davis Medical School had a First Amendment interest in maintaining its affirmative action program for admissions.[39] The Court again cited to the "multitude of tongues" principle from *Keyishian* and the notion that a diverse student population contributes to a "robust exchange of ideas" in *Grutter v. Bollinger*,[40] holding that the University of Michigan Law School's policy of using race as one of many factors in its admissions process did not violate the Due Process Clause of the Fourteenth Amendment.[41] In the Court's most recent ruling on affirmative action in college admissions, upholding the University of Texas' policy of considering race as one of many factors germane to admission, the Court did not cite *Keyishian* but rather added more power to the concept of a university's mission.[42] Justice Anthony Kennedy wrote of the policy:

> A university is in large part defined by those intangible qualities which are incapable of objective measurement but which make for greatness. Considerable deference is owed to a university in defining those intangible characteristics, like student body diversity, that are central to its identity and educational mission. . . . In striking this sensitive balance, public universities, like the States themselves, can serve as laboratories for experimentation.[43]

Put in terms of the marketplace metaphor, the university has the authority to determine who has access (which, for students, means both buyers and sellers) to the marketplace of ideas that it fosters. This has been true since before *Bakke*, *Grutter*, and *Fisher*. As Professor Clay Calvert put it, "entrance and access to the university marketplace of ideas is not free—it is limited by entrance requirements and admissions policies, as well as by physical classroom and dormitory space capacities."[44] Diversity of students is just one of the many ways that the university exercises its freedom to define how it shapes the marketplace of ideas that arises therein.[45] Once these students are on campus, the university further has the freedom to determine how that marketplace is structured, both inside and outside the classroom. As the Supreme Court put it, "a university may determine that its mission is well served if students have the means to engage in dynamic discussions of philosophical, religious, scientific, social, and political subjects in their extracurricular campus life outside the lecture hall."[46]

This view from affirmative theory makes sense in the context of the categorization of most property on public universities as limited or non-public forums. Professor Robert Post offers a helpful interpretation of affirmative theory in such a context, which we borrow here. Post sees *Widmar v. Vincent* as "plainly recogniz[ing] that the university was invested with managerial authority to regulate speech as necessary for the attainment of institutional ends": its educational mission.[47] Post's interpretation does not suggest that public universities would enjoy unfettered discretion on who gets access to their marketplace of ideas. Rather, constitutional scrutiny would be invoked, Post argues, "when members of the general public bring the scope of managerial authority into question."[48] Here, that authority is rooted in public universities' educational missions. To better understand the position of public universities in managing their marketplace of ideas, we must look to how universities define their missions.

THE MEANING OF UNIVERSITIES' MISSIONS

A full account of the nature of universities today and throughout history is beyond the scope of this chapter. Suffice it to say that the role of universities in society has changed a lot over the last couple hundred years. The Founders of the United States saw universities as the essential vehicles through which "the republican values of liberty and self-government were to be reinforced in young people."[49] Such a role broke with traditional European (and namely British) conceptions of universities as conservative institutions devoted to the transmission of traditional knowledge and values to the elite, and instead built a new model that valued the creation of new knowledge through free inquiry.[50] This model gave universities a more public-facing (even if still elitist) mission, whereby "free inquiry . . . manifested in the education of citizens and the provision of knowledge to inform public discussion."[51] In modern terms, a public university's mission was no longer "to instill orthodoxy; it is to encourage inquiry and debate in the unfettered marketplace of ideas."[52] This public mission accelerated after the 1862 Morrill Land-Grant Act, through which the federal government granted newly claimed land to states to establish colleges designed to enrich the agricultural and mechanical arts. The mission of states' flagship land-grant universities that emerged from this law has been threefold: training students in skilled labor, applied research, and democratization.[53] However, as these large public institutions have expanded, so too have their mission. Today, "a proliferation of purposes challenges universities to achieve organizational structures in which the connections among these components become real advantages, not just sources of confusion or complexity."[54]

In the threefold mission of advancing skilled labor, research, and democratization, the first two prongs are self-explanatory. The core definition of the goal of democratization is up for debate. Public universities have fostered the mission of democratization by "anchor[ing] the public sphere of civil society in its debates about key social issues."[55] Hence, freedom of expression appears at the center of this mission. Historically, public universities have also democratized the nation economically, as they have offered millions of Americans from modest means a vehicle of class transcendence.[56] This mission is challenged more and more today as financing a college education falls less on the state and more on students and their families, exacerbating the wealth gap among Americans.[57] To stanch this trend, public universities have sought to position themselves as more open (at least on paper) to fostering the goals of diversity and inclusion. The key question becomes whether public universities can achieve both goals within the same broad mission of democratization.

To better understand this conflict, we examined mission statements from dozens of public universities. Mission statements, whether for companies or universities, are "simple statement[s] of purpose" that "provide a more publicized mission that serves as a portrayal of the organization."[58] In that sense, they mean everything. However, mission statements, particularly at public universities, simply serve "as a collection of stock phrases that are either excessively vague or unrealistically aspirational or both."[59] In that sense, they mean nothing. Indeed, in our analysis, we saw incredible variation: some mission statements are only a short sentence, while others include several sections; some relied mostly on public relations buzzwords, while others read like an academic lecture about what a good education could provide. Nevertheless, as we noted above, the goal of this evidence is to build a better understanding of how public universities conceive of their educational missions today so that we can appreciate their unique positions as institutions equipped to guide public discourse in American democracy.

In our analysis, we found four key themes: social responsibility, inclusion and diversity, knowledge-seeking, and the marketplace of ideas. The first (and overwhelmingly most common) theme, social responsibility, centers on the role of public colleges and universities as laboratories for democracy and civic engagement. As defined by Oregon State University, for example, social responsibility means to "contribute to society's intellectual, cultural, spiritual and economic progress and well-being to the maximum possible extent."[60] Institutions emphasizing this theme regularly describe themselves as a training ground for public dialogue, or a resource that provides value to a healthy democratic society and produces "enlightened citizens," as the University of New Mexico puts it.[61] Common virtues listed throughout this theme include leadership, integrity, stewardship, and service. It is common for institutions to emphasize that in order to build a better society, students must learn that rights come with corresponding duties and obligations. As Middle Tennessee State University expresses it, this helps students "understand the proper role of free expression."[62] This framing does not put community rights and individual rights into conflict, but rather sees these rights as being indelibly linked.

There is also a strong tendency within this theme to tie social responsibility to the mission posed by being public and/or land-grant institutions, often referred to as "heritage." Auburn University provides arguably the strongest definition of what being a land-grant institution means, writing: "Land-grant universities would provide practical solutions to pressing societal problems and provide higher education to a much broader segment of American citizenry. . . . [W]e must never lose sight of the important educational, research and service responsibilities inherent in our land-grant lineage."[63] Elsewhere, the University of Massachusetts-Amherst writes that "the original 'agricultural and mechanical' focus [of land-grant institutions] has broadened into nearly every aspect of modern life and into a larger obligation to the community we serve."[64] The scope of social responsibility is occasionally described exclusively at the state or geographical region, but more commonly begins there and ends on a global scale.

Social responsibility also often positions the university or college as the regulator of student behavior—and possibly even speech. For instance, Boise State University, which has everything related to its mission on a page labeled "Values," writes: "[M]embership in the campus community is a privilege and requires its members to conduct themselves ethically with integrity, . . . demonstrate civility, abide by norms of decorum, and adhere to the principles of civil discourse."[65] This is clearly different from the American public sphere where membership is a right that does not hinge on any preconditions. Institutions that took a maximalist approach to social responsibility generally follow mentions of freedom of expression with calls for corresponding duties. A prime example is Marshall University describing itself as an "Open Community uncompromisingly protecting freedom of thought, belief and expression," while also considering itself a "Civil Community treating all individuals and groups with consideration, decency, and respect, and expressing disagreements in rational ways," and a "Responsible Community accepting obligations and following behavioral guidelines designed to support the common good."[66]

Concern for fostering inclusion and diversity represents a second key theme prominent throughout most of the mission statements. The fact that this concern was rather common reflects the growing trend among public universities to expand their missions to become more welcoming for students of color (or, at least, appear to do so). Some, such as the University of Kansas, also mention a goal of fostering "intellectual diversity,"[67] but most statements focus on cultural and racial diversity. This multiculturalism is often made out to be distinct from politics. The University of Connecticut sought to undercut political critiques by positioning diversity "not as a keyword for token inclusion of the underrepresented, but as a commitment to fostering a welcoming environment in which all individuals can achieve their fullest potential."[68] Diversity is seen throughout as both an end in itself and as a means to excellence, a way to strengthen other virtues. Toleration is sometimes considered a goal and other times something to move beyond to achieve a richer pluralism and acceptance of differences. While some terms such as creative expression, cooperation, equitable treatment, and supportive environment are used, most of the weight of inclusion and diversity is placed on the virtue of respect. For example, in the University of Missouri's statement of values, "[R]espect is essential for nurturing the free and open discourse, exploration and creative expression that characterize a university. . . . Respect is demonstrated by a commitment to act ethically, to welcome difference and to engage in open exchange about both ideas and decisions."[69] Other institutions are more succinct: Louisiana Tech University, for one, states that it "adhere[s] to the equal opportunity provisions of federal and civil rights laws, and does not discriminate."[70]

Many institutions make it clear that violation of their policies would result in sanction because they are a direct threat to their mission, as seen in the University of North Florida's "Statement of Unity."[71] Georgia Tech takes a maximalist approach and includes a separate long ethics section that has multiple components but almost entirely centers around how students should behave in order to respect diversity.[72] Similar stances also often coincide with a positive emphasis on mediating, reconciling, and resolving conflicts that arise due to the long histories of discrimination, with SUNY-Albany even going as far as to emphasize "put[ting] into practice the restorative principle."[73] Diversity is repeatedly described as requiring consideration of context as well as intended and unintended consequences, and statements often include a list of protected classes of people. This approach ranged from simply including a diversity statement below their mission statement to listing the indigenous peoples who used to occupy their current location (as done by the University of Alaska-Anchorage[74]), or underlining institutional identity vis-à-vis protected classes (as seen in Delaware State University labeling itself a Historically Black University,[75] and New Mexico State University describing itself as a Hispanic-Serving institution[76]). Colorado State and Missouri State embrace diversity as a form of "social justice."[77]

The third theme revolves around an institution's knowledge-seeking function. Within this framework, producing research, scholarship, and advancement/dissemination of knowledge through teaching are common goals. The University of Mississippi outlined in the first point of their institutional philosophy that its "identity and purpose [is] fundamentally academic."[78] Knowledge is occasionally outlined as a humanistic end in itself, something that enriches lifelong learning, and includes, as Ohio University writes, "activities both inside and outside the classroom."[79] The University of Pittsburgh provides a common metaphor for describing knowledge-seeking as engaging in "scholarly activities that advance learning through the extension of the frontiers of knowledge and creative endeavor."[80] Knowledge for knowledge's sake is most regularly embodied in the virtue of discovery. As the University of Missouri avows: "Discovery often fractures existing world views and requires acceptance of uncertainty and ambiguity. Therefore, the university must support all its members in this lifelong process that is both challenging and rewarding."[81]

Knowledge is far more commonly framed as a means to tangibly improve the world by applying it to societal problems. In this mode, the common virtues are innovation and entrepreneurship. Even those, such as Indiana University, that outline the "search for truth" as a value then go on to include knowledge's solutions-based characteristics, writing that another core value is the "application of knowledge and discovery to advance the quality of life and economy of the state, the region, and the world."[82] This knowledge-as-means can also be seen in Auburn University's claim that its "duty is to enable our students, graduates, faculty and partners to transform the fruits of our research and scholarship into products, methods, and services that meet our communities' most pressing needs."[83] Similarly, Michigan State University writes that its mission is to conduct "research of the highest caliber that seeks to answer questions and create solutions in order to expand human understanding and make a positive difference."[84] Commonly, there is talk of how critical thinking skills can help meet the specific and unique challenges of the twenty-first century, environmental sustainability being the most popular issue. This is often met with calls for cross-disciplinary collaboration.

The final theme is the marketplace of ideas. Though the term "marketplace," itself, is never used, many institutions referred to a free or open exchange of ideas. Perhaps surprisingly, this theme is the least common of the four themes identified in this analysis. The central notion of this theme is that without free inquiry and debate, human knowledge and experience will be limited, and thus students should encounter a wide range of ideas in and out of the classroom. A large number of public colleges and universities tie their institutional mission in some way to freedom of expression. Some are explicit and specific, such as the University of California, Berkeley directly mentioning its role in the Free Speech Movement in 1964.[85] Some are broader and more ambiguous, such as Kansas State University's statement that it creates "an atmosphere of open inquiry and academic freedom."[86]

Since the goal of fostering a marketplace of ideas can be in tension with the goal of nurturing diversity and inclusion, it is regularly tempered with calls to be equally paired with the virtue of respect and/or civility that are central to the previous two themes. However, Purdue University, in its lengthy section on "Commitment to Freedom of Expression" (adopted from the University of Chicago's renowned "Statement on Free Expression"[87]), directly addresses this conflict between free speech and fostering inclusivity and identifies a winner: "It is not the proper role of the University to attempt to shield individuals from ideas and opinions they find unwelcome, disagreeable, or even deeply offensive. [C]oncerns about civility and mutual respect can never be used as a justification for closing off discussion of ideas, however offensive or disagreeable those ideas may be to some members of our community."[88] This represents the purest marketplace of ideas language found throughout public university missions, explicitly locating freedom of expression as a value that trumps social responsibility and diversity. This cleanly maps onto the previously outlined negative view of free speech that centers on a "freedom from" intervention and relies on human reason for regulation.

Most universities commonly appear to have trouble reconciling free speech and inclusivity, as their mission statements rely heavily on qualifying statements or vague language. The University of Hawaii at Mānoa expresses its dedication to an "ethical learning environment characterized by a free exchange of ideas."[89] The University of Nebraska–Lincoln writes that it "believe[s] in the freedom of speech, and encourage[s] the civil and respectful expression of ideas and opinions."[90] The University of Central Florida cites its commitment to "the free expression of ideas, the equality of all people, and the dignity of the individual."[91] The University of California, Los Angeles writes that it is "committed to academic freedom in its fullest terms: We value open access to information, free and lively debate conducted with mutual respect for individuals, and freedom from intolerance."[92] Colorado State University consecutively lists commitments to "promote freedom of expression" and "demonstrate inclusiveness and diversity" as core values.[93] Similarly, North Carolina State University lists as its values "Freedom—of thought and expression" immediately followed by "Respect—for cultural and intellectual diversity."[94]

Michigan State University's "Statement on Free Speech" represents one of the most straightforward attempts to strike a balance between the marketplace of ideas and responsibilities, underlining reciprocal duties that correspond to free expression rights. It writes that "the University always must strive to strike that balance between maximum freedom and necessary order which best promotes its basic purposes by providing the environment most conducive to the many faceted activities of instruction, research, and service."[95] MSU also outlines specific policies regarding obstruction and disruption of educational activities that appear to provide precise guidelines when a freedom of expression issue occurs.[96]

None of the public colleges and universities that we searched emphasize every one of these themes in the same way, pointing to a wide array of missions. Furthermore, these themes are often so interwoven that it is difficult to categorize distinct missions. Nevertheless, the evidence is revealing—the four themes show that many public universities struggle with balancing missions that tend to be at odds with one another: promoting freedom of speech and fostering diversity and inclusion. The evidence also suggests that public universities seek to tailor their peculiar marketplaces of ideas to meet a broad mission of education, free speech, and diversity. Rather than hamstring schools in their attempts, we contend that courts should allow them to do so. That does not mean public universities should get to craft mission statements that give them a free pass to manage their marketplace of ideas in an arbitrary fashion. Such an approach goes too far and could potentially stifle the free exchange of ideas on campus. Rather, we seek a nuanced approach that properly balances deference to an educational mission with the values of freedom of expression when it comes to the specific challenge of managing extreme and controversial outside speakers. Thus, we turn toward suggesting potential policies that public universities can follow to manage their marketplaces in a way that is consistent with both First Amendment values and public forum doctrine.

MOVING FORWARD

The main argument of this chapter is that public universities should be able to manage the marketplaces of ideas that have (peculiarly) arisen there, thereby playing a leading role in shaping public discourse in American democracy. To this point, our discussion has focused on the theory and doctrine allowing public universities to fulfill such a role. The major question that remains is how public universities should actually fulfill it. Although we do not claim to have the best single specific prescription for how they should do so, we believe that universities must adopt a multifaceted and highly nuanced approach to accomplish this goal, and we sketch out some considerations for such an approach below.

First, public universities must not abandon the importance of freedom of expression to their central educational mission. Indeed, they should continue to embrace free speech and actively encourage it among students, faculty, and staff. In doing so, public universities should also clearly state what First Amendment values they seek to foster. They should come out strongly in favor of both the importance of the marketplace of ideas and the solemn duty they have to ensure that the speech that enters the marketplace best facilitates their educational mission. They should make it clear to their communities that they do not seek to foster freedom for freedom's sake.[97] Rather, they must be transparent about their goal of seeking to actively influence the course of public discourse, and how and why they are trying to do so. Such clear communication also prevents universities from merely paying lip service to free speech. As Professor Harry Chambers put it, "However it defines itself, a university should be honest about its values. A campus that claims to maximize free speech is likely sloganeering."[98]

One suggestion for how public universities can successfully take such a strong and transparent stance is to create an office or standing committee on freedom of expression. Such a body would ideally be made up of senior administrators, as well as the school's general counsel's office, faculty with expertise in the field, staff tasked with implementing policies related to free expression, and student leaders with a robust interest in First Amendment issues. The committee would have the duties of reviewing and revising the university's speech policies, reviewing and managing requests from student groups to bring outside speakers to campus, enforcing the school's speech policies when applicable, and (most important of all) communicating to the university community the values it seeks to uphold through its actions. One goal of creating such an office or committee would be to take the task of governing First Amendment issues out of the hands of an "Office of Student Life," which serves a more general function and may not be in tune with special concerns related to freedom of expression. Another goal of creating such an office would be to remove the risk of giving an administrative office unbridled discretion over the management of speech policies. The mission of such an office should always be to facilitate and encourage robust public discourse on campus. It should act as a more speech-positive alternative to the so-called Bias Assessment and Response Teams (BARTs) now present on many public campuses, whose charge is investigating incidents of hate speech and harassment.[99]

From there, universities should craft policies for managing speech that meet the reasonableness standard articulated above, are narrowly tailored and viewpoint neutral, and offer due process for appeal in a manner that does not place unbridled discretion in one administrative body. Consistent with the precedent highlighted above, a hallmark of these policies would be to distinguish members of the university community and outside speakers. With regard to the former, the university should further distinguish between individual students and student groups that seek official recognition by the university. Individual students should be allowed to participate in the marketplace of ideas and speak their viewpoints however they wish. Consistent with the goals of the limited public forum that it allocates for the recognition of student groups, the university would limit membership to groups that fulfill the educational mission of the school. Through such a policy, the school would easily officially recognize a Campus Republicans club or a Campus Democrats club or a Campus Engineering club, but it would not need to officially recognize a Campus White Supremacist club or a Campus Male Chauvinist club. Such a policy would neither prevent nor punish any student for harboring viewpoints commonly associated with such philosophies. It would neither prevent nor punish a student from *expressing* those views openly in a campus forum; indeed, such a student should be free to face the slings and arrows from his or her fellow students by putting such viewpoints into the marketplace of ideas. The university should simply be allowed to not officially recognize those viewpoints given their incongruency with the school's mission. Furthermore, the university (through the free speech committee proposed above) should actively disavow the speech of such a student, thereby placing its own counter-message into the same marketplace. What's more, it should marshal resources to aid any students who feel legitimately threatened by this student's viewpoints, thereby actively seeking to remedy real harm caused to students without silencing speech in the vague name of "protecting students."

The student group policy would also form the basis for a public university's policy on inviting outside speakers. As Professor Erica Goldberg (author of chapter 9) has argued, "non-student speech . . . is attributable to the student group that has invited the speaker."[100] Such a policy could lower the risk (even if not completely eradicate the possibility) that an extremist speaker would be invited to campus. For instance, a Campus Republicans club would be less likely than a Campus White Supremacists club to request that Richard Spencer be allowed to speak on campus, or a Campus History Nerds club would be less likely than a Campus Holocaust Deniers club to invite David Irving to campus.

The university should be prepared with viewpoint-neutral policies in the event student groups do seek to invite the most extreme speakers to campus. Professor Chambers suggests two criteria for connecting a university's mission with its speech management policies. First, does the speaker advance the university's mission of the pursuit of truth, such that the university could justify investing its scarce resources to support that speaker? For instance, if the History Nerds club sought to officially invite Holocaust denier David Irving, the university could point to its educational mission of the search for truth as justification for denying the invitation of someone who blatantly disregards historical fact. As Professor Chambers suggests, the university would be wasting its precious time and resources on a figure like Irving.[101] Second, Professor Chambers suggests that universities could forge policies for inviting speakers based on objective assessments about the level of academic engagement that a speaker could bring to campus. So, in the event the Campus Republicans sought to officially invite Richard Spencer, the university could consider the type of academic engagement that would transpire at such a speech when weighing its response.[102] Even imagining the most "halcyon" academic discussion between Spencer and one of his critics, the debate would almost certainly devolve into schoolyard taunting ("Whites are the best!" "No, they're not!"). Thus, on the grounds of failing to foster academic engagement—which would fall within the standard of reasonable management of the university's public forums to fulfill its educational mission—the university could justify not inviting him to speak.

Admittedly, there exists a certain class of speaker that seeks to promote controversial viewpoints. On the right are those who harbor ultra-conservative viewpoints, though mostly without endorsing the same extremist ideas of avowed white supremacists. These would be the likes of Pamela Geller, Milo Yiannopoulos, Ann Coulter, and Ben Shapiro, among others. These personae have sparked their share of outrage among progressive college students. On the left are radicals who would advocate for drastic, and sometimes violent, uprisings against the status quo, and some (such as Louis Farrakhan) harbor their own racist ideologies. What's more, political figures of all stripes have all sorts of baggage—from sexual harassment to racist remarks to potential war crimes—that could likewise spark outrage among students. We argue that concern over potential outrage alone does not suffice for a public university to bar such speakers from campus; rather, it would be tantamount to an unconstitutional heckler's veto, whereby angry protesters seek to leverage state action (in the form of a formal prohibition by the university) to censor the speech.[103] In addition, following the criteria suggested by Professor Chambers, a much stronger case could be made for the ability of provocative speakers like these to lead the university community toward truth or to offer fertile ground for academic engagement, which should lead public universities to honor student groups' desires to invite these speakers to campus. However, public universities have a greater degree of leeway in managing the time, place, and manner of speeches by these speakers, so long as their policies and procedures of doing so are content-neutral and consistent with the universities' mission.

One potential option for universities to manage controversial outside speakers is to allocate access to certain facilities based on reasonable concerns related to their educational missions, including concerns for security and management of scarce resources. In a recent law review article, one of us suggested that the University of Minnesota's act of moving Ben Shapiro's February 2019 speech from a larger, centrally located auditorium to a smaller, more suburban venue on a satellite campus was constitutionally sound given the scarcity of the university's resources for maintaining security in a unique setting (i.e., that included public skyways) where controlling large crowds would prove difficult.[104] Put differently, the university did not silence Shapiro's speech or deny students the right to hear it, but rather managed the time, place, and manner of his speech consistent with its educational mission. As long as the policy affords student groups requesting opportunities for Shapiro-like speakers a system of due process and appeal, such a policy could be an important, constitutionally permissible tool for public universities seeking to manage their marketplace of ideas.

However, such a policy would mean nothing if it does not also come with clear and forceful communication by the university regarding its decision-making in such situations. To put it bluntly, public universities must stop hiding behind opaque policies put in the service of well-intentioned attempts to prevent controversial speakers from speaking on campus. If in the future a university follows Minnesota's lead and moves Ben Shapiro's speech to what is undeniably a more favorable place for the university, even if the move is legally sound, the school should own up to its decision and clearly explain why it was made. It must make a clear connection between how the management of its peculiar marketplace of ideas furthers its mission, and it must make it often.

Our argument is grounded in the notion of a university's mission. However, it also depends on the premise that universities have scarce resources to summon to handle issues related to extremist outside speakers (such as security) and that these resources must be used judiciously in the service of the school's mission. Thus, we argue that universities must have clear policies surrounding the management of its resources in the context of outside speakers. Universities could rely on a range of factors to inform such policies. Professor Goldberg suggests that objective factors, such as the number of audience members attending a talk, the number of entrances and exits to a particular venue, and whether the event is open to the public or only to students, should be used to calculate security costs.[105] Meanwhile, Professor Kenneth Lasson has argued "multifarious exigencies occasioned by controversial speakers," including "the tenor of the times, nature of the forum, current tensions on campus, and the size and makeup of the student body," could guide university decision-making over marshaling its resources for security.[106] However universities build their policies, the important point is that the public cannot take the schools at their word that they must move a speaker to a different venue to mitigate security costs. The schools must show their work.

The foregoing are rough sketches of how public universities might maximize the power of their missions in managing their marketplace of ideas in the face of challenges from extremist speakers. We do not purport that they are the final word on this endeavor, nor do we suggest that these are policies that universities must follow. Indeed, a public university could extend an invitation to Richard Spencer and make a convincing argument that doing so is within the purview of its educational mission. We do not seek to deny universities this right, though we would openly question any university's judgment in concluding that inviting Spencer would further its educational mission given that white supremacist views are often used as tools to silence the speech of others, and do not simply serve as another voice of contention in the marketplace of ideas. Rather, we seek only to offer guidance for universities to do more with their missions.

CONCLUSION

Extreme and controversial speakers pose a major challenge to public colleges and universities, and they are not exiting the national dialogue anytime soon.[107] These schools should equip themselves with the tools to manage this challenge. Citing vapid First Amendment platitudes to deny them these tools, framing the debate on free speech on campus in starkly dichotomous terms, or lumping together all free speech issues campuses face rather than treating each on its own merits is not constructive. What's more, these tactics neglect both the current state of the law regarding deference to public universities' educational missions and the multifold and complex nature of such missions as defined by the schools, themselves. We argue that evidence from courts and schools' mission statements, as well as interpretations from scholars and guidance from affirmative First Amendment theory, all point toward one conclusion: public colleges and universities can and should have the right to manage the marketplaces of ideas that, organically and peculiarly, have emerged there. This is not an "anti-speech" argument, as per the rules of the dichotomously framed debate. On the contrary, our argument seeks to bring a nuanced discussion of the values of freedom of expression into the public discourse. One likely outcome of such an effort is instilling greater faith in the role that the First Amendment plays in bringing about positive change in society, something that has been on the wane of late.[108]

From a legal perspective, our position passes constitutional muster. It grants public universities the power to leverage their scarce resources in effective ways, following content-neutral policies, in an effort to further a substantial state interest that courts have long recognized: the schools' educational mission. It is narrowly tailored, focusing only on speakers coming from outside the university community. University policies based on our position would set up a system of substantive due process that avoids amassing unbridled discretion over judgments on speech-related issues in the hands of one administrator or office. From a policy perspective, our position merits attention. It offers universities an opportunity to meet their multiple missions and juggle the needs of their many stakeholders. It gives universities more power to stand up to extremist outside speakers like Richard Spencer, which can enhance their ability to create environments in which students of color can flourish. Indeed, we believe our position can bolster the institution of public higher education by enhancing both the legal and political status of universities' educational missions.

NOTES

1. Suzanne B. Goldberg, "Free Expression on Campus: Mitigating the Costs of Contentious Speakers," *Harvard Journal of Law & Public Policy* 41, no. 1, 163–86 (2018): 167–68 ("Although college and university campuses are hardly the only forums where vigorous debate can take place, they remain among the few locations in American society today where those debates occur in person.").

2. See, e.g., Jeremy Bauer-Wolf, "Reclaiming Their Campuses," *Inside Higher Ed* (March 21, 2018), https://www.insidehighered.com/news/2018/03/21/colleges-changing-their-policies-after-visits-controversial-speakers.

3. See, e.g., Greg Lukianoff and Jonathan Haidt, *The Coddling of the American Mind: How Good Intentions and Bad Ideas Are Setting Up a Generation for Failure* (New York: Penguin-Random House, 2018).

4. *Keyishian v. Regents of the University of the State of New York*, 385 U.S. 589, 603 (1967) (emphasis added).

5. We say "alternative" because the perspective is not new, but rather underappreciated. *See, e.g.*, Henry L. Chambers, Jr., "Curating Campus Speakers," *University of Richmond Law Review* 53, no. Online Edition (May 2019) (arguing that public universities have extensive, though not unlimited, authority to thoughtfully manage their resources to "curate" outside speakers); Vikram David Amar and Alan E. Brownstein, "A Close-up, Modern Look at First Amendment Academic Freedom Rights of Public College Students and Faculty," *Minnesota Law Review* 101, no. 5 (2017): 1955 (suggesting that public universities can "orchestrate" their invitations for outside speakers); Brett G. Johnson and Shane C. Epping, "Forum Delegation: The Birth and Transposition of a New Approach to Public Forum Doctrine," *Hastings Communication & Entertainment Law Journal* 42, no. 1 (2019) (arguing that public universities have the constitutionally sound power to allocate use of their many public forums to manage controversial speakers).

6. Chambers, "Curating Campus Speakers," 3 ("Those who support allowing all controversial speakers to speak on campus tend to be treated as pro-free speech warriors. Those who support preventing some controversial speakers from speaking on campus tend to be painted as anti-free speech. That framing is not particularly helpful.").

7. Derek P. Langhauser, "Free and Regulated Speech on Campus: Using Forum Analysis for Assessing Facility Use, Speech Zones, and Related Expressive Activity," *Journal of College & University Law* 31, no. 3 (2006): 488–89 ("courts are more likely to look favorably upon regulation of external speakers since they are not part

of the immediate community and have, therefore, a less compelling right to be heard in that community.")

8. 454 U.S. 263 (1981).

9. Langhauser, "Free and Regulated Speech on Campus."

10. *Widmar v. Vincent*, 267.

11. Ibid., 276.

12. *Johnston v. University of Pittsburgh of Commonwealth System of Higher Ed.*, 97 F.Supp.3d 657, 668 (W.D. Pa. 2015).

13. *Pugel v. Board of Trustees of the University of Illinois*, 378 F.3d 659, 668 (7th Cir. 2004).

14. *Wozniak v. Adesida*, 368 F.Supp.3d 1217, 1231 (C.D. Ill. 2018).

15. *Iota Xi Chapter of Sigma Chi Fraternity v. George Mason University*, 993 F.2d 386, 395 (4th Cir. 1993) (Murnaghan, J., concurring).

16. *Bowman v. White*, 444 F.3d 967, 978 (8th Cir. 2006).

17. *Glover v. Cole*, 762 F.2d 1197, 1202 (4th Cir. 1995).

18. *Souders v. Lucero*, 196 F.3d 1040, 1045 (9th Cir. 1999).

19. Ibid.

20. *Bloedorn v. Grube*, 631 F.3d 1218, 1240 (11th Cir. 2011).

21. *Sonnier v. Crain*, 613 F.3d 436, 473–74 (5th Cir. 2010) (Dennis, J., concurring in part and dissenting in part).

22. *Lela v. Board of Trustees of Community College Dist. No. 516*, 2015 WL 351243 (N.D. Ill. 2015), 2 (finding reasonable a public community college's "mission to uphold and adhere to the legal requirements for maintaining a non-discriminatory educational environment, free of unlawful hostility."); *Chi Iota Colony of Alpha Epsilon Pi Fraternity v. CUNY*, 502 F.3d 136, 148 (2nd Cir. 2007) (holding that a public university's "interests in applying its non-discrimination policy are substantial.").

23. *Sonnier v. Crain*, 613 F.3d 436, 473–74 (5th Cir. 2010) (Dennis, J., concurring in part and dissenting in part).

24. *Rosenberger v. Rector and Visitors of the University of Virginia*, 515 U.S. 819, 840 (1995).

25. *Tanford v. Brand*, 932 F.Supp. 1139, 1143 (S.D. Ind. 1996).

26. Ibid., 1146.

27. *McCauley v. University of the Virgin Islands*, 618 F.3d 232, 252 (3rd Cir. 2010).

28. *Doe v. Rector and Visitors of George Mason University*, 149 F.Supp.3d 602, 627 (E.D. Va. 2016).

29. *McGlone v. Bell*, 681 F.3d 718, 735 (6th Cir. 2012).

30. Stephen Douglas Bonney, "The University Campus as Public Forum: The Legacy of *Widmar v. Vincent*," *UMKC Law Review* 81, no. 3 (2013): 563.

31. 385 U.S. 589 (1967).

32. Ibid., 603, citing *U.S. v. Associated Press*, 52 F.Supp. 362, 372 (S.D. N.Y. 1943) ("right conclusions are more likely to be gathered out of a multitude of tongues, than through any kind of authoritative selection").

33. See generally, Matthew D. Bunker, *Critiquing Free Speech: First Amendment Theory and the Challenge of Interdisciplinarity* (Mahwah, NJ: Lawrence Erlbaum Associates, 2001), 1–17.

34. Lillian R. Bevier, "Rehabilitating Public Forum Doctrine: In Defense of Categories," *Supreme Court Review* 1992, no. 1 (1992): 113 (arguing that a "chasm separates the agenda of [affirmative theory] from the more modest goals" of negative theory).

35. 497 U.S. 547 (1990).

36. Ibid.

37. 438 U.S. 265 (1978).

38. Ibid.

39. Ibid., 312–13.

40. 539 U.S. 306 (2003).

41. Ibid.

42. *Fisher v. University of Texas-Austin*, 136 S. Ct. 2198 (2016).

43. Ibid., 2214 (internal quotes omitted).

44. Clay Calvert, "Where the Right Went Wrong in Southworth: Underestimating the Power of the Marketplace," *Maine Law Review* 53, no. 1 (2001): 57.

45. See Paul Horwitz, "*Grutter*'s First Amendment," *Boston College Law Review* 46, no. 3 (2005).

46. *Board of Regents of the University of Wisconsin System v. Southworth*, 529 U.S. 217, 233 (2000).

47. Robert C. Post, "Between Governance and Management: The History and Theory of the Public Forum," *UCLA Law Review* 34, nos. 5–6 (1987): 1779.

48. Ibid., 1781. For more on Professor Post's theoretical framework, *see* Robert C. Post, *Constitutional Domains* (Cambridge: Harvard University Press, 1995).

49. John C. Scott, "The Mission of the University: Medieval to Postmodern Transformations," *Journal of Higher Education* 77, no. 1 (2006): 14.

50. Craig Calhoun, "Free Inquiry and Public Mission in the Research University," *Social Research* 76, no. 3 (2009): 902.

51. Ibid., 906.

52. Amar and Brownstein, 1954.

53. Patricia J. Gumport, "Universities as Academic Workplaces," *Daedalus* 126, no. 4 (1997): 116.

54. Calhoun, "Free Inquiry and Public Mission in the Research University," 910.

55. Ibid., 916.

56. Rodney L. Lowman, "Leading the 21st-Century College and University: Managing Multiple Missions and Conflicts of Interest in Higher Education," *The Psychologist-Manager Journal* 13, no. 4 (2010).

57. Kathleen Knight Abowitz, "Imagining Democratic Futures for Public Universities: Education Leadership against Fatalism's Temptations," *Educational Theory* 66, nos. 1–2 (2016).

58. Yvette P. Lopez and William F. Martin, "University Mission Statements and Sustainability Performance," *Business & Society Review* 123, no. 2 (2018): 342.

59. Christopher C. Morphew and Matthew Hartley, "Mission Statements: A Thematic Analysis of Rhetoric Across Institutional Type," *Journal of Higher Education* 77, no. 3 (2006): 457.

60. "Mission, Goals and Values for OSU," *Oregon State University*, https://hr.oregonstate.edu/mission-goals-and-values-osu.

61. "UNM's Mission," *University of New Mexico*, http://www.unm.edu/welcome/mission.html.

62. "Mission Statement," *Middle Tennessee State University*, https://www.mtsu.edu/about/mission.php.

63. "Vision and Mission Statement," *Auburn University*, http://www.auburn.edu/main/welcome/visionandmission.php.

64. "Mission," *University of Massachusetts-Amherst*, https://www.umass.edu/planning/mission.

65. "Statement of Shared Values," *Boise State University*, https://www.boisestate.edu/president/values/statement-of-shared-values/.

66. "Mission, Vision and Creed," *Marshall University*, https://www.marshall.edu/mission/.

67. "Mission," *University of Kansas*, https://chancellor.ku.edu/mission.

68. "Academic Vision," *University of Connecticut*, https://academicvision.uconn.edu/introduction/core-values/.

69. "Mission and Values," *University of Missouri*, https://missouri.edu/mission-values.

70. "Our Mission," *Louisiana Tech University*, https://www.latech.edu/about/mission/.

71. "Mission and Vision Statement," *University of North Florida*, https://www.unf.edu/president/mission_vision.aspx.

72. "Ethics First," *Georgia Institute of Technology*, https://www.gatech.edu/about/ethics.

73. "Mission Statement," *SUNY-Albany*, https://www.albany.edu/communitystandards/mission.php.

74. "Mission, Values, Vision," *University of Alaska-Anchorage*, https://www.uaa.alaska.edu/about/mission-values-vision.cshtml#mission.

75. "Official University Facts," *Delaware State University*, https://www.desu.edu/about/administration/marketing-communications/branding-communications-tool-kit/official-university.

76. "About NMSU," *New Mexico State University*, https://www.nmsu.edu/about_nmsu/index.html.

77. "University Mission, Values, and Guiding Principles," *Colorado State University*, https://catalog.colostate.edu/general-catalog/welcome/mission-values/; "Mission, Vision and Values." *Missouri State University*, https://www.missouristate.edu/about/mission-statement.htm.

78. "Vision, Mission and Core Values," *University of Mississippi*, https://olemiss.edu/aboutum/mission.html.

79. "Mission and Values," *Ohio University*, https://www.ohio.edu/hr/jobs/working-ohio.

80. "Mission Statement," *University of Pittsburgh*, https://www.provost.pitt.edu/faculty-handbook/ch1_mission_stmt.

81. "Mission and Values," *University of Missouri*.

82. "Mission & Vision," *Indiana University*, https://www.iu.edu/about/mission-vision.html.

83. "Vision and Mission Statement," *Auburn University*.

84. "MSU Mission Statement," *Michigan State University*, https://trustees.msu.edu/about/mission.html.

85. "About Berkeley," *University of California, Berkeley*, https://www.berkeley.edu/about.

86. "Kansas State University Mission," *Kansas State University*, https://www.k-state.edu/about/mission/.

87. "Free Expression," *The University of Chicago*, https://freeexpression.uchicago.edu/.

88. "Commitment to Freedom of Expression," *Purdue University*, https://www.purdue.edu/purdue/about/free-speech.php.

89. "Mission and Vision," *University of Hawaii-Mānoa*, https://manoa.hawaii.edu/strategicplan/index.php.

90. "Role, Mission and Values," *University of Nebraska-Lincoln*, https://www.unl.edu/about/role-mission/.

91. "About UCF," *University of Central Florida*, https://catalog.ucf.edu/content.php?catoid=15&navoid=1278.

92. "Mission & Values," *University of California-Los Angeles*, https://www.ucla.edu/about/mission-and-values.

93. "University Mission, Values, and Guiding Principles," *Colorado State University*.

94. "University Mission," *North Carolina State University*, https://leadership.ncsu.edu/university-mission/.

95. "MSU Mission Statement," *Michigan State University*.

96. Ibid.

97. See Morgan N. Weiland, "Expanding the Periphery and Threatening the Core: The Ascendant Libertarian Speech Tradition," *Stanford Law Review* 69, no. 5 (2017): 1418.

98. Chambers, "Curating Campus Speakers," 11.

99. Joseph W. Yockey, "Bias Response on Campus," *Journal of Law & Education* 48, no. 1 (Winter 2019).

100. Erica Goldberg, "Must Universities 'Subsidize' Controversial Ideas? Allocating Security Fees when Student Groups Host Divisive Speakers," *George Mason University Civil Rights Law Journal* 21, no. 3 (2011): 386.

101. Chambers, "Curating Campus Speakers," 12–13 ("debunking already falsified claims wastes the university's most precious resources—the intellectual capacity and time of its constituents. The university's resources should be used on issues that can be reasonably and honestly debated or on topics on which a speaker can shed new light. This is not about ignoring unpopular ideas or supporting orthodoxy, whether conservative or liberal. It is about serving the university's mission.").

102. Ibid., 13.

103. For more on the heckler's veto, *see* Erica Goldberg, "Must Universities 'Subsidize' Controversial Ideas?"; Brett G. Johnson, "The Heckler's Veto: Using First Amendment Theory and Jurisprudence to Understand Current Audience Reactions against Controversial Speech," *Communication Law & Policy* 21, no. 2 (2016); Clay Calvert, "Reconsidering Incitement, Tinker and The Heckler's Veto on College Campuses: Richard Spencer and the Charlottesville Factor," *Northwestern University Law Review* 112, no. Online Edition (2018).

104. Johnson and Epping, "Forum Delegation." As this volume entered its final phase of editing, the U.S. District Court for the District of Minnesota upheld the constitutionality of moving the location of Ben Shapiro's speech by the University of Minnesota. Farrah Mina, "Ben Shapiro Loses Free Speech Lawsuit Againt UMN Over Venue Change," Minnesota Daily (Aug. 30, 2020), https://mndaily.com/261973/news/br-shapiroupdate/.

105. Goldberg, "Must Universities 'Subsidize' Controversial Ideas?," 399.

106. Kenneth Lasson, "Controversial Speakers on Campus: Liberties, Limitations, and Common-Sense Guidelines," *St. Thomas Law Review* 12, no. 1 (1999): 59.

107. Objections to how universities handle these free speech issues has even formed the philosophical foundation for a group of influential commentators that span the political spectrum known as the "Intellectual Dark Web." See Gabriel Parks, "Considering the Purpose of 'An Alternative Sense-Making Collective': A Rhetorical Analysis of the Intellectual Dark Web," *Southern Communication Journal*, 2020.

108. Erik Ugland, "Expanding Media Law and Policy Education: Confronting Power, Defining Freedom, Awakening Participation," *Communication Law & Policy* 24, no. 2 (2019).

Bibliography

"2017 Report on Bias Reporting Systems." Foundation for Individual Rights in Education, https://www.thefire.org/research/publications/bias-response-team-report-2017/report-on-bias-reporting-systems-2017/#12.

"2017 Tennessee Code, Title 49 – Education, Chapter 7 - Postsecondary and Higher Education Generally, Part 24 - Campus Free Speech Protection Act." https://law.justia.com/codes/tennessee/2017/title-49/chapter-7/part-24/.

Abbott, Henry Livermore. *Fallen Leaves: The Civil War Letters of Major Henry Livermore Abbott*. Edited by Robert Garth Scott. Kent State University Press, 1991.

"Abbott Notice of Charge Letter." Foundation for Individual Rights in Education, https://www.thefire.org/abbott-notice-of-charge-letter/.

Abbott v. Pastides, 900 F.3d 160 (4th Cir. 2018).

"About Berkeley." *University of California, Berkeley*, https://www.berkeley.edu/about.

"About NMSU." *New Mexico State University*, https://www.nmsu.edu/about_nmsu/index.html.

"About UCF." *University of Central Florida*, https://catalog.ucf.edu/content.php?catoid=15&navoid=1278.

Abowitz, Kathleen Knight. "Imagining Democratic Futures for Public Universities: Education Leadership Against Fatalism's Temptations." *Educational Theory* 66, nos. 1–2 (April 2016): 181–97.

Abrams v. United States, 250 U.S. 616 (1919).

"Academic Vision." *University of Connecticut*, https://academicvision.uconn.edu/introduction/core-values/.

Adams v. Trustees of the University of North Carolina-Wilmington, 640 F.3d 550 (4th Cir. 2011).

"African 405: The Problem of Whiteness." African Cultural Studies, University of Wisconsin–Madison, https://african.wisc.edu/courses/african-405-the-problem-of-whiteness/.

Ala. Code § 16-68-3 (2020).

Alexander, Evette. "First Amendment Vitals." Knight Foundation, May 13, 2019, https://knightfoundation.org/articles/first-amendment-vitals-gen-z-expression-inclusion.

Allen, Danielle. "The Road To Serfdom: How American Can Become Citizens Again." *The Atlantic,* December 2019, 94–101.

American Freedom Defense Initiative v. Suburban Mobility Authority for Regional Transportation, 698 F.3d 885 (6th Cir. 2012).

"The Alt-Right On Campus: What Students Need to Know." Southern Poverty Law Center, August 10, 2017, https://www.splcenter.org/20170810/alt-right-campus-what-students-need-know.

"Amended Complaint, *Salazar v. JJC*." Foundation for Individual Rights in Education, March 27, 2018, https://www.thefire.org/amended-complaint-salazar-v-jjc-pdf/.

An Act Relating to Higher Education. Fla. Laws Ch. 2018-4, SB4. https://www.flsenate.gov/Session/Bill/2018/0004.

"AN ACT to create 36.02 and 38.05 of the statutes; relating to: free speech at the University of Wisconsin and technical college systems and granting rule-making authority." https://www.wispolitics.com/wp-content/uploads/2017/05/170503VukmirJarchowBill.pdf.

Ariz. Rev. Stat. §§ 15-1864 (2019).

Ark. Code Ann. § 6-60-1003 (2019).

Astor, Aaron. "Partisanship is an American tradition—and good for democracy." *The Washington Post*, July 12, 2017, https://www.washingtonpost.com/news/made-by-history/wp/2017/07/12/partisanship-is-an-american-tradition-and-good-for-democracy/.

Axson-Flynn v. Johnson, 356 F.3d 1277 (10th Cir. 2004).

B.H. ex rel. Hawk v. Easton Area School District, 725 F.3d 293 (3d Cir. 2013).

Bachellar v. Maryland, 397 U.S. 564, 567 (1970).

Barrett, Lisa Feldman. "When Is Speech Violence?" *The New York Times*, July 14, 2017, https://www.nytimes.com/2017/07/14/opinion/sunday/when-is-speech-violence.html.

Barnette v. West Va. Board of Education, 319 U.S. 624 (1943).

Barshay, Jill. "Calculating Faculty Bias Against Conservative Students." *The Hechinger Report,* June 24, 2019, https://hechingerreport.org/calculating-faculty-bias-against-conservative-students/.

Bauer, Scott and Todd Richmond. "Wisconsin Assembly Passes Bill on Campus Free Speech." U.S. News, June 22, 2017, https://www.usnews.com/news/best-states/wisconsin/articles/2017-06-21/wisconsin-assembly-to-vote-on-campus-free-speech.

Bauer-Wolf, Jeremy. "Free Speech Advocate Silenced." *Inside Higher Ed*, October 6, 2017, https://www.insidehighered.com/news/2017/10/06/william-mary-students-who-shut-down-aclu-event-broke-conduct-code.

———. "Free Speech Laws Mushroom in the Wake of Campus Protests." *Insider Higher Ed*, September 16, 2019. https://www.insidehighered.com/news/2019/09/16/states-passing-laws-protect-college-students-free-speech.

———. "Lukewarm Embrace of Free Speech." *Inside Higher Ed*, October 11, 2017, https://www.insidehighered.com/news/2017/10/11/students-opinions-free-speech-divided.

———. "No End in Sight for Campus Free Speech Battles." *Inside Higher Ed*, March 8, 2018, https://www.insidehighered.com/news/2018/03/08/administrators-still-waging-campus-free-speech-wars.

———. "Reclaiming Their Campuses." *Inside Higher Ed*, March 21, 2018, https://www.insidehighered.com/news/2018/03/21/colleges-changing-their-policies-after-visits-controversial-speakers.

———. "Spencer Gets to Speak." *Insider Higher Ed*, October 20, 2017, https://www.insidehighered.com/news/2017/10/20/spencers-talk-florida-met-protests-and-attempts-shout-him-down.

Beauchamp, Zack. "Milo Yiannopoulos: Breitbart's Star Provocateur and Trump Champion, Explained." *Vox,* February 20, 2017, https://www.vox.com/2016/4/4/11355876/milo-yiannopoulos.

Beauharnais v. Illinois, 343 U.S. 250 (1952).

Beck-Coon, Marieke Tuthill. "After Two-Plus Years in Court, Students for Justice in Palestine wins Recognition at Fordham." Foundation for Individual Rights in Education, August 7, 2019, https://www.thefire.org/after-two-plus-years-in-court-students-for-justice-in-palestine-wins-recognition-at-fordham/.

Benford, Robert D. and David A. Snow. "Framing Processes and Social Movements: An Overview and Assessment." *Annual Review of Sociology* 26 (January 2000): 611–39.

Bennett, John. "The Totalitarian Ideological Origins of Hate Speech Regulation." *Capital University Law Review* 46 (Winter 2018): 23–123.

Bennett, John T. "The Harm in Hate Speech: A Critique of the Empirical and Legal Bases of Hate Speech Regulation." *Hastings Constitutional Law Quarterly* 43 (Spring 2016): 445–536.

Berenson, Tessa. "1 in 5: Debating the Most Controversial Sexual Assault Statistic." *Time*, June 27, 2014, http://time.com/2934500/1-in-5%E2%C80%82campus-sexual-assault-statistic.

Berlatsky, Noah. "How Right-Wing Media Has Tried to Stifle Student Speech at Evergreen State College." *Pacific Standard*, July 10, 2018, https://psmag.com/education/the-real-free-speech-story-at-evergreen-college.

Bethel School District No. 403 v. Fraser, 478 U.S. 675 (1986).

Bevier, Lillian R. "Rehabilitating Public Forum Doctrine: In Defense of Categories." *Supreme Court Review* (January 1992): 79–122.

Bible Believers v. Wayne Cty., 805 F. 3d 228 (6th Cir. 2015).

Bice, Sonya. "Tough Talk from the Supreme Court on Free Speech: The Illusory Per Se Rule in Garcetti as Further Evidence of Connick's Unworkable Employee/Citizen Speech Partition." *Journal of Law in Society* 8 (Winter 2008): 45–87.

Blasi, Vincent. "Holmes and the Marketplace of Ideas." *The Supreme Court Review* (2004): 1–46.

Blocher, Joseph. "Viewpoint Neutrality and Government Speech." *Boston College Law Review* 52 (May 2011): 695–767.

Bloedorn v. Grube, 631 F.3d 1218 (11th Cir. 2011).

Bloom, Allan. *The Closing of the American Mind*. New York: Simon & Schuster, 1987.

Board of Educ., Island Trees Union Free School Dist. No. 26 v. Pico, 457 U.S. 853 (1982).

"Board of Regents Agenda and Materials, October 6, 2017." University of Wisconsin System Board of Regents, https://www.wisconsin.edu/regents/download/meeting_materials/2017/october/Board-of-Regents-Friday-Agenda-and-Materials---October-2017.pdf.

Board of Regents of the University of Wisconsin System v. Southworth, 529 U.S. 217 (2000).

Bollinger, Lee C. *The Tolerant Society: Freedom of Speech and Extremist Speech in America*. New York: Oxford University Press, 1986.

———. *Uninhibited, Robust and Wide-Open: A Free Press View for a New Century*. New York: Oxford University Press, 2010.

Bonney, Stephen Douglas. "The University Campus as Public Forum: The Legacy of *Widmar v. Vincent*." *UMKC Law Review* 81 (2013): 545–67.

Bottomly, Therese. "Student Protestors Disrupt University of Oregon's Announcement of $50 Million Gift." *Oregonian*, October 6, 2017, https://www.oregonlive.com/education/2017/10/protesters_disrupt_announcemen.html.

Bouie, Jamelle. "Minor Threat." *Slate*, March 8, 2018, https://slate.com/news-and-politics/2018/03/the-real-threats-to-free-speech-arent-campus-protests.html

Bowman v. White, 444 F.3d 967 (8th Cir. 2006).

Brandenburg v. Ohio, 395 U.S. 444 (1969).

Brooks, Arthur C. "Don't Shun Conservative Professors." *New York Times*, September 15, 2017, https://www.nytimes.com/2017/09/15/opinion/conservative-professors.html.

Brooks, Mo. (@RepMoBrooks), August 25, 2019, https://twitter.com/RepMoBrooks/status/1165706990926086144.

Brown, Elizabeth Nolan. "My Alma Mater American University Cancelled My Title IX 'Hate Speech' Panel." *Reason*, September 29, 2017, https://reason.com/2017/09/29/au-campus-safe-from-title-ix-hate-speech/.

Brown, Sarah and Katherine Mangan. "Trump Can't Cut Off Berkeley's Funds by Himself. His Threat Still Raised Alarms." In *Dealing with Controversial Speakers*, edited by The Chronicle of Higher Education, 7–9, 2017.

Brown v. Entertainment Merchants Association, 564 U.S. 786 (2011).

Brown v. Li, 308 F.3d 939 (9th Cir. 2002).

Brownstein, Ronald. "Red and Blue America Aren't Experiencing the Same Pandemic." *The Atlantic*, March 20, 2020, https://www.theatlantic.com/politics/archive/2020/03/how-republicans-and-democrats-think-about-coronavirus/608395.

Brummans, Boris H. J. M., Linda L. Putnam, Barbara Gray, Ralph Hanke, Roy J. Lewicki, and Carolyn Wiethoff. "Making Sense of Intractable Multiparty Conflict: A Study of Framing in Four Environmental Disputes." *Communication Monographs* 75, no. 1 (March 2008): 25–51. https://doi.org/10.1080/03637750801952735.

Bryant, Jennings. "Media Effects, History of Research On." In *Encyclopedia of Children, Adolescents and the Media*, edited by Jeffrey Jensen Arnett, 509–11. Thousand Oaks, CA: Sage Publications, 2007.

Buckley v. Am. Constitutional Law Found. 525 U.S. 182 (1999).

Bunker, Matthew D. *Critiquing Free Speech: First Amendment Theory and the Challenge of Interdisciplinarity*, Mahwah, NJ: Lawrence Erlbaum Associates, 2001.

Bush v. Gore, 531 U.S. 98 (2000).

Calhoun, Craig. "Free Inquiry and Public Mission in the Research University." *Social Research*, 75, no. 3 (2009): 901–32.

Calvert, Clay. "College Campuses as First Amendment Combat Zones and Theatres of the Absurd: The High Price of Protecting Extremist Speakers for Shouting Matches and Insults." *First Amendment Law Review* 16 (Spring 2018): 454–65.

———. "Reconsidering Incitement, Tinker and The Heckler's Veto on College Campuses: Richard Spencer and the Charlottesville Factor." *Northwestern University Law Review*, Online Edition 112 (2018): 109–32.

———. "Where the Right Went Wrong in Southworth: Underestimating the Power of the Marketplace." *Maine Law Review* 53 (2001): 53–80.

Campbell, Bradley and Jason Manning. *The Rise of Victimhood Culture: Microaggressions, Safe Spaces, and the New Culture Wars.* New York: Palgrave Macmillan, 2018.

Campus Free Speech Protection Act. TENN. CODE ANN. § 49-7-2405 2018, https://law.justia.com/codes/tennessee/2018/title-49/chapter-7/part-24/section-49-7-2405/.

Cantwell v. Connecticut, 310 U.S. 296 (1940).

Ceballos v. Garcetti, 361 F.3d 1168, 1173 (9th Cir. 2004).

Chait, Jonathan. "The Right Is Worse Than the Left on Free Speech. So What?" *New York*, March 20, 2018, https://nymag.com/intelligencer/2018/03/the-right-is-worse-than-the-left-on-free-speech-so-what.html.

Chambers, Jr., Henry L. "Curating Campus Speakers." *University of Richmond Law Review* Online Edition 53 (May 2019): 3–17.

Chang, Clio. "Right Wing Donors Are the Ones Threatening Campus Free Speech, You Idiots." *Splinter*, March 9, 2018, https://splinternews.com/right-wing-donors-are-the-ones-threatening-campus-free-1823651572.

Chaplinsky v. New Hampshire, 315 U.S. 568 (1942).

Charis-Carlson, Jeff. "ISU Settles Lawsuit with Religious Free Speech Group, Changes Harassment Policy." *Des Moines Register*, April 4, 2017, http://www.desmoinesregister.com/story/news/education/2017/04/04/iowa-state-settles-lawsuit-religious-free-speech-group-changes-harassment-policies/100034314.

Cherokee Nations v. Georgia, 30 U.S. 1 (1831).

Chemerinsky, Erwin. "Hate Speech is Protected Free Speech, Even on College Campuses." *Vox*, December 26, 2017, https://www.vox.com/the-big-idea/2017/10/25/16524832/campus-free-speech-first-amendment-protest.

———. "The Free Speech-Hate Speech Trade-off." *The New York Times*, September 13, 2017, https://www.nytimes.com/2017/09/13/opinion/berkeley-dean-erwin-chemerinsky.html.

——— and Howard Gillman. *Free Speech on Campus*. New Haven, CT: Yale University Press, 2017.

Chenoweth, Erica. "Violence Will Only Hurt the Trump Resistance." *The New Republic*, February 7, 2017, https://newrepublic.com/article/140474/violence-will-hurt-trump-resistance.

Christian Legal Society v. Martinez, 561 U.S. 661 (2010).

Chua, Amy. *Political Tribes: Group Instinct and the Fate of Nations*. New York: Penguin Press, 2018.

Citizens United v. FEC, 558 U.S. 310 (2010).

Clark v. Jeter, 486 U.S. 456 (1988).

Closson, Troy, Catherine Henderson, Kristina Karisch, Peter Warren, Christopher Vazquez, Sneha Dey, Evan Robinson-Johnson, Amy Li. "Addressing *The Daily*'s Coverage of Sessions Protests." *The Daily Northwestern*, November 10, 2019, https://dailynorthwestern.com/2019/11/10/lateststories/addressing-the-dailys-coverage-of-sessions-protests/.

Cohen, Richard. "Protestors at Middlebury College Demonstrate 'Cultural Appropriation' – Of Fascism." *The Washington Post*, May 29, 2017, https://www.washingtonpost.com/opinions/protesters-at-middlebury-college-demonstrate-cultural-appropriation--of-fascism/2017/05/29/af2a3548-4241-11e7-9869-bac8b446820a_story.html.

Cohen v. California, 403 U.S. 15 (1971).

Cohn, Joe. "Tennessee Bill to Punish UT for Sex Week Becomes Law." Foundation for Individual Rights in Education, May 23, 2016, https://www.thefire.org/tennessee-bill-to-punish-ut-for-sex-week-becomes-law/.

Cohn, Joe. "First test of Florida's Commitment to Campus Free Speech Looms." Foundation for Individual Rights in Education, April 30, 2019, https://www.thefire.org/first-test-of-floridas-commitment-to-campus-free-speech-looms/.

———. "New Wisconsin Regents Policy Has Problems and Promise." Foundation for Individual Rights in Education, October 10, 2017, https://www.thefire.org/new-wisconsin-regents-policy-has-problems-and-promise/.

———. "Problematic Anti-Semitism Bill Passes in South Carolina." Foundation for Individual Rights in Education, April 17, 2018, https://www.thefire.org/problematic-anti-semitism-bill-passes-in-south-carolina.

———. "Second Wisconsin Bill Addressing Free Speech Presents Significant First Amendment Problems." Foundation for Individual Rights in Education, May 5, 2017, https://www.thefire.org/second-wisconsin-bill-addressing-free-speech-presents-significant-first-amendment-problems/.

———. "Wisconsin Lawmakers Once Again Threaten Academic Freedom." Foundation for Individual Rights in Education, December 21, 2016, https://www.thefire.org/wisconsin-lawmakers-once-again-threaten-academic-freedom/.

Cohn, Richard. "Laws Won't Rein in Hate." *The Washington Post*, August 4, 2009, https://www.washingtonpost.com/wp-dyn/content/article/2009/08/03/AR2009080302222.html?hpid=opinionsbox1.

Coleman, Justine. "University Condemns Islamophobic Fliers Wrongly Posted in YAF's Name." *GW Hatchet*, September 9, 2017, https://www.gwhatchet.com/2017/09/09/university-condemns-islamophobic-fliers-wrongly-posted-in-yafs-name.

College Republicans v. Reed, 523 F. Supp. 2d 1005, 1009 (N.D. Ca. 2007).
College Republicans of University of Washington v. Cauce, 2018 WL 804497 (W.D. Wash. 2018).
Collins, Ronald K.L. (ed.). *The Fundamental Holmes: A Free Speech Chronicle and Reader – Selections from the Opinions, Books, Articles, Speeches, Letters and Other Writings by and About Oliver Wendell Holmes, Jr.* New York: Cambridge University Press, 2010.
———. "Recent Developments Regarding Free Speech on College Campuses." The Free Speech Center, October 27, 2017, https://mtsu.edu/first-amendment/post/65/recent-developments-regarding-free-speech-on-college-campuses.
"Commitment to Freedom of Expression." *Purdue University*, https://www.purdue.edu/purdue/about/free-speech.php.
"Complaint–*Brown v. Jones County Junior College*." Foundation for Individual Rights in Education, September 4, 2019, https://www.thefire.org/complaint-brown-v-jones-county-junior-college/.
Connelly, Michael. *Angels Flight*. New York: Grand Central Publishing, 1999.
"Comprehensive Campus Free Speech Bill Becomes Law in Tennessee." Foundation for Individual Rights in Education, May 10, 2017, https://www.thefire.org/comprehensive-campus-free-speech-bill-becomes-law-in-tennessee/.
Connick v. Myers, 461 U.S 138 (1983).
Cosgrove, Jaclyn and Shelby Grad. "Arrests Made as Hundreds Protest Ann Coulter Speech at UC Berkeley." *Los Angeles Times*, November 20, 2019, https://www.latimes.com/california/story/2019-11-20/arrests-made-as-hundreds-protest-against-ann-coulter-at-uc-berkeley.
"Court Sides with Professor Fired for Expressing Conservative Views in the Classroom." *Pacific Justice Institute*, July 25, 2019. https://www.pacificjustice.org/press/court-sides-with-professor-fired-for-expressing-conservative-views-in-the-classroom/.
Cox v. Louisiana, 379 U.S. 536 (1965).
Creeley, Will. "Fighting a Faculty Gag Order at NY's Nassau Community College." Foundation for Individual Rights in Education, September 28, 2018, https://www.thefire.org/fighting-a-faculty-gag-order-at-nys-nassau-community-college/.
———. "Ignoring Academic Freedom, South Carolina Legislators Aim to Punish Public Colleges for Choice of Books." Foundation for Individual Rights in Education, February 21, 2014, https://www.thefire.org/ignoring-academic-freedom-south-carolina-legislators-aim-to-punish-public-colleges-for-choice-of-books/.
Dariano v. Morgan Hill Unified Sch. Dist., 767 F. 3d 764 (9th Cir. 2014).
Davis, Thomas J. "Assessing Constitutional Challenges to University Free Speech Zones Under Public Forum Doctrine." *Indiana Law Journal* 79, no. 1 (2004): 267–97.
Davis v. Monroe Cty. Bd. of Educ., 526 U.S. 629 (1999).
Davison v. Randall, 912 F.3d 666 (4th Cir. 2019).
Day, Terri R., and Danielle Weatherby. "Speech Narcissism." *Florida Law Review* 70, no. 4 (July 2018): 839–82.
Debs v. United States, 249 U.S. 211 (1919).

DeJohn v. Temple University, 537 F.3d 301 (3d Cir. 2008).

Demers, Demers. *The Ivory Tower of Babel: Why the Social Sciences Are Failing to Live Up to Their Promises*. New York: Algora Publishing, 2011.

Demers v. Austin, 746 F.3d 402, 406 (9th Cir. 2014).

Denniston, Lyle. "Court to Rehear Public Employee Speech Case." Scotusblog, February 17, 2006, https://www.scotusblog.com/2006/02/court-to-rehear-public-employee-speech-case/.

Desanctis, Alexandra. "Anthony Esolen Faces the P.C. Onslaught." *National Review*, November 22, 2016, https://www.nationalreview.com/2016/11/anthony-esolen-providence-college-diversity-dispute/.

de Vogue, Ariane. "How McConnell Won, and Obama Lost, the Merrick Garland Fight." CNN, November 9, 2016, https://www.cnn.com/2016/11/09/politics/merrick-garland-supreme-court/index.html.

Dey, Eric, L, Molly C. Ott, Mary Antonaros, Cassie L. Barnhardt and Matthew A. Holsapple. "Engagging Diverse Viewpoints: What Is the Campus Climate for Perspective-Taking?" American Accociation of Colleges and Universities, 2010, https://www.aacu.org/sites/default/files/files/core_commitments/engaging_diverse_viewpoints.pdf.

Dibble, Madison. "Dean of Massachusetts Nursing School Fired after Saying Everyone's Life Matters." *Washington Examiner*, July 2, 2020, https://www.washingtonexaminer.com/news/dean-of-massachusetts-nursing-school-fired-after-saying-everyones-life-matters.

District of Columbia v. Heller, 554 U.S. 570 (2008).

Doe v. Rector and Visitors of George Mason University, 149 F.Supp.3d 602 (E.D. Va. 2016).

Dred Scott v. Sandford, 60 U.S. (19 How.) 393 (1857).

Dreid, Nadia. "Amid Concerns About Stifling Speech, Colleges Take a New Look at Bias-Response Teams." *The Chronicle of Higher Education*, September 28, 2016, http://www.chronicle.com/article/Amid-Concerns-About-Stifling/237918 (the University of Northern Colorado disbanded its bias-response team).

Driscoll, Matt. "There's More to the Race Protests at Evergreen Than Biology Professor and Viral Videos." *News Tribune (Tacoma)*, June 1, 2017, https://www.thenewstribune.com/news/local/news-columns-blogs/matt-driscoll/article153694734.html.

Driscoll, Sharon. "The Wrongful Convictions Seminar." *Stanford Lawyer* 83, November 4, 2010, https://law.stanford.edu/stanford-lawyer/articles/the-wrongful-convictions-seminar-2/.

Driver, Justin. *The Schoolhouse Gate: Public Education, the Supreme Court, and the Battle for the American Mind*. New York: Vintage Books, 2018.

Dylan, Bob. "With God on Our Side." *The Times They Are A Changin'* (Columbia Records, 1964).

Edwards, Lee. "What Is Conservatism?" *The Heritage Foundation*, October 25, 2018. https://www.heritage.org/conservatism/commentary/what-conservatism.

Edwards v. California, 314 U.S. 160 (1941).

Edwards v. South Carolina, 372 U.S. 229 (1963).

Ellis, Christopher. "Do Americans Support Free Speech on College Campuses? Absolutely. Except Sometimes." *The Washington Post,* November 8, 2017, https://www.washingtonpost.com/news/monkey-cage/wp/2017/11/08/do-americans-support-freespeech-on-college-campuses-absolutely-except-sometimes.

Epstein, Lee, Andrew D. Martin and Kevin Quinn. "6+ Decades of Freedom of Expression in the U.S. Supreme Court." June 30, 2018, http://epstein.wustl.edu/research/FreedomOfExpression.pdf.

Espionage Act of May 16, 1918, 40 Stat. 553 (1918).

"Ethics First." *Georgia Institute of Technology*, https://www.gatech.edu/about/ethics.

Evans, M. Stanton. *The Sharon Statement.* 1960, https://faculty.atu.edu/cbrucker/Amst2003/Texts/Sharon.pdf.

Everson, Ryan. "A University Effectively Fired This Professor After He Spoke at a Conservative Think Tank." *Alliance Defending Freedom*, November 18, 2019, http://centerforacademicfreedom.org/a-university-effectively-fired-this-professor-after-he-spoke-at-a-conservative-think-tank/.

"Executive Order on Improving Free Inquiry, Transparency, and Accountability at Colleges and Universities." March 21, 2019, https://www.whitehouse.gov/ presidential-actions/executive-order-improving-free-inquiry-transparency-accountability- colleges-universities/.

Eyer, Katie R. "The New Jim Crow Is the Old Jim Crow." Review of *Mothers of Massive Resistance: White Women and the Politics of White Supremacy*, by Elizabeth Gillespie McRae and *A More Beautiful and Terrible History: The Uses and Misuses of Civil Rights History*, by Jeanne Theoharis. *Yale Law Journal*, 128 (2019): 1002–77.

Feliciano, Ivette and Zachary Green. "Evergreen Copes with Fallout, Months After 'Day of Absence' Sparked National Debate." *PBS*, January 7, 2018, https://www.pbs.org/newshour/show/evergreen-copes-with-fallout-months-after-day-of-absence-sparked-national-debate.

Feulner, Ed. "Zoning Out on Free Speech: First Amendment Winning Fight Against Campus Free-Speech Zones." *The Washington Times*, February 12, 2018, https://www.washingtontimes.com/news/2018/feb/12/campus-free-speech-zones-are-dying/.

Fields, Suzanne. "The Closing of the American Mouth." *Washington Times*, November 11, 2015, https://www.washingtontimes.com/news/2015/nov/11/suzanne-fields-colleges-teaching-students-what-to-/.

"FIRE Letter to Haskell Indian Nations University, April 24, 2020." Foundation for Individual Rights in Education, https://www.thefire.org/fire-letter-to-haskell-indian-nations-university-april-24-2020/.

"FIRE Letter to Truman State University, December 10, 2019." Foundation for Individual Rights in Education, https://www.thefire.org/fire-letter-to-truman-state-university-december-10-2019/.

"FIRE to Northern Michigan U.: End Ban on Students Discussing Self-Harm." Foundation for Individual Rights in Education, September 22, 2016, https://www.thefire.org/fire-to-northern-michigan-u-end-ban-on-students-discussing-self-harm/.

"FIRE Letter to Scottsdale Community College, May 7, 2020." Foundation for Individual Rights in Education, https://www.thefire.org/fire-letter-to-scottsdale-community-college-may-7-2020/.

"Fire's Stand Up for Speech Litigation Project." Foundation for Individual Rights in Education, https://www.standupforspeech.com.

Fisher v. University of Texas-Austin, 136 S. Ct. 2198 (2016).

Fisher, Thomas C. "'Whatever Happened to Mary Beth Tinker' and Other Sagas in the Academic 'Marketplace of Ideas.'" *Golden Gate Law Review* 23, no. 2 (1993): 351–412.

Fla. Stat. Ann. § 1004.097 (2019).

Flaherty, Colleen. "Evidence of Liberal Academe." *Inside Higher Ed*, October 3, 2016, https://www.insidehighered.com/news/2016/10/03/voter-registration-data-show-democrats-outnumber-republicans-among-social-scientists.

———. "Free Speech for Some, Not All?" *Inside Higher Ed*, November 29, 2018, https://www.insidehighered.com/news/2018/11/29/adult-film-stars-invite-campus-gets-wisconsin-chancellor-trouble-some-see-hypocrisy.

"Florida Becomes Ninth State to Ban Restrictive Campus Free Speech Zones." Foundation for Individual Rights in Education, March 12, 2018, https://www.thefire.org/florida-becomes-ninth-state-to-ban-restrictive-campus-free-speech-zones/.

Foran, Clare. "Trump-Supporting Republicans Face a Backlash on College Campuses." *The Atlantic*, October 31, 2016, https://www.theatlantic.com/politics/archive/2016/10/republicans-trump-racism-sexism/505697/.

Forming Open and Robust University Minds Act, Ohio Laws, Sub. S.B. No. 40. https://www.legislature.ohio.gov/legislation/legislation-documents?id=GA133-SB-40.

Frankel, Jillian. "Conservative Students Face Discrimination, Marginalization at UCLA." *Daily Bruin*, January 18, 2017, http://dailybruin.com/2017/01/18/conservative-students-face-discrimination-marginalization-at-ucla/.

Frankfurter, Felix. "The Appointment of a Justice." In *Felix Frankfurter on the Court: Extrajudicial Essays on the Court and the Constitution. 1882-1965*, edited by Philip B. Kurland, 211–17. Cambridge, MA: Belknap Press of Harvard University Press, 1970.

———. "The Supreme Court and the Public." *Forum* 83 (1930): 333.

Franks, Mary Anne. "The Miseducation of Free Speech." *Virginia Law Review Online* 105 (December 2019): 218–42, https://www.virginialawreview.org/volumes/content/miseducation-free-speech.

"Free Speech Q&A: Elizabeth Warren." PEN America, February 3, 2020, https://pen.org/elizabeth-warren-on-free-expression-in-america.

"Free Speech Zones." Foundation for Individual Rights in Education, May 24, 2019, https://www.thefire.org/issues/free-speech-zones/.

French, David. "Here's How Anti-Conservative Academic Discrimination Works." *National Review*, July 5, 2017, http://www.nationalreview.com/article/449232/conservatives-face-discrimination-colleges-keith-finks-ucla-case.

———. "It's Time to Crush Campus Censorship." *National Review*, April 24, 2017. https://www.nationalreview.com/2017/04/free-speech-campus-censorship-congress-must-punish-universities-indulging-student-mob/.

———. "Yes, Universities Discriminate Against Conservatives." *National Review*, April 1, 2016, https://www.nationalreview.com/corner/yes-universities-discriminate-against-conservative-scholars/.

Friedersdorf, Conor. "A Wisconsin Legislator Models Political Correctness for Students." *The Atlantic*, December 21, 2016, https://www.theatlantic.com/politics/archive/2016/12/a-wisconsin-legislator-models-political-correctness-for-university-students/511337/.

———. "The Perils of Writing a Provocative Email at Yale." *The Atlantic,* May 26, 2016, https://www.theatlantic.com/politics/archive/2016/05/the-peril-of-writing-a-provocative-email-at-yale/484418/.

Frisch, William B. "Hate Speech in the Constitution Law of the United States." *American Journal of Comparative Law* 50 (Fall 2002): 463–92.

Frohwerk v. United States, 249 U.S. 204 (1919).

Fukuyama, Francis. *Identity: The Demand for Dignity and the Politics of Resentment.* New York: Farrar, Straus and Giroux, 2018.

Fuller, Thomas. "A Free Speech Battle At the Birthplace of a Movement at Berkeley." *The New York Times*, February 2, 2017, https://www.nytimes.com/2017/02/02/us/university-california-berkeley-free-speech-milo-yiannopoulos.html.

——— and Stephanie Saul. "Berkeley Is Being Tested on 2 Fronts: Free Speech and Safety." *The New York Times*, April 21, 2017, https://www.nytimes.com/2017/04/21/us/berkeley-ann-coulter-speech.html.

Ga. Code Ann. § 20-3-48 (2018).

Garcetti v. Ceballos, 547 U.S. 410 (2006).

Garris, Carolyn. "Martin Luther King's Conservative Legacy." *The Heritage Foundation*, January 12, 2006, https://www.heritage.org/conservatism/report/martin-luther-kings-conservative-legacy.

Gay & Lesbian Students Ass'n v. Gohn, 850 F.2d 361 (8th Cir. 1988).

Gitlow v. New York, 268 U.S. 652 (1925).

Glover v. Cole, 762 F.2d 1197 (4th Cir. 1995).

Gobitas, Billy. "Letter to Minersville, Pennsylvania, School Directors, Explaining Why the Young Jehovah's Witness Refused to Salute the American flag, 5 November 1935." Library of Congress, https://www.loc.gov/item/mcc.016/.

Gockowski, Anthony. "Socialist Group Calls for the "Extermination" of Capitalists." *Campus Reform*, October 19, 2017, https://www.campusreform.org/?ID=9991.

Goldberg, Erica. "Competing Free Speech Values in an Age of Protest." *Cardozo Law Review*, 38 (August 2018): 2163–213.

———. "Must Universities 'Subsidize' Controversial Ideas? Allocating Security Fees when Student Groups Host Divisive Speakers." *George Mason University Civil Rights Law Journal* 21 (Summer 2011): 349–405.

——— and Kelly Sarabyn. "Measure 'A Degree of Deference': Institutional Academic Freedom in a Post-*Grutter* World." *Santa Clara Law Review* 51 (November 2010): 217–64.

Goldberg, Michelle. "Democracy Grief Is Real." *The New York Times*, December 13, 2019, https://www.nytimes.com/2019/12/13/opinion/sunday/trump-democracy.html.

———. "The Laura Kipnis Melodrama." *The Nation*, March 16, 2015.

Goldberg, Suzanne B. "Free Expression on Campus: Mitigating the Costs of Contentious Speakers." *Harvard Journal of Law & Public Policy* 41 (Winter 2018): 163–86.

"Google Trends: Charles Murray." Google, https://trends.google.com/trends/explore?date=all&geo=US&q=%22charles%20murray%22.

Gorner, Jeremy. "Study Blames 'ACLU Effect' For Spike in Chicago's Crime in 2016, But Experts Differ." *The Chicago Tribune*, March 26, 2018.

Gould, Jon. "The Triumph of Hate Speech Regulation: Why Gender Wins But Race Loses in America." *Michigan Journal of Gender and Law* 6 (1999): 153–220.

Gray, Barbara. "Framing of Environmental Disputes." In *Making Sense of Intractable Environmental Conflicts: Frames and Cases*, edited by Roy J. Lewicki et al., 11–34. Washington, DC: Island Press, 2003.

———. "Strong Opposition: Frame Based Resistance to Collaboration." *Journal of Community and Applied Social Psychology*, 14 (2004): 166–76. https://doi.org/10.1002/casp.773.

Greenawalt, Kent. "Free Speech Justifications." *Columbia Law Review* 89 (January 1989): 119–55.

Greenfield, Scott H. "The Consequences of Free Speech Strike Northwestern." *Simple Justice*, March 21, 2015, https://blog.simplejustice.us/2015/03/21/the-consequences-of-free-speech-strike-northwestern/.

Gregory v. City of Chicago, 394 U.S. 111 (1969).

Gregory, Thomas. "All Disloyal Men Warned." *The New York Times*, November 21, 1917, 3.

Greubel, Greg Harold. "Public Records Reveal Wright State Used Unconstitutional Facebook Page Policy to Censor Pro-union Speech during Historic Faculty Strike." Foundation for Individual Rights in Education, January 24, 2020, https://www.thefire.org/public-records-reveal-wright-state-used-unconstitutional-facebook-page-policy-to-censor-pro-union-speech-during-historic-faculty-strike/.

Griffin, Oren R. "Academic Freedom and Professorial Speech in the Post-Garcetti World." *University of Seattle Law Review* 37 (2013): 1–54.

Griffiths, Paul J. *Lying: An Augustinian Theology of Duplicity*. Ada, MI: Brazos Press, 2004.

Grimshaw, Allen, ed. *A Social History of Racial Violence*. New York: Routledge, 2017.

Grutter v. Bollinger, 539 U.S. 306 (2003).

Gumport, Patricia J. "Universities as Academic Workplaces." *Daedalus*, 1997, 113–36.

Gup, Ted. "Free Speech, but Not for All?" *Chronicle of Higher Education*, April 27, 2017, http://www.chronicle.com/article/Free-Speech-but-Not-for-All-/239909.

Haidt, Jonathan. Personal Interview with Joseph Russomanno, Tempe, AZ, November 9, 2017 (on file with author).

——— and Greg Lukianoff. *The Coddling of the American Mind: How Good Intentions and Bad Ideas Are Setting Up a Generation for Failure*. New York: Penguin, 2018.

Hamilton, Andy. "Conservatism." In *Stanford Encyclopedia of Philosophy*, edited by Edward N. Zalta, Spring 2020, https://plato.stanford.edu/archives/spr2020/entries/conservatism/.

Hanlon, Aaron. "The Real Threat to Free Speech on Campus Isn't Coming from the Left." *The Washington Post*, October 15, 2019, https://www.washingtonpost.com/outlook/2019/10/15/real-threat-free-speech-campus-isnt-coming-left/.

Harris, Samantha. "Fired for His Views: UNT Math Professor Brings Free Speech Lawsuit." *FIRE*, April 27, 2020, https://www.thefire.org/fired-for-his-views-unt-math-professor-brings-free-speech-lawsuit/.

Hart, Bridget. "A Balancing Act for American Universities: Anti-Harassment Policy vs. Free Speech." *Journal of Law and Policy* 25 (December 2016): 399–435.

Hart, Kim. Exclusive Poll: "Most Democrats See Republicans as Racist, Sexist." *Axios*, November 12, 2018, https://www.axios.com/poll-democrats-and-republicans-hate-each-other-racist-ignorant-evil-99ae7afc-5a51-42be-8ee2-3959e43ce320.html.

Hasnas, John. "The One Kind of Diversity Colleges Avoid." *Wall Street Journal*, March 31, 2016, https://www.wsj.com/articles/the-one-kind-of-diversity-colleges-avoid-1459464676.

Hazelwood School District v. Kuhlmeier, 484 U.S. 260 (1988).

Head, Tom. "6 Major U.S. Supreme Court Hate Speech Cases." *ThoughtCo.*, July 18, 2019, https://www.thoughtco.com/hate-speech-cases-721215.

Healy, Thomas. "Who's Afraid of Free Speech? What Critics of the Campus Protest Get Wrong About the State of Public Discourse." *Atlantic*, June 18, 2017, https://www.theatlantic.com/politics/archive/2017/06/whos-afraid-of-free-speech/530094.

Healy v. James, 408 U.S. 169 (1972).

Henry, Jules. *Culture Against Man*. New York: Vintage, 1965.

Heim, Joe, Lori Rosza, Abigail Hausloner, Susan Svrluga. "'Go Home Spencer!' Protestors Disrupt White Nationalists Speech at the University of Florida." *The Washington Post*, October 19, 2017, https://www.washingtonpost.com/news/grade-point/wp/2017/10/18/uf/.

Heins, Marjorie. *Priests of Our Democracy: The Supreme Court, Academic Freedom, and the Anti-Communist Purge*. New York: New York University Press, 2013.

Hentoff, Nat. *Free Speech For Me—But Not For Thee: How the American Left and Right Relentlessly Censor Each Other*. New York: Harper Collins, 1992.

Hetherington, Marc and Jonathan Weiler. *Prius or Pickup? How the Answers to Four Simple Questions Explain America's Great Divide*. New York: Houghton Mifflin Harcourt, 2018.

Hill v. Colorado, 530 U.S. 703 (2000).

Hitchens, Christopher. *Letters to a Young Contrarian*. New York: Basic Books, 2001.

Hofstadter, Richard. *The Idea of a Party System*. Berkeley: University of California Press, 1969.

Hohmann, James. "Trump's Islamophobia Resonates With Base, Not Others." *The Washington Post,* December 9, 2015.

Holmes, Oliver Wendell. "Ideas and Doubts." *Illinois Law Review* 10 (1915): 1–2.

———. "Natural Law." *Harvard Law Review* 32, no. 1 (November 1918): 40–44.

———. "The Path of the Law." *Harvard Law Review*, March 1897, 457–78.

Holmes-Laski Letters: The Correspondence of Mr. Justice Holmes and Harold J. Laski. Edited by Mark DeWolfe Howe, vol. I. Cambridge, MA: Harvard University Press, 1953.

Hondares, Damian. "The Silent Minority: Trump Supporters at Richmond." *Collegian*, Novemebr 7, 2016, http://www.thecollegianur.com/article/2016/11/silent-minority-trump-supporters.

Hook, Janet. "Even the Coronavirus Can't Bridge America's Partisan Divide." *The Los Angeles Times*, March 20, 2020, https://www.latimes.com/politics/story/2020-03-20/coronavirus-crisis-cant-bridge-partisan-divide.

Hopkins, David A. "Why COVID Was Never Going to Produce National Unity." *Honest Graft*, May 26, 2020, http://www.honestgraft.com/2020/05/why-covid-was-never-going-to-produce.html.

Horwitz, Paul. "*Grutter*'s First Amendment." *Boston College Law Review*, May 2005, 461–590.

House Bill 2563, State of Arizona House of Representatives, 2018. https://www.azleg.gov/legtext/53leg/2R/laws/0267.htm.

Houston v. Hill, 482 U.S. 451 (1987).

Hudler, Haley. "New Survey Exposes New Threats to Free Speech On Campus." Foundation for Individual Rights in Education, October 28, 2015, https://www.thefire.org/new-survey-exposes-threats-to-free-speech-on-campus/.

———. "Yale Students Demand Resignations from Faculty Members over Halloween Email." *FIRE*, November 6, 2015, https://www.thefire.org/yale-students-demand-resignations-from-faculty-members-over-halloween-email/.

Hudson, David L., Jr. "Academic Freedom for Public University Professors: Unsettled Questions in the Wake of Garcetti v. Ceballos." Freedom Forum Institute, April 26, 2017, https://www.freedomforuminstitute.org/first-amendment-center/topics/freedom-of-speech-2/free-speech-and-government-employees-overview/academic-freedom-for-public-university-professors-unsettled-questions-in-the-wake-of-garcetti-v-ceballos/.

———. "Are Free Speech and Academic Freedom under Assault at Colleges and Universities?" *ABA Journal*, October 1, 2018, http://www.abajournal.com/magazine/article/free_speech_academic_freedom_buchanan.

———. "Balancing Act: Public Employees and Free Speech." Freedom Forum, December 2002, 23, https://www.freedomforuminstitute.org/wp-content/uploads/2014/09/fac_firstreport_public-employees-free-speech.pdf.

———. "Connick v. Myers: Reflections on Landmark Public Employee Free-Speech Case." Freedom Forum Institute, April 10, 2001, https://www.freedomforuminstitute.org/2001/04/10/connick-v-myers-reflections-on-landmark-public-employee-free-speech-case/.

———. "Controversial Speakers and the Problem of the Heckler's Veto." *Freedom Forum Institute*, April 26, 2017, https://www.freedomforuminstitute.org/2017/04/26/controversial-speakers-and-the-problem-of-the-hecklers-veto/.

———. "Garcettized! 06 Ruling Still Zapping Speech." Freedom Forum Institute, January 5, 2010, https://www.freedomforuminstitute.org/2010/01/15/garcettized-06-ruling-still-zapping-speech/.

———. "Justice Thurgood Marshall, Great Defender of First Amendment Free-Speech Rights for the Powerless." *Howard Human & Civil Rights Law Review* 2 (2018): 167–77.

———. "No First Amendment Protection for Professor Who Spoke Out Against Cheating Students." Freedom Forum Institute, October 24, 2017, https://www.freedomforuminstitute.org/2017/10/24/court-rules-no-first-amendment-protection-for-professor-who-spoke-out-about-cheating-students/.

———. "Teachers Looks Back on Letter That Led to Firing – and Supreme Court Victory." Freedom Forum Institute, July 20, 2001, https://www.freedomforuminstitute.org/2001/07/20/teacher-looks-back-on-letter-that-led-to-firing-and-supreme-court-victory/.

———. "The Supreme Court's Worst Decision in Recent Years – Garcetti v. Ceballos, the Dred Scott Decision for Public Employees." *Mitchell Hamline Law Review* (2020).

Hughes, Brittany M. "Incoming Freshman Says Marquette University Threatened Her Admission over Pro-Trump Video." *MRCTV*, July 9, 2020, https://www.mrctv.org/blog/incoming-freshman-says-marquette-university-threatened-her-admission-over-pro-trump-video.

Hustler v. Falwell, 485 U.S. 46 (1988).

"Investigation of the Baltimore City Police Department." U.S. Department of Justice, Civil Rights Division, August 10, 2016, https://www.justice.gov/opa/file/883366/download.

Iota Xi Chapter of Sigma Chi Fraternity v. George Mason University, 993 F.2d 386 (4th Cir. 1993).

Iowa Code Ann. § 261H.4 (2019).

Isserman, Maurice. "Who Defines 'Acceptable' Speech?" *The Chronicle of Higher Education*, February 18, 2005, B20.

Iuliano, Jason. "The Supreme Court's Noble Lie." *University of California, Davis Law Review* 51 (February 2018): 921–38.

Jackson, Abby. "Liberal Colleges Are Recruiting Conservative Professors to 'Stir up Some Trouble.'" *Business Insider*, August 10, 2017, http://www.businessinsider.com/affirmative-action-conservative-professors-liberal-colleges-2017-8.

Janus v. AFSCME, Council 31, 138 S. Ct. 2448 (2018).

Jaschik, Scott. "Justice Scalia, a Law School and Diversity of Thought." *Inside Higher Ed*, February 19, 2016, https://www.insidehighered.com/news/2016/02/19/georgetown-law-debates-intellectual-diversity-and-institutional-neutrality-wake.

Johnson, Brett G. "The Heckler's Veto: Using First Amendment Theory and Jurisprudence to Understand Current Audience Reactions Against Controversial Speech." *Communication Law & Policy* 21, no. 2 (2016): 175–220.

——— and Shane C. Epping. "Forum Delegation: The Birth and Transposition of a New Approach to Public Forum Doctrine." *Hastings Communication & Entertainment Law Journal* 42, no. 1 (2019): 77–116.

Johnston v. University of Pittsburgh of Commonwealth System of Higher Ed., 97 F.Supp.3d 657, (W.D. Pa. 2015).

"Joliet Junior College—Stand Up for Speech Lawsuit." Foundation for Individual Rights in Education, https://www.thefire.org/cases/joliet-junior-college-stand-up-for-speech-lawsuit/.

Jones, Michael. "Fiery Debate at Penn State After Conservatives Listed as Marginalized Alongside Blacks, Homosexuals, Muslims." *College Fix,* July 6, 2018, https://www.thecollegefix.com/fiery-debate-at-penn-state-after-conservatives-listed-as-marginalized-alongside-blacks-homosexuals-muslims/.

"Joseph Goebbels: 'The Poison Dwarf.'" *Holocaust Education and Archive Research Team.* http://www.holocaustresearchproject.org/holoprelude/goebbels.html.

Judge, Mark. "Why Georgetown University Students Want More Conservative Professors on Campus." *National Review*, October 6, 2017, https://www.nationalreview.com/2017/10/georgetown-conservative-professors-students-intellectual-diversity.

Kahn, Rob. "The Anti-Coddling Narrative and Campus Speech." *University of St. Thomas Law Journal* 15 (2018): 1–25.

Kakutani, Michiko. *The Death of Truth: Notes on Falsehood in the Age of Trump.* New York: Tim Duggan Books, 2018.

Kalman, Laura. *Abe Fortas: A Biography.* New Haven: Yale University Press, 1990.

Kalven, Jr., Harry. "The New York Times Case: A Note on 'The Central Meaning of the First Amendment.'" *Supreme Court Law Review* (1964): 191–221.

"Kansas State University Mission." *Kansas State University*, https://www.k-state.edu/about/mission/.

Kauffman, Gretel. "US No Longer a 'Full Democracy' in 2016 Democracy Index." *Christian Science Monitor*, January 26, 2017, http://www.csmonitor.com/USA/2017/0126/US-nolonger-a-full-democracy-in-2016-Democracy-Index-Where-do-we-go-from-here.

Kendrick, Leslie. "The Answers and the Questions in First Amendment Law." In *Charlottesville 2017: The Legacy of Race and Inequity*, edited by Louis P. Nelson and Claudrena N. Harold, 70–81. Charlottesville: University of Virginia Press, 2018.

Kerr v. Hurd, 694 F.Supp.2d 817, 843–44 (S.D. Ohio 2010).

Keyishian v. Board of Regents, 385 U.S. 589 (1967).

King, Martin Luther. "I Have a Dream." In *American Rhetoric: Top 100 Speeches*, https://www.americanrhetoric.com/speeches/mlkihaveadream.htm.

Kipnis, Laura. "Sexual Paranoia Strikes Academe." *The Chronicle of Higher Education,* 27 February 2015.

Kirchick, James. "No, America Doesn't Need a Hate Speech Law." *The Washington Post*, November 7, 2019, https://www.washingtonpost.com/opinions/2019/11/07/no-america-doesnt-need-hate-speech-law/.

Klaassen v. Atkinson, 348 F. Supp. 3d 1106 (D. Kan. 2018).

Klein, Ezra. *Why We're Polarized.* New York: Avid Reader Press, 2020.

Knight First Amendment Inst. at Columbia Univ. v. Trump, 928 F.3d 226 (2d Cir. 2019).

Korematsu v. United States, 323 U.S. 214 (1944).

Kristof, Nicholas. "The Dangers of Echo Chambers on Campus." *The New York Times,* December 10, 2016, https://www.nytimes.com/2016/12/10/opinion/sunday/the-dangers-of-echo-chambers-on-campus.html.

Kristof, Nicholas. "Beware the Contagion Spread by Blowhards." *The New York Times*, March 8, 2020.

Kruger, Kevin. "Controversial Speech in a Polarized Climate." *Inside Higher Ed*, February 3, 2017, https://www.insidehighered.com/views/2017/02/03/dealing-controversial-speech-campuses-essay.

Kruth, Susan. "Michigan Senate Subcommittee Proposes Penalty for Speech About Labor Unions." Foundation for Individual Rights in Education, April 1, 2014, https://www.thefire.org/michigan-senate-subcommittee-proposes-penalty-for-speech-about-labor-unions/.

Kurtz, Stanley. "The Campus Intellectual Diversity Act: A Proposal." *National Review*, February 12, 2019, https://www.nationalreview.com/corner/the-campus-intellectual-diversity-act-a-proposal.

———, James Manley and Jonathan Butcher. *Campus Free Speech: A Legislative Proposal*. Phoenix: Goldwater Institute, 2017. https://goldwaterinstitute.org/wp-content/uploads/2019/03/Campus-Free-Speech-A-Legislative-Proposal_Web.pdf.

Ky. Rev. Stat. § 164.348 (2019).

La. Rev. Stat., tit. 17, § 3399.35 (2018).

Langbert, Mitchell, Anthony Quain and Daniel Klien. "Faculty Voter Registration in Economics, History, Journalism, Law and Psychology." *Econ Journal Watch,* 13, no. 3 (September 2016): 422–51, https://econjwatch.org/File+download/944/LangbertQuainKleinSept2016.pdf?mimetype=pdf.

Langhauser, Derek P. "Free and Regulated Speech on Campus: Using Forum Analysis for Assessing Facility Use, Speech Zones, and Related Expressive Activity." *Journal of College & University Law* 31, no. 3 (2006): 481–512.

Langhofer, Tyson. "Investigating Speech: When the Process Becomes the Punishment." *ADF Center for Academic Freedom*, November 7, 2017, http://centerforacademicfreedom.org/team/tlanghofer/.

Larson, Jennifer, Mark McNeilly and Timothy J. Ryan. "Free Expression and Constructive Dialogue at the University of North Carolina at Chapel Hill." March 2, 2020, https://fecdsurveyreport.web.unc.edu/files/2020/02/UNC-Free-Expression-Report.pdf.

Lasson, Kenneth. "Controversial Speakers on Campus: Liberties, Limitations, and Common-Sense Guidelines." *St. Thomas Law Review* 12, no. 1 (Fall 1999): 39–94.

———. "The Decline of Free Speech on the Post-Modern Campus: The Troubling Evolution of the Heckler's Veto." *Quinnipiac Law Review* 37 (2018): 1–95.

Lawrence, Charles R. III. "If He Hollers Let Him Go: Regulating Racist Speech on Campus." *Duke Law Journal* (1990): 431–83.

Lederman, Marty. "Ceballos v. Garcetti – What Difference Will Alito Make?" Scotusblog, February 19, 2006, https://www.scotusblog.com/2006/02/ceballos-v-garcetti-what-difference-will-alito-make/.

Lee v. Weisman, 505 U.S. 577 (1992).

Lela v. Board of Trustees of Community College Dist. No. 516, 2015 WL 351243 (N.D. Ill. 2015).

Lemann, Nicholas. *Transaction Man: The Rise of the Deal and the Decline of the American Dream*. New York: Farrar, Straus and Giroux, 2019.

Lemay, J.A. Leo. *The Life of Benjamin Franklin*, vol. 3. Philadelphia: University of Pennsylvania Press, 2009.

Lepore, Jill. "Flip-Flopping on Free Speech: The Fight for the First Amendment on Campuses and Football Fields, From the Sixties to Today." *New Yorker*, October 1, 2017, https://www.newyorker.com/magazine/2017/10/09/flip-flopping-on-free-speech.

———. *These Truths: A History of the United States*. New York: W.W. Norton & Co., 2018.

Lerner, Max. *Nine Scorpions in a Bottle: Great Judges and Cases of the Supreme Court*. New York: Arcade Publishing, 1994.

Levin, Mark. "Professor John Ellis Discusses how American Universities become 'One Party Campuses.'" *Fox News*, June 22, 2020, https://www.foxnews.com/transcript/professor-john-ellis-discusses-how-american-universities-became-one-party-campuses-professor-tim-groseclose-discusses-media-bias.

Levin, Yuval. "How Did Americans Lose Faith in Everything?" *The New York Times*, January 19, 2020, https://www.nytimes.com/2020/01/18/opinion/sunday/institutions-trust.html.

Licea, Melkorka. "NYU Students Who Back Trump Afraid to Show Their Faces." *New York Post,* April 2, 2016, http://nypost.com/2016/04/02/nyu-students-who-back-trump-fear-for-their-safety-on-campus.

Lidsky, Lyrissa Barnett. "Nobody's Fools: The Rational Audience as First Amendment Ideal" *University of Illinois Law Review* (2010): 804–49.

Lilla, Mark. *The Once and Future Liberal: After Identity Politics*. New York: Harper, 2017.

Liptak, Adam. "Hate Speech or Free Speech? What Much of West Bans Is Protected in the U.S." *The New York Times*, June 11, 2008. http://www.nytimes.com/2008/06/11/world/americas/11iht-hate.4.13645369.html.

———. "How Conservatives Weaponized the First Amendment." *The New York Times*, June 30, 2018, https://www.nytimes.com/2018/06/30/us/politics/first-amendent-conservatives-supreme-court.html.

Llorente, Elizabeth. "Growing Number of State Laws Are Passed or Introduced Focusing on Campus Free Speech." *Fox News*, February 9, 2018, http://www.foxnews.com/us/2018/02/09/growing-number-state-laws-are-passed-or-introduced-focusing-on-campus-free-speech.html.

LoMonte, Frank D. "The Legislative Response to a Perceived 'Free Speech Crisis' On Campus." *Communications Lawyer* 34 (Winter 2019): 7–10.

———. "Putting the 'Public' Back into Public Employment: A Roadmap for Challenging Prior Restraints That Prohibit Government Employees from Speaking to the News Media." *Kansas Law Review* 68 (2019): 1–68.

Long, Katherine. "Long Simmering Discord Led to The Evergreen State College's Viral Moment." *Seattle Times*, June 10, 2017, https://www.seattletimes.com/seattle-news/education/discord-at-evergreen-state-simmered-for-a-year-before-it-boiled-over/.

———. "UW to Pay $122,500 in Legal Fees in Settlement with College Republicans over Free Speech." *The Seattle Times*, June 18, 2018, https://www.seattletimes.com/seattle-news/uw-to-pay-127000-in-legal-fees-in-settlement-with-college-republicans-over-free-speech/.

Lopez, Yvette P. and William F. Martin. "University Mission Statements and Sustainability Performance." *Business & Society Review* 123, no. 2 (June 2018): 341–68.

Lowman, Rodney L. "Leading the 21st-Century College and University: Managing Multiple Missions and Conflicts of Interest in Higher Education." *The Psychologist-Manager Journal* 13, no. 4 (October 2010): 237–43.

Lukianoff, Greg and Jonathan Haidt. "The Coddling of the American Mind." *The Atlantic*, September 2015, https://www.theatlantic.com/magazine/archive/2015/09/the-coddling-of-the-american-mind/399356.

———. *The Coddling of the American Mind: How Good Intentions and Bad Ideas Are Setting Up a Generation for Failure.* New York: Penguin Press, 2018.

Lumpkin, Lauren. "University of Massachusetts Professor Removed from Classroom After Showing Hitler Parody." *The Washington Post*, December 16, 2019, https://www.washingtonpost.com/local/education/university-of-massachusetts-professor-removed-from-classroom-after-showing-hitler-parody/2019/12/16/9534a852-1de6-11ea-87f7-f2e91143c60d_story.html.

"MCCCD Statement on Academic Freedom." Maricopa County Community College District Interim Chancellor Dr. Steven R. Gonzales, May 11, 2020, https://news.maricopa.edu/news-articles/mcccd-statement-academic-freedom.

Madison, James. "The Federalist No. 10." In *The Federalist Papers*, edited by Clinton Rossiter, 77–84. New York: Penguin Books, 1961.

———. "The Federalist No. 51." In *The Federalist Papers*, edited by Clinton Rossiter, 320–25. New York: Penguin Books, 1961.

Madway, Brynne. "Berkeley Revises Student Organization Rules in Lawsuit Settlement." *Foundation for Individual Rights in Education*, July 9, 2018, https://www.thefire.org/berkeley-revises-student-organization-rules-in-lawsuit-settlement.

Magarian, Gregory P. "When Audiences Object: Free Speech and Campus Speaker Protests." *University of Colorado Law Review* 90 (2019): 551–92.

Maine v. Taylor, 477 U.S. 131 (1986).

Majeed, Azhar. "Defying the Constitution: The Rise, Persistence and Prevalence of Campus Speech Codes." *Georgetown Journal of Law and Public Policy* 7 (Summer 2009): 483–543.

Marcuse, Herbert. "Repressive Tolerance." In *The Essential Marcuse: Selected Writings of Philosopher and Social Critic Herbert Marcuse*, edited by Andrew Feenberg and William Leiss, 22–59. Boston: Beacon Press, 2007.

Margee v. Trustees of Hamline University, 747 F.3d 532 (8th Cir. 2014).

Masterpiece Cakeshop, Ltd. v. Colo. Civil Rights Comm'n, 138 S.Ct. 1719 (2018).

Mastrangelo, Alana. "Top 10 Craziest Attacks on Campus Conservatives of 2019." *Breitbart*, January 1, 2020, https://www.breitbart.com/tech/2020/01/01/top-10-craziest-attacks-on-campus-conservatives-of-2019/.

Matal v. Tam, 137 S. Ct. 1744 (2017).

Matsuda, Mari J., Charles Lawrence III, Richard Delgado, and Kimberlè Williams Crenshaw. *Words That Wound: Critical Race Theory, Assaultive Speech, and the First Amendment.* New York: Routledge/Westview, 1993.

Matthews, Dylan. "Here's What You Need to Know about Stop and Frisk – and Why Courts Shut It Down." *The New York Times*, August 13, 2003.

Mattis, James. "The Enemy Within." *The Atlantic*, December 2019, 102–104.

Maybee, Julie E. "Hegel's Dialectics." In *Stanford Encyclopedia of Philosophy*, edited by Edward N. Zalta, June 3, 2016, https://plato.stanford.edu/entries/hegel-dialectics/.

Mayer, Bernard. *Staying With Conflict: A Strategic Approach to Ongoing Disputes*. San Francisco: Jossey-Bass, 2009.

McAllister, D.C. "The Sordid History of Liberals Calling Republicans Racist." *PJ Media*, September 13, 2016, https://pjmedia.com/blog/d-c-mcallister/2016/09/13/the-sordid-history-of-liberals-calling-republicans-racists-n5677.

McArdle, Mairead. "Law-School Students Shout Down 'Known Fascist' Christina Hoff Summers." *National Review*, March 6, 2018, https://www.nationalreview.com/2018/03/christina-hoff-sommers-lewis-clark-law-students-shout-down.

McAuliffe v. Mayor of New Bedford, 155 Mass. 216, 220 (1892).

McCauley v. University of the Virgin Islands, 618 F.3d 232, 252 (3rd Cir. 2010).

McClennen, Sophia A. "Enough with the Blue-Baiting: The Biggest Threat on Campus Has Nothing to Do with Free Speech." *Salon*, September 2, 2017, https://www.salon.com/2017/09/02/enough-with-the-blue-baiting-the-biggest-threat-on-campus-has-nothing-to-do-with-free-speech/.

McDonald, Forrest. *Novus Ordo Seclorum: The Intellectual Origins of the Constitution*. Lawrence: University of Kansas Press, 1985.

McGlone v. Bell, 681 F.3d 718 (6th Cir. 2012).

McLaughlin, Sarah. "After Controversy over Dissent Program's Cancellation at Singapore Campus, Yale Faculty Call for Academic Freedom Protections." Foundation for Individual Rights in Education, January 27, 2020, https://www.thefire.org/after-controversy-over-dissent-programs-cancellation-at-singapore-campus-yale-faculty-call-for-academic-freedom-protections/.

———. "After Viewpoint-based Denial, Williams Initiative for Israel finally Receives Recognition." Foundation for Individual Rights in Education, May 16, 2019, https://www.thefire.org/after-viewpoint-based-denial-williams-initiative-for-israel-finally-receives-recognition/.

———. "Fire Raises Questions about UCLA Lecturer Keith Fink's Firing." *FIRE*, August 4, 2017, https://www.thefire.org/fire-raises-questions-about-ucla-lecturer-keith-finks-firing/.

McMurtrie, Beth. "Mayhem at Berkeley Hardens New Battle Lines on Free Speech." In *Dealing with Controversial Speakers*, edited by The Chronicle of Higher Education, 4–6, 2017.

McMullin, Evan. "The Constitution in Danger." *The New York Times*, December 5, 2016, https://www.nytimes.com/2016/12/05/opinion/trumps-threat-to-the-constitution.html.

Meacham, Jon. *The Soul of America: The Battle for Our Better Angels*. New York: Random House, 2018.

Meiklejohn, Alexander. *Free Speech and Its Relation to Self-Government*. New York: Harper & Brothers, 1948.

———. *Political Freedom: The Constitutional Powers of the People*. New York: Harper, 1960.

Mele, Christopher and Annie Correal. "Not Our President: Protests Spread after Donald Trump's Election." *The New York Times*, November 9, 2016, https://www.nytimes.com/2016/11/10/us/trump-election-protests.html.
Menand, Louis. *The Marketplace of Ideas*. New York: W.W. Norton & Co., 2010.
———. *The Metaphysical Club: A Story of Ideas in America*. New York: Farrar, Straus & Giroux, 2001.
Meriwether v. Trustees of Shawnee State Univ., 2019 U.S. Dist. LEXIS 151494 (S.D. Ohio) (9/5/2019).
Metromedia v. FCC, 497 U.S. 547 (1990).
Metromedia, Inc. v. City of San Diego, 453 U.S. 490 (1981).
Mill, John Stuart. *Considerations on Representative Government*. West Strand, England: Parker, Son, & Bourn, 1761.
Miller v. California, 413 U.S. 15 (1973).
Miller, Patrick. "University Regulation of Student Speech: In Search of a Unified Mode of Analysis." *Michigan Law Review* 116, no. 7 (May 2018): 1317–43.
Milligan, Susan. "The Political Divide over the Coronavirus." *U.S. News & World Report*, March 18, 2020, https://www.usnews.com/news/politics/articles/2020-03-18/the-political-divide-over-the-coronavirus.
Milton, John. *Areopagitica*. Edited by Richard C. Jebb. Cambridge: Cambridge University Press, 1644, 1918.
———. *The Prose Works of John Milton*, intro. by Robert Fletcher. London: Westley & Davis, 1835.
Minersville School District v. Gobitis, 310 U.S. 586 (1940).
"Mission & Values." *University of California-Los Angeles*, https://www.ucla.edu/about/mission-and-values.
"Mission & Vision." *Indiana University*, https://www.iu.edu/about/mission-vision.html.
"Mission and Values." *Ohio University*, https://www.ohio.edu/hr/jobs/working-ohio.
"Mission and Values." *University of Missouri*, https://missouri.edu/mission-values.
"Mission and Vision Statement." *University of North Florida*, https://www.unf.edu/president/mission_vision.aspx.
"Mission and Vision." *University of Hawaii-Mānoa*, https://manoa.hawaii.edu/strategicplan/index.php.
"Mission Statement." *Middle Tennessee State University*, https://www.mtsu.edu/about/mission.php.
"Mission Statement." *SUNY-Albany*, https://www.albany.edu/communitystandards/mission.php.
"Mission Statement." *University of Pittsburgh*, https://www.provost.pitt.edu/faculty-handbook/ch1_mission_stmt.
"Mission, Goals and Values for OSU." *Oregon State University*, https://hr.oregonstate.edu/mission-goals-and-values-osu.
"Mission, Values, Vision." *University of Alaska-Anchorage*, https://www.uaa.alaska.edu/about/mission-values-vision.cshtml#mission.
"Mission, Vision and Creed." *Marshall University*, https://www.marshall.edu/mission/.

"Mission, Vision and Values." *Missouri State University*, https://www.missouristate.edu/about/mission-statement.htm.

"Mission." *University of Kansas*, https://chancellor.ku.edu/mission.

"Mission." *University of Massachusetts-Amherst*, https://www.umass.edu/planning/mission.

"MSU Mission Statement." *Michigan State University*, https://trustees.msu.edu/about/mission.html.

Mo. Rev. Stat. § 173.1550 (2015).

Montgomery, David. "The Endless Call." *The Washington Post Magazine*, June 11, 2020, https://www.washingtonpost.com/graphics/2020/lifestyle/magazine/the-endless-call-for-racial-equity-and-justice-in-photos-and-quotes/?itid=hp_magazine-left-8-12_maglead-ans%3Ahomepage%2Fstory-ans.

Morey, Alex. "Georgia Legislator Suggests Professor Be Punished for Comments on Illegal Immigration." Foundation for Individual Rights in Education, June 10, 2019, https://www.thefire.org/georgia-legislator-suggests-professor-be-punished-for-comments-on-illegal-immigration/.

Morey, Alex and Adam Steinbaugh, "Wisconsin Legislator's Threat to Slash UW Budget Over Reading Assignment 'Cuts to the Core of Academic Freedom'." Foundation for Individual Rights in Education, July 8, 2016, https://www.thefire.org/wisconsin-legislators-threat-to-slash-uw-budget-over-reading-assignment-cuts-to-the-core-of-academic-freedom/.

———. "Wrongly Arrested for Racial Slur, UConn Students Sue University over Violation of First Amendment, Court Order [UPDATED]." Foundation for Individual Rights in Education, January 14, 2020, https://www.thefire.org/wrongly-arrested-for-racial-slur-uconn-students-sue-university-over-violation-of-first-amendment-court-order/.

Morphew, Christopher C. and Matthew Hartley. "Mission Statements: A Thematic Analysis of Rhetoric across Institutional Type." *Journal of Higher Education* 77, no. 3 (2006): 456–71.

Morse v. Frederick, 551 U.S. 393 (2007).

Morrar, Sawsan. "'He Should Be Fired': Lawmaker's Resolution Urges Dismissal of UC Davis Prof over Cop Comments." *Modesto Bee*, March 21, 2019, https://www.modbee.com/news/california/article228181294.html.

Moskowitz, P.E. *The Case against Free Speech: The First Amendment, Fascism, and the Future of Dissent*. New York: Bold Type Books, 2019.

N.C. Gen. Stat. §§116-300-116-304 (2018).

N. Dak. Cent. Code Ann. § 15-10.4-02 (2019).

Nahmod, Sheldon. "Public Employee Speech, Categorical Balancing, and §1983: A Critique of Garcetti v. Ceballos." *University of Richmond Law Review* 42 (January 2008): 561–96.

Napolitano, Andrew P. "Protecting Hatred Preserves Freedom: Why Offensive Expression Deserves Constitutional Protection." *Journal of Law and Policy* 25 (December 2016): 161–83.

Nietzsche, Friedrich. "On Truth and Lies in a Nonmoral Sense." In *Truth: Engagements Across Philosophical Traditions*, edited by David Wood and Jose Medina, 17. Malden, MA: Blackwell Publishing, 2005.

New York Times Co. v. Sullivan, 376 U.S. 254 (1964).

"No Comment: Public Universities' Social Media Use and the First Amendment." Foundation for Individual Rights in Education, 2020, https://www.thefire.org/research/publications/miscellaneous-publications/social-media-use-and-the-first-amendment/no-comment-public-universities-social-media-use-and-the-first-amendment/.

Nossel, Suzanne. "No, Hateful Speech Is Not the Same Thing as 'Violence.'" *The Washington Post*, June 22, 2017, https://www.washingtonpost.com/outlook/no-hateful-speech-is-not-the-same-thing-as-violence/2017/06/22/63c2c07a-5137-11e7-be25-3a519335381c_story.html?utm_term=.3a396ce3995.

"Obama Praises University of Missouri Protestors." ABC News, November 15, 2015, https://www.youtube.com/watch?v=8PlcALRh6Og&feature=emb_title.

"Official University Facts." *Delaware State University*, https://www.desu.edu/about/administration/marketing-communications/branding-communications-tool-kit/official-university.

Okla. Stat. tit. 70, § 2120 (2019).

"Oklahoma State Football Coach Takes Million-Dollar Pay Cut after Player Calls Him Out for Wearing T-Shirt Promoting Far-Right News Channel." *Market Watch*, July 3, 2020, https://www.marketwatch.com/story/oklahoma-state-football-coach-takes-million-dollar-pay-cut-after-player-calls-him-out-for-t-shirt-promoting-far-right-news-channel 2020 07 03.

O'Neil, Robert M. *Free Speech in the College Community*. Bloomington, IN: Indiana University Press, 1997.

"Order and Opinion for Motion to Dismiss: Shaw v. Burke." Foundation for Individual Rights in Education, January 18, 2018, https://www.thefire.org/order-and-opinion-pierce-college-shaw-v-burke/.

Orenstein, Walker. "Read the Email Exchange that Sparked Protests Against an Evergreen Professor." *News Tribune (Tacoma)*, June 1, 2017, https://www.thenewstribune.com/news/politics-government/article153826039.html.

"Our Mission." *Louisiana Tech University*, https://www.latech.edu/about/mission/.

"Our Story." *Heterodox Academy*, https://heterodoxacademy.org/our-story/.

Packer, George. "How to Destroy a Government: The President Is Winning His War on American Institutions." *The Atlantic*, April 2020, 54–74.

Pantazi, Andrew and Nate Monroe. "Shouting Match; Hostile Audience Drowns Out White Nationalist's Speech." *Florida Times-Union (Jacksonville)*, October 20, 2017, A-1.

Papish v. Board of Curators, 410 U.S. 667 (1973).

Paris Adult Theatre I v. Slaton, 413 U.S. 49 (1973).

Parker, Kim. "The Growing Partisan Divide in Views of Higher Education." Pew Research Center, August 19, 2019, https://www.pewsocialtrends.org/essay/the-growing-partisan-divide-in-views-of-higher-education.

"Partisanship and Political Animosity in 2016." Pew Research Center, June 22, 2016, http://www.people-press.org/2016/06/22/partisanship-and-political-animosity-in-2016/.

Patel, Vimal. "Students' Attitudes Toward Controversial Speech Are Changing. Here's Why." *Chronicle of Higher Education*, September 22, 2019, https://www.chronicle.com/article/Students-Attitudes-Toward/247167.

Peck, Alison. "Identity-Based Conflicts in Public Policy: Hydraulic Fracturing in Pennsylvania." *University of Pittsburgh Law Review* 79 (Spring 2018): 437–509.

Pepper, Stephen. "Philosophy and Metaphor." *Journal of Philosophy*, 25, no. 5 (March 1928): 130–32.

Perry Educational Association v. Perry Local Educators Association, 460 U.S. 37 (1983).

Peters, Jeremy M. "In Coulter's Free Speech Battle, The Right's Latest Rallying Cry." *The New York Times*, April 26, 2017, A1.

Philadelphia v. New Jersey, 437 U.S. 617 (1978).

Pickering v. Bd. of Educ., 391 U.S. 568 (1968).

Piltch, Jamie. "Free Speech Isn't under Attack on Campuses; It's Just Being Extended to More Groups." *The Washington Post*, December 7, 2017, https://www.washingtonpost.com/news/made-by-history/wp/2017/12/07/free-speech-isnt-under-attack-on-campuses/.

Pinker, Steven. *Enlightenment Now: The Case for Reason, Science, Humanism, and Progress.* New York: Viking, 2018.

Planned Parenthood of Southeastern Pennsylvania v. Casey, 505 U.S. 833 (1992).

Plato. *Republic*. Translated by G.M.A. Grube. Revised by C.D.C. Reeve. Cambridge, MA: Hackett Publishing Company, Inc., 1992.

Plessy v. Ferguson, 163 U.S. 537 (1896).

Poon, Linda and Marie Patino. "CityLab University: A Timeline of U.S. Police Protests." *Bloomberg*, June 9, 2020, https://www.bloomberg.com/news/articles/2020-06-09/a-history-of-protests-against-police-brutality.

Posner, Richard A., ed. *The Essential Holmes*. Chicago: University of Chicago Press, 1997.

———. "Foreword, Symposium: The Path of the Law 100 Years Later: Holmes's Influence on Modern Jurisprudence." *Brooklyn Law Review* 63 (1997): 7–17.

Post, Robert C. "Between Governance and Management: The History and Theory of the Public Forum." *UCLA Law Review* 34 (June/August 1987): 1713–835.

———. *Constitutional Domains*. Cambridge: Harvard University Press, 1995.

———. "Free Speech and Religious, Racial, and Sexual Harassment: Racist Speech, Democracy, and the First Amendment." *William & Mary Law Review* 32 (Winter 1991): 267–327.

———. "The Classic First Amendment Tradition under Stress: Freedom of Speech and the University." Yale Law School, Public Law Research Paper No. 619, September 28, 2017, https://papers.ssrn.com/sol3/papers.cfm?abstract_id=3044434.

———. "There Is No 1st Amendment Right to Speak on a College Campus." *Vox*, December 31, 2017, https://www.vox.com/the-big-idea/2017/10/25/16526442/first-amendment-college-campuses-milo-spencer-protests.

Postsecondary Institutions; Free Expression Policies. Ariz. Sess. Laws Ch. 267, HB 2563. https://www.azleg.gov/legtext/53leg/2R/laws/0267.pdf, accessed July 23, 2020.

"Private Universities." *TheFire.org*, https://www.thefire.org/resources/spotlight/public-and-private-universities/.

Pruitt, Dean G., and Sung Hee Kim. *Social Conflict: Escalation, Stalemate, and Settlement*, 3rd Edition. New York: McGraw Hill, 2004.

"Public University Rejects Animal Rights Club, Citing 'Emotional Risk' to Students." Foundation for Individual Rights in Education. December 10, 2019, https://www.thefire.org/public-university-rejects-animal-rights-club-citing-emotional-risk-to-students/.

Pugel v. Board of Trustees of the University of Illinois, 378 F.3d 659, 668 (7th Cir. 2004).

Quintana, Chris. "At Berkeley, A Speaker's Cancellation Spurs New Battles Over Free Speech." In *Dealing with Controversial Speakers*, edited by The Chronicle of Higher Education, 10–11, 2017.

Quintana, Olivia and Travis Anderson. "Pro-Trump Babson Students Cleared in Wellesley Incident." *Boston Globe*, December 19, 2016, https://www.bostonglobe.com/metro/2016/12/19/pro-trump-babson-students-cleared-wellesley-victory-incident/RsIfPd27sNxqiXvnwOrhTJ/story.html.

R.A.V. v. City of St. Paul, 505 U.S. 377 (1992).

Rabban, David M. "Does Academic Freedom Limit Faculty Autonomy." *Texas Law Review* 66 (June 1988): 1405–30.

———. *Free Speech in Its Forgotten Years*. New York: Cambridge University Press, 1997.

Ramachandran, Shalini, and Joe Palazzolo. "NYU Langone Tells ER Doctors to 'Think More Critically' About Who Gets Ventilators." *Wall Street Journal*, March 30, 2020, https://www.wsj.com/articles/nyu-langone-tells-er-doctors-to-think-more-critically-about-who-gets-ventilators-11585618990.

Rampell, Catherine. "Liberal Intolerance Is on the Rise on America's College Campuses." *The Washington Post*, February 11, 2016, https://www.washingtonpost.com/opinions/liberal but not-tolerant-on-the-nations-college-campuses/2016/02/11/0f79e8e8-d101-11e5-88cd-753e80cd29ad_story.html?utm_term=.786c5263a007.

Rank, Lindsie. "After Scandal, Questions Remain about Central Washington University's New Promise to Support Student Media." Foundation for Individual Rights in Education, January 16, 2020, https://www.thefire.org/after-scandal-questions-remain-about-central-washington-universitys-new-promise-to-support-student-media/.

Reed v. Town of Gilbert, Arizona, 576 U.S. 155 (2015).

Reeves, Inc. v. Stake, 447 U.S. 429 (1980).

"Regent Policy Document 4-21: Commitment to Academic Freedom and Freedom of Expression." University of Wisconsin System Board of Regents, https://www.wisconsin.edu/regents/policies/commitment-to-academic-freedom-and-freedom-of-expression.

Regents of the University of California v. Bakke, 438 U.S. 265 (1978).

Republican National Committee v. Democratic National Committee, 140 S.Ct. 1205 (2020).

"Results of the 2016 University of Michigan Student Campus Climate Survey on Diversity, Equity and Inclusion." *University of Michigan*, https://diversity.umich.edu/wp-content/uploads/2017/11/DEI-STUDENT-REPORT-FINAL.pdf.

Rice-Cameron, John. "Not Backing Down at Berkeley: Free Speech Under Siege." *Stanford Review*, May 29, 2017, https://stanfordreview.org/not-backing-down-at-berkeley-free-speech-under-siege-b596f2d7939e.

Roberts v. Harrigan, 346 F.Supp.2d 853 (N.D. Tex. 2004).

Robinson v. Hunt Cty., 921 F. 3d 440, 447–49 (5th Cir. 2019).

Rodell, Fred. *Nine Men: A Political History of the Supreme Court from 1790 to 1955*, 179–80. New York: Random House, 1955 (quoting Walton Hamilton).

Roe v. Crawford, 514 F.3d 789 (8th Cir. 2008).

Roe v. Wade, 410 U.S. 113 (1973).

Rohde, Stephen. "A Failed Case against Free Speech." *Los Angeles Review of Books*, March 17, 2020, https://lareviewofbooks.org/article/a-failed-case-against-free-speech/.

"Role, Mission and Values." *University of Nebraska-Lincoln*, https://www.unl.edu/about/role-mission/.

Roll, Nick. "Blocking a President from Talking." *Inside Higher Ed*, October 9, 2017, https://www.insidehighered.com/news/2017/10/09/speaker-interruptions-continue-controversial-policy-adopted-wisconsin.

Rose, Joel and Marisa Peñaloza. "Protestors Across the U.S. Decry Policy of Separating Immigrant Families." *NPR*, June 1, 2018, https://www.npr.org/2018/06/01/616257822/immigration-rights-activists-protest-trump-administration-child-separation-polic.

Rosenbaum v. City and County of San Francisco, 484 F. 3d 1182 (9th Cir. 2007).

Rosenberger v. Rector & Visitors of University of Virginia, 515 U.S. 819 (1995).

Ross, Lauren K. "Pursing Academic Freedom after Garcetti v. Ceballos." *Texas Law Review* 91 (April 2013): 1253–81.

Roth, Michael S. *Safe Enough Spaces: A Pragmatist's Approach to Inclusion, Free Speech, and Political Correctness on College Campuses*. New Haven: Yale University Press, 2019.

Roth v. United States, 354 U.S. 476 (1957).

Rozenblit, Bruce. *Us Against Them: How Tribalism Affects the Way We Think*. Kansas City: Transcendent Publications, 2008.

Rubin, Jennifer. "After Brexit, Reason to Be More Sensible." *The Philadelphia Inquirer*, June 26, 2016, C4.

Russomanno, Joseph. "Tribalism on Campus: Factions, iGen and the Threat to Free Speech." *Communication Law and Policy* 24, no. 4 (2019): 539–86.

S. Dak. Codified Laws § 13-53-51 (2019).

Saad, Lydia and Jeffrey M. Jones. "More College Students Than U.S. Adults Say Free Speech Is Secure." Gallup, April 4, 2016, https://news.gallup.com/poll/190442/college-students-adults-say-free-speech-secure.aspx.

Sarabyn, Kelly. "The Twenty-Sixth Amendment: Resolving the Federal Circuit Split Over College Students' First Amendment Rights." *Texas Journal on Civil Liberties and Civil Rights* 14 (Fall 2008): 27–93.

Sachs, Jeffrey Adam, "The 'Campus Free Speech Crisis' Is a Myth. Here Are the Facts." *The Washington Post*, March 16, 2018, https://www.washingtonpost.com

/news/monkey-cage/wp/2018/03/16/the-campus-free-speech-crisis-is-a-myth-here-are-the-facts/.

Saenz v. Roe, 526 U.S. 489 (1999).

Saincome, Matt, "*Berkeley Riots: How Free Speech Debate Launched Violent Campus Showdown*." *Rolling Stone*, February 6, 2017, http://www.rollingstone.com/culture/features/berkeley-riots-inside-the-campus-showdown-over-free-speech-w465151.

Saul, Stephanie. "Dozens of Middlebury Students Are Disciplined for Charles Murray Protest." *The New York Times*, May 24, 2017, https://www.nytimes.com/2017/05/24/us/middlebury-college-charles-murray-bell-curve.html.

Schauer, Frederick. "The Hostile Audience Revisited." *Knight First Amendment Institute*, November 2, 2017, https://knightcolumbia.org/content/hostile-audience-revisited.

Scheinblum, Josh. "Kirkwood Professor: 'I affirm that I am Antifa.'" KCRG, August 22, 2019, https://www.kcrg.com/content/news/Kirkwood-professor-I-affirm-that-I-am-antifa-557897151.html.

Schenck v. United States, 249 U.S. 47 (1919).

Shields, Jon and Joshua Dunn. *Passing on the Right: Conservative Professors in the Progressive University*. New York: Oxford University Press, 2016.

Schill, Michael H. "The Misguided Student Crusade against 'Fascism.'" *The New York Times*, October 23, 2017, https://www.nytimes.com/2017/10/23/opinion/fascism-protest-university-oregon.html.

Schrobsdorff, Susanna. "Teen Depression and Anxiety: Why the Kids Are Not Alright." *Time*, October 26, 2016, http://time.com/4547322/american-teens-anxious-depressed-overwhelmed.

Scott, John C. "The Mission of the University: Medieval to Postmodern Transformations." *Journal of Higher Education*, 77, no. 1 (2006): 1–39.

Secunda, Paul M. "Garcetti's Impact on the First Amendment Speech Rights of Federal Employees." *First Amendment Law Review* 7 (Fall 2008): 117–44.

Seffert v. Los Angeles Transit Lines, 56 Cal. 2d. 498 (Cal. 1961).

Seidman, Louis Michael. "Can Speech Be Progressive?" *Columbia Law Review* 118, no. 7 (November 2018): 2219–49.

Semones, Evan. "Enough Is Enough: Thousands Descend on D.C. for Largest George Floyd Protest Yet." *Politico*, June 6, 2020, https://www.politico.com/news/2020/06/06/george-floyd-blm-protest-washington-304635.

Serwer, Adam, (@adamserwer), August 12, 2017, https://twitter.com/AdamSerwer/status/896413424015560704?s=20.

———. "A Nation of Snowflakes." *The Atlantic*, September 26, 2017, https://www.theatlantic.com/politics/archive/2017/09/it-takes-a-nation-of-snowflakes/541050/.

Shaw, Bernard. *Selections of His Wit and Wisdom*, compilied by Caroline Thomas Harnsberger, 328. Westchester, IL: Follett Publishing Company, 1965.

Shear, Michael D. and Helene Cooper. "Trump Bars Refugees and Citizens of 7 Countries." *New York Times*, January 27, 2017, https://www.nytimes.com/2017/01/27/us/politics/trump-syrian-refugees.html.

Shibley, Robert. "The University of Kansas Controversy: Defending the Freedom to Tweet." Foundation for Individual Rights in Education, September 23, 2013, https://www.thefire.org/the-university-of-kansas-controversy-defending-the-freedom-to-tweet/.

Shiffrin, Steven H. *What's Wrong with the First Amendment?* Cambridge: Cambridge University Press, 2016.

Shmueli, Deborah, Michael Elliott, and Sanda Kaufman. "Frame Changes and the Management of Intractable Conflicts." *Conflict Resolution Quarterly*, 24, no. 2 (Winter 2006): 207–18. https://doi.org/10.1002/crq.169.

Shumate, Ben. "Robert Post Talks Freedom of Expression." *Brown Daily Herald*, November 15, 2016, https://www.browndailyherald.com/2016/11/15/robert-post-talks-freedom-expression/.

Siddiqui, Sabrina. "Kavanaugh Hearing Recalls Clarence Thomas Case." *The Guardian*, September 27, 2018, https://www.theguardian.com/us-news/2018/sep/27/brett-kavanaugh-clarence-thomas-anita-hill-hearings.

Sleeper, Jim. "What the Campus 'Free Speech' Crusade Won't Say." *AlterNet*, September 4, 2016, https://www.alternet.org/2016/09/what-campus-free-speech-crusade-wont-say-0/.

Smolla, Rodney A. *Confessions of a Free Speech Lawyer: Charlottesville and the Politics of Hate*. Ithaca: Cornell University Press, 2020.

———. *The Constitution Goes to College: Five Constitutional Ideas That Have Shaped the American University*. New York: New York University Press, 2011.

———. *Free Speech in an Open Society*. New York: Alfred A. Knopf, 1992.

———. "Speech Overview." *Freedom Forum Institute*, https://www.freedomforuminstitute.org/first-amendment-center/topics/freedom-of-speech-2/speech-overview/.

——— and William Banks. *Constitutional Law: Structural Rights in Our Federal System*, 7th Edition. Durham, NC: Carolina Academic Press, 2019.

"Smothering Speech at Middlebury." Editorial, *The New York Times*, March 7, 2017, https://www.nytimes.com/2017/03/07/opinion/smothering-speech-at-middlebury.html.

Snyder v. Phelps, 562 U.S. 443 (2011).

Sonnier v. Crain, 613 F.3d 436 (5th Cir. 2010).

Souders v. Lucero, 196 F.3d 1040 (9th Cir. 1999).

Southern Pacific Company v. Arizona, 325 U.S. 761 (1945).

Speech First Inc. v. Schlissel, 939 F.3d 756 (6th Cir. 2019).

"Spotlight on Speech Codes 2019." Foundation for Individual Rights in Education, https://www.thefire.org/resources/spotlight/reports/spotlight-on-speech-codes-2019/.

Stanger, Allison. "Middlebury, My Divided Campus." *The New York Times*, April 3, 2017.

———. "Understanding the Angry Mob at Middlebury That Gave Me a Concussion." *The New York Times,* March 13, 2017, https://www.nytimes.com/2017/03/13/opinion/understanding-the-angry-mob-that-gave-me-a-concussion.html.

Stanley, Jason. "When Fascists Weaponize Free Speech Absolutism." *Literary Hub*, September 12, 2018, https://lithub.com/when-fascists-weaponize-free-speech-absolutism/.

"Statement of Shared Values." *Boise State University*, https://www.boisestate.edu/president/values/statement-of-shared-values/.

Steinbaugh, Adam. "Civil liberties Advocates, Celebrities Sign Letter Defending Professor Fired by Babson College, Whose Claimed 'Cooperation' with Police Is in Doubt." Foundation for Individual Rights in Education, January 23, 2020, https://www.thefire.org/civil-liberties-advocates-celebrities-sign-letter-defending-professor-fired-by-babson-college-whose-claimed-cooperation-with-police-is-in-doubt/.

———. "FIRE Warns University of Georgia and State Attorney General to End Speech-Chilling Investigation into TA's Protected Expression." Foundation for Individual Rights in Education, January 25, 2019, https://www.thefire.org/fire-warns-university-of-georgia-and-state-attorney-general-to-end-speech-chilling-investigation-into-tas-protected-expression.

———. "George Washington University Police Investigating Posters Lampooning Conservative Group—Again." Foundation for Individual Rights in Education, September 13, 2017, https://www.thefire.org/george-washington-university-police-investigating-posters-lampooning-conservative-group-again/.

———. "New York Legislators Threaten CUNY Funding, Call for Banishment of Pro-Palestinian Student Group." Foundation for Individual Rights in Education, March 30, 2016, https://www.thefire.org/new-york-legislators-threaten-cuny-funding-call-for-banishment-of-pro-palestinian-student-group/.

Stengel, Richard. "Why America Needs a Hate Speech Law." *The Washington Post*, October 29, 2019, https://www.washingtonpost.com/opinions/2019/10/29/why-america-needs-hate-speech-law/.

Stevens, John Paul. *The Making of a Justice: Reflections on My First 94 Years*. New York: Little, Brown and Company, 2019.

Stone, Geoffrey R. "Aims of Education Address." University of Chicago, 1996, https://college.uchicago.edu/student-life/aims-education-address-2016-geoffrey-r-stone.

———. "Free Expression in Peril." *The Chronicle of Higher Education*, August 26, 2016, https://www.chronicle.com/article/Free-Expression-in-Peril/237568.

———, Marianne Bertrand, Angela Olinto, Mark Siegler, David A. Strauss, Kenneth W. Warren and Amanda Woodward. "University of Chicago, Free Speech on Campus: A Report from the University Faculty Committee." January 6, 2015, http://www.law.uchicago.edu/news/free-speech-campus-report-university-faculty-committee.

———, Marianne Bertrand, Angela Olinto, Mark Siegler, David A. Strauss, Kenneth W. Warren and Amanda Woodward. "University of Chicago, Free Speech on Campus: A Report from the University Faculty Committee." January 6, 2015, http://www.law.uchicago.edu/news/free-speech-campus-report-university-faculty-committee.

Strauss, Leo. "An Epilogue." In *Essays on the Scientific Study of Politics*, edited by Herbert J. Storing, 305. New York: Rinehart & Winston, Inc., 1962.

———. *Liberalism Ancient and Modern*. Chicago: University of Chicago Press, 1968.

Street v. New York, 394 U.S. 576, 592 (1969).

Strossen, Nadine. "Freedom of Speech and Equality: Do We Have to Choose?" *Journal of Law and Policy* 25 (December 2016): 185–225.

"Student Attitudes Free Speech Survey." Foundation for Individual Rights in Education, 2017, https://www.thefire.org/research/publications/student-surveys/student-attitudes-free-speech-survey/.

Sullivan, Andrew. "America Wasn't Built For Humans." *New York*, September 18, 2017, https://nymag.com/intelligencer/2017/09/can-democracy-survive-tribalism.html.

Sunstein, Cass R. "The Law of Group Polarization." John M. Olin Program in Law and Economics Working Paper No. 91, 1999, https://ssrn.com/abstract=199668.

Svrluga, Susan. "Richard Spencer Gets OK to Speak at the University of Florida, His First Campus Event Since U-Va." *The Washington Post*, October 5, 2017, https://www.washingtonpost.com/news/grade-point/wp/2017/10/05/richard-spencer-gets-ok-to-speak-at-the-university-of-florida-his-first-campus-event-since-u-va/.

——— and Joe Heim. "A Washington State College, Caught Up in Racial Turmoil, Remains Closed Friday After Threat of Violence." *The Washington Post*, June 2, 2017, https://www.washingtonpost.com/news/grade-point/wp/2017/06/02/evergreen-state-caught-up-in-racial-turmoil-remains-closed-friday-after-threat-of-violence/.

——— and William Wan. "UC-Berkeley Readies Police, Concerned Ann Coulter Plans to Speak in Public Plaza on Campus." *The Washington Post*, April 25, 2017, https://www.washingtonpost.com/news/grade-point/wp/2017/04/25/uc-berkeley-readies-police-as-ann-coulter-plans-to-speak-in-public-plaza-on-campus/.

Sweezy v. New Hampshire, 354 U.S. 234 (1957).

Swirko, Cindy. "Behind Scenes Logistics at Protests Let Officers Control Chaos. *Gainesville Sun*, October 20, 2017, https://www.gainesville.com/news/20171020/behind-scenes-logistics-at-protest-let-officers-control-chaos.

Sykes, Emerson, and Vera Eidelman. "When Colleges Confine Free Speech to a 'Zone,' It Isn't Free." *ACLU*, February 7, 2019, https://www.aclu.org/blog/free-speech/student-speech-and-privacy/when-colleges-confine-free-speech-zone-it-isnt-free.

Tanford v. Brand, 932 F.Supp. 1139 (S.D. Ind. 1996).

Taylor, Steve. "The Politics of Aging." *Psychology Today*, June 24, 2018, https://www.psychologytoday.com/us/blog/out-the-darkness/201806/the-politics-ageing.

Tenn. Code Ann. § 49-7-2405 (2018).

Terminiello v. Chicago, 337 U.S. 1 (1949).

Terry v. Ohio, 392 U.S. 1 (1968).

Tex. Educ. Code Ann. § 51.9315 (2019).

Texas v. Johnson, 491 U.S. 397 (1989).

Thoreau, Henry David. *Civil Disobedience.* 1849. Reprint, Somerset: Cricket House Books, 2019.

Tierney, John. "Republican Outnumbered in Academia, Studies Find." *The New York Times*, Nov. 18, 2004, https://www.nytimes.com/2004/11/18/education/republicans-outnumbered-in-academia-studies-find.html.

Timpf, Katherine. "University Rejects Animal-Rights Club Over 'Emotional Risk' Concerns." *National Review*, December 17, 2019, https://www.nationalreview

.com/2019/12/truman-state-university-rejects-animal-rights-club-over-emotional-risk-concerns/.

Tinker v. Des Moines Independent Community School District, 393 U.S. 503 (1969).

Trejo, Shane. "ANTIFA Professor Who Wished Genocide on Christians Gets 3+ Years of Pay From College in Settlement." *Big League Politics*, April 28, 2020, https://bigleaguepolitics.com/antifa-professor-who-wished-genocide-on-christians-gets-3-years-of-pay-from-college-in-settlement.

Trump v. Hawaii, 138 S.Ct. 2392 (2018).

Tsesis, Alexander. "Campus Speech and Harassment." *Minnesota Law Review* 101 (May 2017): 1863–917.

Tucker, Jeffrey A. "Why Free Speech on Campus Is under Attack: Blame Marcuse." Foundation for American Freedom, April 22, 2017, https://fee.org/articles/why-free-speech-on-campus-is-under-attack-blame-marcuse/.

Turley, Jonathan. "Cornell Professors Declare 'Informed Commentary' Criticizing the Protests as Racism." *Johnathon Turley*, https://jonathanturley.org/2020/06/12/cornell-professors-declare-informed-commentary-criticizing-the-protests-as-racism/.

Twenge, Jean. "Have Smartphones Destroyed a Generation?" *The Atlantic*, September 2017, https://www.theatlantic.com/magazine/archive/2017/09/has-the-smart- phone-destroyed-a-generation/534198.

———. *iGen: Why Today's Super-Connected Kids Are Growing Up Less Rebellious, More Tolerant, Less Happy – and Completely Unprepared For Adulthood.* New York: Atria Books, 2017.

"UC Berkeley BLOCKS Shapiro Event at University on September 14. Shapiro Vows to Fight Back." *Daily Wire,* July 19, 2017, https://www.dailywire.com/news/18778/uc-berkeley-blocks-shapiro event-university-ben-shapiro.

Ugland, Erik. "Expanding Media Law and Policy Education: Confronting Power, Defining Freedom, Awakening Participation." *Communication Law and Policy* 24, no. 2 (April 2019): 271–306.

UMW Post v. Board of Regents, 774 F. Supp. 1163 (E.D. Wis. 1991).

"UNM's Mission." *University of New Mexico*, http://www.unm.edu/welcome/mission.html.

United States v. Alvarez, 567 U.S. 709 (2012).

United States v. Rumley, 345 U.S. 41 (1953).

United States v. Schwimmer, 279 U.S. 644 (1929).

United States v. Stevens, 559 U.S. 460 (2010).

UWM Post v. Board of Regents of U. of Wis., 774 F. Supp. 1163, 1181 (E.D. Wis. 1991).

"University Mission, Values, and Guiding Principles." *Colorado State University*, https://catalog.colostate.edu/general-catalog/welcome/mission-values.

"University Mission, Values, and Guiding Principles." *Colorado State University*, https://catalog.colostate.edu/general-catalog/welcome/mission-values/.

"University Mission." *North Carolina State University*, https://leadership.ncsu.edu/university-mission/.

"University of Maryland: State Senators Pressure University to Cancel Controversial Film Screening." Foundation for Individual Rights in Education, https://www.the

fire.org/cases/university-of-maryland-state-senators-pressure-university-to-cancel-controversial-film-screening/.

University of Pennsylvania v. E.E.O.C., 493 U.S. 182 (1990).

"University Statement Regarding Offensive Fliers on Campus." The George Washington University, September 9, 2017, https://mediarelations.gwu.edu/university-statement-regarding-offensive-fliers-campus.

"UPDATED: FIRE Statement Regarding Executive Order on Campus Anti-Semitism." Foundation for Individual Rights in Education, December 10, 2019, https://www.thefire.org/fire-statement-regarding-executive-order-on-campus-anti-semitism/.

Uyehara, Mari. "The Free Speech Grifters." *GQ*, March 19, 2018, https://www.gq.com/story/free-speech-grifting.

Va. Code Ann. § 23.1-401 (2019).

Varney, James. "Conservative Students Say Free-Speech Rights Assailed by Anti-Kavanaugh Mob." *The Washington Times*, October 7, 2018, https://www.washingtontimes.com/news/2018/oct/7/texas-conservative-students-say-free-speech-rights/.

Vassiliadis, Kim. "Message from University Leadership: Addressing Threatening Flyers." *UNC News Archives*, February 16, 2017, https://uncnewsarchive.unc.edu/campus-updates/message-from-university-leadership-addressing-threatening-flyers.

Vikram David Amar and Alan E. Brownstein. "A Close-up, Modern Look at First Amendment Academic Freedom Rights of Public College Students and Faculty." *Minnesota Law Review* 101 (May 2017): 1943–85.

Villasenor, John. "Views Among College Students Regarding the First Amendment: Results from a New Survey." Brookings Institution, September 18, 2017, https://www.brookings.edu/blog/fixgov/2017/09/18/views-among-college-students-regarding-the-first-amendment-results-from-a-new-survey/.

"VICTORY: College Settles with 'Antifa' Professor Fired for Criticizing President Trump on Facebook, Avoids First Amendment Lawsuit from FIRE." Foundation for Individual Rights in Education, April 27, 2020, https://www.thefire.org/victory-college-settles-with-antifa-professor-fired-for-criticizing-president-trump-on-facebook-avoids-first-amendment-lawsuit-from-fire/.

Virginia v. Black, 538 U.S. 343 (2003).

"Vision and Mission Statement." *Auburn University*, http://www.auburn.edu/main/welcome/visionandmission.php.

"Vision, Mission and Core Values." *University of Mississippi*, https://olemiss.edu/aboutum/mission.html.

Vitelli, Romeo. "When a Parent Loses a Child: How do People Deal with the Emotional Blow Associated with Child Loss?" *Psychology Today*, February 4, 2013, https://www.psychologytoday.com/us/blog/media-spotlight/201302/when-parent-loses-child.

Vladimirov, Nikita. "Conservative Prof Claims He was Fired over Political Beliefs." *Campus Reform*, May 30, 2018, https://www.campusreform.org/?ID=10960.

Volokh, Eugene. "Protestors at Middlebury College Shout Down Speaker, Attack Him and a Professor." *The Washington Post*, March 4, 2017, https://www.washingt

onpost.com/news/volokh-conspiracy/wp/2017/03/04/protesters-at-middlebury-college-shout-down-speaker-attack-him-and-a-professor/?utm_term=.609350a7b3fb.
Wagner, Helena. "Lawmaker's Bill Aims to Guard Free Speech at Arizona Universities. Critics Decry Censoring." February 17, 2020, *AZcentral,* https://www.azcentral.com/story/news/politics/legislature/2020/02/17/house-bill-2238-sponsored-anthony-kern-would-add-oversight-speakers-arizona-campuses/4626386002/.
Walker, Morgan. "Liberal Profs Outnumber Conservatives 28-to-1." *Campus Reform,* July 6, 2016, https://www.thecollegefix.com/liberal-professors-outnumber-conservatives-28-1-region-known-ivy-league/.
Walker v. Sons of Confederate Veterans, 135 S. Ct. 2239 (2015).
Wampole, Christy. *Rootedness: The Ramifications of a Metaphor.* Chicago: University of Chicago Press, 2016.
Wanshel, Elyse. "Transphobic 'Free Speech Bus' to Tour U.S. With Message of Hate." *Huffington Post*, March 23, 2017, http://www.huffingtonpost.com/entry/transphobic-free-speech-bus-anti-lgbtq_us_58d3ce1be4b0b22b0d1a5022.
Ward v. Rock Against Racism, 491 U.S. 781 (1989).
Washington v. Davis, 426 U.S. 229 (1976).
Weil, Simone. *The Need for Roots: Prelude to a Declaration of Duties Towards Mankind* Translated by Arthur Wills. New York: Routledge 2001.
Weiland, Morgan N. "Expanding the Periphery and Threatening the Core: The Ascendant Libertarian Speech Tradition." *Stanford Law Review* 69, no. 5 (2017): 1389–472.
Weinstein, James. *Hate Speech, Pornography, and the Radical Attack on Free Speech Doctrine*. Boulder: Westview Press, 1990.
Weis, Bari. "When the Left Turns on Its Own." *The New York Times*, June 1, 2017, https://www.nytimes.com/2017/06/01/opinion/when-the-left-turns-on-its-own.html.
Wells, Christina E. "Free Speech Hypocrisy: Campus Free Speech Conflicts and the Sub-legal First Amendment." *University of Colorado Law Review* 89 (2018): 533–64.
Wemple, Erik. "CNN commentator Scottie Nell Hughes: Facts No Longer Exist." *The Washington Post*, December 1, 2016, https://www.washingtonpost.com/blogs/erik-wemple/wp/2016/12/01/cnn-commentator-scottie-nell-hughes-facts-no-longer-exist/
West Virginia Board of Education v. Barnette, 319 U.S. 624 (1943).
Western & Southern Life Ins. v. State Board of California, 451 U.S. 648 (1981).
"WHALE DONE: Animal Rights Club Approved by Public University after FIRE's First Amendment Uproar." Foundation for Individual Rights in Education, February 10, 2020, https://www.thefire.org/whale-done-animal-rights-club-approved-by-public-university-after-fires-first-amendment-uproar.
Whitaker, Charles. "Northwestern's Jeff Sessions Protest Controversy: 'Give the Young People a Break.'" *USA Today,* November 19, 2019, https://www.usatoday.com/story/opinion/2019/11/19/northwestern-university-students-journalists-apology-editorial-jeff-sessions-column/4230002002.

White, Ken. "Some College Thick-Skin Advocates Need a Thicker Skin." *Popehat*, April 18, 2016, https://www.popehat.com/2016/04/18/some-college-thick-skin-advocates-need-a-thicker-skin/.

Whitney v. California, 274 U.S. 357 (1927).

Widmar v. Vincent, 454 U.S. 263, 267 n.5 (1981).

Wiesel, Eli, "Acceptance Speech on the Occasion of the Award of the Nobel Peace Prize." December 10, 1986, http:// www.nobelprize.org/nobel_prizes/peace/laureates/1986/wiesel-acceptance_ en.html).

Williamson-Lott, Joy-Ann. *Jim Crow Campus: Higher Education and the Struggle for a New Southern Social Order*. New York: Teachers College Press, 2018.

Wilson, John K. "The Tennessee Legislature's Defense of Campus Free Speech." *Academe*, May 11, 2017, https://academeblog.org/2017/05/11/the-tennessee-legislatures-defense-of-campus-free-speech/.

Winegard, Bo. "I've Been Fired. If You Value Academic Freedom, That Should Worry You." *Quillette*, March 6, 2020, https://quillette.com/2020/03/06/ive-been-fired-if-you-value-academic-freedom-that-should-worry-you/.

Wis. Assembly Bill 444, September 13, 2019, https://docs.legis.wisconsin.gov/2019/related/proposals/ab444.

Wisconsin v. Mitchell, 508 U.S. 476 (1993).

Woodward, C. Vann, et al. "Report of the Committee on Freedom of Expression at Yale." December 23, 1974, https://yalecollege.yale.edu/get-know-yale-college/office-dean/reports/report-committee-freedom-expression-yale.

Wozniak v. Adesida, 368 F.Supp.3d 1217, 1231 (C.D. Ill. 2018).

Wright, R. George. "Campus Speech and the Functions of the University." *Journal of College and University Law* 43, no. 1 (June 2017): 1–26.

Wright, Wesley. "Ann Coulter: It's Not Just Illegal Immigration That's the Problem; It's All Immigration." Dallas Morning News, June 3, 2015, https://www.dallasnews.com/opinion/commentary/2015/06/03/ann-coulter-it-s-not-just-illegal-immigration-that-s-the-problem-it-s-all-immigration/.

———. "Missouri Governor Signs Law Banning Campus Free Speech Zones." *FIRE*, July 15, 2015, https://www.thefire.org/missouri-governor-signs-law-banning-campus-free-speech-zones/.

———. "Open Letter to Associate Master Christakis." *Down Magazine*, October 31, 2015, https://downatyale.com/open-letter-to-associate-master-christakis/.

———. "Richard Bertrand Spencer." *Southern Poverty Law Center*, https://www.splcenter.org/fighting-hate/extremist-files/individual/richard-bertrand-spencer-0.

———. "Richard Spencer Speech at Florida Campus Sparks Mass Protest." *BBC,* October 20, 2017, https://www.bbc.com/news/world-us-canada-41683713.

Wright, Wesley. "William and Mary Students Protest ACLU Speaker, White Supremacy." *Virginia Gazette (Williamsburg)*, October 6, 2017, https://www.dailypress.com/virginiagazette/news/va-vg-aclu-protest-1007-story.html.

Yagoda, Ben. "Your Lying Mind: The Cognitive Biases Tickling Our Brain." *The Atlantic*, September 2018, https://www.theatlantic.com/magazine/archive/2018/09/cognitive-bias/565775/.

Yockey, Joseph W. "Bias Response on Campus." *Journal of Law and Education* 48, no. 1 (Winter 2019): 1–50.

Young American Foundation v. Napolitano, 2018 WL 1947766 (N.D. Ca. 2018).

Yu, Seth Ian. "College Students Who Openly Support Trump Censored, Threatened, Bullied by Professors, Peers." *College Fix*, September 26, 2016, https://www.thecollegefix.com/college-students-openly-support-trump-censored-threatened-bullied-professors-peers.

Zimmer, Robert J. "President Zimmer's Message on Free Expression and Federal Action." *UChicago News*, March 4, 2019, https://news.uchicago.edu/story/president-zimmers-message-free-expression-and-federal-action.

Zimmerman, Jonathan. "College Campuses Should Not Be Safe Spaces." *Chronicle of Higher Education*, January 17, 2019, https://www.chronicle.com/article/College-Campuses-Should-Not-Be/245505.

Index

About the Contributors

Erwin Chemerinsky is dean of the School of Law at the University of California, Berkeley. He is the author of more than 200 law review articles and 11 books, including leading casebooks and *Freedom of Speech on Campus* (2018) with Howard Gillman. As an attorney, he has argued several cases at the U.S. Supreme Court. A *New York Times* editorial described him as a "much-admired teacher" and "one of the shining lights of legal academia" who "has also taken his profession's public service obligations seriously, working tirelessly for civil liberties."

Ronald K. L. Collins is the co-director of the History Book Festival, is on the editorial board of SCOTUSblog, and is co-chair of the First Amendment Salons. He also writes a weekly blog, First Amendment News. He is the author or co-author of a dozen books including, *The Death of Discourse* (1996), *Robotica: Speech Rights and Artificial Intelligence*, *The Judge: 26 Machiavellian Lessons*, *On Dissent: Its Meaning in America* (2015), *The Fundamental Holmes* (2010), and *We Must Not Be Afraid to be Free* (2011). His scholarly articles have appeared in the *Harvard Law Review*, the *Stanford Law Review*, and the *Supreme Court Law Review*. He is the former Harold S. Shefelman Scholar at the University of Washington and before that was a senior fellow at the Newseum's First Amendment Center in Washington, D.C. His next book, with David Skover, is *Duty as Destiny: Justice Holmes, The Civil War & the Capture of American Law*.

Will Creeley is the senior vice president of Legal and Public Advocacy for the Foundation for Individual Rights in Education (FIRE), a non-partisan organization dedicated to defending student and faculty rights. Will began his work at FIRE in 2006 after graduating from New York University School of Law, where he served as an associate executive editor for the *New York University Law Review*. Will's writing has been published in many outlets, including *The New York Times*, the *Wall Street Journal*, *The Washington Post*, and the *Chronicle of Higher Education*. He has appeared on television and radio on behalf of FIRE, and has spoken to thousands of students, faculty, administrators, and attorneys at events across the country. Barred in New York and Pennsylvania, Will is a member of the First Amendment Lawyers Association and serves as co-chair of the Education Subcommittee of the American Bar Association's Section of Administrative Law and Regulatory Practice. A proud native of Buffalo, New York, Will now lives in New Jersey with his wife and two children.

Joe Dryden is an associate professor in the School of Education at Texas Wesleyan University and an adjunct professor at Texas A&M University School of Law. He earned a JD from California Western School of Law in 1990 and an EdD in Educational Leadership from the University of North Texas in 2010. His experience in education is extensive: a middle school and high school science teacher and coach for eight years; a middle and high school campus administrator for six years; and teaching at the collegiate level since 2005. He has been a member of the Education Law Association since 2010 and served as a member of the Board of Directors of the Education Law Association from 2016–2018. He writes for the School Law Reporter, and contributes chapters for the *Yearbook of Education Law* on K-12 student rights and legal issues in higher education.

Jeremiah P. Fuzy is a doctoral student at the Missouri School of Journalism where his research is focused on media ethics, law, and policy. His interests include normative theories of public communication, journalism's relationship to democracy, political philosophy, cultural and critical studies, First Amendment law, and religion journalism. This has led him to conduct research on topics such as the importance of the news media's interpretive role, freedom of speech and misinformation in the digital era, and how metajournalistic discourse shapes the boundaries of journalism. Fuzy has previous professional experience as the religion editor at RealClearPolitics and as a freelance writer. He received a bachelor's degree in 2011 from Drury University in philosophy/religion and politics and government as well as a master's degree in 2015 from the University of Chicago Divinity School where he studied ethics and religion in America.

Erica Goldberg is a professor at the University of Dayton School of Law. Her scholarship focuses on the intersection of free speech rights and tort law duties, and she approaches these topics from doctrinal, historical, and philosophical perspectives. She has also held academic positions or fellowships at Ohio Northern University Law School, Penn State University Law School, Harvard Law School, and Georgetown's Center for the Constitution. Professor Goldberg is a graduate of Tufts University and Stanford Law School. She clerked on the U.S. Court of Appeals for the Sixth Circuit, practiced appellate litigation, and worked for the *Phnom Penh Post* newspaper and the nonpartisan Foundation for Individual Rights in Education before entering academia. In her spare time, she loves to rock climb (including inventing routes in her home during quarantine) as a way to push her mental and physical limits and learn about physics. She blogs at InaCrowdedTheater.com and believes wholeheartedly in the importance of engaging and interpreting charitably with those with differing opinions and values.

David L. Hudson, Jr. is a First Amendment author and attorney based in Nashville, Tennessee. He is a First Amendment Fellow with the Freedom Forum Institute and a Justice Robert H. Jackson Fellow with the Foundation for Individual Rights in Education. He also is an assistant professor of law at Belmont University College of Law and an adjunct professor at the Nashville School of Law. He is the author, co-author, or co-editor of more than forty books, including *Let the Students Speak: A History of the Fight for Freedom of Expression in American Schools* (2011) and *First Amendment: Freedom of Speech* (2012).

Brett G. Johnson is an assistant professor of journalism studies in the Missouri School of Journalism where he teaches courses in mass communication law. Johnson employs traditional legal research methods as well as mixed- and multi-method approaches to study journalism, law, and technology from a sociological perspective. Johnson's research is grounded in a strong appreciation for the multiple interpretations of First Amendment theory, which allows him to assess the fluid and oft-conflicting interplay between the law and social norms. Johnson has BAs in Spanish and Religious Studies from the University of Iowa, an MA in professional journalism from the University of Iowa, and a PhD from the University of Minnesota.

Joseph Russomanno is a professor at the Walter Cronkite School of Journalism and Mass Communication at Arizona State University. This is the fifth book on which he's been an author and/or editor. Others include *Speaking Our Minds: Conversations With the People Behind Landmark First Amendment Cases* and *Defending the First: Commentary on First Amendment Issues and Cases*. His publications in law reviews often utilize constitutional historicism and theoretical or doctrinal foundations. Those articles include "Tribalism on Campus: Factions, iGen and the Threat to Free Speech" and "Speech On Campus: How America's Crisis in Confidence Is Eroding Free Speech Values." In addition to dozens of presentations domestically, he has also given addresses on speech and press freedom issues in Mexico, Canada, the United Kingdom, Nepal, and Pakistan. His PhD is from the University of Colorado-Boulder.

Rodney A. Smolla is dean and professor of Law at the Delaware Law School at Widener University. He is the author of numerous books, including *The Constitution Goes to College, Deliberate Intent, Jerry Falwell v. Larry Flynt: The First Amendment On Trial, Free Speech in an Open Society* and most recently, *Confessions of a Free Speech Lawyer: Charlottesville and the Politics of Hate*. He is a nationally known scholar, writer, educator, and litigator, and has presented oral arguments in state and federal courts, including at the Supreme Court of the United States. He graduated first in his class at Duke University Law School.

Geoffrey R. Stone is the Edward H. Levi Distinguished Service Professor at the University of Chicago. After serving as a law clerk to Justice William J. Brennan, Jr. of the Supreme Court of the United States, Mr. Stone joined the faculty of the University of Chicago Law School in 1973. Mr. Stone has served as dean of the University of Chicago Law School (1987–1994) and Provost of the University of Chicago (1994–2002). Mr. Stone is the author or co-author of many books on constitutional law, including, among others, *Democracy and Equality: The Enduring Constitutional Vision of the Warren Court* (2020); *The Free Speech Century* (2019); *Sex and the Constitution* (2017); *Top Secret: When Government Keeps Us In the Dark (*2007); and *Perilous Times: Free Speech in Wartime (*2004). Mr. Stone is also the co-editor of one of the nation's leading constitutional law casebooks, chief editor of a twenty-volume series, *Inalienable Rights*, which is published by the Oxford University Press, and an editor of the *Supreme Court Review*. Mr. Stone is a former chair of the Board of the American Constitution Society, a fellow of the American Academy of Arts and Sciences, and a member of the American Philosophical Society, the American Law Institute, and the National Advisory Council of the American Civil Liberties Union.

Christina E. Wells is the *Enoch H. Crowder Professor of Law* at the University of Missouri School of Law in Columbia, Missouri. Professor Wells is an expert in the areas of free speech, including its intersection with dispute resolution and administrative law principles. She is co-author of *The First Amendment: Cases and Theory* (3d ed. Aspen, 2017) and has also authored numerous book chapters, scholarly articles, amicus briefs, and op-eds on freedom of speech, access to government information, and protests. She has written and spoken both nationally and internationally on a variety of free speech issues. Her current work focuses on the First Amendment and conflict surrounding protests. Professor Wells received her JD with honors from the University of Chicago, where she was Comment Editor of the *Law Review*, and her BA *cum laude* from the University of Kansas. She joined the University of Missouri faculty in 1993, after working several years in private practice.